REVELATIONS

REVELATIONS

American History, American Myths

Nathan Irvin Huggins

Edited by Brenda Smith Huggins

New York   Oxford
OXFORD UNIVERSITY PRESS
1995

Oxford University Press

Oxford   New York
Athens   Auckland   Bangkok   Bombay
Calcutta   Cape Town   Dar es Salaam   Delhi
Florence   Hong Kong   Istanbul   Karachi
Kuala Lumpur   Madras   Madrid   Melbourne
Mexico City   Nairobi   Paris   Singapore
Taipei   Tokyo   Toronto

and associated companies in
Berlin   Ibadan

Copyright © 1995 by Brenda Smith Huggins

Published by Oxford University Press, Inc.,
200 Madison Avenue, New York, New York 10016

Library of Congress Cataloging-in-Publication Data

Huggins, Nathan Irvin, 1927-1989
Revelations: American history, American myths / written by Nathan
Irvin Huggins.
p.   cm.
Includes bibliographical references.
ISBN 0-19-508236-2
1. Afro-Americans—History.   I. Title.
E185.H75   1995
973'.0496073—dc20   694-27294

2   4   6   8   9   7   5   3   1

Printed in the United States of America
on acid-free paper

For Nelson Rolihlahla Mandela,
because he embodies the resilient, triumphant
determination to elevate the South African peoples from the
"subjunctive to the declarative."

Acknowledgments

This book is the celebration of a great man and an important scholar. While it is a posthumous work, it is also a work-in-progress. The productive, resilient spirit Nathan ignited in his students—and those of us who had the privilege of knowing and loving him—is alive and well and determined to leave new footprints on the sands.

I am profoundly indebted to Leon Litwack and Lawrence Levine, two highly distinguished scholars who have honored this work by their eloquent revelations and generous contributions.

My heartfelt gratitude to Sheldon Meyer, Senior Vice President, Oxford University Press, who had the idea for this volume and has been a warm and knowledgeable guide. And I wish to thank Joellyn Ausanka for her meticulous and loving care in helping to prepare the manuscript.

I am grateful to Christopher S. Johnson, whose photograph of Nathan graces the jacket, for his artistry and generosity.

My sincere thanks to Werner Sollors and to Josef Jarab, Rector of Palacky University, for their assistance in establishing the Nathan I. Huggins Library for American Studies (Hugginsova knihovna americkych studii) at the University in Olomouc, the Czech Republic.

I especially wish to express my love to those who have been constant sources of inspiration and personal support: Louise Dean Smith, Sue Bailey Thurman, John Fletcher Smith, Mary Wolfman, Barbara Rosenkrantz, Jeff Ferguson, Irving M. Allen, Peter J. Gomes, Lorna Marshall, Lilian and Oscar Handlin, and Gordon P. Golding.

The essays and lectures in this book span two decades, from 1970 to 1989. Some were published previously; others were works-in-progress. No attempt has been made to organize them either thematically or chronologically.

Paris   Brenda Smith Huggins
Summer, 1994

Contents

REVELATIONS

1

The Historical Odyssey of
Nathan Irvin Huggins

LAWRENCE W. LEVINE

In his entry in *Who's Who in America,* Nathan Huggins spoke of the joys of being a historian:

> I find in the study of history the special discipline which forces me to consider peoples and ages, not my own, in their own terms; yet with an informed and critical eye, enhanced by modern analytical tools and the gift of hindsight. It is the most humane of disciplines, and in ways the most humbling. For one cannot ignore those historians of the future who will look back on us in the same way.[1]

In this brief declaration we have a good introduction to Huggins, to his love of what he did, to his desire always to do it with empathy and humility, to his sense of proportion and perspective. Huggins's gift—and it's an essential gift for a good historian—was his ability to feel for and understand those whose shoes he never wore, his ability to make that crucial leap of empathy into the lives and beings of others. Several months after his death, during the memorial meeting we held at the 1990 convention of the Organization of American Historians (OAH), a letter was read from several women who had been students at Radcliffe in the late 1950s and early 1960s when Nat was a graduate student and a young teacher at Harvard. Their memories of Nathan are also a good introduction:

---

*This article is reprinted from *Radical History Review,* Vol. 55 (1993). Reprinted with the permission of Cambridge University Press. It was originally delivered as a lecture in The John Hope Franklin Distinguished Lecture Series at Adelphi University, 5 February 1992.

1. *Who's Who in America,* 42d ed., 1982–1983 (Wilmette, Il.: Marquis, 1982), I, 1600.

Back before it was fashionable for men to do so, Nat Huggins took us seriously. He never patronized; he never treated our aspirations as frivolous; he never used his position as grader, section man, or Radcliffe Freshman adviser to "come on" to us. He liked us; he was comfortable with us; we were not decorative objects. He did not think we were unimportant, either as scholars or as people; he always had time for us. He never used his masculinity to wound our fragile, evolving female egos; instinctively he affirmed our sense of ourselves. It seems now that he knew subliminally and without articulation what women were up against, and he empathized. He was a rare man whose own pain and anger engendered compassion, not bitterness, and served to increase his sense of our common humanity.[2]

These were characteristics that Nathan also exhibited in his scholarship, and while it is always difficult—perhaps impossible—to know with any precision where one's defining character comes from, Nathan's life itself is not a bad place to begin since his life symbolized the complexities, the bewildering intricacies, of American history and society. Nathan was born in Chicago in 1927. His father, Winston J. Huggins, was African American; his mother, whose maiden name was Marie Warsaw, was Jewish. "The fact of the mixed marriage," Huggins was to say in later years, "gave me a keen sense of race rather early." He was to get a keen sense of responsibility rather early as well. After his father, who was a waiter and a railroad worker, left the family, his mother moved with her children to San Francisco. Two years later, when Huggins was only fourteen, his mother died and he and his sister Kathryn, who was two years older, were left on their own. Huggins helped support them by working as a porter, warehouseman, and longshoreman, all to the detriment of his education. When he was drafted late in World War II he still hadn't completed high school. He accomplished this while in the service, and, after the war, he attended the University of California at Berkeley on the GI Bill.[3]

I should mention that at some point during these years Huggins came under the influence of the black minister Howard Thurman and his wife Sue Bailey Thurman, who opened their San Francisco home to Nathan and whom he referred to as his adopted parents. Huggins was influenced by Thurman's pioneering studies of Negro spirituals, but even more so by Thurman's very presence in his life. "Casual Sunday talks with Howard Thurman," he wrote in the acknowledgments to his first book, "while watching televised morality plays in the guise of professional football, unraveled theological knots. In those struggles between

2. Barbara Shortt, Ellen Wolf Schrecker, Patricia Gerald Bourne, and Anne M. Hamilton, "Nathan Irvin Huggins," statement read at the OAH memorial service to Nathan Irvin Huggins in Washington, D.C., spring 1990.

3. George Howe Colt, "Will the Huggins Approach Save Afro-American Studies?," *Harvard Magazine* (September–October 1981), 43, and interview from which these biographical details are taken.

Good and Evil, Evil, true to life, triumphed more often than not." Of
Sue Bailey Thurman, to whom he dedicated his second book, he wrote:
"Her belief in me when there was little to rest it on, was a profound
influence on my spiritual and intellectual development. She reared me
from the subjunctive to the declarative mood."[4]

Attending the University of California was to be one of the turning
points in Huggins's life. Berkeley, he later declared, was "the most
exciting experience I ever had. For the first time I was dealt with as an
adult, and was rewarded for having ideas." Berkeley's very size was
liberating:

> Berkeley was a big school, and I could float my ideas out there on a
> bluebook under the name of Nathan Huggins, and nobody knew
> whether I was a good guy or a bad guy. One always has the suspicion,
> despite claims to the contrary, that somebody knows you are black.
> Blackness is either going to count for you or against you. Because
> Berkeley was so large, they didn't know what color I was until they got
> to know *who* I was, and by then I had established a track record.

Huggins was freed also from one of the things that had most bothered him
in his unhappy high school years: the American history textbooks that he
remembered "painted a rather sunny picture of slavery. They talked
about darkies sitting on the plantation, eating watermelon and singing
songs." These offenses were compounded by the fact that, as he put it,
"the teachers were not likely to be corrective." At Berkeley, Huggins met
Kenneth Stampp, who was then writing his revisionist history of slavery,
The Peculiar Institution. "He gave evidence," Huggins remembered,
"about brutality, coercion, and resistance that one couldn't find in existing texts. He came up with satisfying conclusions."[5]

While he was still quite young, then, the circumstances of Huggins's
life, race, and ethnicity helped him realize that there was something
profoundly wrong in the portrait of themselves that Americans were
learning and perpetuating. "I first began to ponder the meaning of
slavery in American history as a black schoolboy," he later wrote,
"caught by the anomaly of a slave people within a free society and by the
consistent disparity between the principles of American liberty and the
experience of blacks in the United States."[6] Gradually he came to comprehend that it wasn't merely a sin of omission—leaving non-Europeans
out of the equation—but a sin of commission as well, because the omis-
sions distorted the very meaning of America, which was defined by
slavery as well as by freedom, and which had a colonial past in the

4. Huggins mentions his debts to the Thurmans in three of his books: *Protestants
Against Poverty, Boston's Charities, 1870–1900* (Westport, Conn.: Greenwood Publishing
Corporation, 1971), xiv; *Harlem Rennaissance* (New York: Oxford University Press,
1971), xi; and *Black Odyssey: The Afro-American Ordeal in Slavery* (New York: Vintage
Books, 1977), 252.

5. "Will the Huggins Approach Save Afro-American Studies?," 3.

6. Huggins, *Black Odyssey,* ix.

Hispanic settlements of California as well as in the Puritan settlements of Massachusetts. To ignore fundamental elements like these was to deform the truth of the American past.

The immediate problem Nathan faced while completing his studies at Berkeley was, Did it make any sense for a black man to try to untangle the web of the American past by becoming a professional historian?

> Certainly in 1951, one couldn't imagine a black getting a Ph.D. in history and expecting to teach anywhere. Folk wisdom taught us that a black person with a Ph.D. ended up pushing a broom or working at the post office if he was lucky.

The difficulties inherent in his quest convinced Huggins to leave Berkeley after his master's and switch to Harvard, whose doctorate might go further in helping him break into the academic world. "I . . . realized that a Harvard degree would mean more to me in trying to sell myself as a historian, especially considering what I still recognized to be a handicap of race." The move from Berkeley, which he found "much more democratic" than Harvard, was not an easy one:

> I had very real problems at Harvard, but I would have had them had I been white. Harvard is a class-conscious institution, with a sense of social pretension, an elitism based not simply on merit but on the age and pretensions of the institution . . . [the] most austere, uptight place I'd ever seen. In class nobody talked about anything that was being done by anybody outside of Harvard. Everything was here—or it wasn't worth talking about.[7]

Neither Harvard nor the academic world in general encouraged young historians to concentrate on African-American history in the 1950s, and Huggins chose to write his dissertation on charitable institutions in Boston from 1870 to 1900. In addition to his genuine interest in American social history, there was a practical consideration: "I was anxious that no department could pick up my vita and say, Well, he's a Negro historian and that's a field we don't teach."[8] Receiving his Ph.D. in 1962, Huggins spent the rest of the tumultuous decade teaching at California State College at Long Beach, Lake Forest College just outside Chicago, and the University of Massachusetts at Boston. He spent the academic year 1969–70 as a visiting professor at Berkeley and, although we did our best to make him a permanent member of our faculty, we lost him again, this time to Columbia University. I recall vividly Huggins's version of Thomas Wolfe's "you can't go home again." He realized while visiting Berkeley that year that he was no longer a youngster racing through the Berkeley hills in a passion of wonder and discovery. Those years were past, he told me; trying to recapture them would be futile. Thus Huggins

---

7. "Will the Huggins Approach Save Afro-American Studies?," 43–44.
8. Ibid., 44.

went to New York City in 1970, married Brenda Carlita Smith, and spent a very happy and productive decade teaching and writing.

His satisfying sojourn at Columbia ended in 1980, when Harvard University asked him to become chairman of a troubled Afro-American Studies Department and director of the W. E. B. Du Bois Institute for Afro-American Studies. That decision was not an easy one for Huggins. I know this personally because he was living in the Bay Area that year as a Fellow at the Center for Advanced Studies in Palo Alto, and we had a chance to talk. Because I had been asked to join Huggins at Harvard, we had a lot to talk about. Ultimately, I remained in Berkeley and he went to Harvard, and he went for precisely the same reasons he had gone the first time as a graduate student: because it was *Harvard*. I spent many hours discussing the pros and cons of the move with him, and there's no question in my mind that he realized that moving to Harvard would interfere with his research and writing—which it did—and would be personally disrupting because his wife was working in New York. He went nonetheless, because he concluded it was his duty to go. He told me over and over what he was later to tell an interviewer for *Harvard Magazine:*

> If it were just another school, it wouldn't matter. But Harvard means a lot to schools and academics around the country, and the failure of the program here would have an enormous impact. . . . So I felt I should do it, that it was kind of a calling, in a sense. I had a *responsibility* to do it, because I think it can be done and done well, and here's the place to do it.[9]

When Huggins had first gone to Columbia University, his request to teach a course in American intellectual history occasioned some surprise in the history department, some of whose members thought he had come to teach *Afro*-American history exclusively, and some of whose members, Huggins was convinced, wondered if he was competent to teach anything *but* black history. Nathan always fought this kind of compartmentalization, alway resisted being boxed in because of his race. But he also understood—and I think he understood it more clearly as he got older—that being who he was entailed some obligations. In a perfect world there would be no need for departments of or courses in African-American studies, because black people would be an inherent part of the historical fabric. Until that halcyon day arrived, however, there would be a need for both the courses and the departments. But there was no need for either to be parochial or narrowly focused. Indeed, Huggins was convinced that the problem with the way American history itself had been taught and understood in the first place was that it was too parochial, too Europeanized, too certain that everything outside the narrow spectrum of northern European culture was peripheral and uninfluential. The function of African-American history was not to cre-

9. Ibid.

ate another narrow specialty, but to infuse American history with the understanding that from the beginning African Americans have a great deal to do with the distinctiveness of the United States, with what has made America American.[10]

During his decade at Harvard, Huggins became an important force for articulating his conceptions of American history. He built the W. E. B. Du Bois Institute into an active and dynamic institution, but the department itself somehow lagged behind. Huggins was frustrated in making the appointments he envisioned, and at his death the department had only one other tenured member. As a member of the visiting committee to the department for five years, I can attest personally to the impact Huggins had on those students who majored in Afro-American studies, and on Harvard's African-American students in general. Even those who had only peripheral connections with his department came to value Huggins as an adviser and mentor. One young black woman we spoke with, a language major, told of how some of the professors in her major department had made her feel that her interest in Afro-American studies as a minor field was abnormal, and of how important being able to speak with Huggins had been for her. Still, his department never attained the prestige and influence he desired for it, and at his death it remained a department in trouble. Nathan Huggins's primary legacy to us, then, is less institutional than conceptual and intellectual, less embodied in the structures he built than in the books he wrote, which offer the fullest key to Huggins's historical odyssey.

That odyssey took him from one set of assumptions and images about the American past to another. And although it began early in Huggins's life, as we have seen, as was articulated throughout his three decades of teaching, in terms of books it was manifest in one intense period of activity: all four of his books and both of his edited volumes were published from 1971 to 1980.[11] Huggins was an excellent example of what Richard Hofstadter had in mind when he defined the intellectual as someone whose attitudes towards ideas combined playfulness and piety.[12] Certainly, Huggins had an abundance of piety—seriousness about understanding the American past as correctly as he was capable of—but within this circle of piety there was always room for a good deal of playful variety. What he wrote about the poet Countee Cullen: "his poetry remained exercises in verse, never experiment or play,"[13] cannot be said of Hug-

10. This summary of Huggins's views on African-American history is based upon my many conversations with him over the years, as well as upon his published work.

11. *Protestants Against Poverty; Harlem Renaissance; Key Issues in the Afro-American Experience,* ed. Nathan I. Huggins, Martin Kilson, and Daniel M. Fox (New York: Harcourt Brace Jovanovich, 1971); *Voices from the Harlem Renaissance* (New York: Oxford University Press, 1976); *Black Odyssey;* and *Slave and Citizen: The Life of Frederick Douglass* (Boston: Little, Brown, 1980).

12. Richard Hofstadter, *Anti-Intellectualism in American Life* (New York: Alfred A. Knopf, 1963), 27.

13. *Harlem Renaissance,* 213.

gins's own work, for in much of it there is a distinct element of play, of experiment, of variety. Because his study of the Harlem Renaissance involved questions of ethnic identity, he felt free to conclude it with a wonderfully original essay entitled "White/Black Faces—Black Masks," which ranged far beyond the subject of Harlem in the 1920s. Each of his four books is rather distinct in form and essence: *Protestants Against Poverty* is a monograph; *Harlem Renaissance,* a free-ranging essay in intellectual and cultural history; *Black Odyssey,* an imaginative and evocatively written synthesis of the African-American experience in slavery, aimed at a wide audience; *Slave and Citizen,* a brief interpretation of the life of the African-American thinker and politician, Frederick Douglass. The book he was working on in his later years—a large-scale, deeply researched biography of Ralph Bunche—was still another departure for Huggins. Perhaps all of these departures, all of this moving about structurally, was an attempt not to fall into what he saw as the plight of many black writers, such as the poets Countee Cullen and Claude McKay, each of whom was, in Huggins's words "crippled by a tradition not truly the poet's own."[14] It is possible that he was searching for a form of writing history and a voice that were authentically his. Whatever the cause, the structural diversity of his books is striking.

Within that diversity, there are equally striking continuities. The most important of these is his determination to reap whatever benefits he accrued from being black in a white world. Central among these benefits was what Du Bois had called the gift of "second-sight in this American world." Huggins was fascinated with Du Bois's musings about the African-American "double-consciousness, this sense of always looking at one's self through the eyes of others, of measuring one's soul by the tape of a world that looks on in amused contempt and pity." Huggins articulated his own corollary to what he called "this remarkable and profound statement:"

> [T]his "double-consciousness" opens to the Negro—through his own quest and passion—a unique insight into the vulnerable and unfulfilled soul of that other world; a possibility which, once grasped, liberates one forever from the snarls of that other world's measuring tape.[15]

Huggins had grasped that possibility early in his life and tried to utilize the liberation it conferred in all of his work; he strove to benefit as deeply as he could from what he called this "unique insight into the . . . soul of that other world," what Du Bois had called the "gift" of "second-sight in this American world."

This "second-sight" made Huggins particularly sensitive to the paradoxes and ironies that he saw dominating American history. Even in his revised and published doctoral dissertation, *Protestants Against Poverty*—his only book not directly focusing on black history—Nathan

14. Ibid., 214.
15. Ibid., 244–45.

already revealed a fascination with how Americans conceived of and responded to those they relegated to the margins of the society, whether they were poor, immigrant, female, or black. He saw both the folly and the tragedy embedded in the propensity of reformers to create categories and boxes in which to stuff human beings: the "worthy poor" to whom society was always obliged because they retained their self-respect and asked for aid only reluctantly and infrequently, and the "unworthy poor" who too often and too willingly demanded alms "as a right." He grasped the paradox that those who were most in need of aid were deemed the least "worthy," that the cause of poverty was invariably located in the poor themselves, and that "charity reformers never suggested that the poor might have special insight into their own problems; they were the last to be consulted about their interest." Thus the poor "had to be guided, told, scolded, cajoled, pushed and even punished"—treated, in short, like irresponsible children. Huggins was sensitive not only to the paradoxical behavior of the reformers but to the "collisions of cultures" they could never fully perceive, and which separated them from those they were attempting to help. At times, Huggins observed, human voices "broke through the austere records of charitable organizations and the papers of the reformer, so that the reader can sense the poor person as a . . . fellow human creature to be contended with. The voices were rarely heard and never well received." Above all, Huggins was struck by the inability of Boston's charity workers to perceive poverty as a societal rather than a personal problem:

> [T]he reformers were unable to see the simple truth that . . . the problem with the poor is that they have no money. . . . But the implications of that insight are more radical than the genteel charity reformers could have dared to accept. For that would have obliged them to consider ways of distributing the society's wealth so that humanity would not be dishonored by inequity. That is the citadel that any successful war on poverty must control.[16]

These observations concluded Huggins's first book, but not his quest to pursue the entire question of the nation's refusal or inability to perceive the poor, the immigrant, the slave as adults with lives and culture worthy of study rather than as problems to be dealt with, as aberrations which should cause no one to question what he called the "master narrative" of United States history as the progressive triumph of freedom and liberty. His focus now shifted to the black community, and the fullest investigation of this phenomenon was his third book, *Black Odyssey: The Afro-American Ordeal in Slavery.*

In this moving re-creation of the slave experience, Huggins reached out in two new ways: He extended his inquiry from the literate, educated people who had previously occupied him, to a more amorphous

---

16. *Protestants Against Poverty,* 29–30, 181, 183–84, 201.

group we might call the "folk," and he attempted to communicate with a general audience. At the time he was writting it, he told me he was deliberately avoiding any direct bibliographical references in the text or discussion of the scholarly arguments concerning the nature of slavery to prevent academic styles and debates from frightening away potential readers. He was convinced it was possible to write a thoroughly serious book, based upon the latest scholarship, in a way that would command the interest of a diverse audience.

Huggins was particularly anxious to reach a large audience because of what he was trying to accomplish. "The governing word is 'perspective'," he wrote in his introduction to a new edition of *Black Odyssey,* published just after his death. The object was not merely to mention and discuss those who had been marginalized in the standard histories. "Rather it is to understand the past through them, to see history through their eyes, making them essential witnesses to the events historians discussed." It was not sufficient to "integrate" the picture by adding blacks; it was necessary to comprehend that there could be no picture without blacks who were an integral part of it from the beginning. "The challenge of the paradox is that there can be no white history or black history, nor can there be an integrated history that does not begin to comprehend that slavery and freedom, white and black, are joined at the hip . . . we must see them not only as interdependent but as having a common story and necessarily sharing the same fate."[17]

Huggins tells the story of black slaves in America with great force. It is the story of Africans becoming African Americans and adapting their lives and cultures to a new situation. Throughout, Huggins makes us aware of the special dilemmas they faced: "A person from a traditional and static order [the African], was to become part of a modern society whose underlying principle was change. A collective person wrenched from an intimate social context that gave a sense of self, he was thrust into one, against his will, which would isolate and atomize individuals one from another." Throughout, Huggins sensitizes us to the ways in which African-American slaves were able to survive not merely the material, but the spiritual and psychological rigors of the system. He details the cultural adjustments by means of which they were able to resign themselves to slavery without accepting their own inferiority; by means of which they could recognize slavery as "their condition, not their destiny." Huggins allows us to see that ultimately slaves were a troublesome property because even in accommodating to slavery they maintained their humanity. Throughout, Huggins makes it clear that the price slavery exacted was not paid by blacks alone. As time went on, it was not the differences between the races that was threatening: "It was,

17. "The Deforming Mirror of Truth," intro. to the reissued edition of *Black Odyssey: The African-American Ordeal in Slavery* (New York: Vintage Books, 1990), xix–xx, xliv.

rather, the sameness that was the problem. The more white and black, master and slave, shared the same culture, spoke the same language, were tied by kinship and custom, birthplace and lifestyles," the greater the need for structures and fictions that maintained the legal and caste differences between them.

> Southern society had become a monolith, resting upon the single object of preserving and justifying its "peculiar institution." All Southerners, white and black, slave and free, were controlled by the rationalization of slavery's protection. . . . Here was a model totalitarian society supported directly or indirectly by the entire nation. From the perspective of the Afro-American, the United States, by the eve of the Civil War, was what the Founding Fathers meant when they described tyranny.

Black Odyssey is filled with Huggins's sense that history is not a tale to be told for the sake of the telling; that history is something we have to learn from, something that should give us insights into our past and ourselves; that to learn about blacks is to learn about whites—to learn about America itself. The rewards of such learning are not necessarily pleasant; there is no happy ending to *Black Odyssey*. The patience and faith of the slaves were rewarded by a hollow freedom. "For all black men and women, regardless of where they finally settled, the realization sank in that America, not only the South but all of America, would remain for them a land of tyranny." The tragedy was not one for black people alone; the disastrous decision to enslave Africans in the seventeenth century was repeated again and again throughout our history "not just to exploit black people for profit but to despoil other human resources; not just to expropriate the substance of people but to ravage the land and water and air." The result was

> the collective trauma, the loss of communality, that has plagued us as a people. It has meant that when we have most sensed our greatness, we have been made to feel our meanness; when we have proclaimed our freedom most, the ghosts of slaves have sung loudest in our ears, when we would finally grasp the dream, we were stunned by our failure of heart and imagination.

But if there was no happy ending, there was a lesson: "The shadows and ghosts of the past remind us that those who would be tyrants cannot be called free men."[18]

As obviously passionate as Huggins's writing could become, he tried always to walk that delicate line between engagement and objectivity. He could have said along with C. Wright Mills: "I have tried to be objective, but I do not claim to be detached."[19] His final book, *Slave and Citizen*—a brief biography of Frederick Douglass—showed his ability to be critically independent even when writing about a figure he so obvi-

---

18. *Black Odyssey* (1990 edition), 204, 232, 112–13, 242, 246, and passim.
19. C. Wright Mills, *The Marxists* (New York: Dell Publishing Col, 1962), 10.

ously admired and honored. His empathy with Douglass allowed him to show with impressive skill why Douglass, as a black man and an ex-slave, inevitably had to sever his ties with the Garrisonian abolitionists who stressed nonresistance and moral suasion as the means through which to shame Americans into reform. "Such an argument," Huggins maintained, "had very little to say to the slave, or to anyone oppressed," who were most likely to feel that their shame was lodged in their nonre-sistance. "Should a slave not use violence against his master? Should free blacks and fugitives not use violence to protect themselves from slave hunters and kidnappers? The Garrisonians were ambivalent about these questions; Douglass as a black spokesman, could not be." Who Douglass was, Huggins maintains, "where he had come from, the road he traveled were never far from his conscious mind."

The same might well be said of Huggins himself, whose own paths, whose own mobility, whose own sense of being were never far from *his* conscious mind. These similarities were the basis of his profound em-pathy with Douglass, which in turn allowed Huggins to gently criticize and adroitly understand Douglass's growing conservatism after the Civil War. "Cherishing a bit too much the honors that fell to him," Douglass allowed the two very minor posts he was awarded by the Republicans to blunt "the sharpness and power of his social and political critique." But Huggins also demonstrates that Douglass's problem was structural and not merely personal: He, like all other black leaders of the postbellum years, lacked any meaningful political power or base. During the antebel-lum years "his alienation as a black man and radical allowed him the freedom of mind and spirit he would never have again." After the war, his choice was either to alienate himself from the system and once more speak from the outside, or to learn the "art of the possible." Huggins comprehends more than condemns the choices Douglass made in the final decades of his life.

In this book, as in all of his work, Nathan was attempting to under-stand not only the past but something larger, more enduring; he was dealing with not merely the particular subject matter at hand but with the human condition itself. Thus he ended his biography with a parable:

> In 1899 a young man asked Booker T. Washington what he would advise for a young, black man starting into the new century. Washing-ton's answer was characteristic: "Work! Work! Work! Be patient and win by superior service." The same young man had asked Douglass the very same question less than a month before he died. The old man's answer came from the entirety of his life: "Agitate! Agitate! Agitate!" Far into the twentieth century, black Americans would testify that one bit of advice was of little use without the other.[20]

I have saved for last what I consider to be Huggins's most original contribution: *Harlem Renaissance,* his second book and the first book in

20. *Slave and Citizen,* 59, 132, 136, 147, 180, and passim.

which he studied African-American culture and society. It was, and is, a remarkable achievement. It was certainly Nathan's freest and most personal book. *Protestants Against Poverty* was his doctoral dissertation with all of the constraints endemic to that species: the need to please professors, to conform to departmental and university requirements, and so on. *Black Odyssey* was written with a general audience in mind, and that imposes constraints of its own. *Slave and Citizen* was written in the Library of American Biography series, which has a prescribed format and length.

Harlem Renaissance, on the other hand, was the product of Nathan's reflections on the role of black intellectuals at the very moment when he himself was taking his place in the black—and white—intelligentsia. It is thus a work of history with a very personal cast to it. It opens with a beautiful paragraph that gives a wonderful example of Huggins's literary and intellectual style:

> It is a rare and intriguing moment when a people decide that they are the instruments of history-making and race-building. It is common enough to think of oneself as part of some larger meaning in the sweep of history, a part of some grand design. But to presume to be an actor and creator in the special occurrence of a people's birth (or rebirth) requires a singular self-consciousness. In the opening decades of the twentieth century, down to the first years of the Great Depression, black intellectuals in Harlem had just such a self-concept. These Harlemites were so convinced that they were evoking their people's "Dusk of Dawn" that they believed that they marked a renaissance.

Following this introduction, one might expect a celebration of the Harlem Renaissance, but what Huggins gives us is a critical analysis that was and remains the most challenging we have. This was due not only to his critical bent, but also to the fact that in this book especially he was asking questions and mulling over matters that had immediate, as well as historical, relevance to him. He understood that in approaching renaissance intellectuals critically, he was following a precarious course. "Some will argue that in our day of crisis of black identity it is harmful to question *any* Afro-American achievement; positive self-concept needs pure black poets as well as pure black heroes. I have chosen, however, to avoid that condescension which judges all Negro art as required evidence of a black cultural contribution. Who really needs such proof?"

In one important sense Nathan identified closely with the intellectuals he was studying. Their quest to understand their heritage by searching the entire African-American experience for clues paralleled Nathan's own quest as he proceeded from a study of the marginal in white society to a study of those black intellectuals who were attempting to understand and aid their race, to a study of the folk in slavery, to a study of a leader who came from that folk. In his scholarship there was a replication of what he said the renaissance intellectuals were engaged in doing: he shared their sense of obligation to the race, which ultimately led him to Harvard and the building of an Afro-American studies department that could serve as a model for the entire nation. In part, then, the originality and insightfulness of this book certainly stem from the fact that it was the study closest to Huggins's own experiences; but they stem also from his determination to not merely emulate his intellectual forebears, but to understand and learn from their dilemmas and shortcomings.

Afro-American art,, Huggins insists, "bore the special weight of proving racial civility." James Weldon Johnson declared that no "people that has produced great literature and art has ever been looked upon by the world as distinctly inferior." Thus black artists carried a burden not merely of individual achievements but of race advancement—which had to make them and their art self-conscious in a way that could be crippling. In their struggle to prove their worth, they encountered the question of whose standard of art and excellence they were supposed to live up to. Clearly, if they were to win the approval of the larger society, that standard would be the model. But here, Huggins argues, black artists were at a distinct disadvantage when it came to innovation because, only fifty years out of slavery, they had enough to do merely to prove they could learn and emulate the standards, without also having to go beyond them. Black art was too trapped by the past, too much in the grip of the hands of dead men because black artists and writers were trying too hard to be accepted, were carrying too much of the burden of race advancement on their shoulders, were too busy trying to gain entry into the society to be able to devote their energies to breaking out of it, were too unwilling to look within their own traditions and past for their artistic goals and standards. They were, in short, too self-conscious to be truly creative. The renaissance novelist Wallace Thurman depicted the dilemma by imaging Harlem's poet laureate in his creative hours: "eyes on a page of Keats, fingers on a typewriter, mind frantically conjuring African scenes. And there would of course be a Bible nearby."

The final handicap to innovative black art was that the renaissance writers were of necessity writing for a largely white audience that knew relatively little about black culture. This forced black writers to create what Huggins called works of circumstance and context rather than of characterization. In novel after novel, black writers became obsessed with explaining what it meant to be black in America, to describing such phenomena as passing, to proving that there was a black upper class that could discuss novels and art and speak French. There were exceptions in the 1920s—the novelist Jean Toomer and the poets Langston Hughes and Sterling Brown—but their lack of an audience proved the rule.

Where black artistic expression was at its most exciting and innovative in the 1920s was in such areas as music, where it was unself-conscious, where it didn't attempt to emulate standards set for it, where it didn't seek to win the plaudits or gain the acceptance of the larger society. Musicians like Louis Armstrong, Jelly Roll Morton, and Fletcher Henderson were too caught up in their own artistic visions to worry about whether they were achieving the standards of "civilization." Their art came out of their own ethnic context and their own lives, and they found they didn't have to mimic whites; whites were mimicking them—trying to master *their* form and *their* innovations. Unfortunately, their example was too often lost on most of the renaissance writers who saw black jazz and blues as the materials out of which artistic creation might someday be forged, but not as authentic creation itself.

Huggins is perhaps at his most provocative when he discusses the role of Africa in the renaissance. Even as black intellectuals desired to emulate the "European-entranced" white intellectuals, they were also attracted by "the dream of self-definition through the claiming of their inheritance of African culture." He attempts to show the difficulties attendant upon this dual quest. "The Negro intellectual's fascination with primitivism was filled with ironies. Contrary to assertions of the soul-community of blacks, the American Negroes had to *learn* to appreciate the value of African art and culture. Too often they were taught by Europeans. . . ." He tries to demonstrate, too, how *American* their quest was, how related it was to the white intellectuals' tendency to search for *their* roots abroad rather than in their own backyards. "Black Americans, like white Americans, dissatisfied with and unfulfilled by the selves that they had, sought escape in exotica."

The force of these stunning and challenging analyses is how well they often apply to other ethnic groups and to women as well; something I think Huggins was not completely aware of. He tended to stress the distinctions rather than the parallels between blacks and ethnic immigrants: "There is a very real and important difference between being alien and alienated: being a stranger to something which is your becoming, or being native to something of which you are not a part." Huggins, of course, had both of these traditions in his background, but it was his African Americanness that he embraced. Although I knew him well, I can't evaluate what effects, if any, the other part of his identity had upon his work and perceptions, or to what extent it was a part of his identity at all; all of which are interesting questions to contemplate.

What *can* be said without question is that Huggins never abstracts black Americans; he continuously portrays them in the context of the larger culture, which they of course helped to create. "The black-white relationship," he tells us, "has been symbiotic; blacks have been essential to white identity (and whites to blacks). This interdependence has been too profound to be measured by the simple meting out of respective contributions to American symbiosis." It's impossible, ultimately, to do this profound book justice in a brief summary.

In one of his last visits to Berkeley, Huggins gave a speech challenging the Eurocentric bias in education and asked: "How do you get people who believe they are the center of the universe to move over?"[21] During the final summer of his life, Huggins wrote an essay, "The Deforming Mirror of Truth," in which I think he attempted to explain how this could be accomplished.[22] I suspect that he knew this would be his last substantial piece of scholarly writing, his final testament, and it's significant that in it he goes further than he had before; what was implicit in his earlier writings becomes explicit here: We needed—desperately—a new "Master Narrative" of the American past, which would be altered by the "Deforming Mirror of Truth." For Nathan the greatest paradox in our history occurred at its very outset, when the founding fathers sanitized their new creation by ignoring the "inescapable paradox" of a free nation resting on slavery. It was, Huggins comments, "a bad way to start. It encouraged the belief that American history—its institutions, its values, its people—was one thing and racial slavery and oppression were a different story." American historians, Huggins charged, have conspired with the founders to treat racial slavery and oppression not as fundamental parts of the system, but as aberrations which would be corrected as the nation strode towards its destiny. Thus, our national history "continued to amplify the myths of automatic progress, universal freedom, and the American dream." But this "holy history" has become increasingly incapable of explaining our society to its people. "The present challenges the past in ways that cannot be denied. History, even as national myth, must tell us who we are, how and why we are where we are, and how our destinies have been shaped." Our present has become so fragmented that the master narrative no longer serves as universal authority. "Blacks, the poor, and others whom the myth ignores are conspicuously in the center of our present, and they call for a national history that incorporates their experiences."

As he concluded this final piece of historical writing, Huggins almost seemed to give way to despair: "As we enter the final decade of the twentieth century, despondency weighs heavily upon us. The tide seems not to be rising for us." He enumerated our dilemmas: widening maldistribution of wealth, a shrinking middle class, falling living standards, a crisis in education and health, an epidemic of drugs and crime, a decaying infrastructure, an enormous public debt, and an apathetic public. All of which led him to conclude that our times

> seem to call for new myths and a revised master narrative that better inspire and reflect upon our true condition. Such a new narrative would find inspiration, for instance, in an oppressed people who defied social death as slaves and freedmen, insisting on their humanity and creating a culture despite a social consensus that they were a "brutish sort of

21. *Daily Californian* (29 October 1987), 11.

22. This essay was published as the introduction to the 1990 reissued edition of *Black Odyssey*, xi–lxxvi. An abbreviated version, "The Deforming Mirror of Truth: Slavery and the Master Narrative of American History," appeared in *Radical History Review* 49 (Winter 1991): 25–46.

people." Such a new narrative would bring slavery and the persistent oppression of race from the margins to the center, to define the limits and boundaries of the American Dream. Such a new narrative would oblige us to face the deforming mirror of truth.

Thus, I think it's fair to say that until the very end, Huggins continued to believe in the transforming power of history once we learned to read it correctly. To the very end, his despair at what existed was tempered by his sense of what was possible.

I want to conclude these remarks by reflecting on my own friendship with Huggins, which spanned more than a quarter of a century; unfortunately, it also spanned a continent. For most of the years we knew each other we were three thousand miles apart. And so my memories of him are not continuous, but bunched together in a collage of incidents, a few of which I'd like to share because I think they illuminate aspects of his personality and character.

There was the time when he and I lectured at a summer institute for secondary school teachers at Berkeley in the early 1960s. After his exploratory lecture about black poets in the 1920s, one of his earliest expressions of the book he was writing, a black Chicago teacher, enraged that Huggins was intellectually dissecting and even criticizing some of the icons of black American history, came up to him and said: "You forget who you are!" She was, of course, incorrect: as I have tried to show, Huggins never forgot who he was; indeed, it was his profound interest in who he was and how he got there and what his relationship to the larger society was, and what the nature of the African-American group he belonged to was that led to his best work, that helped him become so good a historian. But in another sense, not the sense she intended, she was quite right, for it was Huggins's ability to transcend who he was, to rise above the immediate situation and conditions that defined him, to empathize with the situation and conditions of others, that made him so sensitive and perceptive and powerful a historian.

In the early 1970s, when I was doing research at the Library of Congress, I met a white scholar researching alongside me who asked me if I knew of a good black historian to whom he could give his notes, because he had decided that a white man couldn't—or perhaps it was shouldn't—really write the book on black culture for which he had been doing research. I sent him to talk with Huggins since I knew, or thought I knew, what Huggins would tell him, and it was in fact what he did tell him: that he was being not sensitive but insensitive; that he was insulting black people; that a white scholar could write black history as surely as a black could write white history, or an American could write French history, or a modern scholar could write the history of classical Greece. Huggins simply refused to mystify the history of black people or of any people. He refused to establish barriers, to erect gates and fences, that separated and pigeonholed and limited scholars. That attitude didn't mean that Nat was oblivious to the special insights and perspectives blacks brought to their own experience. I remember how eager he was to have a black artist design the cover of his book *Black Odyssey.* He insisted on it not only to provide work to a black artist in an area where work was often hard to come by, but because he felt an African-American artist would have a special understanding of what Nathan was trying to do in a book that I think was the closest to his affections of all of his books—a book that brought him disappointment because he felt it was never received or understood as he had hoped it would be. In one of my last conversations with him, he told me how delighted he was that the book would be coming out again in a new edition.

There was the time very early in his career, when Huggins got a job without an interview, and only later discovered that he was selected, in part at least—he was always convinced that it was in *large* part—because he was one of the few candidates for the position whose name was not obviously Jewish. When he appeared to begin his duties, his employers found that their zeal to keep Jews out had led them to inadvertently hire a black. Huggins loved to talk about that incident when he was with close friends. He loved the irony of it. He loved to contemplate the ironic in life: he had a gentle ironic sense of humor that lit up his face. It was this sense of the ironies of life that helped him cope with the cruelties and incongruities of his own life and the lives of those he studied. That sense of the ironic was deeply embedded in all of Huggins's mature work, most especially his study of the *Harlem Renaissance.*

In the early 1970s, Huggins and I visited a number of German universities to give separate but related lectures. He spoke about African-American intellectuals and I spoke about the folk. But Huggins kept goading me to form what he called and "act," to give a duet, to weave our lectures together into one performance, and we began to do just that. We stood up together and gave unrehearsed joint interactive lectures that got better every time we did it. Indeed, Huggins used to kid me in later years, saying it was time we went "on the road" again. He loved that kind of spontaneity—he rarely ever *read* a lecture to people. He loved surprising his audiences. He loved the unrehearsed, the spontaneous, the natural.

One night in Berlin in the late 1970s, Huggins and I were in a friend's apartment; it was the early hours of the morning and the subways were no longer running, which gave us the excuse to sit up the entire night with a group of German students talking, drinking beer and wine, and smoking long Russian cigarettes. I still remember how animated Huggins was that night, how full of life and ideas, how articulate he was even as the rest of us began to fade, how lacking in small talk he always was; how much he loved speaking about what he regarded as the significant, which usually meant the deeply human.

Nathan Huggins was in love with ideas, with thought, with the process of thinking. He detested the shoddy, the superficial. He was upset when he first arrived at Columbia University because he felt some of his white colleagues were condescending to black students by not demanding enough of them, by not pushing them sufficiently. But Huggins also expected people—and particularly scholars—to understand the special situation of blacks in American society. In the last year of his life he was furious at a reviewer of Martin Duberman's biography of Paul Robeson because he spent the greater part of his prominent review taking Robeson to task for never breaking with Stalin. Nathan's concern was less the overt red-baiting than the reviewer's total insensitivity to the reasons undergirding Robeson's relationship to the Soviet Union, the Communist Party USA, and American society. Huggins insisted that scholarship be characterized by empathy, by understanding, by a sense of humanity.

Empathy and understanding and humanity characterized his own scholarship. More that that, they also characterized his life.

2

Harlem on My Mind

Harlem! Its very name means black American urban life. Throughout the world, and througout this century, for people with even the slightest notion of the United States, Harlem has been Afro-American life and culture. It has stood for night life and gaiety, jazz and poetry, novels and song. It has also meant poverty and despair, crime and slums, oppression and riots. So jarring and discordant are the images, we can hardly keep them all at once in mind. We think of one side at a time, the sweetness or the bitterness, as it suits us, ignoring the rest until our mood changes. Yet Harlem embodies it all. Like the blues and all of Afro-American life, it is bittersweet. And like the blues, any honest look at Harlem will make you laugh and make you cry, make you feel joy and make you despair. When poet Langston Hughes thought about Harlem, which was just about all the time, he thought of it as a "Dream Deferred."

Harlem is a black word, having lost all meaningful connection with the Dutch who named the river and upper Manhattan. No one even thinks of the solid, middle-class stodginess which characterized the district at the turn of the century, before blacks moved in. At one time it had been rural farmland, before developers, sensing the unrelenting pressure for new housing for affluent whites, turned pastures and cottages into grand avenues, townhouses, and apartment buildings. Harlem was built up to accommodate white folks who had the money to live in bourgeois style and comfort. That explains the tree-lined elegance of Seventh Avenue, the grand and spacious apartment buildings, Stanford White's townhouses on "Striver's Row."

The speculators and developers were to be disappointed. White folks did not come in anything like the expected numbers. Mainly, war in Europe had put a temporary halt to the process where waves of European immigrants pushed older, affluent white residents to seek

*This essay was written in the late 1970s, in conjunction with the Metropolitan Museum of Art's exhibit "Harlem on My Mind."

better housing in newer districts. Harlem was meant for them, but they didn't come.

Black people came instead. Most were newcomers to the city, migrants from the South, pushed by growing poverty and unrelenting racial violence, pulled by the lure of jobs and the promise of freedom in a great northern city. New York City was not alone. Black populations of all the northern cities swelled in the years around World War I—Chicago, Detroit, Cleveland, Philadelphia—wherever there were jobs and the promise of a new life. Each city would develop its own new black district, but Harlem was in New York, and that made it special. It was the emerging business and cultural capital of the New World and, as one saw it in the first decade of the twentieth century, it was the symbol of a new age.

Lacking the expected demand from whites, Harlem real estate went begging. Several enterprising black men, like Henry C. Parker and John E. Nail, took advantage in good American style. They invested in apartment houses, converting them to black occupancy. It was no easy transition, with the old Harlem residents—Germans, German Jews, and Irish—bitterly resisting the racial transformation of their neighborhood. Buildings, streets, and city blocks were struggled over as in house-to-house combat. One after another fell into the hands of blacks. Hardly anyone imagined that Harlem, or any other city neighborhood, could be racially mixed; if it could not be all white, it would be all black. And so it was.

By 1914, it was clear which way things would go. In all of Manhattan, there were little more than 60,000 black people; 50,000 of them lived within a twenty-three-block area of Harlem. Even the most die-hard whites grudgingly gave up and moved to other parts of the city. Major black institutions—churches, fraternal societies, newspapers, social service agencies—moved uptown. By 1920, over 73,000 blacks lived in Harlem. It was as if for the first time, in matters having to do with race, the American system had worked. The supply of housing had surrendered to the demand, regardless of race; the most enterprising and aggressive businessmen had won the day despite the fact that they were black and their competition white. And black people were the apparent victors, the inhabitants of one of the choicest districts in the biggest, best, and busiest city in the world.

So dawned what seemed like a new day for the Afro-American. Emerging from perhaps the darkest period in their history, it would seem that an important corner had been turned. Harlem, in its way, symbolized it.

It had been a half-century since the emancipation of slaves and since the Fourteenth Amendment had included black people to the rights of citizens in the United States. Within that fifty years all hopes of racial justice and fair play had been shattered by fraud and violence, lynching and riots; all while an American people and a national government looked on with indifference. The new century brought a new spirit, the

"New Negro" who would no longer submit to indignities, threats, and violence. The New Negro would fight back and stake out for himself that which he considered rightfully his, and he would defend it and himself; blow for blow if it came to that. Rhetoric and wishful thinking, perhaps, but the blacking of Harlem made it seem real.

The most striking thing about the "New" as opposed to the "Old" Negro was that he was urban, not rural. Blacks might still be exploited in Harlem, but it would not be as sharecroppers, tenant farmers, and peasants locked into the peonage of the post-Reconstruction South. Harlem had been peopled by those who had voted with their feet against southern tyranny, who would not accept their "place" to be that of "uncles," "aunties," and shuffling darkies.

Harlem might be black, but it was also cosmpolitan. The New Negro would have a sense of himself as part of a larger world of black people. Black men and women from the French and British West Indies, Spanish-speaking migrants from Santo Domingo and Puerto Rico settled in the district. Afro-American participation in the European war helped to open the world to them. They were cast among African, East and West Indians, and Asians—all non-white victims of European colonialism. They would find a kinship in race and circumstance, and returning black soldiers would no longer see their predicament as singular and isolated. Harlem would be at the nexus of a world-wide struggle of race, and colored people everywhere would see Harlem as a generating center, the most advanced outpost in the struggle against colonial domination.

Harlem was thus caught in cross currents of world events. Wartime idealism—saving the world for democracy, the self-determination of ethnic peoples—echoed in the journalism and street-corner speeches in Harlem. Fighting for democracy abroad demanded freedom and democracy for black people at home. The same principles justifying the nationalism of the Irish in Dublin, the Magyars in Budapest, and the Serbs in Belgrade supported the demands of black nationalism in America. At the height of the war, A. Philip Randolph, the editor of the *Messenger* and later the founder of the Brotherhood of Sleeping Car Porters, urged blacks not to fight in the European war until their own rights were guaranteed at home. When peace came, W. E. B. Du Bois, editor of the N.A.A.C.P.'s *Crisis,* would petition the councils of the League of Nations against continued colonialism in Africa. Du Bois would be one of the strongest voices for the pan-African movement in the post-war years. Marcus Garvey, a Jamaican, would make Harlem the base for his international organization of blacks supporting black pride, black enterprise, and Africa for Africans. The spirit of the New Negro was in it all; it could be felt in London and Paris, but his home was in Harlem.

The street-corner orator became an institution in Harlem, each arguing his own brand of radicalism: socialism, communism, Africa for Africans, back to Africa, black business, black self-sufficiency, black religion.

Radical rhetoric, however, called forth reaction and repressions. During the war, the Post Office Department confiscated issues of the *Messenger,* and A. Philip Randolph was threatened with jail under charges of sedition. The Garvey movement was harassed, and by the mid-1920s, Marcus Garvey himself would be indicted and convicted of mail fraud, jailed, and ultimately deported from the country. The post-war United States was marked by political repression, and Attorney General Mitchell Palmer initiated raids to suppress leftists and anarchists. In Harlem, as everywhere else in the country, political radicalism suffered.

Despite the muting of the political voice, the New Negro lived on, transformed into cultural forms: literature, theater, music, and art. By 1925, Harlem was being spoken of as the home of the "New Negro Renaissance." Young writers like Langston Hughes, Claude McKay, Countee Cullen, and Rudolph Fisher were getting their first recognition in writing about Harlem and the lives of the people there. There were successful new shows, like Eubie Blake and Noble Sissle's *Shuffle Along.* Black folks' music—ragtime, blues, jazz—was moving into mainstream American culture. Harlem set the tempo and style for the decade F. Scott Fitgerald was to call "The Jazz Age." The literature, like the music and the shows, resonated prohibition: cabarets, speakeasies, bootleg liquor. White writers made more of the exotic Harlem than did black writers. Carl Van Vechten's novel about Harlem, *Nigger Heaven,* sold over 100,000 copies.

As Langston Hughes put it, "The Negro was in vogue." The Jazz Age meant new behavior, new style, new morals, and white Americans were all too eager to break constraints of rural, puritan America. Harlem was the place to go to lose yourself in cabarets and booze and perhaps cocaine, to let yourself go to the rhythms of the Charleston, the Black Bottom, and Snake Hips. Harlem had become the white folks' playground, and most black folks loved it. Musicians and dancers got work at such places as the Cotton Club and Connie's Inn (neither of which catered to black folks), and Small's. White folks brought money uptown, and that was good. It was also fun to watch them act "colored." No white visitor to New York would consider his stay complete without an evening in Harlem. If they were lucky and "in the know," they could get someone like Carl Van Vechten to take them to "authentic" places off the beaten path.

There was a serious side to the culture of the New Negro. The music that was being played and sung—Bessie Smith, Louis Armstrong, "Jelly Roll" Morton, Duke Ellington—would profoundly change American culture; it would never be the same. Books of poetry and fiction were being written by black authors and making their way into the mainstream. And although later the Harlem Renaissance would be called naïve, it was nevertheless an important starting point in Afro-American literature. Some Harlemites, like Arthur Schomburg, began the important work of unearthing the African and Afro-American past. A great

deal of what attracted whites to Harlem in the 1920s was transient indeed, but much they were indifferent to endured and would dominate
the future.

With the Depression of the 1930s, much of the air went out of the
balloon. Everyone got hit, but hard times hit black folks harder than
others. Poverty and squalor had been part of the Harlem scene for a long
time, but no one had wanted to miss the fun and pay attention.

In the crunch of the Depression, even the feeble toehold blacks
had on ownership of Harlem real estate was nearly wiped away. Apartment houses and brownstones had come into black ownership, it is
true, but as is always the case, blacks had to pay more for the privilege
of buying houses and renting apartments. Homeowners, struggling to
keep their heads above water, had taken in lodgers. Apartment house
owners had cut up units so that tenants could afford the rents. More
people had to live in smaller spaces at higher costs. Black folks had
always been forced with limited capital to deal in a restricted real
estate market, making rents and prices high. It had been that dilemma,
after all, that created black Harlem in the first place. It had been the
typical story of ghetto-making.

Reflecting the optimism of the twenties, the poets and writers of the
Harlem Renaisssance had put an amusing face on the poverty and pain
they saw around them. Rent parties had been quaint amusements to
keep landlords at bay. As the Depression deepened and breadlines
lengthened, however, they had to be seen for what they were: one of
many desperate strategies of the poor to survive.

Harlemites had now to look hard at realities. Whatever had been
the wartime promise of advancement and progress, whatever had been
the expectations about Harlem, blacks were still the last hired and the
first fired, and there wasn't much hiring going on. Even though the
district was almost completely black, the white merchants along 125th
Street refused to employ black people as sales clerks or even janitors.
Movie theaters were staffed by white cashiers and ushers. Harlem Hospital allowed neither black nurses or doctors on its staff. As a matter of
fact, black doctors had to turn their patients over to white doctors if they
were to be treated in any New York hospital. Few imagined that just
because Harlem was black everyone who worked there ought to be
black as well, but certainly one could expect some of the money Harlem
spent should return to feed and clothe black people.

The street-corner oratory began now to be peppered with demands
for programs of action. Political agitators joined normally conservative
ministers to boycott the merchants of 125th Street. Picket signs advised
that people should not buy where they could not work. Picketing had to
be selective because in the 1930s, if blacks shopped only where blacks
were hired, they would have had to go without food and clothing.

The boycott movement had its successes. Slowly, store by store,
black faces began to appear as clerks and salespersons; token, certainly,

but steps in the right direction. Each breakthrough seemed like a victory, like a corner had been turned; it seemed that at least in Harlem,
the capital of Afro-America, black folks might get an even break.

Yet such victories could only be small comfort. The great majority of
blacks were still out of work, scratching however they could to make
ends meet. Even public relief and New Deal jobs through the W.P.A.
were administered as if black folks were an afterthought. Parties could
not raise the rent when you couldn't even put up the money for food,
drink, and entertainment, and when people couldn't even afford the
twenty-five cents to get in. Landlords sent their eviction notices. Hardly
a day passed, summer or winter, when one Harlem block or another had
not the pitiful belongings of a family put out on the street.

With the froth and gaity of the twenties blown away, the bitterness
and anger that had always been there showed on the surface of things. On
March 19, 1935, Harlem broke loose. From 116th Street to 145th, along
Fifth, Lenox, and Seventh avenues, people smashed and looted stores.
As Claude McKay remembered, it began in the afternoon and continued
throughout the night. Those who were angry smashed store windows;
those who were hungry looted. Everyone was involved. McKay recalled
seeing a dignified young woman, relative of a conservative minister, carrying a bag of bricks. She was having herself taxied from place to place,
stopping each time to hurl a brick through a store window.

Police brutality was supposed to have set it off. No one seemed to
care much about the why or how of it. Blacks had always complained
about the police treating them with disrespect, acting toward Harlem as
if they were an army of occupation. Whatever the specific incident, it
was remarkable only that this time it set off a riot.

Mayor LaGuardia and city officials would have liked to have pinned
it on the Communist Party and other radicals active in Harlem, but there
was no evidence for it. The riot just happened, and the radicals were as
surprised as anyone. Of course, no one had to look far or think long
about the causes. Racism, joblessness, poverty, all of which characterized the Afro-American condition, seemed to have become the un-
spoken premise of American social policy. City officers and relief workers, policemen and firemen, transit workers and garbagemen, had come
to accept that white folks naturally would get more than black folks,
whatever there was to give. Every black district in the country suffered,
but with Harlem it hurt more because so much more had gone into the
dream.

By 1935, Harlem had become a ghetto in every sense of the word.
What had been a victory before the war—capturing choice real estate
for black residency—had turned sour as the district seemed more like a
quarter overpopulated by victims of social and economic oppression.

When Langston Hughes asked "what happens to a dream deferred,"
he wondered if it would "dry up like a raisin in the sun" or if it would
"explode." In Harlem, it did both. Riots, like that of 1935, would recur

in Harlem in the 1940s and the 1960s, and every major city would in time have its own version. Perhaps the saddest thing about the ghetto that Harlem became was how much of a contrast it was to the vision and dream of those black people who first settled there. Harlem had been their best hope for the future, and it had come to naught.

By the Second World War, Harlem was a place people dreamed of getting out of. Most of New York was decaying, but Harlem faster than the rest. Landlords put little money into their property. Black people could always be forced to pay more for less. Wartime overcrowding took its toll, and continued neglect by the city sped the deterioration of schools, parks, streets, and public transportation. Crime, which had always been relatively high, became more ugly as prostitution and gambling took a back seat to drugs and violent crime. Anyone who could wanted to move into a better neighborhood where children would not be confronted daily with unrelenting despair, where one would not be identified with the sordidness of the ghetto.

Ironically, the liberating forces that made it easier in the 1950s and 1960s for blacks to move out—to Westchester County, to Long Island, to residential boroughs—increased the desperation of Harlem. Whatever else, in the past, a broad socioeconomic spectrum had been represented in Harlem. Doctors and lawyers, teachers and ministers, artists and writers, musicians and hustlers, blue collar workers, and folks on welfare had always made up the Harlem scene. Life styles ranged from dingy rooms to the elegance of Sugar Hill. Although poor folks often complained about the "dictys," they were all in the same boat. But President Kennedy talked about rising expectations, and middle-class blacks quit Harlem as fast as they could; the poor and immobile felt themselves abandoned. Urban riots would shatter the complacency of the "affluent society."

The Civil Rights movement turned into the "black revolution" of the 1960s, and urban disorder reawakened among many blacks the urgency of ethnic identity and community. Harlem gained a new importance. Institutions remained in Harlem: churches, social centers, the Schomburg Library. They insured to Harlem an integrity other black districts lacked. They saved Harlem from the total devastation that wasted the South Bronx. New theater, new literature, new art sprang out of the Harlem ghetto, but unlike the earlier renaissance, it was unromantic, tough, more authentic, and more race conscious. Harlem had survived as a place and a concept to serve a new generation and a new future of Afro-American expression.

There are signs, in the late seventies, of a Harlem revival. The State of New York has built a government center on 125th and Seventh Avenue. A new building to house the Schomburg Center is being constructed at 135th and Lenox. Courageous and visionary enterprises like the Studio Museum and the Dance Theater of Harlem have established themselves and continue to thrive despite chronic shortages of funds.

Middle-class blacks talk about buying some of the still elegant brown-stones and townhouses, returning to the central city. There is faint hope that federal, state, and city governments will channel enough money into the district to turn things around. A new Cotton Club has opened on 125th Street, different from the original in that it welcomes black patrons. The Apollo Theater, after having been forced to close, has reopened and is once again staging live entertainment.

So, Harlem lives. It has stood for too much in the minds and hearts of Afro-Americans to die. It will never again be seen as the "Mecca of the New Negro"; we are too old for such dreams. Harlem will be more real than that, and like the rest of Afro-American life, it will make you laugh and it will make you cry.

3

Pilgrimage for Black Americans: The Slave Castles of West Africa

For good reason, Plymouth Rock is a universal symbol for the American experience. Most Americans shared with the Pilgrims their flight to a promising new land to start a new life. Most Americans, but not all.

In West Africa, along the palm-lined coast of Ghana, are several forts and castles that constitute another symbol; unlike Plymoth Rock, they were points of departure, not arrival, places of despair rather than liberty. They were the embarkation points for hundreds of thousands of men, women, and children who came to America in chains. And now, together with Gorée Island in Senegal, far to the north and west of Ghana, they are the few physical remains of the traffic in human beings that brought many Americans, black Americans, to the United States.

The names of the places are strange—Elmina, Cape Coast Castle, Cormantine, Gorée, Christianborg, Fort Metal Cross—strange even to most black Americans, but they are as much a part of our nation's history as Plymouth Rock. And they are becoming increasingly familiar as more Afro-Americans return to West Africa each year, making visits that are really pilgrimages. Practically every American of African descent has a forebear who suffered in the airless dungeons of these slave castles. And when we visit them today, we experience the emotional shock of common experience in anguish that links us all to those who were confined in these places, made the ghastly Atlantic crossing, and survived the horrors of New World slavery.

*This article appeared in *The New York Times,* Sunday, October 29, 1972. Copyright © 1972 by The New York Times Company. Reprinted by permission.

History's Bad Joke

The name "slave castles" is history's bad joke. They were warehouses for human beings. Slaves were held in them as commodities, merchandise waiting for shipment across the Atlantic. The castles were also military installations: Portuguese, Dutch, French, and British needed them not only to protect their trade in slaves against rivals but also to defend themselves against hostile African tribes and to put down slave insurrections.

From the very beginning, tropical diseases and the power of African tribes prevented the European traders from making real inroads on the continent, so when they established a beachhead on the West African coast they built their castles there. Elsewhere, even on the Niger delta, they were unable to erect such strongholds. There merchants had to trade from their ships and as a consequence left no castles or other physical representations of the slave trade. Their temporary structures, the barracoons used as corrals for slaves, no longer stand.

The history of the castles along the Ghanaian coast reflects the changing trade patterns in the area—from gold to ivory to slaves—as well as the changing fortunes of the European powers. The Portuguese began Elmina ten years before Columbus started his voyage to America. The Swedes began Cape Coast Castle in 1652. Soon afterward, the Danes built Christianborg at Accra, and the English countered with Cormantine. At the same time, over in Senegal, the French fortified Gorée Island. There were many others. What the Dutch wrested from the Portuguese or from the Danes eventually fell into British hands. And each transfer required the help of local African chiefs dependent on European guns and powder.

There is considerable irony to be found in the development of the slave castles. The African chiefs who became partners in the slave trade were unwittingly the agents of their own decline. The coastal castle-forts became the natural focal points for contact between the "advanced" Europeans and the Africans, but this relationship developed from an illusory equality as trading partners to colonial dependency. Only in the last fifteen years has Ghana, for example, become independent from colonial rule. Thus, the slave castles are an integral part of the economic history of Africa, but for the Afro-American it is peripheral history; the slave trade remains the single point of focus.

The castle strongholds were the entrepôts of that trade, which reached hundreds of miles into the interior of West Africa, affecting the history of that region to the present. Men, women, and children were wrenched from the anchor of tradition and family, mixed with other Africans of alien tongue and custom, and herded to the coast.

They passed through many hands and traveled many miles before they reached the castles. While some slaves were captured in raids on villages and some were criminals sentenced to slavery, many were kidnapped or captured by ruse. Alexander Falconbridge, an eighteenth-century observer, reported the capture of one woman: "She was on her return home one evening from some neighbors, to whom she had been making a visit. . . . She was kidnapped; and notwithstanding she was big with child, sold for a slave."

The rivers—Senegal, Gambia, Pra, Niger, Congo—were the major slave highways. But thousands were force-marched overland in slave coffles, caravans of humanity. One African slaver, Theodore Canot, describes how he handled an overland shipment: "Fourteen captives were at once divided into two gangs of seven each. Hoops of bamboo were clasped around their waists; their hands were tied by stout ropes to the hoops, and a long tether was then passed with a slipknot through each rattan belt, so that the slaves were firmly secured to each other. A small coil was also employed to link them in a band by their necks." So bound, thousands of Africans were forced to walk sometimes as much as two hundred miles to reach the dungeons of the castles on the coast.

The oldest of the castles, Elmina, was the center of the Portuguese trade from 1482 until it fell to the Dutch in 1637. It remained in Dutch hands until 1872, when all Dutch holdings on the Gold Coast were sold to the British. The castle was to remain a part of the British colonial administration until Ghana's independence in 1957.

Castle Impregnable

Elmina was built at the point where a river had cut a flat peninsula into the coastline. Considering its use, it was ideal in many ways. The castle rests upon massive rock outcroppings; it was possible to land vessels of up to three hundred tons on the easily defended inlet side of the peninsula, but impossible for hostile ships to get ashore in the rough surf on the seaward side. And the only other approach was along the peninsula itself, which for over a mile was no more than one hundred yards wide.

Within the walls, three-story white buildings form a large, enclosed, rectangular courtyard. Slaves were once herded into this area to be examined and priced. Today the castle is a training school for Ghana's national police, and the courtyard is a drill area.

The upper floors of the buildings, which once housed European soldiers, now serve as barracks for Ghana's police recruits; spacious apartments that once accommodated the castle's commanders and merchants are now occupied by high-ranking African officers.

At the corners of the courtyard, narrow doors lead to the cavernous dungeons where the slaves were kept. Heavy iron gates still stand guard over these huge, airless, lightless, vaulted rooms. Slaves were chained together in these dungeons, sometimes for months, until a ship arrived to take them to an American marketplace.

Before shipment, the process of dehumanization, which began with their capture and forced march, continued. In the open courtyard the slaves would stand, stripped, to be examined and priced. Slave trader Canot described the scene:

As each person was brought before him, Canot wrote, he examined "the subject, without regard to sex, from head to foot. A careful manipulation of the chief muscles, joints, armpits and groins was made, to assure soundness. The mouth, too, was inspected, and if a tooth was missing, it was noted as a defect liable to deduction. Eyes, voice, lungs, fingers and toes were not forgotten."

Before the slaves were sent on board a ship, the captain and surgeon examined them again. The surgeon branded them on the breast with red-hot irons. The air reeked with the smell of burning flesh, the courtyard echoed with cries of agony and terror.

"An Inferior Wine"

The Europeans, according to contemporary accounts, passed the time complaining to one another about the troublesomeness of their business enterprise, the heat of the African day, and the quality of the port wine they were drinking.

The loading of the cargo from the courtyard onto the ships was a critical operation. Uprisings were always possible, and there was never enough space to put all the slaves. Here's how Falconbridge describes a barricade used in the loading process: "It serves to keep the different sexes apart; and as there are small holes in it, wherein blunderbusses are fixed, and sometimes cannon, it is convenient for quelling the insurrections that now and then happen." Canot described the problem of space: "I returned on board to aid in stowing one hundred and eight boys and girls, the eldest of whom did not exceed fifteen years. As I crawled between decks, I could not imagine how this little army was to be packed or draw breath in a hold but twenty-two inches high! Yet the experiment was promptly made, inasmuch as it was necessary to secure them below . . . in order to prevent their leaping overboard. I found it impossible to adjust the whole in a sitting posture; but we made them lie down in each other's laps, like sardines in a can, and in this way obtained space for the entire cargo."

The trip took two months.

The first slaves to arrive in North America were brought to Jamestown, Va., by a Dutch ship in 1619, and they continued to be brought for the next two hundred years by the Spanish, the British, and the French. New England dominated the market, and slaves traded by Newport were sold along rivers in the South. The importation of slaves was brought to an end by the Constitution in 1808, but slaves and the children of slaves already in the United States continued to be traded right up to the Civil War. In 1790, the slave population numbered 700,000; by 1830 it was two million, and by the 1860s four million. Slaves could be bought for $50 in Colonial times, but by 1870 the price had risen to $1,500.

We survived. But today, when we go back to the symbols of our passage to the New World—our Plymouth Rock—we need guides to our past. The guide at Elmina was a police instructor, tall, husky, black, erect, and very proper, suggesting the British influence in his military training. But his discipline and formality failed to conceal his emotion as he stood and talked in the dungeons where at any given time, a thousand human beings had been shackled together. He spoke of food thrown through doors and of the fetid air. Knowing himself how intimate and crucial are the relationships of family, tribe, and tradition to the African's sense of being, his imagination was stunned by the thought of what it must have been like for those thousand who passed through this place. He re-marked that it seemed more like death than life to be torn from family and tribal roots and cast into the bowels of castles and slave ships. It must have seemed that way, too, to the few African girls who escaped through the secret passageways to serve the sexual needs of the Euro-pean officers; it was their only way out. (It is another of those small ironies of the slave trade that much of the small mulatto population along the coast today owes its African-ness to this concubinage.)

A Gem in the Harbor

Elmina might well stand for all the slave castles along the coast, except that each has a special quality, a peculiarity of interest. Gorée Island sits like a gem in Dakar's harbor; the Government of Senegal has tried to make it a comfortable place for tourists to visit. The dungeons of the *Maison des Esclaves* have been painted and equipped with electric lights. There is also a sound-and-light show which gives immediate, dramatic impact to the slave story. Fort Cormantine is currently being restored by Robert and Sarah Lee, two black American dentists who have lived in Ghana for the last seventeen years and have established the African Descendants Aid Fund, a channel through which black Ameri-cans can help with the restoration. Cape Coast Castle, which was the headquarters of British trade on the coast, is now a military barracks and houses a museum affiliated with Cape Coast University. When com-pleted, the museum will be the world's foremost repository of artifacts dealing with the Atlantic slave trade.

No Windows

Cape Coast Castle is overwhelming. Gas torches are needed to see one's way into the dungeons; there are still no windows to admit light and air. A broad curving ramp descends deep under the castle into darkness. The hole is like a cavern, and the torches give too little light to show the full extent of it. But senses other than sight help the visitor to know and feel the place. The stone walls are damp and cold, the air dank and stale. The floors are dirt and, unlike those at Elmina, have absorbed some part of everything that has passed over them. Scratching in that dirt, it is not hard to find the pitiful legacy of the slave trade: beads from women's clothing, pottery, bones. The place gives one the feeling that nothing ever left except the people. Their odors, their breath, their tears, their blood have seeped into the earth; they sweat through the stones of the walls. There is no mistaking it, one is in the presence of those who suffered and died on the site.

Cape Coast Castle is the physical monument to their enslavement; it was built over a stone outcropping which had served, before their subjugation, as a shrine for local African peoples, and that sacred rock forms part of the dungeon's wall.

Now a local priestess comes daily down the ramp to the wall. She pours the libations and says the prayers which evoke all the past spirits of family and tribe into the web that is tradition. Her prayers are not unlike those that were said centuries ago, before the Europeans came. The evolving oral tradition ties her to that distant past, informing her, too, of what has since come to pass. The history of the castle and the slave trade have made a difference. Now her prayers and her libations reach out to those spirits who passed through this place. She prays that they, too, are part of that web and not adrift for eternity.

The slave trade rudely severed the natural family links between past and present generations, which is the essence of African tradition. Normally even the dead remain vital to the African's present. But when Africans were brought into the slave castles and taken in chains to America, they were removed from the consciousness of continuing generations. Slavery did what death could not do. The Cape Coast priestess demonstrates that many Africans cannot rest easy with this rupture in the web. The shrine in Cape Coast Castle served as her means to mend raveled ends; the castle itself serves as ours.

When we, as black Americans, walk through those dungeons and holes, we cannot help but look at the white tourists among us. Whatever their feelings—horror, embarrassment, shame, curiosity—they cannot possibly have the sense of deep personal identification that we Afro-Americans have. These were the places where we stopped being African—Fante, Ashanti, Ga, Bambara, Fulani—and began being American, for good as well as ill. History and circumstance (not will or desire) have obliterated our tribal memories and distinctions and made us into one people. And it started in places like these. Everything that has happened to us since—brutal passage, plantation slavery, centuries of oppression, violence, and discrimination—is all linked to such places. To see the urban ghetto in its fullest perspective, one must walk in the

Cape Coast dungeon. To really understand Attica prison, one must know the meaning of Elmina, and the others, too.

"The Source"

Many black Americans like myself want to find our way back through that horror, into and through those dungeons, to the source of our being. Not because we are so naive as to believe nor because we wish to deny our own history as it has developed from those castles, as brutal and horrible as it has been. We come to find in the experience itself, from the beginning in those dungeons, the essence of our special humanity that the slave experience and all the rest could not destroy.

The guide at Gorée was a Senegalese man. He told the story of the slave castle with genuine passion. He put the slaves' shackles on his legs, wrists, and neck. Chained and hobbled so, he moved before us, pulling us even more into the vortex of the human agony that had taken place there. Then, he looked into my face and said, "For all we know, we may be brothers."

4

The Afro-American, National Character and Community: Toward a New Synthesis

Today, few Afro-Americans would consider integration into American society to be an ultimate objective. Most would at least insist on important qualifications to a goal which would presume the ultimate abandonment of racial identity and the general dispersion of the black population in order to be "blended in." Since the 1960s, "integrationism" and "assimilationism" have been used as terms of derision by many black spokesmen. While few would consider themselves nationalists or segregationists, most would insist on the existence of distinct ethnic values and on the maintenance of racial integrity.

This shift in attitude is remarkable, coming on the heels of the victory for integration in the *Brown* decision (1954). Doubtless, disillusion resulted from the failure of the Supreme Court's decision and the early victories of the Civil Rights movement to bring results. But black ethnocentrism seems to be a part of a broader pattern in American life which rejects the image of the melting pot and emphasizes cultural diversity.

The melting pot assumed a notion of a common American type. The peoples who came to America were "melted down" either to be blended into a new amalgam or to be poured into a mold of the preferred type. Either way, the ultimate goal was an American character, and the evidences of cultural distinctiveness were indications that the process was unfinished. The recent disenchantment with this model is due to its failure to reflect accurately what was actually the experience of many Americans, white and black. Diversity and ethnocentrism have been more the rule than the exception. Furthermore, with the decline of

*This lecture was given in April 1974 at the Center for Afro-American Studies, University of California, Berkeley.

36

WASP influence, there could no longer be a consensus as to an ideal type. Cultural diversity became a positive value, and pluralism the concept to describe the dynamics of American life.

The pluralists describe American society as "fractured into a congeries of hundreds of small 'special interest' groups, with incompletely overlapping memberships, widely differing power bases, and a multitude of techniques for exercising influence on decisions salient to them." These "memberships" are something more than ethnic. Rather, the pluralists generally imagine a diversity in numerous voluntary associations, which are organized to gain their members' share in the commonwealth. Conceivably, these associations might, themselves, be multi-ethnic. They are all competitive. But since none can get what it wants on its own, they all operate through alliances and coalitions, sharing power among themselves.

If Alexis de Tocqueville was not the original pluralist, he was the most imaginative and cogent. The present-day theorists follow him in their construction of an American political order based on the dynamics of competition and cooperation among diverse associations and organizations. The theory has been very useful in the analysis of American politics, especially urban politics. It is attractive, also, because it is an analogue of "free-market" economic theory, which has for a long time appealed to the American mind. In the pluralists' model, as in that of the laissez-faire economists, the way the pie is cut depends on the weight of the competitors and the shrewdness each brings to the "market," not on abstract considerations of justice nor equitable distribution of wealth or power.

As much as Afro-Americans may have found the melting pot an unsatisfactory metaphor for their experience, and as much as they may be contributing to the current vogue in cultural diversity, they will find the pluralists' model just as problematic as any other. There are two reasons. Pluralists, with their emphasis on voluntary associations, despite their awareness of the diversity in American life, do not give adequate weight to the importance of ethnic divisions within interest groups. Secondly, particularly, from the point of view of Afro-Americans, they do not appreciate the limits that race places on coalitions. The second of these problems is of special significance as one considers major patterns of black political behavior.

From the point of view of most Afro-Americans, however one might define "voluntary associations," the ultimate divisions in the United States has been between black and white. History and experience seem to support that view. Despite shared class, occupational, regional, or political interests, blacks have tended to find that their alliances with whites have crumbled when there was an appeal to race interest. Poor whites in the South and poor white ethnics in northern cities have seemed to prefer to languish in poverty rather than join blacks in effective coalitions. If race interests are more important than bread and butter, the pluralist model can work for all except those racial minorities who can never expect to marshal power to overcome the white phalanx arrayed againt them.

It is this perception that has caused black intellectuals, regardless of other persuasions, to sooner or later consider the color-line as the fundamental division in American life. Even in the politics of the Left, theoretical accord has often foundered in the mire of race. Such committed socialists as W. E. B. Du Bois and A. Philip Randolph found the socialist party unprepared to confront race as a different issue than class. Blacks, such as Du Bois and Johnson, always risked the charge of racial chauvinism when they insisted that blacks had special problems in the American society, not the least of which was the ethnocentrism of the working class. Nor was the experience of Afro-Americans different in the Communist party. And the sometimes acrimonious debate to insist on the importance of black voices in the leadership of the moderate NAACP suggests the pervasiveness of an attitude that the goals and tactics of Afro-Americans could best be determined by white men and women of good will.

This view of the intractability of race has sound basis in practical political life. Recent studies of New York City politics have shown the general unwillingness of city bosses to exploit fully the black vote, even when it might have meant a difference in the election. It seems that whites hoped to win without depending on black voters, and that soliciting these votes too eagerly was somehow an act beneath acceptable practice.

Whatever may be said about race as a limit to coalition politics, however, it is also true that the Afro-American style of politics has not been suited to the kind of give-and-take and competition implied by pluralism. The "typical" black spokesman of the nineteenth and early twentieth century followed the style of WASP, mugwump politics. They were "progressives" in sentiment, with a central preoccupation with reform of race relations. Generally speaking, they were disinterested in the kind of precinct organizations and vote grubbing that would produce solid constituencies necessary for urban machines. Without such organization and such political work, black politicians could have little weight to throw into the balance.

Indeed, from Reconstruction to the New Deal, the black style of political leadership was determined by a reliance on the moral obligation that patrons and national leaders could be made to feel about the race issue. Thus, almost all discussions of Afro-American politics during this period turns into a recounting of how one president after another gave fewer political offices to blacks despite efforts of spokesmen to persuade them not to abandon Afro-Americans. Booker T. Washington was the most adept of all of these black men of influence, and he neither asked for nor got more than a voice in the symbolic appointments of black Americans to a few offices.

W. E. B. Du Bois, Monroe Trotter, and others often called for an independent black vote. They threatened from time to time to persuade black voters away from the Republican party (or, in 1916, away from Woodrow Wilson). But these were empty gestures since these men were in no way able to control the vote they attempted to lead. Their style was publicity and moral suasion. They had no political base, and their only influence was through their journalism. So, while they dreamed of a black vote that could swing between the major parties, supporting candidates who promised to serve the interests of the race, they were not inclined to create the kind of political organizations that could make that a reality.

There were exceptions to this mugwump style in black political leadership. Booker T. Washington's lieutenant, Charles W. Anderson, was influential in the Republican party organization of New York City. But, like his mentor, his position seemed to depend on keeping Afro-Americans from effective political organization. Like Washington, he was effective at that. The very special case of black political machine organization in Chicago following World War I may be explained by the especially keen competition between Republicans and Democrats in that city. Marcus Garvey was another exception in his remarkable ability to mobilize and organize blacks at the grass-roots level. But because his objectives were escape and expatriation, his effect in national and local politics was limited.

In general, however, black political leadership, below the level of national spokesmen such as Du Bois, simply tried to sell their influence to white patrons in political office. Martin Kilson, suggesting an analogy of the role of African chiefs to colonial administrations, has aptly called this "client" politics while showing how that style failed to serve the interests of black people. The pattern is significant, when one considers the assumptions of pluralism, because without a political base, blacks were unable to be full competitors.

Pluralism has failed, also, to hold out much hope of social mobility for Afro-Americans. Here, too, it can be argued that social mobility has been largely ethnically determined, and the losers, in time, find themselves struggling against accumulated odds. Stephan Thernstrom has noted that various ethnics have shown different values in their concepts of social mobility. The interplay of values, opportunity, and expectation has caused a distinctive Afro-American approach to mobility. Individuals have generally chosen the professions (teaching, medicine, law, the ministry, and undertaking) and entertainment (including sports). Like other ethnics, blacks have found crime an important means for capital accumulation. But, in crime, America also has its ethnic boundaries, and black Americans have been restricted even there. Except for West Indians, few Afro-Americans have persisted as petty merchants and peddlers in northern cities. Relatively few blacks have found their way up through the city services and the blue-collar trades as represented in organized labor.

It is clear that the routes open to success have been limited. It seems, nevertheless, that Afro-Americans have preferred some ways to others. As characterized in the debate between Booker T. Washington and W. E. B. Du Bois, there was a choice between the artisan trades and the professions. Both Du Bois and Washington wanted to encourage Afro-American business, but neither would have understood business to mean a pushcart enterprise. The story of Mrs. Mary Dean, who transformed a pushcart of "pig feet" into a substantial holding of Harlem real estate, is probably not singular in Afro-American history, but hers has not been the model accepted by most Afro-Americans. Similarly, there has been slight consideration of sanitation, police, and fire services as means of mobility. Of course, there was always pleasure in the news of an appointment or promotion of a black to one of the city services, but Afro-Americans never seemed to assume that they could move in, in large numbers, to make a way for blacks "to take over" in the way that other ethnics have. Certainly, it would have been a futile hope in any case.

Ironically, after World War II, when black Americans were numerous enough in cities to command a place in these services, the terms of entry had been so changed by civil service reform that those ethnics who had found their places in the Police and Fire Departments, the public schools, etc., were entrenched and able to use instruments of reform to hold their places against the pressure from this new quarter.

Furthermore, the unionization of city services has often provided a means for ethnics to maintain places of power. In fact, most of the progressive reforms of the nineteenth and twentieth century have worked to keep black Americans and other "newcomers" from using the same avenues and instruments to power and mobility that white ethnics used before them. So, as it has worked out, white ethnics entrenched in urban bureaucracies, protecting their positions, seem aligned against all other ethnics rather than invited to find coalitions with them.

Generally speaking, the effort of Afro-Americans to find their way into organized labor has also been met with what appears to be a determined "rear guard" of white ethnics protecting their places of power. Historically, black Americans are not newcomers to artisan occupations. In the mid-nineteenth century, there were numerous black craftsmen and laborers. They were displaced by immigrants and other white labor, and labor in America became differentiated along ethnic lines. Undoubtedly, some industrial occupations shifted from English to Irish to Italian to Polish, etc. But from the point of view of black workers, there was little mobility between "white" jobs and "black" jobs. And it seemed that all whites were prepared to keep blacks out of competition for their jobs.

Afro-Americans were used as strike-breakers in the early years of modern labor organizing, so the underlying hostility between unorganized blacks and organized whites had a basis in real conflict. Even those black spokesmen who were consistent in the view that blacks had to take their place in union ranks—men like Du Bois and A. Philip Randolph—

had to apologize for the racist basis of American unions. They had to call for a reform of unions as well as the social fabric of the United States.

Except for some trades and industries—notably the mine workers—Afro-Americans were excluded from organized labor. While this condition changed with the industrial organization under the C.I.O., it was not until after World War II that important racial breakthroughs were made in the ranks of white labor.

American craft unions, governed by principles of "business unionism," attempted to control the labor supply rather than organize all working men. The basis of such unionism was exclusiveness, and blacks were the most convenient to exclude. Thus, black workers have long had to face the fact that newly arrived immigrants, with friends in the right places, could get into the building trades, for instance, while they could not. Race has posed a barrier in American labor history that has been more important than class, and, in many instances, ethnically organized unions, at the height of their power and protective of their "job control," have closed themselves as access for blacks to upward mobility.

The failure to define class identification sharply in America—reflected in the inability of American unions to organize in terms of a working class—has deprived black and white workers of an interest-loyalty that would transcend ethos. Rather, it appears that ethnicity has replaced class-interest as the basis of loyalty. Nathan Glazer goes even farther to say that "ethnicity has become a more effective form [than class] for the pursuit of interest . . . and one reason is that in some way ethnicity is more closely related to feeling and emotion than is the more abstract class loyalty.

The seeming failure of class and group interests to obliterate race identification has dissuaded some black Americans from playing the game of coalitions. When the chips are down, they would say, white men will protect their whiteness before their economic interests. Or, put another way, American history has made whiteness an element of one's economic and social interest. Thus, race has become a part of any equation, such that it would be naive to assume that an "invisible hand" of pluralism and coalition politics can whisk it away.

While race may form an intractable limit to the play of the pluralists' model, few would argue that some gains for blacks could not be won by coalitions. The ability of Afro-Americans to participate effectively is determined by limitations imposed on the group by its historical circumstance and characteristic behavior developed over time.

A concentration of Afro-Americans in places where they were free to act politically was needed before they could compete in pluralistic terms. Such concentration has been a fact of northern urban life for some years, and since the 1960s is becoming a fact of southern life. But North or South, sophisticated political organization of blacks has been a recent phenomenon. There have been some remarkable victories of black politicans in local elections. It remains to be seen how much such political organization can affect the major parties and national policy.

Coalition politics demands an ethnic consciousness and discipline that would urge group-interest over self-interest. There appears, in recent years, to have been a strong development of such race consciousness, race solidarity, and race pride among Afro-Americans. The emergence of African nations in the post-war years has rekindled an affinity to the motherland and African culture. All suggests greater race solidarity than was evident in the past. In this connection, the black power emphasis that marked the end of the civil rights movement seems to have been an effort to galvanize race interests over other loyalties. Some of the substance beneath the black power rhetoric recognized that black people needed ethnic sense, community sense, and the determination to act as a group if coalitions were to work.

Yet, these very features of race solidarity make coalitions difficult to maintain. Appeals to race pride and race loyalty make compromise impossible. The give-and-take that is necessary for coalitions can hardly thrive in an atmosphere of absolute loyalties and non-negotiable objectives.

Associations based on ethnocentric loyalties work against coalition politics in another way. Coalitions are best used when groups can promote programs that are feasible in terms of available resources, serviceable to an actual need, reasonable in terms of a recognized problem, and practicable in terms of administration. Such programs need to appeal across group lines for alliances to make sense. The tendency of ethnocentric groups to *demand* something as "their right" and "their share" works very much against the spirit that would make such programs possible. For black groups, however, it is precisely the sense of futility in coalitions that has made the style of confrontation the apparent practical alternative.

The notion of pluralism, with its dynamics of competition and cooperation, assumes that community interests will be served naturally. Like the model of laissez-faire economics, it is as if by an "invisible hand" the collective interest is formed out of the struggle for self-interest. But it is just the absence of a sense of larger community that has made pluralism a compelling concept. Where a sense of broad community does not exist, it becomes useful to reduce the whole to its parts. The result can seem a collection of groups and interests grabbing whatever they can get, producing little sense of commonwealth.

Insofar as pluralism and ethnocentrism are responses to the lack of an American character that defines all in common and a lack of community that can transcend all ethnic loyalties, they beg rather than answer the question, "who is this American, this new man." For if Americans share only a condition of diversity, and are unified only in their competition, the fundamental questions of nationality and national character are open to debate.

Is there something about Americans, and within the American experience, that sets them off even from their old-world kinsmen? Is there some cohesion in the American setting that calls men to a loyalty beyond particular ethos? When Carl Bridenbaugh delivered his presidential address to the American Historical Association, he complained that what had been a common American history encompassing a national experience had become, in the hands of historians with ethnocentric biases, a history of special and parochial interests. The problem was that the common history in the tradition of George Bancroft was not, in fact, the history of Americans. Thus, the urgency of a focus on the ethnic experience. Yet, the question remains: can a common history emerge from such great diversity as has been the story of the United States?

Some would say that the immigrant experience is the American experience. There is much to be said for that since, in one way or another, all Americans (except Native Americans) have been products of the same drama of separation from the old and reestablishment in the new world. Afro-Americans too, despite the important difference of their history, fit the context of the whole.

When Gerald Mullins discussed the reaction of eighteenth-century African Americans to slavery in Virginia, he sketched out a pattern of assimilation of Africans into new-world life that might have been a model for all immigrants. Briefly, he described "outlandish Africans," still tied to old-world ways, lacking fluency in English as well as a sense of the territory, inclined to seek group ways to react to their condition. Secondly, Mullins described what he calls "New Negroes," who had acquired some English but not a fluency, who had learned to adapt themselves to the particular work system of the plantation, who were still unfamiliar with the territory away from their immediate location, and who thus resisted slavery by truancy from the plantation, inefficiency in work, sabotage and theft. Finally, Mullins referred to the "assimilated" type who had a fluency in English, occupational skills that could be of use anywhere, a good knowledge of the country far beyond their master's place, and a good knowledge of how to get around. The assimilated blacks' style of resistance was to run away, most often by themselves, relying on individual wit and skills.

Mullins restricted his analysis to eighteenth-century blacks, but it applies as well to any immigrant group. The suggested similarity of adaptation and the similar characterization of the ultimate Americanization process points to the possible definition of a national character shared by all who have been molded by this experience.

Ethnic pluralism creates multiple refuges where persons can find a common identity when broader community is in doubt. But these retreats are ultimately narrow and fail to lift the person to participation in a higher unity of nation. There is a need to share in a general community—to look in the face of a fellow being (not of one's church or ancestry) and to acknowledge shared assumptions and values, to anticipate behavior and feeling. Ethnic pluralism does not provide ways to such brotherhood.

It is the need for such community—the sense that one participates in the whole—that explains the persistent appeal of ethnic humor and situation comedy on mass media. One feels a pleasure as one's own argot and special characteristics become a part of (indeed, define) a national humor. Thus, television becomes a means (as did vaudeville and radio before it) for the individual American to become part of the whole. But such pleasure is limited. Ethnic culture, broadcast to the nation, is necessarily diluted and distorted: *Porgy and Bess* at the best, "Amos 'n' Andy" at the worst. Or, as in the case of *Abie's Irish Rose* and its parody on television, "Bridget Loves Bernie," it reduces important matters of ethnic tension to mere banalities.

More is needed. Is there a "new man" in America? Is there an essentially common American experience which can become the point of identity serving all ethnic particulars? Is there a community beyond ethos, which can support such a personality, and which can command a loyalty and a service above particularism? The melting pot image assumed that such a character and such a community existed, or could exist. Can that image be abandoned—as it must—without losing the sense of oneness that was assumed? And, most important, can any such community be realized without the black American being an integral part of it?

National Character

At this moment when the cultural diversity and ethnocentrism of America is being stressed, it is worthwhile to redefine what common qualities there might be in American life. For, whatever the virtues of pluralistic visions, they seem to result from the failure of those centripetal elements that have formerly provided a sense of national order and purpose. There are, I suspect, qualities of common experience and character that make us more like one another than like the peoples in the lands of our forebears. Despite what they may suspect, an Afro-American and the grandson of a Polish immigrant will be better able to take things for granted between themselves than the one could with a Ghanaian or Nigerian and the other could with a Warsaw worker. They, like all other Americans except Indians, are sons of a migrant experience to the "new world" and have shared a continual interface with one another. It has been a rather harsh, bitter, and strained relationship, but it has existed and has been a central element in their consciousnesses.

I have stressed the migrating experience as the central metaphor, providing a shared American eexperience as well as common qualities of American character. This is much preferred to the assumption—especially as it applies to Afro-Americans and non-Europeans—that Americanization was a process of adopting a particular set of European characteristics. The truly important qualities of Americanness were no more part of traditional Europe than of traditional Africa. Individuality, mobility, risk-taking for opportunity, uneasiness with institution, ambivalance about community, are products of the shared experience of migration and settlement. To assume the abandonment of the familiar ways of living and working as well as habits of mind, to be exchanged for some European varieties, is to distort the experience. Neither the African nor the European immigrant was a tabula rasa on which an Anglo-Saxon culture was impressed. Rather, there was a priori "knowledge" which shaped experience in its own terms, manifest not simply in ethnic artifacts or Africanisms, but in subjective areas of belief, myth, style, art, and imagination. As a subterranean influence, ethnic culture participated in standard, American mass culture, by defining it and losing its exclusiveness and distinctiveness in the process.

The Americanization process actually began somewhere else—in the "old world." Africans, Europeans, and Asians had been pulled out of traditional social orders and thrust into what can best be called a modern ethos. Each traditional order, in its own way, was an intricate network of interpersonal relationships and conventions such that each person occupied a relatively fixed place. Such societies were characterized by a slowness of change which promoted the assumption of stability—a static or cyclical order—which helped to guarantee personal identity. Personal relationships, institutional stability, and reliance on conventional behavior and ritual reduced the number of private questions one might ask about oneself, making the self an entity with community.

Out of such a matrix, men were thrust into a context characterized by dynamic and changing institutions, radical social flux, pragmatic and progressive assumptions of change—all future-oriented, with slight reliance on the past and little faith in convention and ritual. This context was the promising and yet frightening "new world."

Social flux and uncertainty made newcomers attempt to reproduce old world institutions and practices where they could. They would try to hold to the church, to the language, to the group, but it was futile. What had been firm and secure became infirm outside the traditional context. Such a "new world" environment required radical shifts in one's sense of self and one's concept of community.

This experience of transformation from the "old world" to the "new world" is the essence of the immigrant experience. At one time or another, it has been an experience shared by all who have come. And the "new world" condition is a continuing one, which has remained distinct even as the "old world" has "modernized" and taken on many of the characteristics of so-called American civilization. It is the historical commonness of this immigrant and the Americanization experience—the obligation, for better or worse—of living together and sharing one another's destinies—that has shaped new men and will define the distinctiveness of American character and American civilization.

While one might speak of an immigrant experience, there were important differences due to time and the character of migration. Surely one cannot claim a perfect identity of the Puritan migration in the seventeenth century with that of southern Europeans in the late nineteenth century. Nor can one act as if the decision of the Swedish farmer to migrate in the 1840s was the same as the forced transport of African village folk in the slave trade in the eighteenth century. Certainly, too, Asian migration had its special quality. Nevertheless, beneath all, there would seem to be an irreducible experience: each had to sever the web that had held him in place and risk becoming an atom, essentially isolated. The process, beginning in the "old world," was centrifugal, and each man, sooner or later, would be destined to continue the process. What this meant to him, and what it has meant to the social order that has been created, goes far toward explaining the problems of ethnicity and pluralism in America. It remains, nevertheless, to consider the African as a part of this same process. His experience explains both the commonness of this general experience and its fundamental inability to reintegrate what had been pulled apart.

That the African was forced into the Atlantic migration and became a commodity in America makes his circumstances strikingly different from those of the typical European immigrant. Yet, a fundamental aspect of the African's experience was common to that of all immigrants.

Force, after all, was not peculiar to the African migrant. Few migrants were simple adventurers; most would have preferred to remain where they were. Generally, however, the European migrant participated in the choice; the African did not. But in neither case was it a matter of *free* will. Furthermore, neither the African nor the European of the seventeenth and eighteenth centuries would be jarred by a condition of unfree labor. The African might well have been forced out of his village by circumstances other than the slave trade; he may indeed have been made a part of the traditional domestic slavery in Africa. However hurtful and sad such events might have been, he would remain in a social context which he comprehended and which comprehended him. Even as a domestic slave, he would be part of a family, village, and community. Only as a convicted criminal or witch would he be abandoned socially in this life or the next. For the Africans, as for the European, force and unfreedom were familiar features of existence. But to be abandoned and isolated from community was the trauma that made "new men" of those who survived.

It is particularly important to understand this source of African transformation because it suggests that the Americanization of the African was not a matter of his abandoning African ways for European ways. Rather, it was a matter of the African, in common with other immigrants, being compelled to change from a traditional orientation to a modern one.

The coming of the African to America did make the African into a new man. In the "old world," there were many Africans. Particularism was, and to a large extent still is, characteristic of African peoples. Tribal differences meant differences in language, religion, principal occupation, family relationship. They were not inconsequential matters. Some Africans were matrilineal, others patrilineal. Some were polygamous, others monogamous. While most who came to America were worshippers of traditional African religion, others were Islamic. They had lived under a wide variety of social and political organizations. While we might find prevalences among the peoples who came, and while we may recognize a general commonality among them, they were preoccupied with the differences. They could not understand one another's language. They might find one another's customs repugnant.

Yet out of this diversity there was created a single people in a much more thorough way than has occurred in the rest of American society. Ethnic pluralism was not allowed the Africans as it was the various Euro-Americans. The slave trade created a new people. Of course, there were in the eighteenth and nineteenth centuries continuing tribal references. And, of course, "Africanisms" remained, but nowhere is *E Pluribus Unum* more appropriate than with the creation of the African American.

We can no longer accept E. Franklin Frasier's assumption that the African's culture was wiped away with the slave trade and slavery, and that the Afro-American absorbed as much of European culture as he was permitted. Africanisms and syncretisms have been too widely observed and discussed. It is worth remarking, however, that the quality of continuing African influence depended on the particular ambience in which the African was placed. In French and Spanish America, that is to say where the Catholic Church was dominant, syncretisms were abundant and obvious. There were analogues to be found between gods and saints, between "fetishes" and relics. Both traditions depended greatly on symbolism and "means" to transport the worshippers to the world of the spirit. The hightly ceremonial Catholicism could be readily adopted by people for whom ceremony and ritual were also central to worship. Catholicism had many doors through which African influence could enter, accommodating and transforming it at the same moment. And those African practices which were not tolerated in the church remained viable for both blacks and whites in the extra-institutional religion of voodoo and magic. Beneath the formal and official descriptions of religious practice in regions where such syncretisms abound, there existed a world of belief and mystery inhabited by both white and black. Neither Europe nor Africa emerged unaffected.

Protestants were much less open to African influence than Catholics. In the colonial South, however, the widespread indifference and even hostility to the Christian conversion of slaves allowed a permissiveness of another kind. Many masters did not want their slaves to become Christians; indeed, many thought it an impossibility. Thus, the religion that slaves adopted, while in the Protestant framework, was in large part an invention of their intuitions, from their religiousity, serving their spiritual needs. Masters did not care much about slave religion conforming to orthodoxy. They were concerned mainly with the problems that slave preachers brought to social control. In such a latitudinarian atmosphere, Africa could sustain itself in the slaves' version of Protestantism.

The Puritan colonies were the least open to Africanisms. On the one hand, they were the most austere of the Protestants—frowning on ceremony, music and dance as part of religious service—and, at the same time, they insisted on conformity to orthodoxy by all members of the community. Where idols, music, and ceremony were suspect as religious practice, there were few doors through which the African influence might enter. But in the realm of imagination, superstition, and magic, Africanisms could still survive. Consider, for instance, the role of Tituba in the Salem witch trials. Consider how she, a black woman with her half-black, half-Indian husband, fed the white community's credulity and hysteria. Coming from different cultural sources, seventeenth-century African and European belief in the effect of spirits and "possession" coincided in almost perfect "understanding."

Far from being alien to the African mind, "possession" was quite the essence of African religion. Africans and Europeans alike could assume that the world of spirits and the physical world intersected: that the will and character of the spirits could be manifest in nature. Indeed, they could both believe that phenomena otherwise not explainable (and sometimes even events with apparently rational explanations) were the consequence of spirits, demons, or gods working their wills in the world of human experience. In this respect, the seventeenth-century European and African cosmologies were not far apart. They could coexist and influence one another. The blending of influence is such that later evidence of myth and superstition in the folk literature of black and white Americans loses all distinctiveness of origins.

For Afro-Americans, the advents of the Great Awakenings, the strong revival current in America, opened up the possibility for "natural" religious expression that was relatively unencumbered by the formalities of theology and institutions. Here could continue the African practice of evoking the spirit within the presence of worshippers. The Afro-American church, in its various manifestations, rests heavily on the American revival tradition, its emotionalism, openness of congregation, and presumption of direct contact with the spirit. Here, too, white and black blended to some extent, with whites capturing some of the African self-expression and Afro-Americans converting Methodist hymns into spirituals.

In those northern areas where music and dance were not frowned upon, African music and dance were remarked as important curiosities. Not only were celebrations in which blacks participated characterized by African-like dancing, but there were also tribal languages, and the "election" of chiefs.

Circumstances and events made the African experience in America depart from that of the European immigrant. Unlike the European immigrants, Afro-Americans were to be cut off from their original cultures. The closing of the slave trade in 1808 effectively ended the importation of new Africans to the United States. The relatively insignificant intercourse between the United States and West Africa in the nineteenth century further limited the African contact. Thus, the Afro-American had little means of regenerating his native tradition and, more than others, was thus nurtured exclusively in the American environment.

Slavery, of course, was a restriction to blacks in both lateral and vertical mobility. As time went on, slaves became less and less able to effect their own destinies. Early in American history, slaves could escape to Spanish Florida or French Louisiana, to one of the several Indian tribes, or into the wilderness to become maroons. But with American expansion—with the removal of "foreign" neighbors and Indians—the Afro-American's mobility became severely reduced. By the 1850s, the only route out of slavery was to the North, and that was no certain escape.

Here, as often in American history, the very elements of American expansion and liberty resulted in greater limitations on black Americans. Racial slavery in the South created a totalitarian world, dominated by a single institution and a monolithic social economy. Blacks were not free, of course. But if you take seriously the complaints of white southerners, their options were also limited by racial slavery and the presence of blacks. To the white southern mind, slavery forced him to make choices among limited options; he was less free than the northern farmer. When he was feeling sorry for himself, the slaveowner could complain how he had become a slave of the system. He could not even abandon his slave property, because that would open the community to the horror of free blacks.

These woes were not wholly imaginary. As slavery became more entrenched as a southern institution, there were greater legal restrictions on the owner as to what he could do with his slave property. And as westward expansion became a matter of national debate between those who wanted to see a national development of free farms and those who wanted freedom to increase their slave population, the continued expansion of the slaveowner's enterprise was in doubt. This is by no means to say that the master's limited options were equivalent to the unfreedom of slavery. It is merely to point out that the African presence—the very machine of southern economic opportunity—resulted in the single institution about which the southerner could not be casual, and which was to dominate his life as neither church, nor state, nor family did.

For the Afro-American, this paradox had bitter and frustrating consequences. Like other Americans, he was a new man in the new world. But the American society and slavery did not permit him to be a new man in the sense that rested on opportunity, mobility, and self-reliance. And yet, having been so transformed, he could never return to traditional life without bringing the assumptions and expectations of the modern world with him.

This impossibility and frustration has characterized all efforts of black Americans to establish themselves in Africa, from the eighteenth century to the present. To "go back" to Africa was to go as a product of the "new world."

Paul Cuffee was born in 1759 of an African father and an Indian mother. He became a Quaker and a prosperous New England merchant. Through the revolutionary years, he was a frequent petitioner to the General Court of Massachusetts, asking that he and other blacks of the Commonwealth be accorded rights assumed under the principles of the "rights of man." He came to feel that life in the United States would remain a constant frustration to Afro-Americans, and he worked for the migration of blacks to the British colony of Sierra Leone.

At his own expense, Cuffee transported thirty-nine free blacks to the colony. Although Cuffee himself was not to live long enough to settle there, he did instruct the families that he brought. He advised that they assemble themselves to worship God. "In this hope, may Ethiopia stretch out her hand to God." He counselled them to have regular meetings "in the Lord, but above all things, let your meetings be owned of the Lord, for he hath told us that where two or three are gathered together in his name, there He would be in the midst of them." He went on to impress upon them the need for "sobriety and steadfastness, with all faithfulness, be recommended, that so professors may be good examples in all things; doing justly, loving mercy, and walking humbly." In all these respects, he echoed John Winthrop's sermon on the *Arabella* of a century and a half earlier. One expects Cuffee to claim Sierra Leone to be a "city upon a hill." One suspects that was in his mind, for if that colony could be successful and Christian, no longer could the Western world despise the African, and the colony could be the instrument by which Africa would be awakened.

Thus Cuffee was not "going back to Africa" in the sense that he was reclaiming his heritage, nor was he abandoning that which he had come to be. He expected Afro-Americans to go to Africa as they were, products of the new world—new men—and, as such, instruments through which Africa itself would be transformed into a Christian commonwealth.

As Paul Cuffee was an agent of the new world, so too were Afro-Americans who followed him in returning to Africa. Neither Bishop Henry McNeil Turner, nor Marcus Garvey, American-Liberians, were different in this respect. However much they might find the plight of the Afro-American in the United States to be intolerable, they were to be agents of that new world in Africa. They were "new men" planning to be instrumental in the creation of a new world.

The Afro-American continues in the twentieth century to sense an attraction to Africa. In this regard of the rediscovery of one's place and origins, the Afro-American finds his greatest difference from the European immigrant. Unlike the Euro-American, he cannot find his village, tribe, or family. Thus, he cannot find his "home" again in the way that it is possible for Italian-, Irish-, or Greek-Americans. It is a felt difference because it deprives the Afro-American of a sense of personal heritage extending beyond the American context.

Once the Euro-American finds the village of his fathers, however, and once he becomes reacquainted with his "family," he is no more likely than his black brother to "fit in" to that social context and thus find his way "home." At best, there is likely to be a strangeness, an alienation, an impatience with the slowness of pace and the fixity of things. After the warmth of reunion and the pleasure of recognizing oneself as part of a heritage, all Americans are likely to discover that they are part of a world different from that of their forebears.

The point is, of course, that they return as new men to the old world. They find an alienation different from the unsettlement and uncertainty they know in America. The original severing of the people from their traditional contexts made the change that could never be repaired.

Quest for Community

The process was begun in the first act of migration. The rendering of community ties in order to migrate, followed by efforts to re-establish community in a new setting, became the drama to be reinacted throughout American history. Each setting—chosen for some convenience—ceased to satisfy some who were then to pick themselves up and go to the next place. Lateral mobility became characteristic of the American experience, and with it a looseness of community relationships. Given the first move and the possibility of migration, subsequent moves became easier—it was easier to leave because ties were unsubstantial, easier to fit into new places, because nothing was rigidly fixed.

But such communities as were established lacked the organic quality, the destiny in which one might find oneself defined and sustained. The old world community—European or African village—could not be reproduced in America. While its absence could be a blessing in the way of fluidity, it could be a curse in the way of impermanence and the relative inconsequential characters of interrelationships. Identity, status, and the nature of social responsibility all became open to question and doubt.

Whatever advantages there were in freedom, the uncertainty made the quest for community and fixed, "normal" social relationships a continuing part of American preoccupations. For those who moved, community was often something left behind. For those who remained, community was often an earlier version of one's town or village, before changes and growth disrupted things. The New England town became, in the

American mind, the ideal community, where freedom and democracy existed within the perfect restraint of community cohesion. However, a closer look reveals it was more an idealized recollection than a reality.

From the beginning, anxieties about community disintegration were unsettling. "Separatism" was John Winthrop's major problem. There were always to be Roger Williamses and Anne Hutchinsons. There would always be new towns splintering off; and each separation was a rending of community and the foreboding of the fabric raveling away. The initial separation started the process that could not be stopped; rather it almost justified each new break.

The Federalist system has created other problems for community. Throughout American history, such fundamental questions as national citizenship have been confused in the uncertainty about sovereignty and nation. The federal government, until the twentieth century, reduced to a minimum its claims on persons. The terms and quality of citizenship became matters of local determination. There were, however, areas of commonness that all free Americans shared: 1) when one was involved with foreign powers—through foreign travel, frontier skirmishes, or Indian relations—one acted as an American; 2) everyone (except slaves and Indians) shared in the Constitution—a binding force which gave a sense of national community; 3) the mythology of the national epic in history projected a sense of a common experience; 4) a developing national legal practice, which gave a sense of a law in common and the expectation that the law would be read the same from one region to another; 5) a national ethos of liberal capitalism which promised progress, reward, and success as a consequence of those very features of independence and enterprise which were assumed to be part of national character.

The uncertainty of community, the absence of a national definition of a common people, and the character of openness in the American society were to have important consequences in the place and condition of Afro-Americans. The very qualities of American life that were attractive to most people—its dynamics, flux, and variety—caused chronic anxiety about disorder and social chaos, where all "civilized" values might be lost. Such anxiety made it crucial that community be defined and distinctions be made among claimants to the commonwealth. From the outset, it has been the fate of black Americans that such community definition has been contrived to exclude them.

British colonization in America seemed to occur in a context of tension in which opportunity and risk were set against community stability and cohesion. Both poles were elements in the motivation of all settlers, but differing values determined how Africans were to be accepted in the settlements. At one extreme is the model of the West Indian colonies. There, the British took full advantage of the opportunity the new world offered, giving minimum concern for community. Because the settlers had little intention of establishing permanent residence in the Islands, they could produce a staple crop with African labor without concern about the African influence on the settlement. Since the colonists' community remained in England, they had little concern for the quality of Island society, except for the efficient production of sugar. The British enclave on the Islands, therefore, had little problem defining the Africans among them. Their relationship was little different than that of similar British settlements in West Africa.

The puritan colonies of New England were in sharp contrast to the Islands. The religious purpose of these colonies made community cohesion and order of such primary importance that the settlers were prepared to forsake considerable opportunity for growth and profit in America. They would prefer to exploit the new world only in ways that would not jeopardize their communities. The presence of Africans, as well as other "foreign" peoples, would always be seen by the New England colonists as a potential threat to order.

New Englanders, therefore, did not encourage the importation of Africans, even as cheap labor. While there was a small slave population in New England, blacks, both slave and free, remained anomalies. They were treated almost as a servant class, subject as whites to the same laws and punishments. And even the growing merchant involvement in the slave trade was not allowed to augment the African population greatly. Thus, Samuel Sewell's antislavery tract, "The Selling of Joseph," stressed the inappropriateness of Africans as labor because they could not be expected to share in such community obligations as the militia. Given the Puritan's sense of the awesome consequences of community disintegration, and given the unavoidable threats the wilderness presented, he did not want to add to his society a people he did not know and could not control.

Virginia, Maryland, and the Carolinas fell between these extremes of the West Indies and New England. On the one hand, the southern settlers tended to be adventurers, much like those on the Islands, who wanted to convert some product into wealth through the mercantile system. On the other hand, they were colonists and settlers, building permanent homes and settlements in a way that the Islanders had not. To take advantage of the opportunities in the new world, they were ready to rely on African labor on a large scale. The sense of home and community coupled with a need for the African presence resulted in a distinctive pattern. The formal establishment of African slavery in these colonies was a way of delimiting the new community to exclude these people who were necessary for the colonies' success, but who were not to be considered part of the commonwealth.

We are reminded of the original insight of Oscar and Mary Handlin in "Origins of the Southern Labor System," in which they argue for the late institutionalization of a system of racial slavery in the southern colonies. The long debate which their article provoked has reduced the matter to a simple question of causality: which came first, racism or slavery? In this form, the argument has distorted the Handlins' original concept. The article did not question the likelihood that Englishmen considered Africans strange and even repulsive. Indeed, it was apparently such ethnocentrism that would explain the colonists' desire to appeal to a dwindling supply of English workers at a time when the future labor of the colonies seemed destined to be African. It was this process that worked to create racial slavery, according to the Handlins. Doubtless they were too mechanistic in their view of the institutionalization of slavery being an inverse relationship to the improvement of the conditions of English indentures. They were, however, correct to focus on community definition rather than on racism. The settlers wanted to reproduce familiar community life if they could. One need not imagine racist fantasies to see how a large black population would undermine that possibility. Furthermore, the Handlins' emphasis is useful in showing that whatever racial attitudes might have been before the institution of slavery, the experience of racial slavery, its necessary oppression and rationalizations, were instrumental in developing racism and racialistic attitudes which were qualitatively different from the bigotry of the typical Englishman of the seventeenth century. The problem for colonists was how to incorporate into their midst an exotic population without losing their own identity.

Those who have emphasized that a priori racism among Englishmen determined a system of racial slavery from the beginning are not wrong, given the need for African labor. But they tend to ignore important considerations. They have relied on an "official" colonial attitude towards blacks, failing to take into account the broad range of cooperation among the Africans and Englishmen who coexisted in the servant class. While they might have been subject to different punishments, blacks and whites did run away together and were otherwise engaged in crime and social disorder. Edmund S. Morgan has illustrated the importance of official colonial concern with disorder among the servant classes for the enslavement of blacks.

There seems to be no record of disorder because of the propinquity of English and African servants. While negative evidence, it would be reasonable to assume that if blacks were generally repugnant to whites, the servant class would have felt some offense at having been cast together with Africans. Even in those laws which do define slavery, it is often ignored that English women were by choice cohabitating with African men. It was not so much that they were "forgetful of their status" as freeborn Englishwomen, but that those who drafted the laws wanted to define a status for them. As much as the laws defined a slave status for blacks, they were imposing upon English men and women limits to their relations with Africans. That, of course, had not been necessary in the mother country, where blacks were no threat to order and community. Englishmen and Africans had been freer to do as they pleased where community was not at stake.

Thus, the slave colonies defined community by the establishment of racial slavery; and the New England colonies sought to strengthen communities by limiting the African presence. Other colonies differed in particulars. But, whatever the pattern, there was always a subtext underlying the dilemma: the acceptance of Africans as a source of labor—a means to wealth and success as a mercantile colony—created another element of disorder and social disintegration. Racial slavery seemed to provide one way out of this dilemma; racial exclusiveness seemed another.

These patterns of racial exclusion or racial slavery marked the development of the nation. The impetus was with the New England model. Article Six in the Northwest Ordinance called for the exclusion of blacks from the land that was to become Ohio, Indiana, and Illinois. While settlers debated the matter, these states developed free constitutions, but they also insisted on restraints against black settlement. Similarly, the principle of Article Six was in the Talmadge Amendment to the Missouri Enabling Act and in the Wilmot Proviso. It was assumed that states could be slave or free—ultimately depending on popular sovereignty—but none of the free states of the West was likely to encourage black settlement. And in the meantime, the status of free blacks in the South became precarious, such that by 1860, the consensus was that free blacks were unwelcome.

The general expansion and liberalization that we associate with the Jacksonian period had restricting consequences for blacks. We think of the period as one of celebration of the common man. It is especially noted for the extension of the franchise, without property qualifications, to all men. Dixon Ryan Fox long ago showed how in New York State, the reform of the franchise by the Democrats was tied to placing special tax qualifications on blacks. Ironically, in the older, aristocratic system of property qualifications, some blacks voted. But under the democratic reforms, where all free men were to be granted a political voice, blacks were placed under special restraints.

The *Dred Scott* case was the most notable effort before the Civil War to get Federal acceptance for the Afro-American as a participant in aspects of citizenship. The result was the assertion that there had been an intentional exclusion of blacks from the community, that the Federal government under the Constitution was powerless to define national development as regards slavery, and that, for practical purposes, citizenship was a matter of local determination. There were dissenting opinions, of course, and Chief Justice Taney's argument was tendentious, but *Dred Scott* represented the official position of the Federal government, as far as the law was concerned, and it was to have an impact on legal interpretation into the twentieth century.

Race became the single determinant of community, especially in those places where slavery obliged special laws defining the Afro-American's place. Even those blacks who were not mere chattel were generally denied minimum citizen rights. They could not own property, make contracts, testify in court; they had no personality in the law. These restrictions made it necessary to construct elaborate formulas defining "Negro" in legal terms. To be a "Negro" meant that one was not considered a person in ordinary terms. Color was not the question, ancestry was. In effect, one could be denied citizenship if it could be successfully asserted that he was to any degree "Negro." Guilt and innocence, performance on contract, marriage and divorce, rightful ownership, inheritance, might rest on the outcome of whether a person was judged "Negro" or white.

Since racial identity meant everything, legal definition was important. Chancellor Harper of the South Carolina Supreme Court gave the clearest, most practical view of the matter. Rejecting the testimony of "experts" in defining a mulatto, Harper said that the term had no technical meaning. Rather, it was a public matter, and the whole question of race identity was a matter of public usage and should be for a jury to decide. Thus, the person might be white or "Negro," depending on his reputation in the community. Harper acknowledged that persons with identical ancestries could be, thus, adjudged differently. But he saw this as a proper means of social control: "It will be a stimulus to the good conduct of [vagabonds] and . . . for the fidelity of citizens."

With the end of the Civil War, the terms changed. The Union victory determined that the southern view of national development would not prevail. With the end of slavery, new terms were to be found to place blacks in the society, but outside the community.

Some had assumed that Reconstruction was to change federal relationships such that the central government could affect social, as well as political and economic, relations among citizens. Furthermore, it was assumed by some that the Fourteenth Amendment was to define, for the first time, a common national citizenship.

> All persons born or naturalized in the United States, and subject to the jurisdiction thereof, are citizens of the United States and of the State wherein they reside. No State shall make or enforce any law which shall abridge the privileges or immunities of citizens of the United States; nor shall any State deprive any person of life, liberty, or property, without due process of law; nor deny to any person within its jurisdiction the equal protection of the laws.

Clearly enough, this amendment answered the Taney contention in *Dred Scott* that Afro-Americans were not citizens. But did the amendment empower the federal government to remove obstacles to the acceptance of blacks in the local community? Did the Fourteenth Amendment change the federal relationships in such a way that the national government could define a standard of rights, privileges, and immunities that would constitute a common citizenship? While some of those who framed the amendment might have thought that was their intent, it turns out that there were many who thought otherwise, and the language of the amendment opened the way to keep Federal distinctions intact.

Beginning with the *Slaughterhouse Cases* (1877) the Supreme Court made a distinction between United States citizenship and citizenship to the States. The language of the amendment was ambiguous enough to permit an interpretation of two citizenships. That had been the assumption in *Dred Scott,* and, indeed, the Court could argue that if the framers had wanted to do away with that distinction they would have been explicit about it.

Following that line of reasoning, the Supreme Court struck down the Civil Rights Bill of 1875 with the *Civil Rights Cases* (1883). The Fourteenth Amendment did not empower Congress to affect community relations, that is the behavior of persons to one another in their states. In short, local determination of how blacks were to be accepted was to remain. It was still for the locality to decide to what extent Afro-Americans were to participate in community. And in *Plessy v. Ferguson* (1896), the Court updated Chancellor Harper's edit on race relations. It would be custom and general social attitude that would determine the place of a person in society. Even, as in this case, where the Commerce Clause of the Constitution gave the federal government clear power to impose a standard, the Court was unwilling to define normal citizen rights.

With the end of slavery and the social disorder in the South, the problem of community definition was again central. The dismantling of the Radical Reconstruction meant the end of that experiment in the shaping of a national people through legislation and public policy. Because the goals of Reconstruction were uncertain, and doubtless unclear even to its advocates, the programs themselves were weak and ambivalent. Even had there been more certainty and purpose, the dreams and hopes of those who saw a national society where blacks and whites would share in the commonwealth flew in the face of a tradition of racial and community dualism that rested on the exclusion of blacks from the community.

The expectations of the "New South"—economic diversity, greater political democracy, and growth—required adaptations of old patterns of race relations. Clearly, slavery was no longer possible or desirable, but neither could Afro-Americans be brought fully into the society. It is really the greater social mobility promised by the "New South" that fed the need for special "Jim Crow" practices that separated blacks from whites as they had never been under the old regime of slavery. The best symbol of the new accommodation is in Booker T. Washington's address at the Atlantic Exposition in 1894. Washington promised that the New South could proceed with industrialization and progress, could seek new means of wealth, could open itself to the change and mobility that would be the spur and result of enterprise, without worry that blacks would do other than serve southern interests. They would, as they always had, be willing to work in the community's interest without asking to share in the commonwealth.

Such formulas were not enough, however. Lacking the institutional restraint of slavery and a free hand, within the law, to control the black population, whites relied on extralegal means to determine the limits of black participation in the society. Lynching, terror, and violence against black Americans had been a growing element of southern life from the Redemption. But it came to characterize race relations in the South into the twentieth century.

Lynching and extralegal violence are important aspects of the failure of community to actually include all who live together. When the community acts as a mob, outside the law, it is assumed that the victim is not part of the society or to be considered a person under the law. Law is an important instrument of community, defining its limits and accepted behavior and procedures. Blacks, as victims of lynching, were signals of a separation from normal procedure. The entire race was considered subject to standards outside what was normal for the community at large. It was not a question of whether or not a particular lynch victim was guilty or innocent of a particular offense. Rather, it was that his alleged offense was especially repugnant because *he* was the offender and that normal standards and procedures of justice could not apply to *him*.

In this regard, this exclusion of black Americans from the community through summary justice is not restricted to mob violence, to the South nor to the past. The special treatment accorded Afro-Americans by law-enforcement agents in northern cities can be understood in the same way. The fact that police and courts may today treat blacks (and other ethnics) in ways not acceptable in the law suggests assumptions that these victims are not thought bona fide citizens of the community. In these terms, the issue of police brutality is crucial in northern cities. The issue for black people is the quality of citizenship itself.

Violence, indeed, is one of the most striking indications of the failure of community in the United States. For law and the expectation of justice, equitable procedures, and punishments are crucial to community definition. The assumption, by law-enforcement officials and ordinary citizens, that one must go outside the law to achieve "justice" reflects doubt about the existence of community under the law. Frontier settlements were violent because "law and order" had not arrived; community life was defined in terms of that concept. But as there is a general feeling among officials that constitutional limitations on official power puts "society" at a disadvantage in the fight with crime and disorder, they become agents of disorder also.

In this respect, too, the experience of black Americans illustrates a broader national problem. The effort to exclude Afro-Americans reflects uncertainty of community and order which has never been resolved. It is symptomatic of deeper social conditions which are part of the nature of American establishment and its immigrant past. The condition of heterogeneity, the lack of certainty at the center of life, the perpetual crises of identity, fosters ethnocentricity and causes us to describe the process as pluralism. But there is no "invisible hand" that can create the sense of oneness that is community.

What has been a history of anxiety about identity, community, and order has been intensified by events in recent years. Afro-Americans, breaking out of the traditional restraints and demanding a new orientation, have challenged the society to adapt itself to changed conditions. The deterioration of institutions and procedures growing from the Vietnam War has caused a challenge to schools and government. With it all, there has been an economic retrenchment that has encouraged ethnocentric protectiveness. Corruption at the highest level of government, the profound challenge to the Constitution, the sense of pervasive corruption in private and public sectors, has caused individuals and ethnic groups to insist on self-interest in the apparent absence of any community interest. The liberalization of standards in education, the advent, for instance, of the structural linguists and their challenge to "proper" English, has given validity to particularism. All of these conditions, events, and tendencies invest pluralism with a new vitality.

That is another argument to show that pluralism leaves community in doubt, indeed, grows from the fact of community uncertainty. There is a need to impose (from without if necessary) standards of community. It used to be argued that legislation in such matters was ineffective because one could not change "the hearts and minds of people through law." Any black person who has traveled in southern cities such as Jackson, Mississippi; New Orleans, Louisiana; Atlanta, Georgia, etc., will now be struck by how the exterior of white and black interaction, covertly at least, has changed for the better since the 1950s. It would seem clear enough that effective community can occur if it is understood and insisted on as a goal. And, it should be borne in mind that lacking the insistence on such standards, violence and disorder may be exacerbated rather than abated.

Civil rights legislation of the 1960s has defined minimum standards of citizenship, and some national administrations have demonstrated some willingness to insist on those standards on the local level. When we accept the notion that there are minimum rights that we as citizens are prepared to extend to our fellows, and which we will insist that government extend, we will have moved toward the acceptance of a national citizenship.

We need to insist on institutional and procedural integrity. While we may permit "compensatory" treatment for those who have been historically deprived, we must not do it in such a way as to undermine institutional integrity. We must find ways to support and sustain centralizing institutions. In a society where institutions such as family and church reflect general social disintegration, the integrity of the law and schools becomes crucial. They remain the institutions that all Americans hold in common. Of course, the question remains: can there be standards of fairness and procedure in law that will be considered *fair* to all; can there be a consensus, based on something other than mere tradition, on which educational institutions can exist?

The single "institution" that would be community-producing is a history which all Americans can recognize as their national as well as their personal story—that they can be a part of a single epic. George Bancroft made such a history for one age. Frederick Jackson Turner's vision created another working model for a national history. But none of these old formulas has been adequate to include the varieties and subtleties of American life. They failed precisely in ignoring the ethnic experiences—most notably they failed to comprehend the significance of the Afro-American in the shaping of the American experience and the American mind.

But ethnic histories are no answer. There is no fairy of laissez-faire, who will, by a magic wand, create a new synthesis out of the many parts. Ethnic history, like pluralism, may be more an expression of failure than of achievement. We may well need to see the need for a synthesis and community before we are willing to transform diversity into unity. Such a synthesis must honor the experiences and special qualities of groups so that all will feel themselves a part. Such a synthesis, such an integration, will make sense to even those Afro-Americans for whom that word has become a term of derision.

5

Foreword to
A World in Shadow

The quality of citizenship and the openness of society in America have not been preoccupations of American historians. Generally, it has been assumed that citizenship has been opened to all born here and to those who have professed a commitment to the nation while demonstrating a minimal knowledge of its laws and institutions. Also, few would question the general thesis that the development of the American nation, from even before the Revolutionary crisis, was toward the openness of liberal capitalism and democracy and away from strictures and limitations on individual freedom.

Of course we have always known of the exceptions to the rule of American life. Slavery meant that a large number of people had no claim to citizenship. The status of Indians in this regard has always been perplexing. Furthermore, we have had to be aware that the maintenance of order—given the institution of slavery—forced antiliberal practices on Americans. Fugitive slave laws have to be considered anomalies in a free society.

However much we have been willing to take the exceptions into account, they have remained merely *exceptions* in our thinking. We have not been willing to define American life and history in terms of the experiences of those who have been excluded from the community of free men. American history has been seen as a story of whites (Anglo-Saxons at that) and free men. All others were peculiarities and their stories excepted from the major themes.

The character of all histories, however, is dependent on perspectives; a change in point of view can make every difference. The spirit of the last decade has compelled us to look at the American past through

*From *A World in Shadow: Free Blacks in Ante-Bellum South Carolina* by Marina Wikramanayake. Published for the South Carolina Tricentennial Commission by the University of South Carolina Press, 1973. Reprinted with permission.

61

new and different eyes: those of blacks, women, Chicanos, Indians, and the "inarticulate." The challenge is formidable, but if good histories are forthcoming from the effort the reward will be a new American history that will be inclusive of the wide variety of human experience that has made it up.

Professor Wikramanayake has taken on a study of a subject that is crucial to the realization of that promise. The free black in the antebellum South has most often been discussed in terms of what he was not. He was not white, he was not a slave, he was not free, he was not a citizen, he was not an alien. He was the most striking peculiarity in a society that defined itself in terms of its "peculiar institution." But to know what he was not is to understand very little about himself and the society of which he was part.

Professor Wikramanayake's study introduces us to the more complicated understanding of what free blacks were. We are shaken from the standard view that they were mainly a poor and pitiful lot. There were among them craftsmen and farmers, the educated and the propertied, and those with a modicum of power and prestige. They were important—perhaps indispensable—to the economies of the societies in which they lived. There were those who were cultivated, according to the standards of the time, as well as those who skirted the margin of acceptable civility. Although free men, they were intimately tied to the institution of slavery. Except for a very few, they gained their status through some act of manumission or purchase through their own or friendly hands. In many ways, the definition of their status turned on their being black men who were not slaves. Yet, fundamentally, the free ground on which they stood was quite infirm. Kidnapping, court action, or impoverishment might undermine their free status into the mire of slavery. Free blacks were like no other Americans in this regard. Freedom and personal liberty were always for them tenuous, and the more precious because it was so.

From the perspective of free blacks, the American experience was quite removed from what we have come to know. Their history was one of more and more sharply defined limits rather than of developing horizons. As white Americans became more convinced that the society they wanted was to be a white society, they became more and more explicit in stipulating the distinctly confined role that non-whites were to play. Therefore, rather than sharing in the gains in personal freedom and liberty that we have associated with the emergence of the "common man" in the early nineteenth century, the free blacks found themselves suffering under greater and greater restraints. Citizenship rights such as voting, holding property, identity before the law, and freedom of movement were challenged or denied rather than recognized and expanded. As time went on, what might have been considered natural rights—to vote, to move, to prosper—were taken away. The very existence of a free black population was ultimately challenged by legal restrictions on manumissions and by promotions of colonization schemes. Indeed, it is not too extreme to say that from the point of view of free blacks, the process of American development was from a relatively opened to an essentially closed society.

Considering the details of life for free blacks in the antebellum South, America was a totalitarian society from every point of view. Its primary and total commitment was to the guarantee of a white society and to the maintenance of black slavery within it. Every other consideration had to conform to those ends. Free blacks thus existed on a sufferance which grew more fragile as whites became convinced that these fundamental objectives were undermined by the former's very presence. It was not merely that free blacks could be denied rights and treated with contempt. Rather, it was that they had no real guarantees of any status. Their liberty would suffer or be sustained through the capriciousness of white men. Individual free blacks depended on the influence and goodwill of whites who favored them. But even that could not be certain when there were imagined threats to public peace. The patrol system converted every white male into a military instrument to enforce the rule of white freedom and black slavery. Modern totalitarian societies have shown few improvements over the states of the antebellum South. Emblematic of the totalitarian character of antebellum South Carolina is the inquisition that followed the disclosure of the Denmark Vesey conspiracy. Here was no testament of a society governed by law rather than men. Here was no subservience of men to the rule of law and principle. Rather, the trials testified to the willingness of white men to use any means necessary to preserve the whiteness of society and slavery within it.

Free blacks, nevertheless, survived and managed under trying circumstances. They had little choice. Escape to the North would have been slight improvement. While some entertained the idea of expatriation to Africa, this too was very problematic. The great majority chose to remain and to try to work out some life for themselves. They quickly learned, however, in the instance of the African Methodist Episcopal Church, that segregation and community-building could be even more offensive to whites than any attempts at accommodation. They worked instead for self-definition through self-distinction. As free men, they were different from slaves, but wealth, property, education, church affiliation, voluntary associations, and skin color became means of finer distinctions of class. Pathetic, in many ways, nevertheless, their efforts were intended to undermine the racist assumption that all blacks were alike. To the extent that distinctions could be recognized and honored, the possibilities of black improvement were enhanced. It may have been a futile hope, but it is one we can understand.

Recent studies of blacks in the North before the Civil War suggest that theirs was a different lot from that of their Southern brothers only in intensity, not in character. Demography and the institution of slavery caused Southern whites to be more direct and purposeful in their control of blacks than were Northerners. Everywhere in antebellum America, blacks were (to use Professor Wikramanayake's word) denizens rather than citizens. And everywhere, while the American society was opening to the "common man," it was closing to blacks. American history from their perspective is quite different from that we have come to accept.

In many ways, Afro-Americans have continued to be plagued by the predicament of their free black forebears. Neither slave nor free, citizen nor alien, blacks took up their role following emancipation. The early characteristics remain with us in many ways, however. Like the free blacks of the antebellum period, present-day Afro-Americans remain the source of the country's deepest problems and anxieties, and because of that they remain, for most, invisible men.

For many reasons, the continuum of the black experience in the United States to our own day is better understood by a study of free blacks than of slaves. It was their condition that the freedmen inherited following the Civil War. And, to a large extent, it was leadership from their population that attempted to direct the race's future in Reconstruction. It will be through their perspective that we will see a very important dimension of American history, that which has always been unfree and closed. Therefore, we can be most grateful to Professor Wikramanayake for this careful study of free blacks in antebellum South Carolina. For she takes us far along the way we must go.

6

The Freeman Lectures

I. Biography as Art and History

When speaking of biography and history, the central question is why historians should bother with biography at all. As the Psalmist asked: "What is man that thou art mindful of him?" If, indeed, the task of the historian is to explain how the present got to be the way it is—how our society got to be the way it is—it is well the historian should ask, "What is man, any man, that we should be mindful of him?" Do individual personalities matter enough historically to command our attention? Should we recommend to readers as history the stories we as historians construct of individual lives?

Our answers to these questions have changed with time depending on how we have perceived humanity to be in control over circumstance and destiny. When we have imagined man heroic and compelling, we have assumed that to know the great men, the public men, the movers and shakers was to know all we need know about their times. When, on the other hand, we have thought man impotent, the victim of circumstance, our attention has gone to context, the age, the underlying determining forces. Over the last thirty years, we have witnessed a change in view, diminishing the role of individual lives.

It is not the first time fashion in historical biography has responded to sea changes in the relationship between the individual and the world. The modern tradition begins with Plutarch, author of lives of Greeks and Romans who lived in the first century. In his preface to the *Life of Alexander* he wrote:

> It must be borne in mind that my purpose is not to write histories, but lives. . . . As portrait-painters are more exact in the forms and features of the face, in which character is seen, than in the other parts of the

*Douglas Southall Freeman Lecture Series, March 1986, University of Richmond, Richmond, Virginia.

body, so I must be allowed to give my more particular attention to the marks and indications of the souls of men.

In the late seventeenth century, John Dryden, in his preface to *Plutarch's Lives,* recognized the implicit conflict between biography and history; in biography, he wrote:

> There is a descent into minute circumstances of trivial passages of life . . . which the dignity of (history) will not admit. . . . You see the poor reasonable animal, as naked as ever nature made him; are made acquainted with his passions and follies and find the Demi-God, a man.

Dryden saw, nevertheless, that biography excels over history in "pleasure" to the reader.

Where both Plutarch and Dryden saw biography and history as occupying separate realms, Thomas Carlyle saw them as joined:

> The history of mankind [Carlyle wrote] is the history of its great men: to find out these, clean the dirt from them, and place them on their proper pedestals.

It was Carlyle's romantic and heroic view, making history the signature of great men, that has influenced English and American historical writing into the twentieth century. History became the way of celebrating the individual spirit.

Concerning this dichotomy, two images come to mind, both from traveling on railroads. In the first, the train is momentarily stopped at a small-town depot. Looking out the window one sees a person, citizen of Yorkville, or Smith Junction, or whatever its name. As we look into this person's face, at his clothes, watch him pet his dog or knock the ashes from his pipe, we fancy that were we able to solve the enigma of his face and life, we would know about that town and his place in it.

In the second image, the train enters Manhattan from the north. The train often stops momentarily at the northern part of the island before going into the tunnel on its way to Grand Central Station. While the train stands, one sees walls of windows of tenements. It is always summer as, my eye recalls it, the windows open and the curtains blowing in whatever breeze there is. It is six o'clock and people are faceless, indistinguishable. While the mind tells us that each person is an individual, the scene and its context defies us to find personality or individual significance. There is no discernible individual through whom to imagine the whole story. Meaning must be derived from the aggregate. In such an image—in such a world—what is a man, indeed, that we should be mindful of him?

It is fitting to address the subject of historical biography in lectures named for Douglas Southall Freeman, an American historian whose greatest works were monumental biographies, those of Robert E. Lee (four volumes, winner of the 1934 Pulitzer Prize) and George Washington (six volumes—the sixth posthumous). They were monumental in two ways: first, in scale, in the grandness of the works; and second, in intent to be monuments to the subjects—to be definitive.

It is fitting for me also, because, despite an intellectual indisposition to the form, I myself have been the author of a biography of Frederick Douglass and I am presently engaged in a major study of the life of Ralph Bunche. As I think about that, I am a little surprised at myself, given attitudes I have harbored since my days as a graduate student. Thus, the mere act of standing before you and speaking about historical biography has forced me to raise questions about myself and about the form.

Everything in my training would have sent me in other scholarly directions. My teachers and the American historians who had the greatest influence on my generation (those in graduate schools between World War II and the mid-sixties) were little interested in personalities. The "Great Man" as a mover and shaker in history had suffered some hard knocks and had been pretty much deflated by progressive historians going back to Charles Beard, and by revisionist and iconoclastic historians like Kenneth Stampp and Richard Hofstadter. I readily accepted the view that Great Men were mere men after all, with ordinary, recognizable human motivations, foibles, and limitations; and, that the reasons of history should be sought in conditions, contexts, and social structure rather than in the lives and personalities of men, however celebrated and important.

Because of my interest in African-American history, I was especially taken with this message. After all, the profession did not take seriously the historical importance of Afro-Americans as actors, other than mere victims in American history. Except for Frederick Douglass and Booker T. Washington, no black personalities would have been considered worthy of historical attention.

There were too few celebrated black figures, and those who were had not been so institutionally based as to support the view that they had changed history by the force of their personalities. In terms of manifest history—the headlines of the past—they had not made a difference. And few Afro-Americans had the archives—the papers, diaries, journals, memoirs—historical biographies depend on. To the extent that history was seen as the whim, will, and behavior of individual men, there would be little historical reason to look at African Americans.

As I saw it, whatever might be the case for others, the history of black Americans would have to come from context, from condition, from the aggregate of men and women who were mute in conventional historical documents; whose testimony had to be discovered by extraordinary means. There were others besides Afro-Americans, of course—women, the poor, farmers, laborers, ordinary people—who had been "left out" of American history. In the late 1950s, we talked of writing history "from the bottom up," including in our history the previously unrepresented. That would of course mean Afro-Americans.

We were moved not only by ideological dispositions that were sympathetic to the poor and dispossessed, but also by the arrival of high-speed computers and methodologies, making it possible to digest and analyse vast amounts of data to answer demographic, social, economic, and political questions about the past (and groups in the past previously not considered.

What I have been describing is my generation's intellectual weaning from dependence on great personalities in history, under the shaping influence of times in which the individual had lost central place.

In the 1950s, when I was a student, few thought to answer historical questions, or achieve subtle and complex understanding of the past, through study of individual lives. The brilliant iconoclasm of Richard Hofstadter was for me the final word on great men. The notable "biographers" among my teachers, Arthur Schlesinger, Jr. and Frank Freidel, cast their work in terms of the age rather than the personality.

Little wonder. My teachers had become revisionists and iconoclasts in the 1930s and 1940s, working against the background of various forms of collectivism: fascism, communism, the corporate and the welfare state. We were not so much persuaded by facile theories of historical determinism. Rather, we were sensible to such social theorists as Durkheim, Weber, and Marx, who provided us analytical means to understand how social structure and social institutions shaped, limited, and determined individual choices and directions. In the mid-twentieth century, how could it be meaningful to say with Carlyle that the "history of mankind is the history of great men"?

Most of the history written well into the twentieth century was *"manifest history."* That is, history of events which contemporaries were well aware of, the headline events of their time. The documentation was from public records, from the personal archives of great men much involved in those very manifest events. This meant that individual players in the manifest events would occupy a central position in the resulting histories. And it meant that historians would pay but little attention to those who did not figure in public records, who kept no private archives, journals, diaries, and other papers. The historian-biographer was spared defending the historical significance of his subject by virtue of the importance of the manifest events in which his subject was an actor. Much the way we might see our citizen in the small town railroad station, the historian biographer sought to transfer the meaning of the whole onto a study of the particular personality.

That was the tradition. But as students we were all too aware of social structure and other systemic determinants of historical change to pay much attention to individuals. The "new social history" and the Annalistes captured our imaginations. We cared about people, of course, but we knew we could learn more about history by studying people in the aggregate: a reasonable and expected result from scholars shaped in our lives by mass culture and mass society; by the window-walled tenement rather than the small-town depot.

A different problem existed for the Afro-American historian. There remained those huge gaps where, from the point of view of African Americans, there were no icons to break; no history at all for that matter.

It was the consciousness of these gaps in the history that prompted historians in the 1950s and 1960s to argue for a "history from the bottom up." That meant deliberately to seek ways to tell the story of the inarticulate, the historically mute. For those of us who were interested in the history of black people and women, this was a brisk and tonic development.

Yet, the new methodologies which made it possible to define and articulate the *latent* history could not fully satisfy the needs we felt in Afro-American and women's history. These techniques described, defined, and analysed aggregates, not units; and whatever significance one might, through them, breathe into classes and categories of people, they diminished the significance of the individual. Like the faceless tenement dweller we see from our passing train, his importance is not in a personality which we cannot discern, but in his collective condition. Such aggregate history might be a perfect corrective to the traditional, overweening preoccupation with great, white men; but it only meets limited needs of African Americans and women, who would find the traditional landscape barren of significant personalities.

Taking mid-century, 1950, as a point of reference, it is interesting to consider the names of Afro-Americans most recognizable to the ordinary student of American history (excluding athletes and entertainers); the most likely candidates would have been: Nat Turner, Frederick Douglass, George Washington Carver, Mary McLeod Bethune, Marcus Garvey, and W. E. B. Du Bois. You might add some names to this list, but I think I have been generous. In 1950, however, only one of these figures, Frederick Douglass, had received full biographical treatment by a professional historian—the black historian Benjamin Quarles.

On the other hand, the typical college history student would probably not have heard any of the following names: Salem Poor, David Walker, Benjamin Banneker, Alexander Crummell, Bishop Henry McNeil Turner; nor, the names of any senator, congressman, or public officer during Reconstruction, such as T. Thomas Fortune or Ida Wells-Barnett. Of course, one could add to this list, but you get my point.

The first task of Afro-American history was, therefore, to make the names and achievements of such individuals conspicuous parts of the historical landscape. That meant running counter to what I have been describing as a major sea change in history—away from emphasis on the individual personality. It has only been in the last decade that support could be found for the publication of papers of black major figures such as Douglass, Garvey, and Du Bois. This need to illuminate the lives of historically important black men and women is far more a matter of filling in a wide gap of ignorance than it is a lingering fascination with "great personalities."

This necessary and understandable emphasis by Afro-American historians on biography has, however, three hazards:

(1) In the enthusiasm to discover and make public the importance of black people one risks the breathless, "Gee Whiz!" approach to discoveries. "Did you know that George Grant, an African American, invented the golf tee?" The understandable desire to remark on every achievement, every contribution, diminishes the historian's most important concern—historical relevance. Even while we look at the man in the train station, our real interest has to remain the town.

(2) Ironic: the collective need to celebrate heroes and heroines acts to create public figures—heroes rather than human beings—submerging (if not destroying) that individual essence that reveals self-doubt and weakness. Ethnic histories, like nationalistic histories, compel their individual subjects to serve collective ends, thus converting individuals into aggregates of another kind—stock, monumental characters which lack individual personalities.

(3) The "new social history" dominates and defines the profession such that the major historical questions being asked now are those best answered by the techniques and methodologies of that history; and they are not likely to be approached (let alone answered) by biographical studies. This could mean that, to the extent that Afro-American historians concentrate on biography, they will be peripheral to the central historical work being done. Their work won't make a difference!

These theoretical and historiographical questions govern any consideration of historical biography. But these last observations reveal the fundamental limitation of the new social history: while it serves the social science side of history well, it serves less well the humanistic side. And it is on this humanistic side that historical biography—with all its faults and problems—is at its best. What we look for in individual lives is not scientific solutions, but the awakening of our human sensibilities. Here, I would quote one of the greatest biographers in the English language, Samuel Johnson, who described biography as "what comes near to us, what we can turn to use." Johnson believed that hardly a single life had been lived from which we could not learn something if told with complete honesty. Johnson, even then, was doubtlessly thinking of how isolated and compartmentalized all of us really are, and how much we all need to touch hands with others, to learn from each other's experience and to get whatever encouragement we can.

In this sense, the biography is neither about the town nor about the tenement. Rather, it is about the individual human being, herself or himself, within the problematic contexts we have come to understand. The biographer wants to find out how those we consider great experiencing natures ever managed to become what they were—"what they had to struggle against, and above all, what they had to struggle against in themselves." Pertinent are Samuel Johnson's comments to the Shakespearean scholar Edmond Malone:

> If nothing but the bright side of characters should be shewn, we should sit down in despondency, and think it utterly impossible to imitate them in anything. The sacred writers . . . related the vicious as well as the virtuous actions of men; which had this moral effect, that it kept mankind from despair.

These observations help to explain why biography continues to be the most popular form of non-fiction, and probably the means by which most readers involve themselves in history. It also explains why the historian has a responsibility to present lives in human and complex terms so that their readers can find within those lives—so far distant from their own—the shock of their kinship recognition.

In my next lecture, I will step back from these rather theoretical considerations and address the subject as it relates to African Americans specifically.

II. African Americans and Historical Biography

In my previous lecture, I asked you to think with me about some theoretical problems with historical biography. Specifically, I wanted us to consider how our changed view of the importance of the individual has affected biography in history. We look less to the individual great man or woman to explain our past than we once did. Yet I argued that because some groups (Afro-Americans and women for instance) have been so thinly represented and understood in traditional history, we have a reasonable desire (and a reasonable need) to discover and illuminate the salient lives previously ignored or undervalued. I concluded by saying that left at that, however, such efforts in African-American history (or women's history) will continue to be marginal and of limited influence on mainstream historical scholarship which seeks to discuss questions about which individual lives can offer little more than anecdotal evidence.

I would like in this lecture to address more directly some problems I see facing historians wanting to do biographies of Afro-Americans. I wish merely to discuss historical biography and so some definitions are called for.

First, I would remove from our discussion autobiographical literature, which I estimate constitutes a remarkably large percentage of the printed pages about black individuals. I would consider as autobiographical the compilations of slave narratives and other such oral histories. Oral histories are autobiographical even where the scholar has played a crucial role in getting the life in print and before the public, as in the case of Theodore Rosengarten's *All God's Dangers: The Life of Nate Shaw,* and Nell Irvin Painter's *Hosea Hudson.*

The scholar's role is the important determinant. Whether as compiler, editor, or even as amanuensis, the scholar in these works serves merely to make a primary source available to the public and to other scholars. The scholar stands outside the work, providing, if anything, commentary on the source. In fact, the authenticity of the source depends on our certainty of the scholar's "distance" from it.

Second, I also exclude that kind of literary biography (including biographies of scientists, artists, musicians, etc.) which focuses on the subject's own "authorship." Historical biography should rest on something broader, a historical relevancy. When choosing a subject for biography, the historian should believe that the completed work will cause us to understand better or differently something of historical significance. A literary biography of W. E. B. Du Bois, such as Arnold Rampersad's *The Art and Imagination of W. E. B. Du Bois* (1976), need not go much beyond Du Bois's voluminous writings; whereas a historical biography would have to reach into the political, intellectual, social, and institutional contexts in which the subject moved. Because Du Bois's life was so long, so involved in manifest events, historical significance can be assured as long as the scholar brings to the work questions the history wants answered.

To state it positively, what makes biography historical is the attempt to answer historical questions, to give readers a particular perspective from which to view certain historical events, to enhance their personal empathy and involvement in times and experiences remote from themselves. The historical biography is constructed through scholarship which exploits a variety of sources (only some of which may be produced by the subject), reconstructing the personality, the context, and the events as the scholar sees them. Thus, the accuracy, validity, and significance of the work is the responsibility of the scholar and not that of the subject.

As I mentioned yesterday, as late as 1950 we could find but one book-length biography of an Afro-American written by a professional historian, that being Benjamin Quarles's *Frederick Douglass* (1944). There were two reasons for that; one of them subject to change, the other not.

The first and changeable reason was the profession's general rejection of the testimony of black Americans, whatever their condition or circumstance. White American historians (which of course almost defined the profession) tended to view African Americans and slavery as anomalous or marginal to the mainstream of American history—a history, incidentally, they would define as free and progressive. Because the history of black Americans was as slaves and oppressed, it was convenient to consider them outside the norm; their witness would be seen as biased and irrelevant to the central story. Historians would not, therefore, use slave narratives as a means of understanding slavery. They tended to see black activists as mere pawns or mouthpieces of white reformers and politicians. The presumption was that Afro-Americans had an axe to grind; only white historians could be unbiased.

It must have taken considerable courage, therefore, for Benjamin Quarles to do the Douglass biography under William Hesseltine at the University of Wisconsin. Courage to face the cynical condescension for doing "Negro history," and courage to endure detailed scrutiny for evidence of bias. The book shows it. The work is carefully "scientific," thorough, and dispassionate. Throughout, Quarles deliberately signals distance between himself and his subject. Although Afro-American, he could be "objective" about Douglass, slavery, and abolition. The goal was to achieve such distance that the reader would be unable to tell that the author was black—certainly an important, if unstated, criterion by which the profession would measure any black scholar. Quarles achieved it admirably.

Those attitudes and assumptions have changed remarkably in our own time. American historians have come to see African Americans as important witnesses and have come to recognize bias, predisposition, and point of view as inescapable (and even desirable) elements in historical writing. This change is reflected in the number of biographies of black Americans published since the mid-1960s.

The second reason for the scarcity of black biography was not so open to change, and it persists. The subjects of historical biography are most likely to be persons so located socially as to be actors, shapers, or witnesses to *manifest* events—those headline events or occurrences in history. They need not be *great men* or *great women,* but they should be strategically placed and sufficiently involved so that their lives reveal to us matters we consider of historical importance.

Most importantly, they must be highly literate, with the peculiarity of mind that makes them think their thoughts and observations are important and will be seen so by others. Such people keep diaries and journals; write memoirs and autobiographies; save letters. Furthermore, they cohabit a special world with others who do the same.

In short, the historical biographer requires archives of documents— public papers, private papers, etc.—and the more there are and the more varied they are, the better. The biographer wants points of view different from that of his subject, points of view from the subject's friends and foes alike. Dare I say it? We want gossip!

Basically, we want to make the subject human—dimples, warts, and all. That is why a community of letters makes better biography.

In light of this second reason, it becomes clear why, until the mid-nineteenth century, few black Americans invited biography. They did not consider themselves historically placed; they did not think of themselves, their thoughts and behavior, as historically significant; and they did not find themselves among others who did.

This is not to say that there are not African Americans about whom we would love to have good historical biographies: Paul Cuffee, Denmark Vesey, Absolom Jones, David Walker, Sojourner Truth, Harriet Tubman, Nat Turner, to name a few. We can tell their stories, but we cannot get enough into their thoughts, their lives, and their circumstances to flesh out the biography and use their lives as an entrée into broader historical understanding.

So our history, through much of the nineteenth century, compels us to turn more to aggregates than individuals. From the beginning of the century, black Americans in increasing numbers are found in places of leadership and consequence, institutionally and politically. Since World War I, more and more of the "manifest" events which make our traditional history have had to do with African Americans and had blacks as at least minor players. Since the 1960s, some Afro-Americans have been major players and some have been so situated in public office as to attract historical attention outside Afro-American history per se.

Two examples of this last point. If a historian wishes to write about the Department of Housing and Urban Development, he must write about Robert Weaver, its first secretary and the builder of the department. Or when historians write about the national budget and deficit crises of 1985, they must write of Congressman William Gray, chairman of the House Budget Committee and a major player in budget legislation. Not to mention the political effect black Americans have in national and local politics in general: the Black Caucus, black mayors and administrators. This trend would suggest that at some future time, students of American history will know about black men and women as a part of the manifest events of general American life, and not particularly as related to Afro-American concerns.

Since the late nineteenth century more African Americans are likely to have left papers in a usable form that can now be found in archives. Few blacks or whites of the twentieth century are as historically minded as were earlier Americans, and that sensibility seems to have diminished as the century has grown old. Nevertheless, there are resources, however thin, despite the fragmented and atomized literary community. All of this is to say, my second explanation for few Afro-American biographies will be less consequential in the coming years.

Still there will be problems all historians will face in writing biographies of twentieth-century figures. The problems are general, but some have greater relevance to those working with Afro-American subjects.

The most general problem has to do with the quality of the documents that will be available to us. This problem stems from the ubiquitousness of technology in our society. We now have the capacity (and apparently the inclination) to produce vast amounts of paper, much of which will, alas, make up the archives. Despite the bulk, however, the kind of insight the historian hopes to find with regard to decision-making or personal judgment is less likely to appear and be preserved than in an age of diaries, letters, and journals. Much of what the historian-biographer will want to know about his subject's thought and judgment will be lost because of telephones and changed habits of confidence. Less of what we want to know will actually be in the papers; and we will have to plow through a growing bulk of paper to discover less of value.

We have yet to know and can only imagine the consequences on biographical research of computer and electronic technology. So much can be stored and lost through the agency of the microchip that I fear future historians will have both a lot more, and a great deal less.

Another general problem for biographers is the tendency for public figures, the most likely candidates for historical biography, to be circumspect, enigmatic, and even mute on those issues of greatest interest to the historian. A public person is likely to create a public *persona,* a self always aware of public scrutiny, and always careful not to be candid about others or reveal self-doubt, ambivalence, or uncertainty. One's loyalties to leader, party, or group controls not only one's speech but what one puts in writing.

This is certainly true of the major figures of black biography. Afro-Americans who would be leaders have been controlled by a common compelling fact: they were, and they were perceived to be, singular representatives of a race which was poor, oppressed, and struggling for freedom and genuine citizenship. All Afro-Americans of aspiration and achievement saw themselves (and were forced by others to see themselves) as exemplars of their race. They could, it was imagined, show black people, by their achievement and behavior, the way out of second-class citizenship. Likewise, they could show to whites and the world the potentialities and the promise of the mass of black Americans whom they were thought to represent.

This can be seen clearly in the lives of Douglass, Washington, and Du Bois. Their lives and their reputations were their principal assets and principal instruments for reform. Du Bois, in his *Dusk of Dawn,* uses his life to describe the anomaly and the tragedy of the color line. Douglass wrote three autobiographical works. His abolitionist role was to tell and retell his experiences in slavery and his escape to freedom. It was his life and what he had become which he and his abolitionist colleagues saw to be the most damning argument against slavery. So concerned were his friends that he be a convincing instrument of reform that some urged him to speak a poorer English, a dialect—at least one instance when the desire to be a good tool for reform ran counter to the desire to exemplify the human potential of slaves.

Washington made Tuskegee to stand upon the evidence of his life. His journey, "up from slavery," is calculated to bring hope to white philanthropists—eager to see an untroubled racial future—and to black Americans, hopeful to find patterns and formulas which enlist essential white good will and support. Louis Harlan has been able to cut beneath the public person of Washington to reveal a more interesting and more historically significant person than Washington would want us to see.

Douglass, however, is a much more difficult case. His public self was so at one with his private self that hardly any existing document reveals a face beneath the mask. It is as if he were born anew after his escape, searched for a new self as well as a new name, and became the "representative man" totally and completely. Preston Dickson, using local records from the Eastern Shore of Maryland, has been able to show in his *Young Frederick Douglass* the probable year of Douglass's birth (which Douglass did not know), and to show that Douglass misremembered his past so as to better serve abolitionism. Dickson, a white native of the Eastern Shore, wanted to show that Douglass knew more about his family than he revealed, and that he was rather well treated and a relatively privileged slave. Dickson's version is doubtless closer to the truth than Douglass's, but it would have been less dramatic on the abolitionist stump.

Two romantic assumptions influenced Du Bois's thought about himself. First was a romantic view of history, demiurgic and global. And second was his fascination with great men and heroes who could translate into an Emersonian "Representative Man." Du Bois's three valedictory addresses—one at Great Barrington High School, one at Fisk University in 1888, and the third at Harvard College in 1890—took as subjects "great men": Wendell Phillips, Bismarck, and Jefferson Davis respectively. Much of his writing is autobiographical, often repeating in different places the same story for different results. That is why he can assume to illustrate a global problem of racism through telling the story of his own life. Thus, *Dusk of Dawn* bears the subtitle: *An Autobiography of Race Concept* and in it he attempts to show the "problem of the 20th century as that of the Color-line."

This problem of the self-conscious exemplar extends beyond the great historical figures. In my current work on the life of Ralph Bunche, I have found very little in over 180 boxes of his papers that is of an unofficial and private character. He, too, was always on stage, and knew it. Like most black achievers of his generation, he knew that he stood for more than himself at UCLA, at Harvard, and in the world. That onus, special to black men and women, was one of the elements selecting out individuals on the way up. It took an extraordinary capacity to take the tension of being a "credit to the race," to get along and to achieve. As Bunche moved up in his career—OSS, State Department, The United Nations—the burden of confidentiality and secrecy associated with his work added to this natural reticence, circumspection, and conservatism. Like other diplomats and career civil servants, Bunche became even more circumspect in what he put on paper.

In a sense, most black figures, thinking about themselves and their lives as likely historical subjects (and this well into the twentieth century), saw themselves monumentally: as exemplars whose lives and achievements weighed into the ongoing American debate over racial justice. If one can think of ideal models, it would be of the great men and women about whom biographies had been written. They saw themselves as models to be emulated, great men and women, heroes and heroines whose slightest slip could be an embarrassment and a setback to the race. What was open to others—drinking, gambling, sexual involvements—was closed to them even in the most modest forms. This helps to explain why such potential leaders as T. Thomas Fortune were forced to remain in the shadows, as secondary figures. It also alerts us to some important changes in the twentieth century, when such figures as Adam Clayton Powell, Jr. and Malcom X could reject some aspect of the exemplary model. Similarly, it is noteworthy that revelations of the sexual indiscretions of the Reverend Martin Luther King, Jr. were far less damaging to him than similar charges would have been to Frederick Douglass or Booker T. Washington.

Nevertheless, such an exemplary view of oneself cramps and confines one's behavior and sanitizes what one is likely to reveal about inner feelings, doubts, or personal conflict, defying the historian to discover the human side. Lacking a social context in which colleagues might also leave papers—which has too often been the case with important African-American figures—the historian has difficulty triangulating to discover perspectives that the subject would not provide.

The historical importance of the lives of black individuals of achievement cannot be gainsaid. What we come to know about the fabric of Afro-American history, especially until World War II, will be learned through individual lives and not through institutions, public policy, and manifest events.

The historian, therefore, has to be even more careful to ensure that the subject of his biography is the history it can illuminate and not merely the personality. It is the town we want to know about, not the man in the station. Historians have to avoid succumbing to the idea the subject would like to project: that he is exemplary. To write good Afro-American history, the biographer must deliberately and persistently insist that the subject tell us something beyond himself and his achievements. This is hard to do because of the thinness of sources, and because the subject—who often seems to stand alone in his time—encourages our focus on his uniqueness.

This task was made easier for me in my book on Frederick Douglass because, by the time I wrote it, there were three other biographies on him, and I did not feel the need to persuade my readers of Douglass's greatness. I could give attention to such issues as the tension between Douglass and his abolitionist friends and enemies; to his political conflicts and inconsistencies (and, thus, to the significance to Afro-Americans of the political tumult of the 1840s and 1850s); to the problems of black leadership in the post-war years; to the dilemma of African Americans in the late-nineteenth-century Republican politics. Through it all, Douglass does not always appear in heroic light, but he becomes more interesting as a human being and more interesting historically.

I detect a rather important change over the past generation in the way we view personality and ourselves. We are no longer able to accept easily the idea of heroes. This change stems from the realism or cynicism which has spurred the historical iconoclasm of the past half century; from a mass culture which produces celebrities rather than heroes; from our felt importance in the face of a technology we barely understand and cannot control, in a universe in which we find ourselves shrinking in significance. Our Napoleons have become in our eyes martinets and megalomaniacs.

To this change I ascribe differences in the way we look at biography and in the character of the papers and autobiographical writing of our contemporaries. I notice two characteristics: (1) a self-serving tendentiousness, especially of public figures, and (2) a willingness, no, an eagerness, to reveal personal angst and to assume the role of antihero.

As to the first, this is an age of tendentiousness. Since nothing is really provable, everything is arguable. Public figures more and more attend mainly to their ideological commitments (their faiths), selecting from within the world of evidence "facts" to argue their point with no attempt to understand others. We do not expect from the memoirs of Kissinger, Nixon, Carter, or anyone else deliberate and honest reflection on major events of their lives. Autobiography in our time has become more special pleading than at any time in our past. What is the future historian to do with such sources as evidence of the true world outside the subject's own self-absorption and self-defense?

Likewise, what will the future Afro-American historian do with autobiographies of those who see their lives as examples not of a race's potentiality, but of a race's suffering or pathology. Specifically, what is the historian to do with the selves portrayed by Claude Brown (*Manchild in the Promised Land*), Malcolm X (*The Autobiography of Malcolm X*), or Eldridge Cleaver (*Soul on Ice*)? In some of these works, fact and fiction have been so joined that they resemble more a work of Ishmael Reed, E. L. Doctorow, or Tom Wolfe than efforts at a true representation of actual lives. As with so much in our time, lives become symbolically true. The historian has to distinguish.

Nevertheless, biography will remain an important element of historical writing. Biography is, and will undoubtedly continue to be, the most popular form of nonfiction. And, probably, most Americans' continuing knowledge of history will come through biography and historical fiction. Here, we might remember Samuel Johnson's intent in writing biography: "what comes near to us, what we can turn to use." Not the hero, the monumental figure, the demi-god, but men and women like ourselves. It is because of our felt isolation and impotence in the modern world, its atomization, our compartmentalization that we need "to touch hands with others, to learn from each other's experience and to get whatever encouragement we can."

Is this new focus on personality a return to the Great Man? I think not. Putting aside the question of those previously left out of history (Afro-Americans and women), the facts of lives tell us of our impotence. Our great men are powerless in the Atomic Age. Even as we watch them go through the motions and the pretense, when we dare to be honest we discern that they too are ignorant, as we all are; the more certainty they claim, the more they reveal their ignorance. Our political reality seems to show a broad societal conviction that the image is more than the substance. The sense of human powerlessness to events draws one in curiosity to the study of the individual wrestling with history and forces he cannot change.

One looks at Ralph Bunche—his dreams in the United Nations and international organizations for world peace, his extraordinary equipment of intellect and character—and one sees the life spin out in his own, personal disappointment (despite all of his achievements), and one is persuaded of the inevitability of that result. We see hubris and tragedy more likely than our nineteenth-century antecedents.

Yet, what we see is inspiring because the dream can be so grand, the vision so ideal, the effort so superior. It sounds like neo-romanticism: not the romantic view of man represented in a Napoleon or Nietzsche's superman, rather that sense of hubris as represented in Faust.

7

W. E. B. Du Bois and Heroes

W. E. B. Du Bois celebrated his twenty-fifth birthday in Berlin where he had come after having graduated, first from Fisk University in Tennessee and then from Harvard. He took the passage of the quarter-century of his life with due weight and seriousness. He staged a private ritual—between himself and his god—with appropriate music, reflection (the reading of old letters, memories of his dead parents), "sacrifice to the Zeitgeist" which he defined as "mercy-God-work,"[1] candlelight libations of Greek wine. From his description it might have been a scene from Wagner—a ritual of dedication and self sacrifice.

So, Du Bois recorded the event. It was a self-conscious, happy, and eager taking stock of his youthful life already notable and auspicious for a black American, and an equally deliberate and self-conscious dedication of his adult life to a grand and worthy purpose: to race building, nation building, advancing civilization. He recorded the ceremony and his thoughts as if it were a covenant, a pact with God in the devotion of his life. His was a grand vision, reflecting his sense of the great need of his race, and reflecting, also, a grand conception of the potential of the Great Man and of Great Leadership.

A child of the nineteenth century, Du Bois would move into the twentieth century with a deeply rooted and well cultivated romantic imagination. As any romantic, he had an exceptional regard for the individual, the great man in history. Being an Afro-American, however, he saw greatness and power through the eyes of an oppressed and powerless people. Thus, while he was fascinated with the idea of the hero—imagining, doubtless, like many of his contemporaries, that black Americans awaited a great leader, a Moses, to transform them into a people—

*From *Amerikastudien: Eine Vierteljahrsschrift*, Jahrgang 34 (1988). Wilhelm Fink Verlag, München.

1. "Celebrating His Twenty-fifth Birthday," in *Against Racism: Unpublished Essays, Papers, Addresses by W. E. B. Du Bois*, ed. Herbert Aptheker (Amherst: University of Massachusetts Press, 1985), pp. 26–29.

seeing them from below, the heroes of the Western World were also oppressors—often brutes. That perspective kept him from simple hero worship.

His fascination and ambivalence about great men and heroes was well marked before his twenty-fifth birthday ritual. He had celebrated three heroes in the three valedictory addresses he had given, at his high school, at Fisk, and at Harvard. At his high school graduation, he spoke of Wendell Phillips, the American abolitionist, who had only recently died and whose deep and uncompromising commitment to human freedom and empowerment drove his advocacy for the slave, for women, and for the laborer. When Du Bois graduated from Fisk in 1888, he gave a commencement address on Bismarck. Two years later, at his Harvard graduation, Du Bois spoke to his Harvard audience on "Jefferson Davis as a Representative of Civilization."[2]

When Du Bois spoke at Fisk, Bismarck was still living and would live another decade. Du Bois merely told the story of Bismarck's rise to power—the identity of the self as the measure and determinant of rightness, the powerful man and ego which was at one with the creation of the powerful state. There could have been no better example in the modern age of the dominant personality shaping the times in which he lived and stamping that time with the character of his personality. What Napoleon Bonaparte had been nearly a century before, Bismarck was to the *fin de siècle*.

For Du Bois, Bismarck was an attractive subject because the promise and the problems raised by the Bismarck phenomenon spoke to two pressing needs in American life:

(1) the needs of a nation still in the throes of reformation and redefinition resulting from the shock and trauma of the Civil War;

(2) the needs of shaping and defining of the Afro-American people, still, in his time, unformed as a people or a nation. These dual problems of nationhood and peoplehood determined Du Bois's choice of subject to his southern black college just twenty-three years following the end of the Civil War. Bismarck appealed strongly to him: single minded, egocentric, focused on the one and only goal of nation building; so powerful in character and force of personality as to overcome the great opposition of parties, public opinion, and craven would-be leaders, forging his personal will and vision into a tangible, compelling, irresistible reality and fact.

Du Bois, however, was quick to see that the audacity and greatness of Bismarck came at a price. Great as he was, Bismarck was an illiberal force, placing himself against progressive and democratic currents in Germany and Europe. Whatever was gained for Germany in nation

2. "Bismarck" remains unpublished and may be found in the Du Bois Papers, University of Massachusetts, Amherst. "Jefferson Davis as a Representative of Civilization" is in W. E. B. Du Bois, *Writings*, ed. Nathan I. Huggins (New York: Library of America, 1986), pp. 811–14.

building, much more was lost as that nation, in Du Bois's view became an instrument of political conservatism and reaction. Bismarck, the single-minded hero, was amoral—seeing himself beyond good and evil. That, to Du Bois, led to a corrupting of self and society. Thus, he concluded his address to his classmates:

> The life of this powerful Chancellor illustrates the power of purpose, the force of an idea. It shows what a man can do if he will. But it carries with it a warning lest we sacrifice a lasting good to temporary advantage; lest we raise a nation and forget the people, become a Bismarck and not a Moses. To the one object of his life Bismarck sacrificed even truth and liberty. No lie ever stood between him and success; no popular right ever hindered that ruthless hand of iron.[3]

Bismarck, Du Bois added, gained a "fearful power and wields it . . ." but "he has made Germany a nation that knows not the first principle of self government, that must have a Bismarck or after Bismarck the deluge."

Just two years later, Du Bois delivered a valedictory at Harvard. This time his subject was Jefferson Davis, the late President of the Confederacy and symbolic leader in the failed effort at southern nationality: "Jefferson Davis as a Representative of Civilization."

The ironies could hardly be missed. Here was a black American youth speaking of the greatness of this champion of the South, this defender of slavery. Du Bois, furthermore, was to deliver his speech to a largely Yankee audience at Harvard. He would speak from the stage in Sanders Theater, built just sixteen years earlier as part of Harvard's Memorial Hall, which had been constructed to memorialize Harvard men who had lost their lives fighting to defeat the Confederacy,[4] to preserve the Union, and (perhaps incidentally) to free Afro-American slaves. In every niche and corner of that great hall were busts of men in heroic aspect who had fought in the Union's war, and chiseled onto marble plaques were the names of the Harvard war dead—an awesome toll of the "flower of New England."

Du Bois's address was a masterful manipulation of interrelated themes, worked toward surprising results: Jefferson Davis, the hero, the personality, individualism, the strong man, the strong nation (the value of strength and power in the strong individual and the strong state), civilization as defined and sustained by such values, race as an extension

---

3. "Bismarck," see Du Bois Papers, Amherst.

4. Recently, in the past year, there has been an unsuccessful move to bring into Memorial Hall the names of Harvard men who died in the Civil War on the Confederate side. It appears that the subscriptions which raised the money for the building specifically claimed the intention of memorializing Harvard men who died fighting *to preserve the Union*. While the passions connected with that war have cooled, if not died, opposition remains significant and sufficient to resist any change. Such resistance is "legalistic" (the original intent was clear and should not be countermanded) and from blacks for whom the symbolism of the Civil War and the Confederacy remain powerfully alive.

of civilization, and pluralism as a constructive and healthy alternative. The address begins, seemingly, as a celebration of the great man and the hero; it ends as a sharp critique and challenge to both and the assertion of the need for complementary values and a broader conception of civilization than that represented by Davis.

Actually, Du Bois has little to say about Jefferson Davis, the man. After the second paragraph, he scarcely mentions the name. He sets out to identify Jefferson Davis with the "civilization" which will become the actual subject of the speech. Davis is defined in the first sentence as a "typical Teutonic hero."[5] That, for Du Bois, is identical with the "Strong Man." The Anglo-Saxon—generally used as interchangeable with Teuton—"loves a soldier—Jefferson Davis was an Anglo-Saxon,[6] Jefferson Davis was a soldier." It is about these values, attributed to "Teutonic" or "Anglo-Saxon" civilization which would become the subject of his remarks.

As "typical" or representative of that "civilization," Davis personified its characteristics, which Du Bois set out to describe in terms one might associate with medieval romance. Davis was "fiery and impetuous," "cool and ambitious," "imperious." His physical description fit the type: "thin nervous lips and flashing eyes," with a body which would not be defeated and "never surrendered." Du Bois's characterization of Davis—undoubtedly Davis's view of himself—was like a medieval knight of romance: "a soldier," "a lover," "a ruler," "passionate, ambitious and indomitable; bold and reckless guardian of the people's All."

It was, nevertheless, a description filled with ambivalence: like a wonder-filled notice of an avatar, a living relic of a dead and dying past, wearing still the odor of glory mixed with the corruption of disease and death—Du Bois speaks of Davis's "cadaverous" and "diseased" body. Judged "by the whole standard of Teutonic civilization," Du Bois proclaimed, "there is something noble in the figure of Jefferson Davis." Recognizing that "nobility," he was, nevertheless, quick to tell his audience that "judged by every canon of human justice, there is something fundamentally incomplete about that standard."

Thus, Du Bois makes clear that his subject is really not Davis, but civilization, and not just civilization but "Teutonic civilization." We need remind ourselves, then, what, in 1890, "Teutonic" and "Anglo-Saxon" meant to an American audience.

Americans, following some Western European thinkers, had come to accept and amplify theories of the Germanic origins of modern, western political institutions. This claim dates at least to the eighteenth century and the Frenchman Count de Boulainvilliers and, especially for Americans, to the Englishman Samuel Squiers. Their theories and argu-

---

5. All quotations from this address are taken from Du Bois, *Writings,* ed. Nathan I. Huggins.

6. Actually, Jefferson Davis was from Welsh immigrant stock. He was, therefore, strictly speaking, of Celtic origin rather than Anglo-Saxon.

ments stemmed from their reading of Tacitus and such Enlightenment figures as Montesquieu, who had found in Tacitus appreciation for the German's love of liberty and, by inheritance, English political and social institutions. American Enlightenment thinkers were so taken by the uniquely progressive character of American institutions that they would attribute it to some special genius in the English-Anglo-Saxon race, the germ of those ideas and institutions originating in the German forests. Thomas Jefferson thought it important enough to study the Anglo-Saxon language.

"Germ theory" and notions of Teutonic origins of American institutions became part of a theory of racial superiority which would explain and justify American and Anglo-Saxon domination over other peoples— Manifest Destiny. As Bishop William Stubbs of Oxford would put it:

> It is to ancient Germany that we must look for the earliest trace of our forefathers, for the best part of almost all of us is originally German; though we call ourselves Britons, the name was only a geographical significance.

Such theorizing relied on Tacitus and the Anglo-Saxon Chronicles. Americans, as heirs of the English civilization and confronting conflict of race and nation, echoed the theories. Even Ralph Waldo Emerson:

> It is race, is it not? that puts the hundred miliions of India under the dominion of a remote island in the north of Europe. Race avails much, if that be true, which is alleged, that all Celts are Catholics, and all Saxons are Protestants; that Celts love unity of power, and Saxons the representative principle. Race is a controlling influence in the Jew, who for two millenniums, under every climate, has preserved the same character and employments. Race in the negro is of appalling importance. The French in Canada, cut off from all intercourse with the parent people, have held their national traits. . . . I found abundant points of resemblance between the Germans of the forests, and our *hoosiers,* . . . of the American woods.[7]

Henry Adams in 1873–1874 conducted a special seminar to study Teutonic and Anglo-Saxon institutions. "The State and the Law," he would say, "may have originated there." Herbert Baxter Adams, the historian, argued that the New England Town meeting was a resurrection of Teutonic councils.

The central notion, common in the 1890s, was that Teutonic, Anglo-Saxon race was indomitable. It was the carrier of "civilization" across the world. It was a notion which supported expansionist's dreams of Manifest Destiny and the Providential character of American history and development. Before the advance of the Anglo-Saxon—the vanguard of civilization—the lesser races (Celts, Indians, Africans, Jews)

7. Ralph Waldo Emerson, "Race," in *English Traits,* ed. Howard Mumford Jones (Cambridge, Mass.: Harvard University Press, 1966), p. 75.

swooned into thralldom or death. Even such a radical abolitionist as Theodore Parker[8] wrote of the irresistible power of the awful Anglo-Saxon blood. And nowhere were the racist assumptions of Teutonism and Anglo-Saxonism more pronounced than in the epic written by American historians: George Bancroft, Francis Parkman, William Prescott, and John Lothrop Motley.

It is in this network of meaning that Du Bois's audience would understand his references to Teutonic civilization. Nearly all would have seen themselves as racial or cultural heirs to that civilization. They were the more alert to racial distinctions as they worried over the consequences on American society of the so-called "new immigrant"—the non–Anglo-Saxons from Southern and Eastern Europe adding their huge numbers to the earlier waves of non–Anglo-Saxon Irish. Sitting in Sanders Theater, Du Bois's Yankee audience's pride of race was embedded in theories of an Anglo-Saxon civilization, irresistible and transcendent, pushing lesser peoples aside or underfoot and marching triumphantly into the twentieth century.

Du Bois's strategy was to get his racially prideful audience to view themselves—and what they called civilization—through an epitome of their values, yet one who was, to them, an antihero. The strategy was to get them to see that which was insufficient and "incomplete" in Jefferson Davis as wanting in them as well.

His first step was to characterize the basis of their civilization as the source of glorification of the hero, the martial hero, the soldier. That, in turn, became the justification of the Strong Man: "Individualism coupled with the rule of might." It was the ground on which such men as Bismarck and Davis could stand. So, also, would stand the bully, the outlaw, the tyrant. Power in such a civilization became all, so that despite human evolution the compelling reason "even of modern history, [was] the cool logic of the Club." So, Davis, the heir of the medieval knight, could be "brave" and "generous" while "advancing civilization by mudering Indians," being hero to the "national disgrace" of the Mexican War, and "crowning the absurdity, the peculiar champion of a people fighting to be free in order that another prople should not be free."

With a mere shift of language, the Strong Man became the Strong Nation, the Strong State. What was in the individual egocentrism and self-will—the "overweening sense of the I and the consequent forgetting the Thou"—became in the nation, "national selfishness," aggression and imperialism. The I, the nation, was all. The Thou—other cultures and peoples—were mere obstacles to national will. Power, the "cool logic of the Club," was the single instrument of advance. It has become, Du Bois argued, "well nigh impossible for a new race to introduce a new idea into the world except by means of the cudgel."

8. See his *Rights of Man* (New York: Negro University Press, 1969), p. 320.

The same rhetorical strategy which had converted Davis, the hero, to the Strong Man, to the Strong State, now transformed "civilization" into "race." The civilization and race Jefferson Davis represented deified "stalwart manhood" and "heroic character," but at the same time "moral obtuseness" and "refined brutality." These were the contradictions in seeing Teutonic civilization as the highest end of mankind. Some important elements were missing. For the highest human achievement something was needed to complement the Teuton and Northern civilization. The answer, according to Du Bois, would be found in Southern cultures.

He pointed to the apparent rise of the South. New nations and new peoples coming to the attention of the Western world. Here, then, was the crux of Du Bois's strategy. It was the "Negro"—the black man—to appear in contrast (the necessary complement) to the Teuton.[9] The question is what they bring to the equation. The "glamorous history" has always shown the strong man "crushing out effete civilization." "That brutality buried aught else beside Rome when it descended golden haired and drunk from the blue north has scarcely entered human imagination." Du Bois would argue that something else was lost, in softness, in art, in sensibility. That is the clue to what he thinks the Negro brings, coming not as a "muscular warrior" but the "cringing slave." The "Teutonic met civilization and crushed it." So, the Teuton, now, becomes not the agent of civilization but the destroyer of it. The "Negro met civilization and was crushed by it." The one, Du Bois claimed, was "the hero the world has ever worshipped," the other the "personification of dogged patience bending to the inevitable and waiting." Nothing could be more sharply in contrast. Yet that, too, was a virtue, the stoicism he characterized as "Negro." They were qualities associated in his audience's mind with blacks, powerfully characterized by Harriet Beecher Stowe in her character Uncle Tom.

Du Bois argued that one did not find in blacks the Teutonic deification of self and the single-minded acceptance of brute force as the ultimate value. Black virtues were, rather, in submission "apart from cowardice, laziness or stupidity." The complement to the Teutonic strong man was what he called the "doctrine of the Submissive man," the submission of the strength of the Strong to the advance of all. Not in mere "aimless sacrifice, but recognizing the fact that, 'to no one type of mind is it given to discern the totality of Truth.' The submission to the Thou is the highest form of Individualism."

Du Bois accepts standard racialist characterizations conventionally used to rationalize white or Anglo-Saxon superiority, but he turns them into claims of deficiency and limitation. Granting them their power,

9. This idea of the Afro-American having special racial qualities necessary to complement the white (or the American) culture becomes an important element in his *Souls of Black Folk*, 1903.

whites lack something essential and they would find it in the racial spirit and genius of blacks.

Thus, the Teuton and the black are drawn in sharp contrasts, personal assertion vs. personal submission. Du Bois's argument is that true civilization needs both. "No matter how great and striking the Teutonic type of impetuous manhood may be, it must receive the cool purposeful '*Ich dien*'[10] of the African for its round and full development."

The African (particularly the Afro-American) people are, in Du Bois's argument, crucial to civilization's advance, not through conversion into Anglo-Saxons, but for essential qualities inherent in the race.

Until the last sentences of his address, Du Bois kept his subject distant to himself and his audience. Their association with Jefferson Davis, with Anglo-Saxon or Teutonic civilization, was only as they might assume the values Du Bois attributed to them. In the penultimate sentence, however, Du Bois shifts to the personal pronoun, "you," forcefully associating his audience with the values, the qualities, the limitations he has described.

> In the rise of Negro people and development of this idea, you whose nation was founded on the loftiest ideals, and who [not which] many times forgot those ideals with a strange forgetfulness, have more than a sentimental interest, more than a sentimental duty.[11]

The point is driven home in the final sentence: "You owe a debt to humanity for this Ethiopia of the Out-stretched Arm, who has made her beauty, patience, and her grandeur law."[12] The gender shift re-enforces the argument: the complementary characteristics of race and civilization, the nonthreatening but enriching addition of submission to assertion, the female to the male.

Du Bois would attempt to put the principles into his own life—the I to serve the Thou; the self at the service of race and civilization. It was this principle which inspired his twenty-fifth birthday valedictory and ritual.

"This night before my life's altar," he would write. Then, after reflecting on his life, his friends, his loves, he especially recalled, "Harvard—scholarships, high marks, Boylston prizes Cambridge applauded, Commencement when the Harvard applause awoke echoes in the world" capping "five and twenty years of my apprenticeship." But what was he apprentice to? What was his calling, his great service?

---

10. "I serve" is an ironic allusion to the *noblesse oblige* assumed traditional with medieval knighthood. "Ich dien" is also the motto of the Prince of Wales.

11. The use of "sentimental" here should be noted. It is to say, it is not a matter of gratuity, good will or generosity. It is rather a matter of urgency, necessity, obligation. It is, furthermore, not the nation which forgot, but "you" who forgot, "you" who are obliged.

12. The reference to Ethiopia is a near-quote from *Psalms*, 68.31: "Princes shall come out of Egypt; Ethiopia shall soon stretch out her hands unto God." Ethiopia is often given feminine personification. It is, nevertheless, significant in the context of this argument which poses martial and male virtues against "submission" and "patience."

"These are my plans," he wrote, "to make a name in science, to make a name in literature and thus to raise my race. Or perhaps to raise a visible empire in Africa thro' England, France, or Germany." What would be the outcome, he asked, and answered, "Who knows?"

But dedication was clear. "I will go unto the king," he wrote, "which is not according to the law and if I perish—I perish."

8

Martin Luther King, Jr.:
Charisma and Leadership

The historical importance of Martin Luther King, Jr., goes beyond his work in the civil rights movement, as important as that was. To begin with, King represents a kind of black leadership generally unknown at earlier periods in United States history. In the past, black leaders, for the most part, whether they were reform minded or accommodationists, had very little tie to a power base. (By and large, black leaders could be characterized as spokesmen and brokers between white power and blacks.[1]) King, however, rested his leadership on a religious establishment that extended beyond his particular church, on a constituency (both white and black) that followed him for reasons of ideology and strategy.

He also differed from conventional black leaders by his seeming independence from party machinery, from institutional constraints.[2] He was free to address himself to issues broader than race and racial justice. Despite objections from conventional leaders in the movement, King spoke out on poverty and economic injustice. He was most daring

*From *Journal of American History,* 74 (Sept. 1987), 477–81. Copyright © Organization of American Historians, 1987.

1. There were exceptions. Obviously, elected politicians, such as Oscar De Priest, William Dawson, and Adam Clayton Powell, Jr., had local power bases. See Rayford W. Logan and Michael R. Winston, eds., *Dictionary of American Negro Biography* (New York, 1982). Ministers who acted as leaders outside their churches also had a base in their institutions. Similarly, A. Philip Randolph can be said to have had a power base in the Brotherhood of Sleeping Car Porters.

2. Compared with a Walter White within the ideological and strategic constraints of the National Association for the Advancement of Colored People, which W. E. B. Du Bois had to struggle free from, Martin Luther King, Jr., had greater freedom to define his own program with an expectation his constituency would remain with him. It is important, as others have emphasized, that many were involved in shaping King's program, but it is precisely the interdependent relationship between leader and constituents that I find distinctive in the character of King's leadership.

and independent in his outspoken criticism of the war in Vietnam despite angry opposition from the president and the leadership of the Democratic party. Many liberal leaders, especially blacks in conventional organizations, did not hide their fear that King might help accelerate a shift of national interest from civil rights to peace. Furthermore, the traditional arena for black protest was racial justice and domestic issues akin to race relations. King, however, took his leadership off conventional turf.

The authors of all the papers express some discomfort in singling out Martin Luther King to honor. He was only one man in a movement, although a very prominent one. Focus on him is very likely to cause us to ignore the hundreds of leaders and heroes who were crucial to the movement. Some are troubled by the "great man" implications of such celebrations as this. After all, what happened in the 1960s had more to do with broad social and economic changes and with the wave of young and old people who were willing to put their bodies on the line than with personality and oratory. Others are troubled that such celebrations as this will end in trivializing or co-opting the memory of Martin Luther King. Consider the incongruity of the Marine band concert as a part of the festivities honoring the nonviolent Dr. King. Some are troubled by charismatic leadership itself, wanting to deny the implication that people must await another such individual before the movement can be reborn.

No one is more troubled than I am by Great Man approaches to historical events. We can be sure that some of what occurred in the 1960s would have occurred without any given individual, Martin Luther King included. Yet it is foolish to imagine that the individual actors were interchangeable parts and that, without the particular personality of Martin Luther King, someone else would have served as well. Individuals do make a difference, and when they play such important roles as did Dr. King, we must give them great attention.

Of course it is impossible, counterfactually, to remove Dr. King from those events to see how they would have been different. We know, however, that they would have been very different. And I believe, as I am sure some of you believe, the movement and the rest of us would have been much the losers without him. That means we must study him, and that we are able, by memorializing him, to recapture many of the ideals, aims, and achievements of the movement. Those who were not active in the movement (a number which will grow as years pass) will be unable to rediscover the movement as well by studying any of the other leaders, however heroic and deserving they might be. Because King's role was more central—his vision more inclusive—than those of others, he will offer a better lens through which to see the movement.

Our difficulty with charismatic leadership comes, I believe, from our distrust of the nonrational. We, as scholars, are intellectuals and, for the most part, rationalists. We are also aware that masses who are galvanized by one man for good ends may be subject to capture by another for evil ends. Some of the most fearful and inhuman moments in recent history have been results of some charismatic leader. Furthermore, we would like to think that men and women can organize themselves to act politically without the magnet of someone's intense vision and message.

Yet the nonrational is central to our political and social lives. Lacking strong institutional ties, Americans (white and black) are likely to be organized and moved by individuals with the power to make us believe in their visions. We should not forget that charisma is an *exchange* between the leader and the group. There are values, myths, hopes, fears, anxieties awaiting expression in the crowd to which the charismatic leader gives voice. The exchange is not completely mindless, and charisma touches something genuine, or else it does not exist.

Just as we historians find it difficult to deal with nonrational charisma, we are ill at ease with true religious phenomena. As David J. Garrow has pointed out, Martin Luther King saw the prayerful moment in his kitchen as the turning point in his understanding of his "call." He sat at his table in his Montgomery home, near despair. His earthly father, who had always before been his guide and counselor, was in Atlanta. He said that at that juncture he turned to his "heavenly father," and he was told the way to go. From that point on, there would be other moments of dejection and depression, but he never again doubted his purpose, and he would again and again recall that Montgomery moment as the sign, the signal. The moment in the kitchen that King described (although he does not use the words) was the sort of religious experience central to the Christian tradition.

What is the historian to do with that? We mention it of course, but we are poorly equipped to discuss the inner terrain of spirit and mind that was transformed by that event. As social scientists or humanists, our training gives us little to work on. The central point is that Martin Luther King believed in God, in a Christian God, and his life was shaped by that fact, from the inside out. For most of us, that belief remains a mystery. We are products of a secular age in which religion is trivialized or popularized to make it palatable to all. We all will admit to the importance of the black church, but few of us are able to see beyond its institutional character.[3]

Both the religious and spiritual character of Martin Luther King and the charismatic factor challenge us to look deeper into the nonrational and spiritual dimensions of the man and the movement. Sadly, however, we have few scholarly examples to show us the way. Psychology might seem a possible source of guidance, but it is difficult to shake the focus on the pathological in its methodology. I have been drawn again to William James's *Varieties of Religious Experience.* What is remarkable about the

---

3. We acknowledge the importance of the black church since the civil rights movement, anyway. Before the 1960s few social scientists had much hope for the black church as a progressive force or for its ministers as progressive leaders.

lectures contained in that volume is that James takes the religious experience seriously. That is, he does not assume reason to be the norm, and nonrational experience to be in some sense perverse. His lectures in the book—"The Divided Self," "Conversion," and "Saintliness"—are much to the point of Martin Luther King's experience.[4]

Dr. King encouraged us to understand his tactics of nonviolent resistance as deriving from Gandhi. While there was no doubt a Gandhian influence, I think it much more important to understand nonviolence in relation to the tradition of the southern black Christian. At least one of King's teachers at Boston University, Howard Thurman, had visited Gandhi and had incorporated some of the Eastern vision into his theology. But the tactic worked in the southern setting because of the deep tradition of Christian stoicism in the black community. Blacks had long appreciated the moral superiority of those who continued to do right despite violence and oppression. When King repeated again and again that "undeserved suffering is redemptive," he was merely iterating a value that his southern black audiences had lived their lives by. Christian stoicism was the traditional base on which southern blacks engrafted King's message of nonviolence.[5]

That it did not work well in the North is not surprising. Northern blacks had lived in a world where institutions like the church were relatively weakened in their influence on individual lives. Theirs was a competitive world in which the "payoff" was all that mattered in the end. Pragmatism was the touchstone of northern urban life. Does it pay? Will we win? Does it work? Those were the questions that nonviolent tactics had to answer, and for King's leadership, the answers were too slow in coming. Nonviolence seemed to mean acquiescing in violence against blacks with no real payoff. By 1965–1966 , nonviolence had even played out in the South. The message of leaders like Malcolm X had greater power in northern cities and among the young people in the movement.

King and his nonviolence, nevertheless, had a kind of power that alternate strategies lacked. His message was *inclusive.* He spoke always of love, without boundary of race, class, or nation. His audience, from wherever it came, could feel included, invited to join the march to racial and human justice. There was a place for everyone, white and black, Jew and Gentile. That inclusiveness characterized that part of the movement, that phase of the movement, which King dominated. The move away from nonviolence, however understandable, came at the cost of

    4. William James, *The Varieties of Religious Experience: A Study in Human Nature* (New York, 1929), 163–319.

    5. King's views on nonviolence are most readily available in James M. Washington, ed., *A Testament of Hope: The Essential Writings of Martin Luther King, Jr.* (San Francisco, 1986). The comment on undeserved suffering was often repeated by Dr. King; see *ibid.,* 18. Of the several books by Thurman, the most relevant for this point is Howard Thurman, *Jesus and the Disinherited* (Rockford, Ill., 1981).

universality. Malcolm X, for example, implied boundaries. Self-defense, after all, *excludes* those other than "self."

Finally, to return to the general concern of many of the papers in this conference: the focus on the man rather than the movement. It is my view that we have to focus on the man precisely because he gives us a lens through which to see the larger picture, a picture otherwise lost to those not participants in the movement. It is, nevertheless, right to be cautious lest one surrender to hero worship. Fortunately, we know enough of the humanness of King to keep us from that trap.

Robert Moses has spoken of the movement as an ocean, with individuals (Dr. King among them) as waves on that ocean. Without the ocean the individuals would be of little significance. He would have us focus on the movement and not the man.[6] For myself, I am no more comfortable with metaphors of oceans and waves that I am of focus on the central individual. Likening the movement to an ocean implies that it has a constant flood and direction, which frees us from the endless wait for the individual leader. But we have no better understanding of the lunar phases that cause the tides of the movement than we do of the lodestars that come from time to time into our view to give us direction. There is as much danger in romanticizing movements as in romanticizing individual leaders.

6. Robert Parris Moses, "Commentary," at the conference, "Martin Luther King, Jr.: The Leader and the Legacy," Washington, D.C., Oct. 15, 1986 (in Robert Parris Moses's possession).

9

Black Biography:
Reflections of a Historian

A common complaint of scholars studying the Afro-American experience is that blacks have left too scant a historical record. Written evidence, such as diaries, memoirs, autobiographies, and correspondence, is rare. It is said that, too often, researchers have been forced to see black Americans through the eyes of whites and through white-controlled institutions.

That was certainly true of the nineteenth century and earlier when few of those black Americans who were literate were so placed in society as to assume historical celebrity for themselves and their work (such as in business, politics, or the arts). Fewer still valued themselves enough to consider that a record of their life and work would be of worth to future historians. It takes a special self-concept to keep such papers and write such journals and autobiographies.

Judging from the historical sources deposited in archives throughout the country, whites had that self-concept in abundance and black Americans did not. There were exceptions of course: the various slave narratives by Frederick Douglass, Charlotte Forten, and of course Booker T. Washington in the twentieth century, come to mind, but they are exceptional and reinforce the point.

Even those personal records we have are curiously impersonal. Black Americans who wrote them were keenly aware of the burden of the race's reputation. Slave narratives were not merely personal stories—they were abolitionist propaganda. The autobiographer saw himself as an exemplar whose life and works would both point the way for other Afro-Americans and persuade whites of the race's potential. One looks to them in vain for the kind of candid, inside, self-evaluative and self-critical perspective on events and people historians most seek in personal accounts. They are, rather, careful and correct.

*This article is reprinted from *CAAS Newsletter,* Vol. 9, No. 1 (1985), UCLA Center for Afro-American Studies. Copyright © The Regents of the University of California.

We have seen this scarcity of personal records as a particular handi-cap for Afro-American historians, and we have had to use ingenious and heroic devices to reconstruct the history of black people. We have turned to oral history, and some have used quantitative techniques to great effect. Afro-American historians have, therefore, been in the van-guard of the effort to write history "from the bottom up," as much out of necessity as out of interest in this technique.

A few years ago, I completed a biography of Frederic Douglass.[1] In doing that work, I was struck by the fact that Douglass had, like all public figures, created a public self, a persona for the world to see. He had come, in the public's mind, to stand for the full human potential of black Americans. His message was clear: "How evil is a system that would enslave such a man as me!" The more reason no shadow should fall on his honor and reputation. Fair enough, all of us wear masks in public.

Most of us harbor our private sensibilities, our questions, our doubts about which we dare not speak lest we undermine some work or thing or person we want most to support and protect. Yet, in private, unguarded moments we are apt to reveal these deep-felt, private selves. There was once a time when people did that in their diaries. For Douglass, how-ever, the public self—the persona—became so dominant that there was no discernible private self. I believe that to be true of most black leaders into the twentieth century.

We have reason to hope that twentieth-century black leaders will leave historians a fuller record than those of the nineteenth. Since World War I, and at an accelerating pace since the New Deal, larger numbers of black Americans have found themselves in organizations and institu-tions which have historical significance. More have taken leadership roles in organizations and movements which have so changed our way of life as to oblige historians to search out and include their witness of changing times. It remains to be seen, however, how many of them will leave important papers or write autobiographies.[2] We may continue to have to rely on extraordinary means to discover the true mind and thought of black men and women of influence.

The problem of sources is by no means new to historians, nor is the problem peculiar to black historical figures. From our earliest training in the research and writing of history, we were cautioned about the use of personal records. We have been constantly reminded that even at their most candid, diaries, journals, memoirs, autobiographies, and even let-ters are not always accurate or honest; human beings do, after all, have a penchant for self-deception. The aspect of this problem that has espe-cially troubled Afro-American historians is the scarcity of such material

---

1. *Slave and Citizen: The Life of Frederick Douglass* (Boston: Little, Brown, 1981).

2. I wonder, for instance, if the Reverend Jesse Jackson has systematically kept his papers, if he has a diary or journal, and if he will write his autobiography (preferably without the services of an amanuensis).

for the period antedating World War I. That which exists is uniformly guarded, self-protective, didactic, and "official" in character. We know that for the mid- and late-twentieth century the scarcity of such sources will be less of a problem, but we may wonder if modern black subjects will be more forthcoming than those of the past.

There is reason to believe that all twentieth-century historians and biographers will have to learn to work with data and documents that will be less than meets the eye. Modern men and women are not as apt to keep diaries and journals as were their forebears. Time, the sense of urgency, the pace of life have changed both the way and the amount we read and write. It was not uncommon, formerly, to pen notes and letters even to neighbors and associates close at hand. Educated people were accustomed to reading lengthy and expansive prose (in fiction and non-fiction) and considered it part of their civility and station to write at length about their thoughts and behavior—incidentally leaving a written record of both bulk and substance. Technology, as well as the pace of life, has so affected us moderns as to change all that.

The media, especially television and film, have profoundly affected our leisure. In the aggregate, we may not read fewer books than our nineteenth-century counterparts, but the size, purpose, and character of our reading is greatly different. The power of visual images has come to so dominate our imaginations as to displace the word (both written and spoken) from its once-central place in expression and communication.

For the historian, the greatest culprit is the telephone. Seldom, now, do we put anything on paper that can be said by phone. Whether in public office, business, or private life, modern men and women are more apt to voice their most candid, private, and personal thoughts by phone than by written word. Much of that which the historian will want most to document will therefore be lost in electronic dissipation.

Another problem, no less worrisome, is the increasing tendency for American celebrities and persons in public life to use professional writers as collaborators on an autobiography. It is impossible to measure the effect of third persons on the substantive outcomes of such works. The very fact of their "professional" interests (i.e., market, ease of reading, audience, and attention to the vogue) are very likely to move the work away from the subject's true mind and preoccupations, at the very least coloring it with the tone and sensibility of a mass culture.[3]

Such problems will exist equally for those working with white and black subjects. The problem for the Afro-American historian, and for those who would do biographies of modern black figures, is whether what I discern to be a chronic reticence of Afro-Americans to "tell all" will continue to add to their problem. Since the end of World War II, there has been a growing body of what I would call "confes-

---

3. Such writers may also have been chosen in order to protect the subject's reputation.

sional literature" from black Americans, all having an autobiographical character.[4]

I have recently come to think about these questions because of my work on a biography of Ralph Bunche. There is little doubt that Bunche's life will reveal a great deal about black professional and middle-class life from the 1930s through the 1960s. By focusing on him, I will be able to delineate the effect of shifting values and attitudes about race, race relations, and protest over this crucial period.

Considering Bunche's family and upbringing, for instance, I am struck by how fully they accepted the values of individualism, optimism, and achievement. He came from a lower-middle-class family,[5] whose pride would cause them to take offense at the suggestion that they were from slave origins or that Ralph's childhood was spent in the ghetto. They were not much different from many of their black contemporaries—stoic, hardworking, moral, upright achievers. While they were outspoken in protest about racial slights and insults, and unwavering in their insistence on reform for equality and fairness, they seemed persuaded that industry and the moral, exemplary life would ultimately cause them to prevail.

Bunche was an academic, training himself at UCLA and Harvard University, at a time when blacks with professional aspirations were generally restricted to law, medicine, the ministry, teaching, and undertaking. When Bunche got his Ph.D. at Harvard, it was unheard of that a black American would hold a position at a northern university or college. Moreover, his discipline, political science, was in its infancy and there were hardly any Americans in his field of study, African colonial administration. In time, he was to find political science inadequate to study black Africa, and his scholarly interests expanded to include anthropology.

Through Bunche's life one can get a glimpse into the pre-war black college and the professional lives of black academics. From a distance, many of us have discerned something of the politics and tensions associated with traditionally black schools, and we have hints of the burden black scholars worked under to be productive in institutions fraught with jealousies and petty bickering, and which were, at best, ambivalent about scholarship. Had Bunche been forthcoming and candid, he could have told us much about that experience and about the black bourgeoisie, professional life, and prospects.

Similarly, his professional work—on *The American Dilemma,* in the

4. I think of such works as Eldridge Cleaver, *Soul on Ice;* Claude Brown, *Manchild in the Promised Land; The Autobiography of Malcolm X;* and Maya Angelou's quasi-autobiographical *I Know Why the Caged Bird Sings.* While all of these works would appear to be very personal and candid, they are not intended as autobiographies in the way that, say, Frederick Douglass's *The Life and Times of Frederick Douglass* was, and the historian would have to be very cautious in using any of them as a source.

5. Defined by modes of property ownership, education, and values.

State Department at the opening of World War II, in the O.S.S. during the war, in the shaping of the United Nations—can have enormous historical significance. Through his work on the development of the U.N.'s Trusteeship Council, we can catch glimpses of the U.S. policy toward decolonization and the shaping of Third World politics as we have come to know them.

Finally, of course, there is Bunche's work in the United Nations itself. His direct and formative work on major questions—Palestine, Kashmir, and the Congo—as well as his work in the Secretariat made him one of the most important figures in that organization in its formative years.

On the surface, the historian and biographer will have ample material to work with. Ralph Bunche's papers are housed in the Special Collections at UCLA. They are wonderfully managed by an excellent staff, and are fairly well organized. Over 180 boxes of these papers are now open to the public.[6] Other sources should be available at Howard University, the National Archives, and the United Nations archives, among others.

From the evidence at UCLA, however, the bulk of these papers is deceiving. Bunche seemed to keep everything, from college notebooks to social invitations and greeting cards. A great amount of his letters in "correspondence" consists of courteous and sometimes perfunctory responses to letters written to him. Incidentally, Bunche seemed to answer all letters, from a child's request for an autograph to the numerous requests which came to him for jobs at the U.N. All of that is to say that one has to go through a lot of paper to get a worthwhile yield. Of course, that is what historians do.

There is little in these papers one could consider private or personal in character. Seldom does Bunche commit to paper true confidences or judgments which might reveal something beneath the public self. Bunche seems consistently aware of a public self and an office which demands discretion. That style and voice develops especially from his days in the State Department.

I have come to believe that civil servants and bureaucrats in such public offices develop a kind of written style which is elliptical and noncommittal. One does not mention the names of third persons, they are referred to by initials. The actual subject of letters may not be made explicit, but rather one writes with the understanding that the reader knows without explicit reference. Any comment generally adds up to: "I'll tell you when I see you."

Some of this may be attributable to the great wartime concern for secrecy ("A slip of the lip might sink a ship."). Correspondence could fall into the wrong hands. But it is also, I think, a conventional style

---

6. There is an unknown quantity restricted, owing to sensitivity and pertaining to the United Nations.

developed by men and women whose jobs and careers placed a high value on reticence and circumspection. One does not want judgments on paper until they are nearly accepted and official. Bunche learned to write that way in the State Department, and kept the style through his U.N. days.

Bunche's role in the U.N. made him especially guarded. He liked to describe himself as an international civil servant. It was a role that obliged him to act officially and publically as if he had no private or personal interests in the issues the world organization took up. While he was an American citizen—he was quick and ready to proclaim that—he could not act so as to suggest that he was serving American interests in the U.N.

During the McCarthy hysteria, the U.N. came under organized and powerful attack in the United States.[7] Bunche found it necessary to defend the organization more and more, and was therefore more on guard lest he give a hint or suggestion that could become ammunition to be used against it. If anything, his language became more careful and deliberate. He had become an exemplar not only for the race, but also for a beleaguered world organization which had been the dream of his life.

He continued to speak out on matters having to do with racial justice in the United States. He supported Martin Luther King, Jr. He went on the Selma March, despite the great pain it caused to his legs. He would even engage in public pressure to break down racial barriers. In the 1950s, Bunche made public the West Side Tennis Club's (Forest Hills) refusal to admit his son to membership. Then a student at Choate, his son was clearly turned down on racial grounds.[8] A barrage of letters resulted in a change of both policy and management. By that time, however, black Americans' attitudes toward race, reform, and protest had so changed that Bunche got as many criticisms (because it was seen as a class issue) as compliments.

The challenge of biography is no less reduced because we now have papers available to us in large bulk. The case of Ralph Bunche indicates that the historian and the biographer must still find ingenious ways to bring historical significance and meaning to the lives of twentieth-century Afro-Americans.

7. The slogan was: "Get the U.N. out of the U.S.; get the U.S. out of the U.N."
8. The club had a policy of excluding blacks and Jews.

10

Herbert Gutman and
Afro-American History

The problematic of Afro-American history is obvious. Black Americans have been central to a national history driven by ideological assumptions of natural rights, equality of opportunity, providentially shaped destiny, national calling, and progress. Within this world view and national self-concept, it is challenging to explain how it came about that a significant and conspicuous part of the population—elemental to its history—was unfree and oppressed for much of the nation's history; subordinated, exploited, and oppressed for the rest of it. It would seem that the American historian, facing the fact of the Afro-American experience, would be forced to expose profound social, moral, and intellectual contradiction or describe the history, as Gunnar Myrdal did, as a societal dilemma.[1]

Until the late 1960s American historians did neither one nor the other. Rather, they took one of three tacks: (1) they chose to see Afro-Americans as anomalous—because of race or culture outside the definition of American people and, therefore, in no real way definitive of the national history;[2] (2) Afro-American experience was anomalous owing to the perverse persistence of slavery—an institution uncharacteristic of American civilization—and of the unnatural, aristocratic pretensions of those who would be a master class;[3] (3) not to consider Afro-Americans

---

*This article is reprinted from *Labor History,* Summer 1988. Copyright © 1988, *Labor History.*

1. Gunnar Myrdal, *The American Dilemma* (New York, 1944).

2. Both Thomas Jefferson and George Bancroft would argue that it was a fortuitous matter that Europeans and Africans would be brought together "under a temperate clime." Once done, however, it would be inevitable that the European would subjugate the African.

3. A version of this view is to see slavery as a feudal hangover from European history and institutions or, differently, to see race attitude (or racism) as an inheritance of Europe.

at all until coincidentally forced by one's topic to do so. And then when forced, to choose tack #1 or #2.

It is fair to say that by the 1960s, except for some of the work of a few black historians,[4] there was little in the historical literature about the Afro-American experience itself. American historians contented themselves to explain how—sadly, tragically, or ironically—black Americans were rightly a subject people in a land without subjects; or, on the other hand, how Afro-Americans were exploited or oppressed by a perverse or twisted pursuit of the American Dream.

The complaint so often heard from black Americans in the 1960s was that they had been left out of American history. That, of course, was not exactly true. Blacks were included in the history, but mainly in the terms I have mentioned. In short, they were used principally to explain white men and white institutions. In either view of the anomaly of the Afro-American experience black men and women came off as victims, not as historical actors in their own right. They were either victims of the historical chance that brought them to the New World where they would necessarily be subjugated to a dominant and progressive race, or they were victims of the greedy exploitation of men who would pervert religious or political principles for their own power, comfort, and gain.

Being portrayed as victim is not without its attractions. It brings focus on the oppressor as culpable, and it reinforces any moral claim the group makes on the present generation. Black scholars understandably contributed to this view of black Americans as victim, often to explain the persistence of racial inequality. While undoubtedly without intention, Stanley Elkins's *Slavery*[5] awakened both black and white scholars from their slumbers.

Although *Slavery* was seriously flawed in almost all it set out to say—misunderstanding slavery in the United States and elsewhere in the hemisphere, misunderstanding the effects on Jews of the concentration camp experience, misunderstanding and oversimplifying personality theory—the book had an enormous influence. Elkins made the bold claim that the historiography of American slavery was sharply divided between that which followed a pro-slavery tradition and that which followed the abolitionist, that this debate should be ended with Kenneth Stampp having the last word,[6] and that historians' attention should now better be given to questions social scientists might ask about institutions and personality. Particularly, Elkins addressed the effect of slavery on the slave's personality. In doing that, and owing to the controversy his book provoked, he helped speed the shift of historians' attention, as if for the first time, to focus on the slave and free black, and thus on *Afro-Americans' history.*

4. For instance, Rayford Logan, John Hope Franklin, and Benjamin Quarles.
5. Stanley Elkins, *Slavery* (Chicago, 1959).
6. Kenneth M. Stampp, *The Peculiar Institution* (New York, 1957).

Two of Elkins's assertions are of concern to us. The first was his claim that there was no possibility of institutional support of personality definition for slaves, no place in the law, the church, the family, etc. The second is the conclusion that the slave personality can be described accurately by what we might otherwise take as stereotypes; that "Sambo" was the dominant character of the slave personality. Whether intended or not, Elkins had fashioned the ultimate interpretation of slaves (and by extension blacks in general?) as victims. Not only had they no control over their lives and destinies, they had no self-concept worthy of the term, and they had no basis for a will to be other than what they were.

Oddly, for those who wanted to describe slavery as the most unmitigated evil and as an institution of total repression, *Slavery* was grist for their mill. One, however, could not follow that path long without confronting the dilemma it posed. If the slave experience was so destructive to black life and consciousness as Elkins would suggest, if it left slaves so devoid of characteristics of adult, responsible humanity, it would have produced by 1865 four million zombies, hardly capable of freedom in any society and hardly legitimate candidates for citizenship in the United States. That was certainly not the case—there were too many non-Sambo blacks in and out of slavery to support such an idea. Such a naked and unadorned view of blacks as victim was offensive to what historical evidence was known, and offensive as well to Afro-Americans.

John Blassingame's *The Slave Community*[7] was the first major reinterpretation of slavery to follow Elkins's book. It is also, in my view, the first book by an American historian to seriously attempt to explain slavery from *within* the slave experience. As a conscious and deliberate answer to Elkins, however, Blassingame accepted Elkins's paradigms and formulation of the questions. He merely argues that slaves were not devoid of institutional support: there was a "slave community" which comprised slave religion (a church), and a family with males as dominant figures (despite assaults on the slave family through sex and sale). There was not just one personality type: Blassingame would accept Elkins's Sambo as realistic, but he would give us two others—Jack (the trickster) and Nat (the rebel).

In general, it was a more satisfying picture. It was, however, limited necessarily by the problematic character of Elkins's original conceptualization of the matter. The claim of a "slave community" seemed also to beg the question. The assertion of a slave family in the problematic circumstances Blassingame described was ambiguous to say the least. While three personality types are better than one, no number of "types" is sufficient to explain something so complex as the slave personality.[8]

In the terms of personality as posed by Elkins, it is my view that

7. John Blassingame, *The Slave Community* (New York, 1972).
8. Neither Elkins's nor Blassingame's "types" incorporate the possibility of females. Indeed, it is no exaggeration to say that the family in *The Slave Community* is defined in terms of male influence and leadership.

Blassingame put the matter to rest. In any case, there has been little further effort to pursue these questions in such terms. But on the broader questions addressed by both Elkins and Blassingame, those having to do with insitutions, religion, family, consciousness, etc., very important work was done in the 1970s,[9] and I think the most important of these was Herbert Gutman's book on the black family. I think it the most important because it radically changed the way we look at the historical black family, because it successfully broke from conventional wisdom on the black family and black consciousness, because it exemplified that aspect of the "new social history" that wanted to voice the experience and values of the historically mute and inarticulate, and because it did what is so rare in American history—it provided *new* evidence.

To understand Gutman's contribution to Afro-American history we should first consider where it fits in scholarly literature on the black family. Almost all of this literature, before the 1970s, was not in history at all but in other social sciences. Indeed, very little historical work had been done on the American family. The generalizations we accepted as true were those made by sociologists and some social psychologists. It is worth recalling here the nature of those generalizations.

In the 1960s, conventional wisdom about the black family came from generalizations and interpretations by a group of sociologists, principally E. Franklin Frazier and Charles S. Johnson.[10] Scholars trained in the Chicago School of Robert E. Park,[11] they set out to describe the black family as they thought it to be, and to explain how and why it differed from what was taken to be the normal American family.

Whether in the general study of Frazier or that of rural life in Johnson, the black family was seen to have certain dysfunctional characteristics: (1) it tended to lack a stable male head of household; (2) it tended to be controlled, led, or dominated by women (mothers, grandmothers, aunts, etc.); (3) pre-marital sex (and, therefore, pre-marital pregnancies) were more common among blacks than among whites; (4) unwed mothers and their children were more tolerated among blacks than among whites; and (5) the black family, therefore, lacked the capacity for stable economic support and inner discipline normal in the society at large.

What was described was clearly class-determined. As Frazier was quick to point out, as one moved to what might be described as middle-class families, one came closer to family life and experience which com-

9. I would mention Lawrence Levine, *Black Culture and Black Consciousness,* 1976; Eugene Genovese, *Roll, Jordan, Roll,* 1977; Nathan Huggins, *Black Odyssey,* 1978; and Herbert Gutman, *The Black Family in Slavery and Freedom,* 1976.

10. E. Franklin Frazier, *The Negro Family* (Chicago, 1941); Charles S. Johnson, *Shadow of the Plantation* (Chicago, 1936).

11. See John H. Stanfield, *Philanthropy and Jim Crow in American Social Science* (Westport, Conn., 1985) for an insightful discussion of Park and his influence.

ported well with the norm. The problem of explaining the phenomenon of the black family, therefore, was partly to explain economic circumstances (i.e., economic instability of black males). But that seemed not enough, for implicit in the circumstances was the possibility that there was something inherent in the black population, something native to them (a culture perhaps), which made the described patterns natural among them. In other words, were these characteristics of the black family signs of imperfect assimilation by persons of African (and civilized) heritage into an advanced western culture? Maybe blacks were just backward.

It is in response to this implied question that Park, Johnson, and Frazier would construct a historical explanation which would do two things: (1) deny any continuing influence of Africa and African culture on Afro-Americans, and (2) find the historical causes to be within the American experience and within American institutions.

To serve the first objective, it was important to posit a sharp and nearly absolute break between Africa and the New World. As Robert Park put it:

> My own impression is that the amount of African tradition which the Negro brought to the United States was very small. In fact, there is every reason to believe, it seems to me, that the Negro, when he landed . . . left behind him almost everything but his dark complexion and his tropical temperament. It is very difficult to find in the South today anything that can be traced directly back to Africa.[12]

Frazier was to press this view even further, arguing that Africa had been destroyed in American slavery, and the Afro-American was further deprived of any culture, African or Euro-American:

> Probably never before in history has a people been so nearly completely stripped of its social heritage as the Negroes who were brought to America. . . . Through force of circumstances, they had to acquire a new language, adopt new habits of labor, and take over, *however imperfectly,* the folkways of the American environment. . . . But of the habits and customs as well as the hopes and fears that characterized the life of their forebearers [*sic*] in Africa, nothing remains.[13]

As Charles S. Johnson would have it, slaves were deprived of any full culture:

> The Negro of the plantation came into the picture with a completely broken cultural heritage. . . . What he knew of life was what he could learn from other slaves or from the examples set by the white planters themselves.[14]

12. Robert E. Park, "The Conflict and Fusion of Cultures with Special Reference to the Negro," *Journal of Negro History,* 4 (1919), 119.

13. E. Franklin Frazier, *The Negro Family in the United States* (Chicago, 1939), 21ff. Emphsis is mine.

14. Johnson, *Shadow of the Plantation,* 3.

Eric B. Reuter, another student of Park, would make explicit the implications for family life: "The native forms of family life and the codes and customs of sex control were destroyed by the circumstances of slave life; and procreation and the relations of the sexes were reduced to a simple and primitive level. . . ."[15]

According to this view, whatever cultural or institutional support the African family might have enjoyed was destroyed in the process of American slavery. And slavery, contrary to the claim of some that it was a "school" of civilization, deprived blacks of full acculturation and for economic reasons undermined the institution of marriage and the family. With neither a past nor an adequate present, the Afro-American slave (and, by extension, black Americans in general) were forced to develop crippled and dysfunctional institutions. Johnson, looking at Afro-Americans in rural Alabama in the early 1930s, and Frazier, surveying the black family later in that decade, would explain what they saw as the heritage of slavery. The onus was on a history of oppression, and black Americans in the present were victims of the past.

It is important to point out that another, and earlier, comment on the black family by W. E. B. Du Bois observed much the same phenomenon, but tended more to explain it in terms of present economic discrimination.[16]

This view, of course, did not go unchallenged. Frazier and the anthropologist Melville J. Herskovits framed the terms of a classic debate as to the importance of Africanism and African culture in Afro-American thought and life.[17]

These studies, as works of sociology, had another characteristic that is important to us. They approached their subject guided by Webberian "idea-types." That is, they had a priori notions of what an American family was and should be. Both implicitly and explicitly, they assumed a model family which was nuclear, with a male head of household acting as authority (and as principal breadwinner), and with children who were nurtured and disciplined within its context.

Their attention understandably focused on how and why Afro-Americans failed to conform to the model or norm. In one of their works, therefore, do we find consideration of how the family managed despite aberrations from this norm. Mind you, these works were not based on what we would now accept as good empirical evidence, either to verify the application of the model as the American norm or to measure the extent to which the general observations applied to black families. Furthermore, the generalizations in these works about history resulted from no historical inquiry, but rested only upon impressions and the uncritical acceptance of what was taken as historical common sense.

15. E. B. Reuter, review of *The Negro Family in the United States,* appearing in *The American Journal of Sociology,* 14 (1940), 799.

16. W. E. B. Du Bois, *The Philadelphia Negro* (Philadelphia, 1899).

17. Melville J. Herskovits, *The Myth of the Negro Past* (New York, 1941).

Until the 1960s, our understanding of the slave family rested wholly upon this kind of generalization and rationalization. We assumed that all institutions and cultural life were destroyed for slaves, and that slaves brought out of slavery social institutions which were crippled and flawed and consequently subject to warped values which were transmitted over generations under continued racial oppression and discrimination. So much was this the conventional wisdom that influential works in several fields of the social sciences, addressing black family and black personality, would simply assert this "history" as fact.[18]

Curiously, everyone, including black Americans, seemed content enough with this historical interpretation until the mid-1960s. After all, one edge of this sword cut deeply into the pretensions of slavery apologists, exposing as oppressive and immoral slave holders and the society that white Americans tolerated. It seemed possible to ignore the sword's other edge, which while revealing blacks as victims also exposed them as socially and morally crippled, enmeshed in a historic pathology from which there seemed no escape.

The "Moynihan Report"[19] brought that problem sharply into focus at a time when Afro-Americans wanted history to do more than reveal the ugliness of the white world. The search to discover black history was a search to bring to life the black experience as seen through the eyes of those who lived it. Now, it was to understand how people "coped" under oppressive circumstances. One had to believe that black men and women had some control over their lives and imaginations, and to the extent they did have control, they exercised it in normal and healthy ways. The desire and the need to have heroes clashed with the traditional view of blacks as victims.

Moynihan's report said nothing more offensive than what had been said by Frazier and Johnson earlier. He, in fact, provides data updating observations that had been made by Du Bois, Frazier, and Johnson. He took over, without question, the historical assumptions of these scholars, which had, it is fair to say, remained unchallenged or unthought about until 1965. One important difference from the earlier work was that there was a welfare system and expectations of a public policy responsibility. The Moynihan Report was recommending to the Nixon Administration a "benign neglect" of that responsibility.

Moreover, Moynihan's rhetoric seemed provocative to some. His characterization of the black family as ensnared in a "tangle of pathology"[20] was especially irksome, as many charged that American social scientists habitually studied black Americans as if they were merely an infirm social element. In any case, the "Report" caused a firestorm of protest by blacks and whites, scholar and non-scholar.

18. See for instance, Abraham Kardiner and Lionel Ovesey, *Mark of Oppression* (New York, 1956), "Preface."

19. U.S. Department of Labor, Office of Policy Planning and Research, *The Negro Family: The Case for National Action* (Washingon, D.C., 1965).

20. Ibid., 47. The term was first employed in this context by Kenneth Clark.

American historians had their own particular complaint; it was as much against historians who had gone before as it could have been against Moynihan. What Moynihan took as the conventional historical wisdom was nothing more than the impressions and deductions of earlier sociologists. Historians had provided no respectable knowledge about the black family in slavery or freedom. To say, as Moynihan would, that "it was by destroying the Negro family that white America broke the will of the Negro people," that three centuries of "injustice" had caused "deep-seated structural distortions in the life of the Negro American,"[21] was, beyond its rhetoric, making historical assertions about cause where there was no historical literature to support it. Were the present-day disabilities of the black family (whatever they were) an inheritance of slavery and history, or were they more traceable to contemporary conditions of labor and employment?

How could we know what the black family was (or the black experience in slavery was for that matter)? Just as it had been assumed that slaves had no culture or independent values, it had been assumed that they had no voice. They had not left personal accounts historians normally use to get within the human experiences of the past. We had assumed that Afro-Americans, along with much of the laboring classes, were mute witnesses, and so impressions and deductions were the best to be had. Yet, by the mid-1960s, social historians were straining to break that convention of the discipline of history which studied men and institutions of power to the exclusion of all else. The cry was to write "history from the bottom up," to find new ways of getting within the lives and experiences of those who did not leave letters, journals, diaries, etc. That meant that more had to be asked of the past of blacks and slaves than we had asked before. And that means that long-standing assumptions Moynihan and others could adopt without question, had to be questioned. It is this challenge which Herbert Gutman took up when he set out to study the black family.[22]

The most immediate and obvious influence on Gutman's thinking was the work of British labor historians E. P. Thompson and Asa Briggs. Their basic assumption was that there was a working-class culture, and that for the historian to understand the history of that class it was necessary to stand within that culture. Gutman would write: "The behavior of black (and white) workers can be fully understood only by a careful delineation of the external and internal context that helped shape such behavior."[23] Gutman assumed, as earlier scholars had not, that there was a "culture" which slaves made and in which they lived.

He approached the subject of the slave family with expectations of finding clues to the slave experience and the slave culture, and like an archaeologist working over the shards of an ancient people, he expected

21. Ibid.
22. Herbert Gutman, *The Black Family in Slavery and Freedom* (New York, 1976).
23. Milton Cantor, ed., *Black Labor in America* (Westport, Conn., 1969). "Introduction," xi.

to find these clues not through their explicit testimony but through the evidentiary remains.

The remains were massive in quantity. There were planter records and the journals of slave holders, probate records, records of the Freemen's Bureau, etc. They had all been used by scholars before. Gutman, however, brought two new elements to the search: (1) he believed, as others had not, that there was a slave culture or mentality worthy of articulating, and (2) he brought to the work quantitative skills and high-speed computers which could quickly analyze and rationalize vast amounts of data.

He brought also a different frame of mind—influenced by the work of anthropologist Sidney Mintz. Unlike his predecessors who had worked within sociological assumptions of models and norms, Gutman approached the questions of family and culture more as an anthropologist would. Rather than assume models against which to measure what he found, considering deviations as evidence of pathology and dysfunction, Gutman asked the question of how family existed among slaves. Granting the oppressive character of slavery, how could slaves adapt themselves and experience the necessary functions and ideas associated with family? He looked with the expectation of finding something to describe, and he found a great deal.

Gutman was admittedly provoked by the Moynihan report. In an early work with Lawrence A. Glasco, he asked the question: if the characteristics of fatherless, matrifocal homes was an effect of slavery and was strong enough to continue into the twentieth century, then would it not be more strong and more obvious in the years nearest to and following emancipation? Studying black families in Buffalo, New York, from 1855 to 1875 they found that lower class black Americans in Buffalo bore no visible relationship to the "tangle of pathology" described by Frazier and others.[24] He encouraged his students on kindred questions, generally showing the adaptive capacities of poor immigrant groups.[25]

Turning to the matter of the slave family, there were several compelling questions: Was there something that could legitimately be called a slave family? Was there a genuine sense of kinship and family among slaves? Was there in slavery such a preponderantly matrifocal emphasis as to support a claim of historical cause or tradition? Were whatever moral values and standards associated with family life imposed from without the slave family or could there be said to be values of internal origin?

The first contribution of Gutman's study was to establish the terms in which the slave family could be said to have meaning. By using plantation records as no others had, he was able to place families to-

24. Ibid., 18.
25. He mentions especially the work on the Irish by Carole Groneman.

gether. By using naming practices he was not only able to discern family groups, but also to trace them longitudinally over several generations. In short, perhaps the most spectacular result of his scholarship was the graphic display of family trees on several plantations.

Out of this came a firm sense of kinship networks, extending in meaningful ways our sense of family. It gave us to understand how in a region (of counties, etc.) slave family and kinship could (and did) extend well beyond the property confines defined by slavery and the plantation. It also gave us a clearer appreciation of how family breakups among slaves could be felt and mourned outside the immediate "nuclear" family setting.

Through analysis of naming patterns, Gutman was able to show both how slaves were self-governing in the naming of their children, and how the names they chose described and honored kin often several generations removed. By the same token, males as well as females were named and honored, indicating the influence of male figures throughout.

Through analysis of Freedman's Bureau records, Gutman was able to show how these family and kinship linkages extended over time and lengthy separations of slave families. At the end of the Civil War, slaves were insisting on being married properly and legally. They were traveling hundreds of miles to rediscover family they had been seperated from by sale. Husbands sought wives and children; wives and children sought husbands and fathers. Here was no picture of a people reduced to primitive values of sex and family.

The assumption that slaves could merely mimic the master's institutions and values, and that only imperfectly, implied that whatever slaves did or believed would be a pitiful corruption of standard Euro-American values. Whatever they had was the grudging contribution of white men and women. In this view, they would be a mere subject people, completely the victim of the whim and will of their oppressors. From this analysis of kinship and naming patterns, Gutman made two important observations. There was a significant frequency of names of African origin persisting throughout the period. Even some of the apparently Anglo-Saxon names were in fact sometimes mere adaptations from African practice, notably the use of day-names such as Monday, etc. The second observation was the clear evidence of slave exogamy, taboos against cousin marriages.[26] This practice was a fact in the face of the endogamous practices general among the Anglo-Americans who were the master class.

These two observations supported two important claims. First, this was more evidence supporting the idea of continued African influence on Afro-Americans well after the end of massive slave importations. Second, support was given for the claim that a slave belief-system existed independent of the master. Here was the kind of evidence for

26. This evidence is also supported in folklore and in folk songs.

assumptions of slave culture and slave community that had previously been so elusive.

It was these last points that Gutman believed were his most important discoveries. They created the basis on which to consider slaves on their own terms rather than as failed white men. It gave one a sense of a moral character among slaves despite an oppressive system which had no moral character.

Since Herbert Gutman's study, the conventional wisdom on which Moynihan and others relied is no longer intact. Gutman's work (along with that produced by others) has shown the way (and set a new standard) for inquiring into the experience and culture of blacks. Most importantly, Gutman has given us *new* evidence in his constructions of families and kinships, using data many had not exploited before him. Thanks to him we will never be able to see the slave past and the past of African Americans the same as we once did.

11

Alain Locke:
Aesthetic Value-System
and Afro-American Art

Alain Locke would be especially gratified that a symposium of this character, sponsored by the *Harvard Advocate,* is given in his honor. His gratitude would go beyond his pleasure in being honored at Harvard, the University of his graduate training. It would stem, rather, from the fact that the *Harvard Advocate,* long an organ generating Euro-American letters, has at last made itself instrumental in celebrating Afro-American writers. From Locke's point of view, this symposium would mark a coming of age for both the *Advocate* and black American literature.

For almost half a century, Alain Locke has been respected for his role as interpreter of the Harlem Renaissance, for his identifying and support of young black artists, for his unfailing enthusiasm about the high cultural calling of black men and women of talent. But we have tended to use Locke as a lens through which to see writers like Langston Hughes, Countee Cullen, and Sterling Brown, and artists like Aaron Douglas; and we have tended to ignore the philosophical and theoretical grounds on which all of his efforts rested. This is especially ironic since his academic training was in philosophy, and since it has often been noted that his special interest was aesthetics. We should have wanted to look deeper, to understand the source of Locke's thought. It was not until I read his dissertation that I realized how much of a single piece was his scholarly work and his criticism.

Locke's dissertation, entitled "The Problem of Classification in Theory of Value," which was done here at Harvard in 1917, is a quite technical work which proposes, for all fields of value, a classification system suitable for comparison and analysis across the various fields.

*This lecture was given as part of the Alain L. Locke Symposium at Harvard University, December 1, 1973.

111

Locke had no intention of attacking traditional views of aesthetic values, which held aesthetics to be strictly contemplative and sui generis. Rather, he wanted to find, in the roots of human experience, the genetic source—the blueprint—from which ultimate aesthetic value could be derived.

Traditional thinking did not allow for the possibility that human experience directed toward other values—economic, hedonistic, moral, or ethical—could produce the psychological circumstances in which aesthetic values could be realized. If you found pleasure eating, you could not derive from that experience any aesthetic value.

Locke denied this. He claimed that through the experience, one could discover "enjoyment beyond mere satisfaction in eating." Likewise, one could discover in the religious experience, or the jazz performance, those qualities which stood on their own grounds as values in themselves.

To use his words, "psychologically" such aesthetic value "consists of such relationships that the presentation as a whole or the activity as a process induces a form-quality in feeling, which as long as it lasts or holds is felt to be the intrinsic ground of its own valuation and [the intrinsic ground] of wishing to persist . . . for the sake of maintaining the attitude and its component feeling qualities."

These qualities, growing out of generalized experience, Locke called pre-aesthetic values. But he found in them those genetic patterns of the form-feeling which would be manifest, in its purest state, in the fully developed and abstract aesthetic values. In other words, one could find inherent in the most ordinary and generalized experience a sense of contrast, a sense of rhythm, a sense of climatic order, a sense of summating. However primitive these senses might be in any given experience, they may evoke, according to Locke, rudimentary aesthetic values which are suggestions of themselves in a purer, abstract state.

Alain Locke's role in the 1920s and 1930s can be understood in terms of these ideas. They formed the basis for the cultural pluralism that characterized his work; they explain his persistent demand that Afro-American art achieve universalizing forms; they explain his belief in a process by which art-forms (such as jazz and dance), emerging out of generalized human experience, could ultimately be developed and abstracted into the quintessential purity of form to be found in fully developed aesthetic values. One can see here a debt to two of his teachers at Harvard: it is a fusing of the philosophical idealism of Josiah Royce with the psychology of William James. But Locke's thinking had a special charge: to serve the refinement of Afro-American culture.

We can now understand why African art had such a special meaning for Locke. Here was an art, created out of the religious and community experiences of a non-white people, that exhibited the discipline and purity of form that could be called *classic*. In every sense, African art demonstrated intrinsic aesthetic value.

This not only supported his theory but also represented the promise of Afro-American art. He did not expect Afro-American art to imitate African forms, but he hoped that the existence of African art would suggest to black Americans the possibilities of their own expression.

Locke acted as agent for the realization of sophisticated Afro-American art. There was, in his mind, a need for an authoritative voice to assert the validity of the Afro-American art enterprise. There was a need for someone to mediate between the folk art and the goals of classical expression, to articulate and define possibilities, to point the way. There was a need for someone to identify those values and techniques, derived from Afro-American sources, which had found their way into universal currency. Alain Locke wanted to fulfill all those needs.

To Locke, the Afro-American had to be held to his true experience. The temptation to imitate, to merely please and entertain, was the greatest danger, especially since black Americans had been persuaded that such was their role. Black artists could learn from Africa. But even there they had to be careful. The Afro-American, according to Locke, was actually the African "turned inside out." Whereas the African's dominant arts were decorative and craft arts—sculpture, metal working, weaving—the Afro-American's had been literature, song, dance, music, and later, poetry. The African was technical, rigid, controlled, disciplined, "thus, characteristic African art expression is sober, heavily conventionalized, restrained." On the other hand, black Americans were "freely emotional, sentimental and exuberant, so that even the emotional temper of the American Negro represents a reversal of his African temperament." Locke did not intend that the Afro-American give up his character, but he did hope that he could learn from the African to have a respect for technique and craft, a respect for discipline and form, and, through the agency of African art, an appreciation of forms of beauty that would better fit his own reality than those imposed by European sources.

Interestingly enough, Locke's notion of the African's character stood at odds with the characterizations of naïve exuberance, spontaneity, and sentimentality which were being imagined by Claude McKay and Countee Cullen, and which were, in time, to define negritude.

Doubtless the best example of Locke's theory at work is his discussion of jazz. For him, there were two types of worthwhile jazz: first, "that which, rising from the level of ordinary popular music, usually in the limited dance and song-ballad forms, achieves creative musical excellence." This we may call the "jazz classic." The other is that type of music which successfully transposes the elements of folk music, in this case jazz idioms, to the more sophisticated and traditional music forms. This latter type has become known as "classical jazz."

While he was appreciative of both the "jazz classic" and "classical jazz," it is clearly the latter he valued most, since only it could realize what he called universal and sophisticated values. He found in some Afro-Cuban music the development of formal ballet and chamber music, which were to him suggestive of the future of jazz.

In 1936, when he wrote *The Negro and His Music,* Locke found the influence of jazz already widespread. "It has educated the general musical ear to subtler rhythms, unfinished and closer harmonies, and unusual cadences and tone qualities. It has also introduced new systems of harmony, new instrumental techniques, and novel instrumental combinations."

And as if to demonstrate the validity of his theory of progress of pre-aesthetic values, he asserted, "The greatest accomplishment to date excepting the joy of the music itself, lies in the fact that there is now no deep divide between our folk music and the main stream of world music. That critical transition between being a half-understood musical dialect and a compelling variety of world speech has been successfully made."

For Locke, it was all progressive: stages leading to higher stages until it was all capped by universal values and forms. As he put it, "Every successive step in the general popularity of the Negro theme brings the Negro and the white American artist closer together, in this common interest of the promotion of Negro art over the common denominatory of the development of native American art." The ultimate end was an American art, in part defined by Afro-American forms, participating in universal aesthetic value.

It is hard to know how Locke would view it all now. But if music, dance, and theater are any measure, the vital force of Afro-American expression has so perfused American culture that it is sometimes impossible to recognize it for what it is. That might please him, but he would still want to search for his universal forms.

12

"Here to Stay"

With blues as your muse you expect to be down even when you're on top of things. In February 1941, when Arnold Rampersad takes up the second part of his comprehensive study of Langston Hughes, the poet was certainly down in every way. He was under debilitating medication in a California hospital, recovering from a long and painful bout with gonorrhea. He was dead broke and forced once more to rely on the generosity of friends. He was being hounded by the political right for his early sympathy for the Soviet Union and for his youthful attacks on the hypocrisy of Christianity. He got out of that hole, and others, as his reputation and fortunes waxed and waned over the next two decades. But there was never an upbeat that did not echo the down.

Like the bluesman, heroism for Hughes was the persistence of self with integrity, perspective and humor. A defiant cry—"Still Here" (1941), "Here to Stay" (1953)—runs as a refrain through his work. The abiding and indestructible self, however, is not Langston Hughes but the spirit and soul of black folks, which he assumes as a persona. Such a survival had to be negotiated in full awareness of the inescapable irony and ultimate absurdity of life. Being black in America makes one confront that irony and absurdity as white folks need not. That is why blues is a black folks' idiom, and to that testimony Langston Hughes committed himself.

Hughes, alone of the young writers from the Harlem Renaissance, persisted with his original voice and vision into the 1960s. Rudolph Fisher and Wallace Thurman died in 1930. Jean Toomer abandoned writing for a comfortable marriage and religious mysticism. The careers of Nella Larsen, Countee Cullen and Claude McKay foundered in the 1940s, well before their deaths. Zora Neale Hurston's work only found much deserved attention more than a decade after her sad and unremarked death in 1960. Hughes's friend Arna Bontemps, having a family and mouths

*This article is reprinted from *The Nation* magazine, October 10, 1988. Copyright © The Nation Company, Inc.

other than his own to feed, settled into a job as librarian at Fisk University and subordinated his writing to necessity. It was not merely that Hughes lived longer; it was the intensity and single-mindedness of his commitment that made the difference.

In 1926, in the pages of *The Nation,* Langston Hughes proclaimed his manifesto, "The Negro Artist and the Racial Mountain." Black Americans had an identity, a spirit, a perspective on life, a culture, an idiom, which was articulated in their speech and music (the blues more than spirituals) and it was the responsibility of black writers to craft their art from that medium. In his lifetime he would write hundreds of poems, some librettos for musical theater and operas, a novel and countless pages of prose, plays and other dramatic works. Hardly a word of it can be said to contradict that vision.

He wrote a lot, and he liked to give the impression that his writing (especially his poetry) was instinctive or intuitive, like jazz riffs and innovations; it was supposed to be natural, never worked at in a studied way. He was criticized for that. Some complained that his poetry sometimes resembled doggerel. James Baldwin charged that he had "stopped thinking." Ralph Ellison dismissed him as "incapable of sustained labor on a single, epic enterprise." Strange. Hughes had imagined his entire professional life had been just such a labor.

From the beginning Hughes swore himself to making his living from his writing. He would not take jobs unrelated to his art, like teaching, editing or portering. That, in the 1920s, was a courageous or foolhardy thing for a black man to do. The market open to black writers was thin and fickle, and poetry was a notoriously poor way to make a living. Standard American magazines and journals would not welcome Hughes's material, and radio and film were closed to black writers. Hughes's career was, therefore, within the range of his vision, opportunistic. He agreed to almost any proposition that would pay him for his writing: children's books, plays, stories, newspaper columns, operas, oratorios, translations from Spanish and French, what have you. For most of his life, he would rely on reading his poetry throughout the country, especially to Southern black communities and universities—after each reading, selling his books with a smile and an autograph.

Writing was a contingent and fragile livelihood, and that is why the unrelenting hounding by the political right threatened disaster. In 1941 Hughes recanted as youthful indiscretions two poems of the 1930s: "Goodbye Christ" and "Put one more 'S' in USA," but to no avail. He denied being a Communist, but he never denounced the left. Slowly and without display, he withdrew from association with groups that might bring him trouble, and he found a comfortable retreat in the Red-baiting N.A.A.C.P. As a final obsequence, he submitted himself to the humiliation of a "honorable surrender" before Senator McCarthy and his committee. He quietly explained to Roy Cohn, Joseph McCarthy, Everett Dirksen, John McClellan et al. about irony, about the voice of the poem not necessarily being that of the poet, about why a black American might have had a youthful infatuation with the young Soviet Union, the only nation to have officially denounced racism. While he did not name names or denounce anyone or anything, he performed sufficiently the rites of exorcism: openly acknowledging his brush with the devil, persuading the tribunal he was no longer possessed. He even admitted some sixteen of his books probably ought not to be in the United States's overseas libraries; but with an eye always on survival he suggested his "more recent books" should be there. Hughes distinctly remembered that at the end of the ordeal, just as he was being dismissed, Senator McCarthy actually winked at him—lest he forget the absurd.

Persistence through the 1940s and 1950s was the more difficult because no matter how much he produced, in whatever genre, Hughes never seemed able to break through to the public recognition and reputation he wanted and thought he deserved. Even his successful collaboration with Elmer Rice and Kurt Weill on *Street Scene* led to nothing in particular. He wrote the libretto for William Grant Still's opera *Troubled Island,* but Still's kind of music was in the losing camp in the struggle between champions of "American" music led by Howard Hanson and the European-influenced "American modernism" that would later be expressed by such composers as Aaron Copland. It was nearly impossible to get the opera performed, and it met a cool if not hostile reception when, after many years, it was finally heard. The composer Jan Meyerowitz persuaded Hughes to join in several ambitious projects, each opening to a lukewarm reception; each time Hughes complained that his words couldn't be heard over Meyerowitz's modernistic music.

More troubling, Langston Hughes would see his career eclipsed by younger black writers. He had always been generous with young writers, and all the black writers who came into prominence in the postwar years owed Hughes something, not only as someone who had prepared the way but as one quick with encouragement and support. But as with every generational transition, this one raised conflicting values and gave Hughes intimations of his mortality.

He was particularly annoyed by the successes of Richard Wright, Ralph Ellison, and James Baldwin. In spite of himself, he could not resist a bit of envy and even some resentment that none of his work received the acclaim or the rewards that came to these authors. Something about his style—his *sans souci,* his genial personality—made it difficult to take him really seriously, even when he was most acerbic and critical. The ironic voice, the blues muse, has that problem: Its most poignant insight issues forth in a wry and knowing smile rather than in purposeful rage. The novels of these three younger writers demanded attention. Like them or not, they were social, politiccal, and humanistic critiques one could not ignore.

Equally distressing for Hughes was how the works of these young writers, although they wrote about blacks, departed from the vision of his 1926 manifesto. Having wrestled with racial angst, they came out not revealing the Negro's soul but celebrating the individual self, at best, and negation, at worst. They attempted to buy a personal salvation through an intellectual or ideological distancing.

Like Hughes, both Richard Wright and Ralph Ellison had, in the 1930s, flirted with Marxism and Communism. Unlike Hughes, it seems, they expected the left to offer solutions to the quandaries of race in America. Their disillusionment was the greater for it. The same reliance on reason that tempted them to embrace Marxism propelled them toward other rational systems once that god failed. For Hughes, it was all a denial of the "racial mountain."

Hughes certainly did not admire Wright's brutal naturalism in *Native Son*. He thought it sordid and contemptuous of black people. He liked even less Wright's later plunge into nihilism and negation. He did not like the literary modernism, *de rigueur* in the 1950s, that informed Ralph Ellison's art. Ellison's tireless work on his masterpiece, his refusal to publish parts as they came along, was hard for Hughes to comprehend. He was bemused, nevertheless, and genially encouraging until the spectacular reception of *Invisible Man*—as if America had finally found its black novel and its black writer. Beyond envy and resentment, Hughes was alien to the mind behind that work, finding its existentialism merely another kind of distancing from race.

He was no more impressed by what he saw to be a trend among black writers toward a confessional literature, in which personal *angst* became the source of a public wail, to be "felt-sorry-for by your own self." So he found little to like in the words of James Baldwin and Chester Himes. Hughes would echo Richard Wright's comment about Baldwin: "This man disgusts, there is a kind of shameful weeping in what he writes." Such self-absorption was its own rejection of the racial mountain. Wright, Baldwin, and Himes would go the whole way by their expatriation to Europe. *Invisible Man*'s protagonist, escaping to his cellar, was a kind of expatriate. And Ellison, in his aerie on Riverside Drive, might as well have been.

It was Ralph Ellison who pointed to what made Hughes different from the rest. For Hughes, Ellison complained, race was the source of everything. "To me," he said, "it was simply lazy-mindedness on Langston's part." Hughes would not assume responsibility for his artistic growth and change, invoking instead "the excuse of racism." Ellison and the others were very much aware of the changing literary forms and techniques, and of the need to master them "in order to get in the game," to use Ellison's figure. "But Langston," he went on, "had stopped thinking. He had cut himself off from what was really important in art and the intellectual life." Hughes, for his part, saw modernism as intellectually pretentious, fundamentally alien to the spirit and source of Afro-American genius—an escape from the racial mountain.

In April 1967, just weeks before Langston Hughes died, I had a chance to interview him after a typically warm and moving public reading of his poetry, this time to benefit the newly founded Museum of Afro-American History in Boston. We talked of the Harlem Renaissance, of course, to help me with a book I was writing. We also talked of "modernism" and what it meant for Afro-American poetry. And that made him tell a story about his poet friend Melvin Tolson.

According to Hughes, he and Tolson had often commiserated over the fact that their poetry was totally ignored by the intellectuals and was never taught in colleges. Tolson argued that with the "New Critics" in the driver's seat, poets could only get attention with work no one could understand. He vowed, said Hughes, to write a book of poetry with so many and such arcane references as to make T.S. Eliot pray for footnotes.

If that was his intent, he certainly succeeded in his *Harlem Gallery* (1965), a work of extraordinary complexity and erudition. It would seem by that work's reception that Tolson had gotten "in the game." The book won ringing praise from *both* Alan Tate and Karl Shapiro. Alan Tate found Tolson the first Negro poet to have "assimilated completely . . . the language of the Anglo-American poetic tradition." Shapiro asserted that "Tolson writes in Negro."

Despite such praise, Hughes would surely not be surprised that, "in the game" or not, *Harlem Gallery* has not been much discussed since, and Tolson is still not read by undergraduates or graduate students of American literature. For him, if not for Ellison, it would be further proof of the persistent absurdity of American culture, where everything comes down to race in the end.

Hughes was not so depressed by the successes of all black writers of the time. He eagerly applauded Gwendolyn Brooks's winning the 1949 Pulitzer Prize for poetry. He had been a support and encouragement to her, and she readily acknowledged her debt to him. He also liked the work of Ann Petry and Paule Marshall. He felt a genuine pride in the success of Lorraine Hansberry's play *A Raisin in the Sun,* taking deserved pleasure from the fact that his poetry had been an inspiration. Was it mere coincidence that he liked the women writers most? Or was it that they found it possible to continue an unambiguous love of the Negro people as the source of their art while they wrote with unflinching realism?

This second volume of Arnold Rampersad's two-part biography reveals how consistent and unswerving Langston Hughes was to his original vision and commitment to race, in spite of the extraordinary diffusion of his artistic interests and energies. The dominant irony in the blues fixed his point of view; the absurdity of race in America was compelling and inescapable. His response was neither anger nor rage but a genial stoicism.

Some of Rampersad's best pages are those devoted to Jesse B. Semple, the character Hughes created in 1943 for a column in the Chicago *Defender.* Those columns developed as an ongoing dialogue between the narrator, Boyd, and Semple, whom Boyd called "my simple-minded friend." Boyd was bourgeois, educated, reasonable, and a bit stuffy. "Simple," as he came to be called, saw everything as a "race man." For him, there was no reason mitigating the fact of race. Simple is probably Hughes's most powerful creation—Simple and Boyd comprising the permanent poles of Afro-American consciousness. They are, doubtless, Hughes's own voices: "myself," as he put it, "talking to me. Or else me talking to myself." Few black writers could, as Hughes did, embrace and expose to public view the Simple in themselves.

Any final literary assessment of Hughes and his work will be disputed, and Rampersad does not venture any here. He approaches the biography as one would approach *cinéma vérité*, revealing the life as it unfolds with only occasional and slight comment or judgment. This volume, like the first, is rich in detail, intelligent and well written. It satisfies admirably our need for a full understanding of the life and career of Langston Hughes. The author has, however, left unanswered questions about Hughes's significance for American literature and culture.

These volumes will, nevertheless, allow cultural historians to appreciate the rich insights Hughes's opus offers into the life, language, culture, and mentality of Afro-Americans during the middle years of the twentieth century. The idiom, the rhythms and sensibilities of urban black America are captured in Hughes's language more and better than anywhere else. As for originality, he created new forms by successfully wedding urban black idioms to conventional forms. It was Hughes's creation of gospel theater in such works as *Black Nativity* and *Tambourines to Glory* that opened new possibilities for the sacred and profane in American culture. We shall live off that investment for some time to come.

Hughes's purpose in life and art was to persist for himself and for the race:

> But I'm here, still here—
> And I intend to be!
> It'll never be *that* easy, white folks,
> To get rid of me.

Even death could not efface the wry smile, the irony. Hughes's final words for his funeral were from an Ellington tune:

> Do nothing till you hear from me.

13

The Purest Kind of a Guy

Devoid of heroes, awash in TV images of the pathetic and the banal, we do not know how to respond to tragedy in its classic form. Yet Paul Robeson was a true tragic figure, an avatar from a more heroic age. He and his life were just the right stuff for an Aeschylus, for King Lear's or Othello's Shakespeare. He was a man of such enormous natural endowment in talent and in his physical being as to seem almost godlike. His strength of character, consistency, and loyalty to transcendent values would be seen as political naïveté and would, in the end, ensnare him as a victim of swarming Lilliputians.

It is the wonderful achievement of Martin Bauml Duberman to have recaptured the greatness of Paul Robeson and the ambiguity and treacherousness of his time, while guarding his own critical sense, avoiding many partisan and ideological traps.

Robeson was born in 1898 in Princeton, New Jersey. His father, who escaped from slavery in 1860, was a minister. His mother, a schoolteacher, died when he was six years old. Character and honesty were essential elements in his upbringing, and he always found his rock and moral sustenance in the black church and community.

Robeson seemed special from the beginning. He excelled—indeed, triumphed—at everything to which he put his hand or mind. He was an extraordinary athlete and scholar. All-American in football at Rutgers University, he graduated Phi Beta Kappa and valedictorian of his class. He worked hard for these achievements, and he faced, as did other black men, the extra hurdles and obstacles of racism. But his slightest effort seemed to level the barriers, and his warm good humor seemed disdainfully to dismiss racists who would stand in his way.

While taking his law degree at Columbia University, he began performing small theatrical roles. He jumped at the chance to play the lead in Eugene O'Neill's *All God's Chillun Got Wings* when it opened in

*This article is reprinted from *The Nation* magazine, March 20, 1989. Copyright © The Nation Company, Inc.

1924. He also took the lead in *The Emperor Jones,* which for a while ran on alternate nights from *All God's Chillun.* The plays got mixed notices, but Paul Robeson was hailed.

Robeson's mere presence onstage brought a dynamic charge. It was his body of course, his size and effortless command of self and scene, but it was also some quality of character that read to an audience. You do not work at it or learn it—you either have it or not. Robeson had it. Throughout his professional life, regardless of the type of production or the vagaries of performance, his presence was hailed by audiences and critics.

In 1925, Robeson launched his career as a concert singer, giving solo performances of spirituals and work songs. In this, he found the finest expression of his talent. His genuine awe of and love for the common people and their music flourished throughout his life and became his emotional and spiritual center. Whatever his ventures into theater, film or politics, he would always find his home in the songs of everyday people and in his magnificent voice.

The great triumph in the theater for Robeson was his Othello, which he first performed in London in 1930. It was a historic event, as a black actor had not played the role in England in a century. Despite his great success, it would be more than a decade before Robeson could open in *Othello* on Broadway. It was unheard of for a black man to play a romantic lead in the United States, especially against a white woman. But Robeson's *Othello* was even greater here than it had been in England: The New York production had 296 performances, a record for Shakespeare on Broadway at the time.

Richly endowed black men have a hard lesson to learn. All the talent in the world, all the charm or charisma, will not of themselves convert a world corrupted by racism. In Robeson's case, what opened his eyes was a failed romance with a white British woman, Yolande Jackson. They had been deeply in love and planned to marry after Paul divorced his wife, Eslanda. Social and family pressure, however, persuaded Jackson to walk away from what she had professed was the love of her life.

It had all been too easy for Robeson in the beginning. He had met and confronted racism, but he had never before been defeated by it. His painful experience with Yolande Jackson forced upon him a different consciousness. While in London in the 1930s he also came to know Africans like Jomo Kenyatta and learned about the African independence movement. In 1934 he visited the Soviet Union, where he became friends with filmmaker Sergei Eisenstein, and where he was idolized. He fell in love with the Russian language (in which he would become fluent) and added Russian songs to his repertory, as he did the songs of working people and peasants around the world.

From the mid-1930s Robeson viewed himself and his art as serving the struggle for racial justice for non-whites and economic justice for the workers of the world. In 1938 he went to Spain to lend his support to the

Republic's war against Franco and Fascism. By the outbreak of World War II, there seemed to him to be a single, global conflict, between the progressive forces working for democracy, socialism, and equality and the Fascist ones defending colonialism, racism, and exploitation. He had no doubt that the Soviet Union, which he saw as in the vanguard of the new age, was on the right side of that struggle.

During the war years, Robeson was optimistic that progressive forces in the United States (the labor movement, those fighting Jim Crow, the New Deal's left, the left in general) would emerge triumphant. He was dismayed, however, by post-war policy. He saw an American government all too eager to take up the colonial powers' burden in Asia and Africa, preferring cold war to peaceful coexistence with the Soviet Union, launching what he saw as a purge of the progressive left by means of anti-Communist hysteria.

He threw himself into the 1948 campaign for Henry Wallace and the Progressive party. With that defeat, there seemed even more reason to marshal international and domestic forces for peace, racial justice, and the self-determination of colonized peoples. This political agenda aligned him with the professed aims of the Soviet Union and put him at odds with American cold war policy. As the pro-Soviet left in the United States came under heavier attack, Robeson became more determined in its defense.

In 1949, speaking in Paris to the Congress of the World Partisans of Peace, Robeson said that neither black nor white workers would make war against the Soviet Union or anyone else. Misquoted at home, his words were taken to mean that blacks would not defend the United States in a war against the Soviet Union, suggesting a primary loyalty to the latter. Robeson became a major target in the witch hunt. Black leaders were especially eager to establish their anti-Communist credentials by distancing themselves from him. In 1949 it would require deft contortions for A. Philip Randolph, Roy Wilkins, and much of the black press to find an acceptable position on the bloody and racist-inspired Peekskill riot organized to block a Robeson concert.

Robeson stood firm during these post-war years despite, as Duberman's biography suggests, his possible disillusionment with the Soviet Union. On a visit to the Soviet Union in 1949 he insisted on seeing his friend Itzik Feffer, a Russian-Jewish writer who had been arrested by Soviet authorities. Feffer told him of widespread oppression and of brutality toward Russian Jews. At his Moscow concert ending this visit, Robeson spoke publicly of Feffer and then, after reciting the words in Russian, sang in Yiddish the Warsaw Ghetto resistance song. But on returning to the West, Robeson was deceptive and evasive about the plight of the Jews in Russia. Even after Feffer disappeared years later, Robeson was silent. The cause, to his mind, was much larger than the Soviet Union, and he would do nothing to sustain the feeding frenzy of the American right.

In 1950 the State Department took Robeson's passport, claiming his travel abroad would be "contrary to the best interests of the United States." Promoters refused to book him and concerts were cancelled, but there was little liberal or mainstream protest. Black audiences and churches remained loyal to him, regardless of what they thought of his politics. That small group, and the diminished left, could hardly sustain a career. The State Department remained adamant, despite protests both here and abroad. In defiance, Robeson had his voice amplified across the Canadian border, and he once telephoned a concert to an enthusiastic audience in Britain, but he was effectively silenced.

Deprived for eight years of his right to travel abroad, he remained popular overseas nevertheless, returning in 1958 to enthusiastic audiences in Britain and the Soviet Union. But the physical and psychological cost had been high. He suffered serious depressions from 1956 on; in 1961, while in Moscow, he slit his wrists. Except for brief periods he spent the remaining fifteen years of his life in psychic retreat and pain—treated for much of the time by electroshock therapy and heavy medication. He returned to the United States in December 1963 and lived in seclusion until a fatal stroke in January 1976. His ventures into public were rare in the intervening years, but in each he was warmed by the unflagging affection that black people had for him. Except for W. E. B. Du Bois, no other black American had ever been so great that the mobilized and monstrous might of the United States government was required to chain him.

Martin Duberman has done a masterful job in this biography. Robeson left only a small written record, and much had to come from the papers of his wife, the very opinionated and truly remarkable Eslanda. Duberman has balanced her account—consulting other archives, conducting more than 135 interviews and exploiting those F.B.I. documents he could get at by way of the Freedom of Information Act. He has been courageous in confronting frankly all the political and personal questions raised by Robeson's life. Controversy will persist, but all will concede that Duberman's work is thorough, balanced, and wholly engaging.

Tragedy should finally be ennobling, and so this story will be once the dust has settled. Paul Robeson might have served drama better had he gone out of life raging in madness rather than in the awful pain of depression. He was forced in the end to retreat into a wilderness with his ghosts. He was, alas, more Lear than Othello. Martin Duberman has made both that pain and that glory accessible to us.

14

Integrating
Afro-American History into
American History

"Most people think American history is the story of white men, and that is why blacks want a history of their own." I began an essay in 1971 with that sentence. A blunt statement, but fair enough. American history seemed the story of white men and their institutions until the onrush of historical writing and reinterpretation that began in the late 1960s. Now that more than a decade has passed, it is a good time to rethink that statement. Until the mid-1960s it was impossible to describe what was then called Negro history as a legitimate field. Now one can hardly read a college catalog, a bibliography, or a publisher's list without a sense of remarkable change. Before the 1960s, those wanting to publish articles in Afro-American history were limited to the pages of the *Journal of Negro History*. Unless an article about blacks could pass as something on the Old South, Civil War, Reconstruction, or some such area, it would not likely find a place in the pages of "main-line" scholarly journals. The clamorous protests of the 1960s helped change things.

But this protest and agitation about race exclusion from American history was only part of the story. The triumph of the "new social history," the maturing of techniques of quantification (whereby previously mute and unsummoned witnesses could offer testimony), the ability of high-speed computers to make use of previously indigestible data, the vocal demands of women and others for acknowledgment in history, all contributed to a broad and deep change in American historiography. It was a collaborative and complementary (if not a cooperative) process; it was not just Afro-American history that marked the change. It is important to bear this in mind, because the revision has not been merely additive, that is to say just more about blacks included in historical writing and discourse. The character of the discourse has changed as historical problems have been freshly conceptualized, as the context has been enriched by a more heterogeneous history.

This is especially clear in fields like colonial history, where most of what has changed has been the work of historians not noted for their involvement in Afro-American history. Peter Wood, Edmund Morgan, Bernard Bailyn, and many others have, through their attention to ethnicity and race, changed profoundly how we think about the seventeeth and eighteenth centuries. It is certainly a far different social history from that of Carl Bridenbaugh.

Professor Bailyn, in his presidential address before the American Historical Association, described himself as having been a historian of the "Anglo-American experience," but went on to describe his present major project, which will include the peopling of America: people from the Congo as well as people from Northern Europe.[1] Similarly, we can see the great change in the history of slavery brought about by historians like John Blassingame, Leslie Owens, Herbert Gutman, George Rawick, Eugene Genovese, and others.

In Reconstruction, perhaps the liveliest American field at the moment, the works of Ransom and Sutch, Robert Higgs, Thomas Holt, Leon Litwack, and the forthcoming work of Eric Foner will transform our thinking about the period. Similarly, the works of Lawrence Levine, Sterling Stuckey, and Vincent Harding have changed the way we think about American culture in general.

Still, Afro-American history, like women's history, is a bit peculiar. These are not quite fields of history in the way that, say, social, economic, and intellectual history are. In such fields we are aware that history is being looked at through the prism of a specific discipline. Within either periods or fields, we assume that some centralizing principle or confluence of events offers special insight into a procession of events. The problem for Afro-American and women's history is that they are so essential to American history that it is perverse to think of it without them. A white American history and a male history ought to be, common sense tells us, unthinkable.

When I say that, I am also saying that we have read a lot—indeed, been brought up on—a lot of perverse history. But to pull these essential elements out for separate study does not, lacking a more realistic synthesis, produce a better history. Afro-American history as a subfield, therefore, is at once distinguishable, yet necessarily *within* the fabric. Much of what we do in the field is to bring a different angle of vision to well-known subjects and issues (i.e., Slavery and Reconstruction) or focus

1. Bernard Bailyn, "The Challenge of Modern Historiography," *American Historical Review,* cxxxvii (February, 1982), 1–24.

upon movements and their leaders (e.g., Nell Painter's *The Exodusters* or her *Hosea Hudson*) or to bring attention through monographs to an important moment in time, an important issue in time, or a change that has occurred that makes a difference, that has consequence (e.g., Darlene Hine's *Black Victory*). These should inform us and make us sensitive to the complexities and subtleties of the black experience.

That experience is illuminated, too, by biographies, which have increased greatly over the past decade. From Booker T. Washington to Langston Hughes, many black lives are now in published form, the obscure as well as the famous. Important collections of papers have been accessible to scholars (e.g., Herbert Aptheker's *Du Bois,* John Blassingame's *Douglass,* and Robert Hill's *Garvey*). In short, the work over the past decade has been to bring into view what has been latent in the warp and woof of American history.

As important as have been the accomplishments of the past two decades, we should not forget that the end of our study of history is the fabric itself. What we should expect in the end is no less than the reconstruction of American history. My metaphor of latent strands within fabric comports well with the rhetoric that was common in the 1960s, demanding history "from the bottom up." What we have witnessed is this latent matter being brought to the surface so that our view of the fabric is different. When we look at the whole, we ought to be seeing something different.

That American history is not what it once was is greeted by most of us with a great deal of satisfaction. The story of America I was told as a boy began with *our* pilgrim fathers and ended with my school days' present—the New Deal. That story, that continuum, that wholeness, that narrative is no longer available to us precisely because of changes brought about by the "new social" history, women's history, black history, etc. There has been a fragmenting and a faceting of the history so that the wholeness of the narrative no longer can contain all we now know to have been real, important, essential.

It has been a cause of complaint for a number of historians that the narrative is passé. While much of that complaint comes from conservative and reactionary impulses—the wish to hold to old values and clear away competing claims to historical significance—it is, nonetheless, important that we recognize that in an important way the *story* is what history is about. We all need to be calling for a new narrative, a new synthesis taking into account the new history. It is especially important for Afro-American historians, unless we are content merely to work in an eddy of the larger stream.

Afro-American history and American history are not only essential to one another. They share a common historical fate. Both the American nation and the Afro-American people are creations of the New World. Both were ruptured from tradition. History for both, therefore, has been problematic. Tradition is a legitimizing phenomenon. All peoples and all nations want to tie themselves to an ancient past (ideally, preliterate and mythic). The traditions are often related to place or to migration where antiquity alone would explain the *naturalness* and *rightness* of the present. Medieval political leaders liked to relate themselves (often as illicit offspring) to the myths of Homer and Virgil.[2] The modern state of Israel rests its territorial claims and its foreign policy on the Old Testament. Certainly, a nation born of revolution in a "New World" and a people snatched from the web of their tradition would face a similar problem of finding their legitimacy in history.[3]

The Founding Fathers were conscious that the actual history could not be the rationale on which their new nation could rest. They wanted to found their roots in a classical and honored past, while they were deliberately severing themselves from the one tradition that gave them place and reason. Afro-Americans, too, are new, a new people brought into being as a consequence of American history, a new people for whom after several generations in America it was impossible to trace back to any tradition beyond the American experience itself. This newness of people and nation has caused in both a problematic relationship with tradition.

Consider the generation of the so-called Founding Fathers. Here was a nation which they themselves had established, deliberately breaking from their immediate connections with the past. At the same time, nevertheless, they tried heroically to place themselves in a real, identifiable, classical tradition—one which could explain their present, more so than their past. America, the land and its native peoples, of course, had its own past, but it was not one that Anglo-American newcomers could honor (nor would that indigenous past honor them). America was not Britain or France or Italy or Greece, where the earth itself yielded up evidence that its contemporary generation belonged to something extending back beyond recorded time.

In America there were no ruins (except for Indian mounds) to be dug up, no statues as in Greece, the Holy Land, or Italy; no arches as in Rome; no Colosseum, none of that sort of thing. Yet, at the same time, this generation of new Americans went about identifying and naming their cities Rome and Troy and Athens and Syracuse and Ithaca and Utica and Alexandria and Augusta, names that clearly associated the present with an ancient past. And they did not simply choose place names, but they called on tradition to name the very institutions of their newly established polity. They might have called themselves a *commonwealth*, but they turned to the Roman *res publica* for *republic*. For their

2. A number of still unpublished papers which were delivered at a conference at the Maison des Sciences de l'Homme in Paris, July 7–9, 1982, amplify this general idea. Susan Reynolds's "Medieval *Origines Gentium* and the Continuity of the Realm" is especially relevant. The conference addressed the general topic "Legitimation by Descent."

3. See my own paper at this conference: "The Afro-American and the Myth of American History."

new leader, they thought of titles such as "His Mightiness," "His Highness," "Protector," "Regent," or "Serenity"; they chose "President" from *praesidens*. When they established themselves a legislature, it was not a "parliament," but a "congress," from *congressus*. Through it all, one sees this deliberate effort to establish a legitimacy with an ancient and glorious past.

As a further illustration, take the symbolism on the dollar bill. The great seal of the United States bears an eagle which, except for being an American bald eagle, suggests the eagle of the Roman legions. Both the olive branch and the sheaf of arrows it clasps—emblems of peace and war—have classical connotations and were not common symbols in this country before the Revolution. Then, the Latin phrase, *E pluribus unum*. On the obverse side, above the truncated pyramid, above the triangle in glory with the eye of God, one reads: *annuit coeptis*—he has favored our beginnings. Below the pyramid is *Novus ordo seclorum*—a new order of the ages. And at the base of the pyramid, in Roman numerals for greater dignity and authority, is MDCCLXXVI, which is when the new order of ages began. The Founding Fathers wanted to imbue 1776 with ancient virtue.[4]

In these pretenses the Founding Fathers were no different from Hugue Capet establishing a myth of descent from Aeneas, no different from all peoples who through myth and symbol attached themselves to a grand tradition from which they gain legitimacy and meaning. It was the rupture from their immediate and natural tradition (the final achievement of which was the American Revolution), the need to establish new birthright claims, that made their deliberate and self-conscious link with the classical past necessary.

Africans who were brought to America suffered a similar rupture from their immediate and natural tradition. They, too, were to become a new people, but it would not be easy to find a satisfactory linkage with any past known to them. The ancient European tradition was impossible, and the developing American myth of a providentially designed free society of democratic institutions did not accord with the black experience. For many, Christianity made possible the identification with the Children of Israel of the Old Testament.

But Afro-Americans lacked a specific and direct tie to Africa; we were alienated from, yet elemental to, the New World. Dissatisfied with our own history of slavery and oppression, we have desired to leap over the Afro-American experience altogether, to place ourselves in a tradition which is not immediately ours but certain to give us a sense of grandeur and legitimacy. Such mythologizing is not what we professional historians mean by historical study, but it is a deep human and social need which insinuates itself into our scholarship and criticism.

Even we professionals want history to give us legitimacy as a people

4. Howard Mumford Jones, *O Strange New World* (New York, 1963), 229.

or as a nation, and this is true whether we are Afro-Americans thinking of ourselves as a people or Americans thinking of ourselves as a nation. That is why the dominant Anglo-Saxon story of American history, that is to say the Bancroftian myth, persisted so long and with such strength in our historiography. The black and nonwhite experiences never comported well with the central myth—thus the tendency to deal with such groups as anomalous or egregious. That is why Afro-Americans have from the nineteenth century wanted to use the same history of America to demonstrate that we were here "before the Mayflower," that we were part of a developing nation and its history, and thus use American history to establish our birthright.

Consider the Sally Hemings story, the power of it, its persistence. The evidence is circumstantial; we will never establish a *truth* all will accept. Certainly, we will never get Thomas Jefferson or Sally Hemings to testify to the facts. There are those people, custodians of the Jefferson legacy, who have a clear stake in protecting not only his historical reputation but his progeny from the taint of race mixture. Similarly, there are those—I venture to say most black people—who *know* the rumors are essentially true despite gaps and problems with the evidence. Why is it so important? Sally Hemings was certainly not the first or the only black woman so used. Why the fuss? It is not Sally Hemings, but Thomas Jefferson who makes the difference. He was a Founding Father of the nation, and, the rumor had it, he sired children by a slave woman. In the overall effect of that story, it does not matter whether or not it was *actually* true. It is *symbolically* true. The story, like so many legitimizing myths, symbolically ties a people (through Sally Hemings) to the founding of the nation. It is ironic, too, because of the illicit means of establishing legitimacy. That, too, is common in such birthright myths.

Alex Haley's *Roots,* to point to another example, for all of its many historical problems, captured the American imagination—white and black—like no recent work of history has. It accomplished two important things: (1) It evidenced the direct and specific connection between an Afro-American and a traditional Old World culture. It authenticated the Afro-American experience by means of an oral tradition, similar to the Old Testament and the *Iliad.* It autheticated an individual black man, a family, a family enlarged into the Afro-American people. (2) It integrated itself into the dominant Bancroftian myth of providential destiny of America, the American people and nation. The story ends with that onward, upward, progressive vision so characteristic of the American faith. Through *Roots,* black people could be mythically integrated into the American Dream. It does not matter whether or not Haley *actually* traced his family back to a West African village. Whatever the truth, the story will continue to stand as emotionally and symbolically true.

In 1971, I was inclined to dismiss myth as not the proper work of historians. Although I still believe that professional historians have a responsibility not to pander to primal emotional needs and fantasies, I have come to appreciate better how the mythic can suggest itself into the most scholarly work. We blacks writing Afro-American history, no matter how much distance we like to maintain, are drawn to "tell the story of our people" in epic scale.

Vincent Harding's *There Is a River* and my own *Black Odyssey* are works driven by such need. There are many differences between these two works: differences in scale, in vision, in sense of history. Yet the similarities are noteworthy: their literary character, the use of literary devices to insinuate oneself and one's ideas into the experience of both the subject and the reader. Both attempt to include the reader into the *we* of the history. These are not *they* and *me* books. *We* and *our* are the dominant (though often implied) pronouns: we as reader, we as writer, we as Africans, we as Afro-Americans, we as slaves.

They are similar in another way: each has a dominant theme making the book cohere. That theme is explicit and relentless in Harding's work. In my own it is implicit, but nonetheless deliberate and obvious. Harding tells the history of black Americans as a story of resistance, with the "river" of resistance being the central metaphor. For my part, I make the slave experience one of transcendence of tyranny. The themes are not only narrative devices, they are instruments of historical selection and interpretation. The strokes are broad, antithesis muted or denied. In short, both works are attempts at epic.

In the attempt, however, both authors illustrate the problematic character of an Afro-American epic written in the late twentieth century. For, as one is asked to focus on the theme of resistance, the power of the oppressor necessarily remains dominant. As one is invited to celebrate the victory of the slave's humanity over the tyranny of his condition, one is drawn to the unmoved and immovable tyrant. It only reminds us (for those who need reminding) of the paradoxical character of the Afro-American experience. There is no way out of it. History "from the bottom up," as important as that is, will not turn the world upside down. Our reading of Harding or Huggins serves finally to convince us that the "river" and the "transcendence"—the oppression and tyranny that spawn them—have gone on, will continue to go on, far into the future. It is, perhaps, this problem that prompted August Meier to characterize *There Is a River* as "pessimistic."[5]

In a more general sense, these remarks suggest the central problem of the narrative (as well as the epic) for American history. One cannot imagine an updated George Bancroft persuading us. Contemporary Bancroftians like Carl Degler[6] bring our attention to the anomalies (blacks, at least) just as Harding and Huggins give silent authority to oppressors and tyrants. The modern American epic will have to discover the theme

---

5. August Meier, Review of Vincent Harding's *There Is a River* (New York, 1981).
6. Carl Degler, *Out of Our Past* (New York, 1959).

or metaphor that can bring all of the parts together in a common American story. Such a theme is latent in the American imagination. I think of the central idea in Martin Luther King, Jr.'s "I Have a Dream," as a force for unity, a river different from Harding's. It is surely more compelling and enduring than Booker T. Washington's metaphor of the hand and the fingers. As a practical matter, however, no such epic theme can work without the factual and experiential basis on which to make it credible. So far, such optimistic themes work better as dreams of future possibility and as America's unrealized calling than as history.[7]

Black Americans, like the American nation itself, will be forever searching into the past to provide a sense of legitimacy and historical purpose, forever bound and frustrated in the effort. I do not suggest this is something they ought not to do, but that it must be done again and again, never with satisfaction. In this regard, black Americans who work in this field are different from their white colleagues. It is *their* history, and in a deep, personal and emotional way they will never be able to escape their personal identification with it however much scholarly distance is achieved. That is fair enough and no different from other historians with what they consider *their* history.

I mean this to be neither a validating nor an invalidating idea regarding black or white historians working in the field. It is merely to state the obvious. I hope we have moved beyond the view, pervasive within the profession before the 1960s, that a black historian's judgment about slavery, etc., had to be discounted as naturally biased, while whites had no ax to grind, and the equally foolish idea of the 1960s and 1970s that white historians could not write or comment on the black experience. I mean only to point to the dual character of history. We need to know how and why we use history: to serve both our needs of personal and group identity as well as for the more "scientific" and humanistic purposes of historical analysis. We should know the differences and not confound them.

Most of what we read as Afro-American history is really not so cosmic as all of this. Rather, it is quite limited, particular, and precise. Most do not address large, ideational issues. Most, I am forced to say, are rather parochial. It has been an "archaeological" work, digging and opening new ground. It brings to our attention particulars, data that is new to us. These shards, in themselves, are not startling discoveries, but they constitute a new history as far as Americans are concerned. We now have a number of monographs that have made genuine contributions.

So you get studies of blacks in Kentucky, blacks in Illinois, blacks in Indiana, or wherever. The history gets repeated again and again; we

7. What George Bancroft, Alex Haley, Carl Degler, et al. have in common is the implicit sense of destiny moving toward some promise in the future, "The Dream." Such histories would seem to preempt the future, characterizing this "epic" story as American and unlike such classic epics as the *Iliad*.

need the reiteration, each with its particular or special angle or twist. We need to know the sameness to discover in it what is unique. Sometimes the angle of vision is only slightly shifted: now it is "black men," now it is "black women." We take old, much-studied issues and institutions and reconsider them with blacks in mind. We look at individual lives, often by means of oral histories and interviews, to bring into our consciousness ranges of human experience previously remote or inaccessible to us. It is all extremely important work, and the production of the past decade has been impressive.

The danger, however, is that we see this work as the end and purpose of Afro-American history—creating a narrow specialty over which we establish a proprietary interest, squeezing our concerns to the point of historical insignificance. It is a danger because the American academic professions encourage such mindless territoriality, and because many are fearful to venture beyond their carefully cultivated certitudes.

We ought, rather, to see this work as the building blocks of a new synthesis, a new American history. Would that the work should raise such fundamental questions of American society as to provoke discourse among American historians to change the history they write. We are able now to say, as we were not fifteen years ago, that blacks (black leaders, the black experience, etc.) are *included* in the textbooks. That is not enough.

Recently, I was asked to review a manuscript for a college textbook in American history. It seemed all right; it omitted no notable group; it made no mistakes; it covered all the bases. It was, nevertheless, a poor history. The authors had a chapter on mid-nineteenth-century reform. William Lloyd Garrison and the abolitionists were there. Frederick Douglass was not. He was in another chapter, the one on blacks. Surely we must know that what actually happened in that historical moment was a consequence of the interaction between Douglass and Garrison. It cannot be told as a story of *black history* and *white history*. It must be told as one. While that idea is simple enough—a truism indeed—too few of us accept the radical implications of it. We do not put it into our thinking, our writing, our courses. That idea, nevertheless, is a key to any new, successful narrative of American history.

It may be that the Afro-American story remains too discordant with progressive assumptions to be comfortably incorporated into the American story, Alex Haley notwithstanding. Dominant, national narratives, after all, are *selected* from a matrix of historical experience. What is chosen, and how it is put together, tells us how a people would like to perceive themselves—their future as well as their past. As Americans, we have liked the succession of events to move in ever-ascending stages, each today better than all yesterdays. Surely there were problems, but there were reforms and resolutions. Things worked out. All national histories are not so optimistic and progressive as our own. Some are characteristically ironic, some cyclical, some fatalistic.[8]

Except for Alex Haley's *Roots,* I know of no treatment of the Afro-American story that shares the dominant optimism and faith in progress, certainly not one written in the late twentieth century. The Afro-American story has more been told in terms of failed hopes, frustrated and ambiguous victories, dreams deferred. In contrast to the dominant American story, it is most often characterized as tragic.[9] It may well be that the new American narrative, when it is written, will resonate to a more experienced, a wiser, nation. We might, then, see as if for the first time, the elemental truth in the black American experience; rather than being an anomaly, it is central to the story. That would result in a new American history, indeed.

We need not wait for such grand, synthetic efforts; there is much to be done. Old questions in American history demand new answers from the angle of vision of Afro-American history. Old topics seem different from that perspective: the city, economic development, citizenship, federalism, majority rule, and so on. On the scale of dissertation and monograph, with a new vision there is a new history to be written if historians and teachers are willing to be genuinely challenging. Moreover, historians of the Afro-American experience must reach beyond ethnic history by choosing topics having historical significance beyond narrow bounds of race, by developing the implications of their work for the general history, and by raising through their work general questions, provoking discourse among historians and contributing to the new American history.

8. Hayden White, "Introduction," *Metahistory, the Historical Imagination in Nineteenth-Century Europe* (Baltimore, 1973).
9. Ibid.

15

The Constitution and Civil Rights

I. Tale of Two Documents

The Declaration of Independence and the Constitution are often considered two documents at odds, the one an expression of freedom, the other of restraint. The Declaration of Independence justifies disorder and dissolution; the Constitution creates structure and defines a new order, a "more perfect union." The Declaration of Independence freely asserts the *right* to revolution; the Constitution protects against domestic insurrection and might be said to be *counter-revolutionary*. The Declaration of Independence proclaims and celebrates the Rights of Man; the Constitution guards against human impulses, weaknesses, and foibles.

It is not surprising that black Americans have tended to find inspiration and support for freedom and civil rights in the Declaration more than in the Constitution. It is the Declaration, after all, which makes the claim that "all men are created equal" and ascribes to all men the "inalienable" rights of life, liberty, and the freedom to pursue happiness (commonly taken to mean freedom of opportunity). The Constitution, on the other hand, is silent about such general principles, requiring as an afterthought that their legal guarantees be added to the document in the Bill of Rights.

In the years before the Civil War, those abolitionists who followed William Lloyd Garrison argued that the Constitution was in fact (or at least in effect) a document supporting slavery. It did so, they argued, in the several compromises and references to slavery. It did so in guaranteeing to slaveholders federal protection against slave revolts or uprisings. It did so in its blanket protection of private property, in its implication that Congress was empowered to legislate the return of fugitive slaves to

*This lecture was given at the Tocqueville Forum, Wake Forest University, 1989.

their owners.[1] It did so in the very federal union it created, powerful enough (unlike the union under the Articles of Confederation) to quell domestic disorder (i.e., slave revolts) but impotent to regulate or abolish slavery in any direct way.

There were, of course, those abolitionists like Gerrit Smith, James Birney, and Theodore Dwight Weld who saw the possibility of reform—and eventual abolition—through electoral politics and thus through the Constitution. For them, the Constitution was sufficiently neutral on the question of slavery so as not to exclude the possibility of change through a moral-political crusade.

Black Americans found themselves following either camp, often owing to the influence one or the other had in a region. Frederick Douglass, himself a fugitive from slavery, began his career in New England as a Garrisonian, expressing deep reservations about the possibility of abolition under the Constitution. He began to moderate his views on the Constitution after moving to Rochester, New York, starting his paper, *The North Star,* and falling under the patronage and influence of Gerrit Smith. Suffering the hostility of Garrison and his followers, Douglass moved in time to support the Liberty and Abolition parties, the Free Soil party, and the Republican party. Even so, he was never comfortable or optimistic about the prospects of political change through the Constitution, and he was by 1859 so disillusioned that he thought seriously about his own expatriation.[2]

For Douglass, as for most black Americans, the Civil War was from its outset going to be the crucial test of the Union. Not a test of the Union as Abraham Lincoln wanted it to be, but a test of whether the United States could *become* a free society—for the first time. Douglass saw the war as revolutionary in character, forcing a grudging and reluctant nation to confront the slavery issue and to end it. However Lincoln might have wanted it to be, Douglass (and all thinking black Americans) understood that a Union victory had to be an abolitionist victory; because war, itself, is radically transforming, because the Union would have to rely on black troops (many of them refugees from slavery) to defeat the Confederacy. Emancipation became a way (perhaps the only way) for the Union to win the war.

Frederick Douglass, like most Afro-Americans, saw the Union victory as not only the end of slavery but also the establishment of a *new national era.*[3] Not only was the South (the most recent and strongest advocates of states' rights) defeated, but also the Constitution itself was changed. The Thirteenth Amendment gave national authority to abolish slavery and involuntary servitude, challenging even the lingering "badges

1. Cf. footnote 8 below.
2. Remarkable because Douglass had always been the most powerful and consistent critic of those who advocated expatriation or colonization.
3. The "New National Era" was to be the title of the paper Douglass would edit in the post-war years.

of servitude." The Fourteenth Amendment for the first time in the Constitution defined citizenship in the United States, denying states the right to those aspects of sovereignty which recognize (or refuse to recognize) citizenship status. That amendment seemed to have given the federal government and Congress the power to guarantee equal rights and equal protection to all citizens. The Fifteenth Amendment, in another federal limit to state authority, took from states the right to deny a citizen the right to vote because of "race, color, or previous condition of servitude." It was reasonable, on the face of it, to believe that a new national union had been created in the aftermath of the war. That new nation would have the power to protect and guarantee the citizenship rights of all, reaching over states when necessary.

Those like Douglass who optimistically believed so (or hoped so), however, would be sorely disappointed. Surely as far as race was concerned, Congress would be made impotent once again by a Supreme Court intent on keeping federalism alive and negating. The Court's reading of the Constitution well into the twentieth century would be narrow and restrictive as it was asked to disallow the establishment in law and practice of white supremacy and racist totalitarianism. Blacks would have reason, once again, to raise the question of whether the document, from its framing, did not invite and support such restrictive and exclusionary results.

II. Constitution—Restrictive and Exclusionary

The Declaration of Independence addresses "mankind" and speaks of and for the "rights of man," all men. It is thus an inclusive instrument, proclaiming that the principles on which it stands derive from natural law and are thus universal. Thomas Jefferson's private beliefs about black Americans and Native Americans, notwithstanding, he did not inscribe doubts, limits, or exceptions in the document. The sweeping character of the claims in the Declaration would, in time, embarrass many Americans (including Jefferson and, later, John C. Calhoun) who could not fail to see the contradiction between those lofty principles and the reality of racial slavery in the United States.

The Constitution's only claim to inclusiveness is in its first phrase: "We the people of the United States. . . ." That language is unclear, however. One might assume, given eighteenth-century Enlightenment rhetoric, that "people" meant everyone who inhabited the United States. More likely, the meaning would be closer to the French *le peuple,* than to *les gens.* "People," in this sense, are the legitimate and legitimizing folk, those who have authority to establish government, and from whom government derives its powers. The pronoun "We" supports that reading. For, who are "We"?

Although a plural pronoun, "we" is both personal and exclusive. It is personal in that it identifies the self (the speaker) at the center of those who make up the subject. It is exclusive in that it assumes or understands there to be a "thou," not within the subject. To say "we" is, at the same time, to say "not you," and "not they." Unquestionably, "We the people of the United States" includes the authors, the framers, and their constituencies, but who is excluded?

The language in Article I: Section 2 is to the point.

> Representation and taxes shall be apportioned . . . according to their respective numbers, which shall be determined by adding the whole number of free persons, including those bound to service for a term of years, and excluding Indians not taxed, three fifths of all other persons.

"We the people" is here defined. The people include all free persons, even those bound by indenture. The people does not include untaxed Indians and "other persons." We know those other persons to be slaves, considered only for purposes of apportionment for representation and taxation. Here, as elsewhere in the document, slaves are merely alluded to, never identified or referred to by direct language. Slaves, thus, are excluded not only as ordinary persons, but they are also excluded from the language of the Constitution.

Slaves, though not necessarily all black people, fell into the category of "other persons," not among "We, the people." It is a matter of historical fact that there were free blacks in both the North and the South who might, lacking other evidence, have been accepted among the "we." Race, as such, was not in the framers' minds a category worthy of distinction or of special mention. As we will see, by the mid-nineteenth century, a racial as well as a status distinction would be inferred from "other persons" by the Supreme Court.

III. The Constitution, a Legitimizing and Centralizing Document

For the American people, as well as the American nation, the Constitution is a legitimizing document. We are distinctive, both as a people and as a nation, in that we were founded—created, established—within memorable history. The Constitution is like a written covenant which establishes the fact of our being.

Traditional peoples are established out of the fullness of time, beyond memory or even history. Their origins are told in myth and folklore, out of the reach of historical calculation and judgment. They are a people because of the land they stand on, because of the land from which their common ancestor migrated, because they are linked by shared mystery and music and tongue.

In contrast, America[4] and Americans came into being owing to delib-

---

4. I am obviously referring to the United States. I do not intend to imply that America and Native Americans did not exist before the European migrations.

erate acts of statecraft, and we have a document to prove it. The opening line of Robert Frost's "A Gift Outright" captures the sense of it:

> The land was ours before we were the land's.

Our legitimacy had to be established by a formal, political instrument rather than from traditional birthright claims. And that document speaks in the name of "We, the people."

The nation's motto, *E Pluribus Unum,* reflects another aspect of the matter. It has sometimes been taken, as a Federalist's avowal, to mean one nation out of several states. More generally, however, and from the eighteenth century—Tom Paine, Samuel Adams, Walt Whitman, Frederick Douglass—Americans have understood it to mean one people out of many. That was Walt Whitman's, Frederick Douglass's, and W. E. B. Du Bois's meaning in their phrase, "a nation of nations."

There is, however, a problem in that. For *E Pluribus Unum* implies original parts—original peoples—whose legitimacy (or identity) derives a priori from the act of union. The act of union denies the many in creating the one. The motto—like pluralism itself—is at once nation building and nation destroying. It creates one nation at the expense of the many.

The major political and social struggles marking American history have been fights to exclude or to include, more or less, into the pronoun "we," into "the [legitimate and legitimated] people." Thus seen, the Constitution is a centering document. That is to say, it provides the norm and the standard of peoplehood in the nation. Those who are comfortably included in the "We" see themselves as legitimized and authorized by it. They are the norm against which all others are measured; all others become marginalized thereby.

The history of the Afro-American people can thus be seen as persistent appeals and claims to inclusion into the Constitution's "people." Blacks have wanted the custodians of constitutional interpretation to recognize Afro-American birthright in fact as well as in principle. That means being taken into account, not studiously ignored as in the framers' tortured language: "other persons" for slaves,[5] and "the migration and importation of such persons" for the slave trade.[6]

The first full statement of the problem came in *Dred Scott v. Sandford* (1857). Chief Justice Roger Taney's majority opinion in that case was, in fact, a political decision designed to reclaim the center for the South and slaveholders. As early as the Northwest Ordinance of 1787, there was strong evidence that the future of the United States (as reflected in the development of new territory) was to be inhospitable to slavery. Article 6 of the Ordinance prohibited slavery and involuntary servitude in the Northwest Territories. That same sentiment was echoed,

5. Article I, section 2.
6. Article I, section 9.

albeit in modified form, in the compromises of 1820 and 1850 in which it had been assumed that slavery could be restricted from some territories. It was of little consequence that these restrictions be obtained by geographical division as in the Missouri Compromise or by popular sovereignty as introduced in the Compromise of 1850. The principle that slaveholders and the South could not share fully in the nation's future growth was marginalizing to the South and slaveholding interests.

The center was being politically pre-empted by the North and the West. The Free Soil party and the emerging Republican party intended to define the nation's future in terms of free farming and free labor, relegating the slave South to the backwash of American progress.

From Chief Justice Taney's point of view (and from the point of view of the South), the most important part of the Dred Scott decision was the flat and unequivocal rejection of the assumption that slavery could be restricted from any part of the United States.[7] It disallowed in one stroke the Compromise of 1820 and much of the Compromise of 1850. It remained open to debate whether settlers through popular vote could exclude slavery from their territory.[8] Taney's decision recentered the South and slavery while incidentally formalizing the marginalization of Afro-Americans.

What concerned black Americans at the time, and what should concern us now, is that Taney's decision denied citizenship or even personhood to those of African descent. In 1788–89, there were a number of African-Americans who did not fall under the catch-all, "all other persons." They were free men and women, both in the South and the North. Taney, for the first time in constitutional interpretation, read blanket racial qualifications for citizenship, for inclusion into the "we." The force of the decision fell on free blacks only. None would have assumed slaves to have been considered citizens under the Constitution. After all, that document had already dismissed them as "other."

Taney lumped all African Americans together as a degraded race, saying, in effect, that the Constitution had established a white man's country. All black Americans were part of a degraded class who "had been a race subjugated by the dominant race, and whether emancipated or not, remained subject to their authority." In the Court's view, the framers could not have intended to include Afro-Americans in the polity because, at the time, they "had no rights which the white man was bound to respect." The Chief Justice, writing for the Court's majority, read the Court's own views on race into the intentions of the framers.

---

7. Don E. Fehrenbacher, *The Dred Scott Case: Its Significance in American Law and Politics* (New York: Oxford University Press, 1978).

8. An issue taken up in the Lincoln-Douglas debates resulting in Douglas's Freeport Doctrine in which Douglas held that a majority would have to take positive action in passing laws supporting slavery for it to exist, e.g., a de facto popular sovereignty. Freeport, Illinois, 27 August 1858.

Not only did they exclude black Americans from citizenship but also from the protection given to *persons* under the Constitution.

As a political decision, *Dred Scott* was merely an early salvo in the struggle between the North and South over the definition and dominance of the nation's future. As a historical document, as a reading of the Constitution, however, it succeeded in reading into that document the social and racial assumptions of white political and judicial leadership of the 1850s, not the 1780s. It should be noted that while several of the justices wrote independent opinions, taking issue with one or another point of Taney's decision, only two justices expressed themselves in opposition to Taney's views on Afro-American citizenship.

The war which ensued ended in a northern victory and a series of constitutional amendments designed to settle the question of race and servitude that had been raised by Taney.

Thirteenth Amendment
Neither slavery nor involuntary servitude, except as a punishment for a crime whereof the party shall have been duly convicted, shall exist within the United States, or any place subject to their jurisdiction.

Slavery was ended, and the former slaves became free men and women. The problem was not only a legal status as chattel or free. The Reconstruction Congress understood that, as had Roger Taney in his own way. He had written in *Dred Scott* that black Americans had become "a subordinate and inferior class of beings . . . [with] deep and enduring marks of inferiority and degradation." From ratification of the Thirteenth Amendment, many argued that Congress was authorized by it to enact laws to eradicate the "badges of servitude" as well as slavery itself. Early on, the Supreme Court accepted this view but withdrew from it in the 1880s.[9]

Fourteenth Amendment
Section 1. All persons born or naturalized in the United States, and subject to the jurisdiction thereof, are citizens of the United States and of the State wherein they reside. No State shall make or enforce any law which shall abridge the privileges or immunities of citizens of the United States; nor shall any State deprive any person of life, liberty, or property, without due process of law; nor deny to any person within its jurisdiction the equal protection of the laws.

Here, for the first time in the Constitution, citizenship was defined, and it was defined deliberately to include African Americans. The federal government, furthermore, was empowered, indeed obliged, to guard the rights of its citizens.

9. The Court reverted to the original view by the late 1960s. In *Jones v. Alfred H. Mayer Co.* (1968), the Court was willing to say that racial discrimination was the sort of "badge of servitude" that Congress could prohibit.

Fifteenth Amendment
The right of citizens of the United States to vote shall not be denied or
abridged by the United States or by any State on account of race, color,
or previous condition of servitude.

This was not a positive grant of the franchise to citizens, nor was it a
removal from the states their authority and responsibility to regulate and
stipulate the requirements for voting. It merely denied states the right to
restrict the franchise on the ground of race, color, or previous condition
of servitude.[10]

These amendments would seem to have centered black Americans
by (1) recognizing their existence within the Constitution. No longer
"other persons," and no longer described in Court opinions as a degraded class, race was in the Constitution but as a protection and affirma-
tion of black citizenship; (2) by denying the legitimacy of racial or class
distinctions; and (3) by committing the federal government to protect
and defend the citizenship rights of Afro-Americans.

IV. Federalism: A New National Era?

Frederick Douglass and other abolitionists imagined that the Civil War
had ended forever any question regarding supremacy of the federal over
the state governments. The federal order established under the Constitution left areas of authority and power unclear. Dual sovereignty allowed
the evasion of problems wherever there could be uncertainty. The more
difficult, the more fundamental the problem, the more likely no
government—state or federal—would address it squarely.

So with slavery. The political leadership in slaveholding states was
committed to the defense and preservation of slavery. It was to the
political interests of the owners of slaves to see the developing West
open to slavery. One could not, therefore, expect those states to address
or reform their peculiar institution. Those who saw slavery as a serious
problem for the nation's future were located in states where there were
no slaves, and the federal government—except for its power to regulate
interstate commerce, its governance of the District of Columbia, and its
involvement in the return of fugitive slaves—had no clear authority to
address the issue of slavery.

In the antebellum period, Congress was divided just like the nation,
and it could not be persuaded to address slavery forthrightly even where
it had authority. Congress did have the power under the Constitution to
regulate the interstate slave trade, and any effective prohibition of interstate slave traffic would have been damaging, if not crippling, to the
institution. It never chose to exercise that power. On the other hand, the
federal government's right to legislate to aid in the return of fugitive

10. States could and would discover ways of restricting the vote through taxes and
literacy tests, the administration of which had the effect of racial disenfranchisement.

slaves who had crossed state lines was at least questionable. Congress, nevertheless, did enact fugitive slave laws.[11]

To Frederick Douglass, a nation which could not act on matters crucial to its character and survival was hardly a nation at all. With the war's end and the passage of Reconstruction amendments, he thought all that was changed. He was quick to call the post-war years "the national era," signaling the character of that change.[12] Now the federal government could act to assure the liberty and the quality of citizenship of its people, black and white. And now there could be no doubt in his mind that African Americans were part of the "we," part of the legitimizing *people*.

V. Post-Reconstruction

The question remained whether by the reconstruction amendments the federal government had been empowered to guarantee the civil rights of black Americans against not only state action but against the fallout from an atmosphere of general racial hostility. Douglass believed that to have been Congress's real intent on framing and adopting those amendments, and he could not imagine there to be much doubt about it. However, he hoped for too much. He would live to see a conservative Supreme Court sharply rein in Congress and narrowly limit the Reconstruction amendments as they affected the civil rights of Afro-Americans.

In 1883 the Court decided five cases stemming from the enforcement of the Civil Rights Act of 1875. Assuming it had the power from the Fourteenth Amendment, Congress included in this legislation prohibitions against racial discrimination in places of public accommodation. The cases involved innkeepers, theater owners, and a railroad company. The Court, however, saw the Fourteenth Amendment as prohibiting only state action. Justice Joseph Bradley chose to read the language of the Amendment narrowly, denying any implication that Congress had been empowered to enforce more than the prohibition against a state action which might be discriminatory. Nor did he entertain the thought that places of public accommodation such as inns,[13] theaters, and public carriers such as railroads,[14] operating under the aegis of state authority, were clothed with public interest. For Bradley, writing for an eight-to-one majority, the Civil Rights Act was merely an invasion of local law by

11. The fugitive slave laws operated on *private individuals* (as would the Civil Rights Act of 1875), and they were based on Article 4, section 2, paragraph 3 that did not, in fact, empower Congress to legislate. The clause merely provided that a fugitive slave be delivered up upon the claim of his owner, yet the Supreme Court sustained the acts of 1793 (*Prigg v. Pennsylvania,* 1842) and 1850 (*Ableman v. Booth,* 1859) but would deny Congress such power for the Civil Rights Act of 1875 (*Civil Rights Cases,* 1883).

12. In 1870, Douglass acquired ownership of a paper—*The New Era*—which he would edit, significantly under a new name, *The New National Era.*

13. Obliged under ancient common law to serve the wayfarer.

14. Each requiring licenses from the state.

the national government and contrary to the "reserved powers" of the Tenth Amendment.

The Court ruled in the *Civil Rights Cases* that the complaints were of acts by individuals against individuals. That was, Bradley claimed, outside the reach of Congress. Only when the state acts adversely to the rights of citizens could Congress act. For the Court, racial discrimination was something of a social more, a custom, and not a "badge of slavery."

Justice John Marshall Harlan wrote a sharp dissent. He argued that the Fourteenth Amendment established a national citizenship, and its intent was to assure that freedmen would have the same rights as white men. The act of 1875 was aimed at erasing assumptions of inferiority. For Harlan, individuals and corporations do, under certain circumstances, exercise the power and authority of the state. Common law had since ancient times considered highways (railroads) and inns quasi public and thus not strictly a private interest or property. For Harlan, they were clothed in public interest and their actions, therefore, could be seen as extensions of state action.

It was clear enough to Harlan, as it should be clear to us, that principles and theoretical constructions of federalism were only an excuse by the Court to deny to Congress and the federal government power to do what the Court's majority did not want done. Harlan pointed out that federalism had not prevented the Court from supporting congressional acts which protected slavery. There had been no expressed power in the Constitution giving Congress the power to legislate for the return of fugitive slaves. It did so legislate, and the Court approved it as an "implied power."[15]

The *Civil Rights Cases* returned ambiguity to the citizenship status of African Americans. While black Americans were included in "We the People," *le peuple* were viewed by the Court through bifocal lenses. Echoing Taney in *Dred Scott,* the Court now recognized a dual citizenship: one was a citizen of the United States and a citizen of the state wherein one resided. One had certain rights and privileges as a citizen of the United States, and they could not be abridged by the action of any state. As a citizen of a state, however, one was unprotected in one's private associations with other individuals except to the extent the state was willing to act. For black Americans residing in former slave states, that was in effect a major qualification to the substance of citizenship. As long as racial discrimination could avoid blatant and evident state action, neither the Congress nor the Court could be expected to act.

Contrary to Douglass's hopes, the late nineteenth century would see a *new federalism* rather than a *new nationalism*. It was, in effect, to hold individuals at arm's length from the government of the United States. That meant for Afro-Americans another kind of exclusion.

Thirteen years after the *Civil Rights Cases* the Court took up the

15. Cf. footnote 8.

challenge of a Louisiana statute ordering segregation in *intra-state* transportation brought by a mulatto named Homer A. Plessy. Here was state action, pure and simple, but the question was whether a state could determine racial segregation to be in the public good. Justice Henry Brown chose also to question whether racial segregation was in fact actually discriminatory.

Brown found little trouble with either question. He found the statute a reasonable use of the state's police power and "not for the annoyance or oppression of a particular class." It was an exercise of police power to prevent threats to public peace by the "commingling of the races." Brown and the Court assumed that the racial assumptions of the white majority, and the racial etiquette imposed by them, were such deeply ingrained social mores that they could not be reached by legislation. Reasonableness, according to Brown, must be determined with reference "to the established usages, customs and traditions" of *the people* of the state. The Court seemed not to imagine that "the people" of the state were black people as well as white people. The people, the norm, the standard had once again become white people.

The Court assumed the naturalness of separation owing to what it referred to as "racial instincts." Legislation was futile against passions and feelings of such inherent character. Equal rights, it concluded, could not be gained by "enforced commingling."

The Court's majority found a suitable formula in Lemuel Shaw's separate-but-equal doctrine.[16] The principle was that there was nothing discriminatory in segregation, per se. As long as facilities were equal, they could be separate. Justice Harlan, again in lone dissent, argued that such statutes codified practices which were badges of slavery, and the majority decision permitted "the seeds of race hate to be planted under the sanction of law." The argument that prejudice could not be legislated away overlooked the extent to which prejudice had been legislated into existence by such statutes.

Aside from the famous doctrine enunciated in *Plessy,* and the peculiar sociological and psychological assumptions on which the majority decision rested, it is notable that black Americans were not taken into account as people, subjects, or citizens. It was curious, to say the least, for Brown to argue state-imposed segregation did not "necessarily imply the inferiority of either race to the other," followed by the denial that "the enforced separation of the two races stamps the colored race with a badge of inferiority. If this be so, it is not by reason of anything found in the act, but solely because the colored races chooses to put that construction on it." Even if that were true, a significant portion of the citizenry deserves to have their construction taken into account. Otherwise, they themselves are not taken into account.

Plessy cleared the way for separation of the races in all places of

16. *Roberts v. Boston* (1851).

public accommodation, and as Justice Harlan predicted, it gave the sanction of the Court to practices of racial discrimination which conveyed the badge of servitude and inferiority for over half a century. From 1896 to *Brown v. Board of Education* in 1954, advocates of the civil rights of Afro-Americans kept cutting away at the racial partition that was erected in *Plessy*. They would be successful in individual cases, but their victories touched only the surface and not the substance of the doctrine.

In case after case, plaintiffs were able to show that equality was not achieved in particular instances or applications of racial separation. In the 1930s and 1940s, cases having to do with graduate schools and law schools pushed the tests of equality beyond the mere fact of separate facilities. A quickly made up law school for Afro-Americans in Texas could not be equal to that of the University of Texas with its numerous and celebrated faculty, its large library, its students, etc. To duplicate such an institution in quality would, if even possible, be unbearably expensive. During these years, neither the Court nor the attorneys for black plaintiffs addressed the central assumption of *Plessy:* that state-imposed racial segregation was discriminatory in nature and adversely affected one part of the population.

The importance of *Brown* is that it was that precise question which the Court addressed and answered, nullifying the separate-but-equal doctrine.[17] Significantly, it did so by taking into account—as far as the best social science could inform them on the subject—the psychological and social effects of racial segregation on black children. The Court, in fact, cited the sources for its judgment in these matters in its famous footnote 11, which has become the target of most critics of the decision.[18] In *Plessy,* Justice Brown could write that if the "enforced separation of the two races stamps the colored race with a badge of inferiority . . . it is not by reason of anything found in the act, but solely because the colored race chooses to put that construction on it." In *Brown,* Chief Justice Earl Warren could write, based on his understanding of the psychological consequences of state-imposed segregation, that it negatively affected the "hearts and minds" of black children.

Beyond the matter of school segregation itself, the most important change that *Brown* marked was the deliberate and conscious taking into account of black people, the negative impact of certain public policy on

17. The Court did so without actually declaring *Plessy* null and void.

18. Critics complain about the court's use of social science evidence in this decision to support its conclusions that racial segregation had a negative effect on black children. Courts had previously taken racial domination as a fact, justifying legislation against blacks. Taney, in *Dred Scott,* considered blacks a degraded class who "had been subjugated by the dominant race, and, whether emancipated or not, yet remained subject to their authority." He would have had no doubt but that such domination and subjugation would have an effect on blacks. Brown, in *Plessy,* merely accepted what he viewed as racial convention and ignored the effect on blacks of the official endorsement of those practices.

them. Whereas Justice Brown, in *Plessy,* would say it's only in their minds, Warren, in *Brown,* would say that because it's in their minds, we must change these practices.

That was a major step in American constitutional history as far as "We, the People" is concerned. *Brown* makes Afro-Americans a part of "We, the People" such as they had never before been. The government and the Court would henceforth be obliged to take the realities of race into account as the founding fathers failed to do.

16

Ethnic Americans

First: the subtitle of *Ethnic America: A History,* by Thomas Sowell, should be *A Comparison*. It assumes that ethnic groups in America can be compared, one with another, better to understand why some succeed well and others not at all. It imagines the American social economy to be something of a variable escalator, each immigrant group climbing on at a given point in history, but each rising at a rate determined by its peculiar characters and circumstance. The normative experience in America, as Thomas Sowell sees it, is upward mobility, and those groups which have failed to achieve are victims of some social, psychological, or cultural pathology that has ill-equipped them for the struggle and opportunities of American life. William Graham Sumner's "The Drunk deserves his ditch" describes well Sowell's point of view. In any case, *"A History"* this is not, for reasons I will address further on.

A more cautious mind would hardly have ventured into a thicket of ethnic comparisons. Not merely because it is bound to raise hackles (as it surely will), but because the effort itself is so problematic. Sowell takes on nine groups (Irish, Germans, Jews, Italians, Chinese, Japanese, Afro-Americans, Puerto Ricans, and Mexicans). Not only are they widely different in culture, but each arrived at a different point in American history—each moment having its own demands and limitations—and each met a different character of resistance to its efforts at achievement. Unless one is prepared to do exhaustive and careful work on each group—which Sowell has not done—the result is bound to be merely invidious comparison. This book is certainly that. There are only slight attempts to disguise its judgmental character. Sowell is in awe of the Jews, the Japanese, the Chinese. He is mildly approving of the Germans and the Italians, downright disdainful of the Irish, patronizing to blacks, and vaguely confused about Puerto Ricans and Mexicans. The message is clear: there is something exemplary in the Jews, Japanese, and Chi-

*This article is reprinted from *The Yale Review*. Copyright © 1982 Yale University Press.

nese, and it would be well—especially for blacks—to find out what it is and follow, follow, follow.

The social changes beginning in the 1950s—heightening ethnic consciousness in the 1960s—have made such comparisons irresistible. They have become popular, vulgar exercises permitting even the most heady intellectual to indulge prejudices about his pet incompetent ethnic. The favorite target is blacks, because it would seem that despite all their "demands" and significant legislative and judicial victories, and despite some modest "improvement" in the black middle class, the great bulk of the black population has not moved upward and seems more than likely to move *down*. How long, it is asked, must society pay for the inequities of slavery? When will blacks stop blaming their failures on history and society and take responsibility (as everyone else has had to) for their own destiny? Are not blacks, somehow, responsible for their own plight? Are not all ethnic tubs really on their own bottoms, and rightly so?

These questions are the subtext of Thomas Sowell's book, and they are the kinds of questions which are answered in the asking. Since all groups have suffered, all have had barriers to overcome. Some have made it, some not. It is time, therefore, for blacks to stop *demanding* social justice and start *earning* it. Abandon the welfare mentality, the dependency on public support, the assumption of "entitlements," the self-deprecation and self-destruction that comes from giving over to the state and to society one's destiny, and assume responsibility for oneself. That is Sowell's message to his people. Compete and win. There are models to follow.

Before we reject this argument as insensible or insincere, we must accept a kind of validity in it. One can call on society only so long, and only to a limited extent, to rectify historical or cosmic injustice. The most tolerant and sympathetic grow tired in due time, and few are willing to give in a shrinking economy when the job that is given may be one's own. For tactical reasons it might be wise for blacks to sing a new tune. Certainly lasting success will more likely come from group cohesion and economic power than from moral suasion. If, however, one takes it more seriously than that—as Thomas Sowell does—if one believes he has discovered some profound social truth by denying the distinction between racism and bigotry and by rejecting racial discrimination as a significant economic factor, then one has been maddened by too much learning, blinded to the distinctions between theory and life.

This effort to treat blacks as just another group of immigrant ethnics dates back to the late 1950s, when thinkers like Oscar Handlin, Irving Kristol, and Nathan Glazer argued that blacks were merely the last of the immigrants into urban industrial America. Their struggle was similar to the struggle of all immigrant groups, and one could expect that blacks, too, would in time move into the economic mainstream as the others had. It was to say there was nothing unusual about blacks having a disproportionately small share of society's wealth. Time and the system would be fair, and no extraordinary or heroic public effort need be exerted in their behalf. Nor, it would seem, should society feel any special remorse at their plight. Bizarre and tortured comparison as that analysis was, it continues to serve dogma, and so it is useful to those of conservative persuasion.

There are several reasons the comparison is inappropriate for twentieth-century blacks. In the first place, blacks had been willing competitors in northern cities throughout the nineteenth century, much before the massive migration began. Theirs was not an experience of moving, in the course of time, up the economic scale. It was much more characteristic that their jobs and positions would be lost at the slightest challenge from white competition, whether immigrant or native. Second, blacks as presumptive citizens were seen as a threat to conventional political order (white men's rule) as the immigrants were not. The anxieties arising from this concern explain the vigilante control of blacks in the South and the riots and racial upheaval on their arrival in the North. Finally, blacks were a native population, at home in America even when they moved to a different region of the country. They were Protestant and English-speaking, sharing more of the culture of the Anglo-Saxon majority than any of the newcomers. They had historic claims to birthright citizenship; they were an *alienated* population, not an *alien* one.

It is this last question, that of birthright, that makes all the difference in attitude between immigrants and the native born. It has been, historically, the highest priority for Afro-Americans, often taking precedence over matters more strictly economic. It is in these terms that one should consider the much-discussed dispute between W. E. B. Du Bois and Booker T. Washington. Washington was willing to defer birthright considerations at least for a generation, trusting in the ultimate fairness of the economic system to reward efficiency and production. Du Bois, on the other hand, while not denying the importance of black self-help, insisted that the rights of citizenship were paramount for self-respect and dignity. Thomas Sowell leaves little doubt that his sentiments are on the Washington side of the question. Sowell, like Washington, has unqualified faith in the "market" to reward the most productive and efficient person, discounting in the course of time all factors—such as racial prejudice—which have nothing to do with making a better product cheaper. Because of Washington's enigmatic and duplicitous character, it is impossible to know whether he really believed what he preached or merely thought it expedient. He nevertheless urged southern blacks to learn agricultural and artisan skills which, whatever else might be said, ill prepared his students for the industrial world where such skills were outmoded.

The claim to birthright is a powerful and compelling incentive, impossible to factor into economic models. Yet it explains a great deal, such as why much black reform effort has gone into symbolic rather than substantive change; why blacks have found it difficult to form class alliances with immigrant workers; why blacks have rarely challenged the system. It is birthright which explains the power of the desegregation issue. Few blacks would deny the possibility of superior black schools. No one knowing the universally inferior Boston public schools could believe that poorly educated black kids were improved by mingling with poorly educated Irish kids in South Boston. To accept segregation, however, even if one were to achieve a separate-but-equal reality, would be to deny a historic claim to being sharing partners in the commonwealth. This claim has not always resulted in rational strategies and priorities, but it has been essential to the Afro-American experience and will doubtless continue so.

Immigrants have not borne that particular emotional burden. Their birthright claims—their alienation and wounds of separation—remain with the old country, not America, their host. This is not to deny real barriers and discrimination against them, but as aliens they are free from deeply emotional and historic association with such treatment. This difference helps explain Sowell's observation that West Indian blacks have been much more successful than native Afro-Americans. Success is not "in their blood" or genes; West Indians are not notable achievers on the islands. Why in the United States? It has I think to do with the selective and liberating force of immigration. At the same time, West Indian immigrants to Great Britain have not made similarly dramatic strides. As "British subjects," these black men and women carry to England birthright claims not appropriate in the United States.

If native blacks are to be compared to any group of Americans, it should be to native Anglo-Saxons, a group which Sowell does not discuss. When blacks moved to the northern cities in waves cresting around the two world wars, they were not "newcomers," the latest group of immigrants. Rather, they were akin in this in-migration to Okies and migrants from the Appalachians. All were impoverished, all forced by economic circumstance to leave the land on which they had eked out subsistence, all drawn by a promised opportunity in another part of *their* country. In what Sowell calls "human capital," they were not much different. How did they fare? Sowell does not tell us.

Let us take the American "Class of 1810," two years after the official close of the African slave trade. If we were to consider the accumulated American population to date, we would have the bulk of the "seed" Anglo-Saxon population and practically all that would sire Afro-Americans until the twentieth century. Were there some accounting technique to weigh out the advantages and disadvantages of freedom and slavery—the ability to accumulate property and capital as against the fate of being used as capital—my hunch is that the progeny of those blacks would not compare unfavorably with their Anglo-Saxon counterparts. There would be a significant gap, certainly, between the parallel trajectories of black and Anglo-Saxon careers, but the slope would be about the same. After the first great spurt of accumulation and achievement, there was a leveling off of the native-born. By the 1840s there were growing complaints of loss of status, what some have called downward mobility.

The point is that the native population—white or black—does not compare well to most immigrant groups in the terms of Sowell's measures. In fact, in one of his tables indicating relative family income, Anglo-Saxons rank just above the Irish and well below Jews, Japanese, Polish, Chinese, and Italians. All of which is to say that there are better ways to think about this problem, and the task Sowell set for himself is far more protean and problematic than he pretends.

Were his clumsy comparisons merely innocent intellectual parlor games they would be bad enough, but because he is a social scientist of high repute Sowell's work has a pernicious influence. He invites bigotry and pandering in stereotypes. Indeed, he is himself promiscuous.

He is clearly disappointed in the Irish. They came with advantages over other immigrants. They spoke English. Except for their Catholicism, they were culturally close to Anglo-Americans. They had organizational and political skills. They were white, for what that was worth. The Irish, nonetheless, have not done so well on Sowell's scales. He is at great pains to explain this "failure," and it comes down to certain character traits. They drink a lot: "Ireland produced some of the finest whiskey in the world, and the economic and social climate produced ample reasons for drinking it." They were not industrious: "the 'laziness' or 'improvidence' of the Irish became a familiar refrain among contemporaries in Ireland—and later in America—and among sympathizers as well as critics, both scholarly and popular. The point is not to assign blame but to recognize a factor that was to have continuing influence." They crowded into cities because American farming was "foreign to the gregarious Irish." Their poor hygiene and lack of discipline made them disproportionately subject to diseases like cholera and tuberculosis, to crime and disorderly behavior, and to a "high rate of insanity." Even their unusual political skills resulted in heavy reliance on the public payroll, on party or public bureaucracy.

Sowell's mind works in such stereotypes. He seems willing to accept any generalization which serves his argument. Germans, thus, were disciplined, possessing technical and managerial skills, but given to "jovial, yet orderly" recreations—"hearty and harmless diversions." Italians were closely tied to families, had low rates of alcoholism (they drank wine), were dependable but lacking in initiative. Like all stereotypes, these have some basis in behavior, but Thomas Sowell explains reality in terms of them. Joan Moore, in her *Mexican Americans,* tried to explain the high incidence of fatal automobile accidents among Mexican Americans as owing to their poverty and the decrepit cars they drive. Sowell knows better. He attributes it to the fact that they are "young men in a group that stresses machismo." Take your choice.

For Sowell, nothing succeeds like success, and no group intrigues him more than Jews. They seemed to do everything right. They were industrious, frugal, philanthropic, cohesive, aspiring, temperate, and disciplined. They turned to education and valued culture, but not to a fault. They were responsible citizens, but they did not become dependent on the political process. "Rather than surrender to despair or exhaust themselves in trying to reform others, the Jews found or made their own opportunities." Sowell's chapter on Jews might well be called: "The Jewish Ethic and the Rise of David Levinsky."

Nobody's perfect, and Sowell admits that Jews had one failure: agriculture. Of those few who settled on the land, "all failed financially. Centuries of urban life in Europe lay behind their failure as well as their many successes." But, alas! he is wrong. Just to his north, in Petaluma, California, he can find a number of Jews who have succeeded in poultry farming despite their urban, European past.

He gets quite excited by the figures. While explaining that education was not the reason for the upward mobility of the Jews, Sowell expands:

> As of 1908, 16 percent of Jewish youngsters graduated from high school, and although that was well in excess of such groups as the Irish or Italians, it could hardly explain the rise of the other 84 percent of Jews.

Which means, it would seem, that 100 percent of the Jewish population "rose." That will surprise many.

Similarly, Sowell is loose in using IQ data. He attempts by them to make comparisons within groups (Russian Jews versus German Jews) as well as between a given group and the general population. He never tells us what we are to understand from these comparisons, whether he thinks that intelligence is group determined (cultural or genetic), or, more important, whether there can be *any* meaningful correlation between IQ scores and upward mobility. In fact, our present understanding is that within a quite broad range (and except perhaps for academic and some professional work) there is minimal correlation between IQ scores and successful performance in business and life. Sowell, nevertheless, uses his comparisons as if they were telling and determining facts of ethnic life.

Furthermore, he is uncritical of the data he uses. He continually applies, without comment, the United States Army's intelligence tests of the First World War. We learn, for instance, that Russian Jews "averaged among the lowest mental scores of any of the ethnic groups tested"; or, again, that "Polish Americans had average IQs around 85 during the 1920s . . . but in the 1970s, their IQ level was 109." Whatever these data may *actually* mean, Sowell uses them as an index of upward mobility. The general problems of intelligence testing aside, Sowell seems unaware of the deeply flawed character of the Army tests in particular. They were conceptually problematic in the first place, and they were not

administered in a way that could result in good, reliable data. Nevertheless, he uses them when they serve his argument.

I want, now, to return to my charge that whatever this book is, it is
not *"A History,"* as the subtitle promises. Of course, in a work such as
this, it would be too much to expect research in primary sources. Sowell
is, therefore, dependent on secondary literature. The quality and quantity of that literature varies among these groups, and that explains the
thinness of chapters on Mexican-Americans and Puerto Ricans. It also
explains why two interesting groups, Filipinos and Greeks (both more
numerous than Japanese or Chinese), were not included at all. It is no
crime to rely on secondary material, but Sowell uses it as if he were at a
smorgasbord. He picks and chooses only what he likes, ignoring all the
rest. Consider his treatment of slavery.

Sowell wants slaves to be inefficient, unskilled, unproductive, and
ignorant, so he uses Ulrich B. Phillips as his authority on slave character.
He imagines slave spouses were forcibly separated with "considerable
frequency," and he finds something in Robert Fogel and Stanley Engerman's *Time on the Cross* to support it. He wants slave families to be
stable and autonomous of master definition and domination, and he
turns to Herbert Gutman's *The Black Family in Slavery and Freedom.*
Then he calls upon Eugene Genovese's *Roll, Jordan, Roll* to sustain his
notions that slaves' incompetence caused them to break tools, and that
their coherent slave community inhibited them from informing the master on their fellows.

It does not matter to Sowell that Phillips is possibly the worst authority on slave character he could find, that Fogel and Engerman actually
minimize the number of family breakups and depict slaves as being very
efficient and productive labor (out-producing northern free framers),
that Gutman and Genovese are in deep disagreement about the nature
of the slave family, and that none of the living authorities on slavery he
cites would agree with the picture he draws. Needless to say, these
historians are at odds among themselves. Rather than take such disagree-
ments into account, Sowell uses what he wants from wherever he can
find it. His ideology requires a particular, simple-minded view of history; complexities and contradictions are inconvenient. Shielding himself from the problems, he shields his readers as well. Rather than
writing a history, he has engaged in historical plunder.

Perhaps, however, all these questions are not central to the problem
of this book. They assume a scholarly effort, an intent to produce a work
of balanced and rational discourse. Sowell appears, rather, to be something of an evangelist, a "true believer" who has for some time been
"saved" from any skepticism which might force him to question his
assumptions. Despite the footnotes and other pretensions of scholarship, we have a work of dogma.

We are quick to condemn the doctrinaire determinism of old-line
Marxists, but we are tolerant still of "Marketists" like Sowell, for whom

all social and economic questions are ultimately reducible to equilibrium analysis. The mischief is sobering enough in the daily press, but in such work as this, we find history reshaped and distorted, better to conform to dogma.

It is a vision of life which equates "isness" with "oughtness"; not that life is good for everyone, but that any freeze-frame of social history would find most people with what they deserve, nothing more and nothing less. Preoccupations with reform, social inequities, and so forth are wasteful in energy and result in no improvement because, in the aggregate, one will command no more than the market determines.

Those, like blacks, who have imagined their plight to be owing to a history of discrimination and racial oppression are, according to Sowell, mistaken. Except for slavery, when they were not, strictly speaking, part of the market system, blacks have earned pretty much what the market determined their skills and talents to be worth. Since, as he sees it, the freedmen had almost nothing to offer except the crudest agricultural labor—no managerial, industrial, or entrepreneurial experience—they were, alas, best suited for tenant farming. Relying on Robert Higgs's *Competition and Coercion,* Sowell claims that blacks got as much for their labor as whites doing the same work.

Racial discrimination does not make economic good sense and must, therefore, not exist as a significant economic factor determining a group's status relative to the rest of society. "Translating subjective prejudice into overt economic discrimination is costly for profit-seeking competitive firms." Presumably, if you can produce more efficiently, you will be hired, regardless of race. Sowell does not deny the fact of discrimination: most of the groups in this book have been subject to it—Chinese, Japanese, and Jews, as well as blacks and Hispanics. Since some groups have risen against these obstacles, it is not the barriers which are to blame. Individuals, he says, may be "devastated by discrimination," but that "does not explain the economic condition of the group as a whole."

Typically, Sowell turns to historical authority—this time, W. E. B. Du Bois. Citing Du Bois's sociological study, *The Philadelphia Negro* (1899), Sowell quotes him to the effect that " 'representative Negroes' were . . . 'probably best fitted for the work they are doing,' " and that if prejudice were removed, it " 'would not make very much difference in the positions occupied by Negroes' as a whole, although some few would get new places 'but the masses would remain as they are.' " So, Du Bois is enlisted to support the notion that racial discrimination does not hold the group back.

What Du Bois actually wrote was this:

> Most of them are best fitted for the work they are doing, but a large percentage *deserve better ways to display their talents and better remuneration.* [*The Philadelphia Negro;* my emphasis.]

and:

> Probably a change in public opinion on this point [discrimination] to-
> morrow would not make very much difference in the positions occu-
> pied by Negroes in the city: some few would be promoted, some few
> would get new places—the mass would remain as they are; but it would
> make one vast difference: it would inspire the young to try harder, it
> would stimulate the idle and discouraged and it would take away from
> this race the omnipresent excuse for failure: prejudice.

In 1899, W. E. B. Du Bois understood the matter differently from (and
better than) Thomas Sowell. How sad to see him misread thus.

If the history of the South is an example, Thomas Sowell is right
about one thing: racial discrimination is economically costly. He fails,
however, to appreciate the central fact of that history: Southern whites
were willing to pay those costs to maintain their sense of order. Even if
one accepts Robert Higgs's questionable claim of white-black wage equity in Reconstruction, both whites and blacks suffered, the region depressed, because economic choice was narrowed by preoccupation with
white supremacy.

Northerners, too, were willing to pay the price. Racial discrimination resulted not so much in blacks being paid less than whites, but in
their being narrowly restricted in the work they were hired to do. That is
what Du Bois says in the passage Sowell misreads. It would seem there
was a social taboo against blacks and whites competing in a free market;
it was not blacks who shrank from the opportunity.

Into the mid-twentieth century, the convention of "Negro jobs" removed blacks from competition with whites in the labor market. European immigrants learned the system fast; being white was a privilege.
There was something morally offensive about hiring blacks to do work
that whites were able and willing to do—that is to say free blacks; as
slaves blacks had larger occupational opportunity. Blacks who established themselves in traditional crafts—barbering, catering—and semi-
skilled labor would have to give ground as immigrants and other whites
found those occupations desirable. Studies like Elizabeth Hafkin Pleck's
Black Migration and Poverty, Boston 1865–1900 make clear the narrow
limits of black opportunity in the late nineteenth century. Rather than
expanding, opportunities were shrinking in the face of white immigrant
pressure and racial discrimination. Properly understood, that, too, is the
point of *The Philadelphia Negro.*

Consider the railroads. In the nineteenth century, blacks had worked
on southern railroads in a variety of jobs, including the positions of
brakemen and firemen. They were, in time, excluded from these positions, not because they lacked skills, but because theirs became white
men's jobs. Or, more familiarly, Pullman porters and dining car waiters
(black jobs) commonly did the work of conductors and stewards (white
jobs), but they were never compensated for their work, nor was it thought

possible to appoint blacks to the managerial posts they sometimes were obliged to occupy. Indirectly, the railroads did play an important role in black upward mobility. There is hardly a black professional man in his late fifties or older who has not, at one time, worked as a porter, waiter, or redcap to help put himself through school. But no realistic black man would have seen the railroad—or any similar industry—as providing him an *internal* ladder for upward mobility.

The fact that Thomas Sowell's book is problematic, both conceptually and methodologically, does not diminish the central questions he wishes to raise. Can a history of discrimination (and even oppression) continue to explain a group's limitations in a time when most of the obvious barriers to progress are removed? Is it not possible that a group's preoccupation with its victimization can make its members victims, helpless and dependent? Is it not probable that present economic weakness (among blacks, say) has as much to do with deteriorating institutions—family, church, community—as with a history of racial discrimination? And is not that deterioration exacerbated rather than cured by demands on the public, with expectations of "entitlements"? Is it not probable that the economic and social salvation of members of the so-called underclass will come (if it comes at all) from their discovery within themselves of those virtues of self-help and discipline which have been essential to mobility in America? Is not the leadership, particularly the black leadership, too enthralled with New Deal modes of reform to address these fundamental questions?

We are clearly at a crucial point in public policy, requiring fresh formulations. It is no longer sufficient for black leadership, for instance, to make demands simply on the basis of past inequities and their legacy. It is fair to say that much that we consider reform has benefited mainly the middle class, serving the poor badly.

I believe this was what Thomas Sowell had in mind in writing this book. I believe, further, that his principal interest is that of blacks. It would have been a better book, but by no means a less controversial one, had he taken that as his focus rather than to assume the pretense of social history on such a grand scale.

17

Modernism and
the Harlem Renaissance

The standard judgment is that until the 1940s, Afro-American writers were rather conservative or conventional. One can find Afro-American representatives among the various schools of novelists: realists, like Charles W. Chestnutt, Paul Laurence Dunbar (as novelist), Jessie Fauset, Nella Larsen, Wallace Thurman, Chester Himes; local colorists like Zora Neale Hurston, and Claude McKay (in *Home to Harlem*); naturalists like Richard Wright and Williard Motley. With, perhaps, the single exception of Jean Toomer, no black writer would be considered a "modernist" until Ralph Ellison.

What I wish to suggest is that black writers and artists (with the exception of musicians) had a problematic relationship with the modern. In my book *Harlem Renaissance,* I used the image of provincial vs. metropolitan culture to identify the problem. By that image I wanted to suggest two things: First, American critics and custodians of culture were, in their own self-concept, "provincials" to a European culture. They measured themselves and the work that came before them by what they understood to be a European (most especially English) standard for high culture. Even those who could beat the drum for American culture, like Van Wyck Brooks,[1] were anticipating an American literature and culture which would be distinctive yet measure up to the European. Second, the Afro-American writers and artists stood in a similar relationship as provincials to a metropolitan culture which was defined by those very critics and custodians of culture who looked to Europe for their guide. My point was, of course, that under these circumstances, one could expect little else from Afro-American writers of the 1920s than variations on rather staid conventions.

*This article is reprinted from the German journal *Americana,* Vol. 2, No. 1 (1988).

1. Van Wyck Brooks, *America's Coming of Age* (1915).

That conception and image was another way of addressing the question of modernism and the relationship of the artist to the modern. The *provincial/metropolitan* model has, however, a pejorative implication about which we should be cautious when discussing Harlem Renaissance writers. The mentality which I could describe as provincial also has a special attitude and relationship to "tradition" and the "traditional" which is central to any consideration of the "modern." The provincial mind is obliged to lean on what is seen to be tradition as a guarantee and authentication of standards. The provincial mind is uneasy with the "modern" because it, by definition, departs from tradition, risking and creating new standards.

America and Tradition

America is synonymous with the modern. For Europeans and Africans, it was a "new found land," discovered and its culture created out of the common experiences of uprooting from the "old world," adventure into the "wilderness," and the forced living together of peoples of diverse races and cultures. America has been truly a "New World," where everyone (including Native Americans) has been forced to rupture lines to the past and to tradition. Becoming American is like being "born again," alienated from tradition.

Being modern, however, means a problematic relationship to the past and tradition. "What means America to me?" the Harlem poet Countee Cullen would write. His poem "Heritage" expresses the troubled and ambiguous relationship of the Afro-American to his African past. All Americans might well write similarly about the "old world" traditions from which they came.

American culture is in the present, in the NOW. When Americans are at their best, they are optimistic and have an eye on the future where, they are convinced, every problem can be solved, every trouble transformed. Their energy is also in the present, their challenge to innovate, to re-create, to "make it new." "Make it new" is the shibboleth of the jazz musician, and it is this spirit of immediacy, now-ness, and improvisation which makes jazz the truest and best representation of America.

But Americans are not always at their best. Sometimes the future is bleak and obscure, sometimes they have doubts about their energy and capacity to transform and re-create. Then, in those moments, the NOW is insufficient and they search for roots and heritage. They would like, in such moments of "identity crisis," to find themselves authenticated in an honorable and revered tradition.

This dichotomy, as I pose it, is merely a convenience of speech. In fact, the problem is more complex. Americans are never one without the other, never in the NOW without lurking anxieties about the ground they stand on. The point I wish to make, starkly put, is that once having rejected tradition, Americans have no living tradition out of which to grow and are, therefore, fated either to indifference or to awe.[2] They are thus locked in "modernity" because they have no choice.

We could follow the track of this American ambivalence with its "modern" condition from the seventeenth century. We need not do that here, but it is important to recall that in the years following the First World War, American writers, artists, and critics were in one of the most aggravated episodes of this chronic identity crisis. From the pre-war years there had been a steady erosion of the accepted ground of American arts and letters;[3] an attack on the so-called Genteel Tradition[4] had deprived the custodians of culture of their earlier certitude.

We need to understand that what we call the Harlem Renaissance occurred in the context of the dramatic challenge and change we know to be the 1920s in American literature. The 1920s have been seen as one *Coming of Age* of American letters. We think of the authors Ernest Hemingway, F. Scott Fitzgerald, E. E. Cummings, T. S. Eliot, Ezra Pound, etc., and we immediately understand the magnitude of the challenge and change. Yet, as we look at the novels and poetry produced by black writers of the Harlem Renaissance, we do not see anything like the assertion of the modern that we find in white American writers. We should state the exception in Jean Toomer who, though black, was tied more to Greenwich Village (Waldo Frank and Hart Crane) than to Harlem writers. Toomer's *Cane* (1923) was, and continues to be, an experimental and innovative book and one of the most "modern" of the period. Langston Hughes, in his poetry, attempted to exploit jazz themes and thus depart from conventional poetic voice and diction.

Otherwise, one finds in the poetry and fiction of the Harlem Renaissance not only efforts to work within convention, but, as in the case of Claude McKay's sonnets and Countee Cullen's echoes of Keats, conservative (if not reactionary) form. Often the content of these poems and novels was inappropriate to the gentility of the form. The question, then, is why was not the Harlem Renaissance more centrally a part of the restatement of American modernism in the 1920s?

2. This point of American "exceptionalism" has been made before by Tocqueville, among others. My own argument develops from the political analysis central in Louis Hartz, *The Liberal Tradition* (1955), which explains the failure of a conservative tradition in the United States.

3. See especially Henry F. May, *End of American Innocence* (New York, 1959).

4. Genteel Tradition was defined by the philosopher George Santayana in a lecture at the University of California, Berkeley, in 1916. Santayana understood that tradition to have been rooted in the moral charge of Puritanism and the idealism of Transcendentalism. But, he argued, those sources had attenuated so that the tradition was a mere shell, lacking the emotive or imaginative power of its sources. One might say the fate of modern society is its inability to sustain its own tradition.

Blacks and Modernism

The answer to that question is to be found in the special relationship of blacks to art and culture at the time. In those post-war years, black intellectuals were self-conscious of being only fifty years away from slavery. The history of black people in America had been, from the beginning, under the shadow of doubt as to their humanity, capacity, civility, and culture. The fifty years that followed emancipation merely intensified the challenge by whites and the white society as they erected social and economic barriers to deny them equality and citizenship. For black intellectuals, literacy and culture were to be markers which would prove Afro-American capacity and promise. Thus, blacks' relationship to literature as culture was problematic.

The dilemmas were torturous. Blacks would want to prove themselves as "civilized" through their creation of "high" art, but the white custodians of culture (and white audiences and readers) were reluctant or unwilling to accept Afro-Americans except in stereotypical rôles—the minstrel mask. The easiest path was to work within the stereo type, writing dialect verse like Paul Laurence Dunbar. Editors, like William Dean Howells, were comfortable with such work. But Dunbar saw the challenge of breaking the barrier and the stereotype and writing in standard English, and he remained bitter and frustrated that he was unable to break free.[5] The relevant point is that such a struggle placed an unusual premium on breaking into conventions, on proving oneself in terms of established standards.

The curious self-consciousness about culture and literature by black intellectuals of the period is best expressed by James Weldon Johnson in his "Preface" to *The Book of American Negro Poetry*.[6]

> A people may become great through many means, but there is only one measure by which its greatness is recognized and acknowledged. The final measure of the greatness of all peoples is the amount and standard of the literature and art they have produced. The world does not know that a people is great until that people produces great literature and art. No people that has produced great literature and art has ever been looked upon by the world as distinctly inferior.
>
> The status of the Negro in the United States is more a question of national mental attitude toward the race than of actual conditions. And nothing will do more to change that mental attitude and raise his status than a demonstration of intellectual parity of the Negro through the production of literature and art.[7]

5. For a different point of view on this issue, see Houston Baker, Jr., *Modernism and the Harlem Renaissance* (Chicago, 1988).

6. James Weldon Johnson, ed., *The Book of American Negro Poetry* (New York, 1921 and 1931). Both editions have the same "Preface," deliberately unchanged in the 1931 edition except for commentary with some footnotes.

7. Rpt. in Nathan I. Huggins, ed., *Voices from the Harlem Renaissance* (New York, 1976), pp. 281–304. Quote from p. 281.

In this statement, the burden on the artist and art was clear: it would be the artist and his work which would raise blacks in the estimate of the white world. That, basically, was the problem of race in America. The task was to demonstrate "intellectual parity" through literature and art. Parity, of course, implies a common standard, and that necessarily would have to be a standard drawn from the past. Afro-Americans would have to write poems that looked like, and read like, poems of high quality. Of unusual importance was the *recognition* of the work as art and culture rather than nonsense. That expectation and requirement imposes a conservative constraint. The challenge, here, is not invention, innovation, or "making it new." James Weldon Johnson was asking the black writer and poet, in contrast to the jazz musician, to be a mimic.

The problem, also, was that black intellectuals in the 1920s would not have recognized a black tradition on which to build. All had good words to say for the spiritual and the special qualities of Afro-American music, but the Afro-American past was of slavery and oppression. While one could identify heroes and heroines from that slave past, few would wish to identify a literary or artistic tradition if there was one.

For the Afro-American in the 1920s, being a "New Negro" was being "modern." And being a "New Negro" meant, largely, not being an "Old Negro," disassociating oneself from the symbols and legacy of slavery—being urbane, assertive, militant. Abandoning dialect and the signs of submissiveness in the literature was one way of being a "New Negro." For Dunbar, that had been writing in standard English. It was for James Weldon Johnson the refusal to write in dialect. It was for McKay the rejection of the dialect poems of the *Contab Ballads* for the sonnet. And it was for Cullen to echo the English Romantics. That kind of modernism, however, looks very old hat.

There remained, nevertheless, a desire among some to create a tradition that was Afro-American. If it could not conveniently rest upon an antebellum past, then it could perhaps recross the Atlantic and find its roots in Africa. The desire among Afro-Americans to find themselves a part of an African tradition is of long standing. It, too, has been problematic for a number of reasons, not the least being continued black ambivalence over both European and African culture. In the 1920s, this fascination with Africa is documented by a number of poems: Cullen's "Heritage" is the best known; but there is also Langston Hughes's "Afro-American Fragment":

> So long,
> So far away
> is Africa.
> Not even memories alive
> Save those that history books create,
> Save those that songs
> Beat back into the blood—

Beat out of blood with words sad-sung
In strange un-Negro tongue—
So long, So far away
Is Africa.

Alain Locke, one of the promoters of the Harlem Renaissance, saw possibilities as well as impossibilities in African art. While they might have been the black American's "Ancestral Arts," they were nonetheless foreign and unrelated.

[The] American Negro, even when he confronts the various forms of African art expression with a sense of its ethnic claims upon him, meets them in as alienated and misunderstanding an attitude as the average European Westerner. . . . So there would be little hope of an influence of African art upon the western African descendants if there were not at present a growing influence of African art upon European art in general.[8]

The legacy was nonetheless essential. The mere knowledge of the skill and craft of Africans to dispel the stereotype of them as savages was of value to the Afro-American sense of self. Equally, the realization that the "Negro is not a cultural founding without his own inheritance . . . [could correct their] timid and apologetic imitativeness and overburdening sense of cultural indebtedness."

But what the Negro artist of today has most to gain from the arts of the forefathers is perhaps not cultural inspiration or technical innovation, but the lesson of a classical background, the lesson of discipline, of style, of technical control pushed to the limits of technical mastery.[9]

Both James Weldon Johnson and Alain Locke assumed that the central problem of race in America was one of attitude and reputation. They accepted the notion that art was a primary way in which reputation could be enhanced. Art and culture gained respect for a race and a people. Locke's consideration of Africa and African art weighed more on racial self-respect, while Johnson saw the enhancement of reputation in the eye of the onlooker—the white culture. Both Johnson and Locke, notably, saw tradition and heritage as crucial. Blacks had to prove themselves in terms of a respected tradition of culture. To use Locke's word, blacks needed to show themselves as other than "cultural foundlings."

As I have wanted to stress, it is indeed the character of the "modern" to be a foundling; that is to say, in a problematic relationship to heritage and tradition. In the 1920s, Afro-Americans were struggling with all their might to become accepted and established within a known and respected tradition.

8. Alain Locke, "The Legacy of the Ancestral Arts," in Alain Locke, ed., *The New Negro* (New York, 1925). Quoted in Nathan I. Huggins, *Voices*, p. 137.
9. *Ibid.*, p. 138.

Making It New

Being black and literary in the 1920s was an innovation of a kind to the white American mind. That is why the Harlem Renaissance was considered a remarkable phenomenon outside Afro-American life. White writers and critics, like Carl Van Vechten and H. L. Mencken, doted on their "discoveries" of black writers and poets. The reading public got the idea, making Van Vechten's Harlem novel and Claude McKay's *Home to Harlem* both bestsellers.

For the general American public, the 1920s was the "Jazz Age," as Fitzgerald had named it, and that was defined by jazz, and Harlem, and black people writing poems and stories about themselves—coming of age as it were. From the broad American view, then, Afro-Americans and their literature (regardless of how conventional and conservative it was) was what made America "modern." Some of the Afro-American writers managed to challenge conventions, if not the forms. Those challenges were often in the themes about which they wrote. Claude McKay's second novel, *Banjo* (1929), for instance, breaks conventional form in the novel as well as challenging the moral conventions of the old genteel tradition. Both of Nella Larsen's novels, *Quicksand* (1928) and *Passing* (1929), challenge sexual taboos.[10] Zora Neale Hurston's interest in folklore and folk culture, her implied rejection of the urban, industrial, and scientific suggest that she is other than "modern" in outlook; she fits more closely with those white southern conservatives, "The Fugitives." A little-known poet, Helene Johnson, could break conventions of form, subject, and diction in "Poem."

Breaking the Mold

Two conceptions held black writers of the 1920s within conservative constraints. The first was a view which placed the burden of the race's reputation on art and culture. That view valued demonstration of art and culture within a tradition and, therefore, imitation. Furthermore, it viewed alienation from such a tradition as being a "cultural foundling." The second, and related view was the consciousness of Afro-American writers that their audience was largely white, and that there were expectations one needed to attend. It is clear enough when one considers William Dean Howells's urging Paul Laurence Dunbar to write dialect verse rather than in standard English. The argument was, that was what his readers wanted and would tolerate. The influence of a white audience's expectations are also clear in Claude McKay's *Home to Harlem* and the early writings of Zora Neale Hurston. White "friends" of the Harlem Renaissance like Carl Van Vechten and H. L. Mencken pressed home their notions of audience expectations and tolerance.

10. See Deborah McDowell's "Preface" in her edition of Nella Larsen's *Quicksand and Passing* (1987).

For black writers to break free of these constraints, something in the underlying conception had to change. As early as the 1930s, one sees evidence that the view of culture Johnson and Locke shared had been undermined by the hardships of the Depression and the "social realism" in art that accompanied it. Art as politics, social critique, and weapon replaced the notion of culture as the ground for racial respectability. Black writers like Richard Wright and Chester Himes had no view of themselves or their art as means of improving the reputation of blacks among whites. For Wright at least, a Marxist critique supported a view of Afro-American writing as a galvanizing, race-building, mobilizing, and revolutionary instrument.[11] Accompanying this liberation was the idea that the audience would find the literature, educating itself when necessary to understand it.

The change in both assumptions has been the liberation of Afro-American writers and artists. It has allowed some to move off into "mainstream modernism,"[12] while others have explored the prospects of a black aesthetic.[13] Without this transformation there could have been no Alice Walker or Toni Morrison or Gloria Naylor or John Wideman or Ishmael Reed, to name the most prominent of our contemporary black writers.

Significantly, as we search for the modern in American literature today, unlike the 1920s, we are most apt to define it in terms of some of these writers, the women and the men.

11. Richard Wright, "A Blueprint for Negro Writing," in Huggins, *Voices,* pp. 394–401.

12. By this I refer to the modernism of Eliot and Pound, and in the 1950s that represented by the "New Critics," but also their antagonists, the Beats. On the one hand, one has the poet Melvin Tolson and the novelist Ralph Ellison; on the other hand, one has LeRoi Jones (Imamu Amiri Baraka), William Gibson, etc.

13. Addison Gayle, Jr., ed., *The Black Aesthetic* (New York, 1972). Houston Baker, Jr., continues in this line.

18

American History and the Idea of Common Culture

All history is abstraction, generalizations on human experience. I think none of us would make the mistake of assuming that the history we teach and write about is identical to what happened in the past—the events and experiences themselves. Students and teachers of history have long looked at written history as deliberately selective. The historian chooses his subject, asks what he considers the most crucial and necessary questions, selects his data, and constructs his argument and narrative with an eye toward discriminating between that which he finds compelling and essential and that which appears incidental and of no consequence.

Different moments, we all know, urge different necessities; and in a different time, a different historian will ask different questions, discover significance in data others consider dross, construct different order, and tell a different story.

Generally, those who make these commonplace observations want to remind us of the essentially creative and subjective character of history—at bottom always one of the humanities, even as it borrows heavily from the methodologies and techniques of the social sciences. I wish, instead, to make a different kind of point or, rather, to emphasize a different facet. The necessarily discriminatory character of historical writing and teaching makes the product an abstraction of experience, not the comprehensive experience itself.

History orders and gives meaning to experience *because* it is selective. Of course, it is unthinkable to try to be comprehensive and inclusive, even about the smallest slice of history. There are too many angels on the head of a pin, one might say, to count them all individually. As we give meaning and order to the jumble of the past, we should always be aware that something or, rather, some things are being left out—things

*This lecture was given at the University of California, Berkeley, on September 23, 1987.

that are important and meaningful in themselves and to those who find themselves bound to kindred experiences and destinies. Another kind of historical dispensation may feature what others ignored.

History, then, is in some sense like a road map. It abstracts reality so as to give shape and possible utility. Many towns do not appear on even the best road maps, and it does not really matter to us as we whiz past on the expressway. We can ignore that geographical spot and its inhabitants, all incognito, and we won't lose our way. At the same time, however, we must understand that the place has enormous importance for its residents, who would be lost if they did not exist on their own "maps." Chances are, those town folk see the surrounding territory, their state, the nation, and the world in some sense differently, precisely because they are not "on the map." Part of the argument for our thinking about them as we contemplate the "big picture" is that their view is likely to be a useful distortion of reality divergent from our own.

At the risk of going on too long with this analogy, we should think about how people at different times have conceived of regions of the world as reflected in cartographical representations. We do not have to go too far back into the past to find on contemporary maps vast regions of terra incognita, often thought of as uninhabited. Time, exploration, and knowledge subsequently have filled in those blank spaces with physical characteristics—mountains, rivers, deserts, and even evidence of human habitation. It is important to make conscious note of the obvious: those spaces never were *really* empty except for those who found in them no useful meaning. It is our loss that we are likely never to know what view of the world the inhabitants of those regions had.

Only when we think about the past in this way can we appreciate the chauvinism and ethnocentrism in concepts of discovery. It is more than a clever twist of words to say that Native Americans "discovered" Europeans only when they landed on these shores. If we could understand both attitudes of that process of mutual discovery, we might gain useful insight into a moment of history unavailable to us who have been taught that the only reality was that as perceived by those considered to be our cultural forebears.

This is of capital importance when we think of how American history has been written and taught. We have allowed vast areas to be dismissed as terra incognita. We have imagined that for all practical purposes the continent was empty until the coming of English settlers—American Indians often being confounded with the wilderness. We have essentially dismissed French and Spanish settlement in the "New World"—even on territory which would later become part of the United States—until contact or westward expansion made it necessary to include it in telling the story. Written American history said virtually nothing about Spanish culture in the West and Southwest, not to mention its ignorance of French Louisiana. By now, it is well enough known how African Americans, Asians, Native Americans, and other ethnics and "minorities" have been treated: until the past decade or so, they were "not on the map" of American history. But that is only a small part of the matter. The history we have written, read, and taught has so generally assumed that American history was about New England, New York City, and something generally vague called the South (meaning slavery, plantations, aristocracy, poverty, backwardness, and racism) that we are at a loss to understand regions of our country that are now beginning to determine much of the country's politics and character.

Experience and necessity, however, are determining. Empty spaces in the historical landscape do get filled in when demands of the present—our need to understand our lives, our problems, where we are—compel us to give concrete representation to what we might earlier have dismissed as "not on the map." The reason historians turn their attention to peoples and subjects once ignored is that the problems of our time now demand a knowledge of them. True, some historians may have taken up African-American, Asian-American, Native-American, and other ethnic histories out of a sense of fairness to "victims" of the past; but the reason these studies will continue to have a place (and a growing importance) in American historiography is because we have learned that we must know about them to know anything well. We are told that California in the 1990s will be a "third-world state." If we are to produce good histories of California for that future population, we are going to have to know a lot more than we now do about the experiences of Native Americans, peoples from the Pacific, and immigrants from Mexico, Central America, and the Caribbean Basin. It is not merely because it is a nice thing to let such people learn about themselves, but because no one can understand the territory without such knowledge.

This is an important distinction. Those who wish to argue for American history as "common culture" do not, to my mind, fully understand the new emphasis on ethnic histories. They assume some unfair imbalance in past histories that perhaps needed redressing. "Of course," they say, "blacks should not have been left out of American history. But we have gone far enough now to guarantee them visibility and fair treatment. The danger is that we have gone too far; our history is fragmented. By our focus on the particular, we have lost sight of the whole. What is needed now is to rearticulate those common values that make us all Americans. We need the kind of American history we used to have, that told essentially *one* story to *one* people." The problem is, however, that our social geography is far different from that of two decades ago— spaces we once thought empty are now too insistent and demanding. We do not know enough yet about what fills those spaces to understand fully how they inform our present and future; but we cannot be as complacent in our ignorance as we once were. Understanding what we used to call "our Pilgrim Fathers" has helped us to understand something about America and California; but now we will also need to know a great deal that departs from that tradition.

The history that will best serve the coming generation will be no less an abstraction of the American past than those we have studied and written. What is included, however, will have to give shape and meaning to the past for a population quite different from that of this generation. A shift of focus and emphasis will mean that some values once thought of as dominant will be subordinated to others. Coming generations of Americans are likely to find a reality that discovers meaning and importance more in pluralism than in oneness. The dominant historical questions will naturally reflect that shift even at the cost of presumed "common culture." Those who most fear such a result see it as a loss of national unity and identity. What, after all, is the principal reason for studying national history if not to see oneself as part of a large tradition and order?

The problem raised by the question of "common culture" is really the problem of a national history. If by nature history is an abstraction, national histories are so in a special way. The need to define the nation as a coherent whole obliges one to obliterate or subordinate those particular groups who would lay claim to an independent or an alternative generalization. The nation-state came about by subsuming the many into one; and it succeeds best when individual groups are able to submerge themselves comfortably into the large abstraction of the nation.

This is an implicit problem in United States history. Always a pluralistic nation, we have become more dramatically and divergently so in the late twentieth century. Historians have dealt with the problem in various ways. We thought of the frontier as the Americanizing experience. Significantly, historians discovered the power of the frontier only when it was perceived by some to be closing in the face of rising immigration. Then there was the melting pot—the assumption that the crucible of the American experience would produce an "American" from the polyglot population that streamed to these shores. At no time—certainly not since the Civil War—have Americans ever been comfortable with the pluralistic reality of the American nation. That reality notwithstanding, we have tried to fashion a story to serve as the nation's common history—subordinating a great deal of human experience and particularity by the way. A lot of what has happened in the last twenty years attests to the failure of that story. Now the question is, can we fashion a new one? Should we?

While the problem of national history has a special force in America, it is certainly not peculiar to Americans. Merely glancing at other national histories with which we might be familiar, we see how the Welsh and the Scots resist being swallowed into a common British history. The same can be said of the Celts in Brittany who want to keep their language and culture from being erased by a dominant French history, in the name of nationality. Surely the same point can be made for minorities in Italy, Germany, Eastern Europe, and the Soviet Union. Those of us who prefer the superhighways of national history feel no great loss in not knowing much about these groups and their aspirations. But what some would dismiss as mere particularism means a great deal to those involved. History has shown that such groups will not efface themselves for our sakes; indeed, they show universally a remarkable and often annoying tenacity. We would do well to know more about particular ethnic elements in those countries than about some abstraction called the nation. That, too, is true of America. National histories basically are ideological constructions, which rest on the premise that the defined whole is greater than the sum of its parts—an assumption always contradicted by those who feel themselves defined as much by the part as by the whole.

A stress on "common culture" turns history into a tool of national unity, mandated principally by those anxious about national order and coherence. Leaving aside the vague and unscientific use of the term "culture," we see nonetheless that without some organizing principles, some imposed structure, something we all can assent to as ours, the radical variety of experience threatens chaos.

At a very abstract level, all humankind shares common values, aspirations, and "culture." In the years immediately following World War II, a photographic exhibit at New York's Museum of Modern Art entitled "The Family of Man" wanted to make exactly that point. But the concept is too abstract and general to serve national needs. That which could serve as a common heritage (values or what have you) must be general enough to cover the kaleidoscopic variety of our social life, yet particular enough to distinguish us from others. It is not a simple task. Those pushing for a "common culture," however, seem to believe that repeatedly asserting the need for discovering the formula is enough.

I suspect that advocates of "common culture" do not see their position as debatable because they do not recognize the sources of their concerns as ideological. Like most ideologues, they consider their arguments common sense; and they have no problem understanding and defining the shared, common "culture"—it is, simply, what they recognize as their own. I have heard no advocate of "common culture" who did not assume that "everyone should recognize *my* story is *our* story." During a long part of American history, immigrants and others seemed willing to try it; there will always be those who will accept whatever is the dominant "culture" as their own. But it will not work for long, and what was accepted as dominant will change.

Until the end of World War II, in one form or another, the Bancroft myth of American history served as a frame within which to build the national myth and history. It defined the common culture in terms of an Anglo-Saxon tradition that, however badly it fit reality, was generally accepted. The first cracks in that structure, that myth, appeared in the 1940s and 1950s—which saw a growing emphasis on social history and a new focus on particular peoples and their experiences. Some complained, seeing that these changes shattered the common history that had served the nation since the nineteenth century. But the problem was that the children of immigrants wanted to change the story. In 1962 Carl Bridenbaugh voiced these anxieties in his presidential address to the American Historical Association:

> Historians of our Recent Past shared a common culture, a body of literary knowledge to which allusion could be usefully made. . . . Today we must face the discouraging prospect that we all, teachers and pupils alike, have lost much of what this earlier generation possessed, the priceless asset of a shared culture. Today imaginations have become starved or stunted, and wit and humor, let alone laughter and a healthy frivolity, are seldom encountered. Furthermore, many of the younger practitioners of our craft, and those who are still apprentices, are products of lower middle-class or foreign origins, and their emotions not infrequently get in the way of historical reconstruction. They find themselves in a very real sense outsiders of our past and feel themselves shut out. This is certainly not their fault but it is true. They have no experience to assist them, and the chasm between them and the Remote Past widens every hour. . . . What I fear is that the changes observant in the background and training of the present generation will make it impossible for them to communicate to and reconstruct the past for future generations.

Bridenbaugh's anxieties are shared by those of us today who are concerned with the "common culture." Now, ironically, the problem is being raised by the very people whom Bridenbaugh described as "outsiders." By birth and class, Bridenbaugh saw himself as conversant with what he called the "Remote Past," which he feared was being lost forever. The present group at least grants the possibility of sharing, within the radical diversity. It is more democratic. Yet, I disagree with them all because I believe they are unaware of what drives their demands— which I see as ideological sets leading to a national and inspirational history. Too many descendants of immigrants would have all students finishing high school American History knowing that they are "American" and exactly why they should be proud of it. "Common culture," in this sense, is an indoctrination into normative standards and "values" (another vague word now in favor).

Though I do not like this rather benign formulation, I sense something even more ominous when I hear casual talk of teaching "our common values." Given its normative implications, it translates into indoctrination as to how we *ought* to think about things. I am more comfortable with variety than conformity, and I think our values will manage to get across without being deliberately promoted.

The questions to be raised in history are not so much the values we do or do not share but, rather, how we interpret past events. Those very elements that advocates of "common culture" consider most to be taken for granted are the crux of the dispute, because they point to the differing perspectives on the past. The Declaration of Independence is the most frequently used illustration of values Americans hold in common: all men are created equal, and so on. Putting aside for the moment a fact that every student of American history should know—that there always were and continue to be Americans who do not subscribe to these values—and even assuming that all do accept such statements as describing our national ideals, we will nevertheless diverge sharply and reasonably about how those ideals relate to American history.

We might all agree that American history reveals a gap between ideals and reality. Some might say that the important thing is to bridge the gap by accepting such values, taking them seriously, and trying, however imperfectly, to live up to them. Others, looking at the same history, would stress the persistence of the gap—that is, the failure of Americans to honor the principle except when forced to by circumstance. The question is whether the glass is half full or half empty—not a matter of values but one of ideological perspective. I do not think it the historian's role to insist, for reasons of national interest, that the more positive perspective is more valid, while the other is mere cynicism. The historian should see questions from as many perspectives as possible. The historian should find it a blessing rather than a burden that variety—ethnic, regional, or what have you—forces him to look at the same problem from different angles. My point is not that the historian should avoid having a personal point of view. But he should recognize that it is but one among several; and he should be willing to give respectful attention to perspectives not his own.

I would argue, further, that the role of history is not to promote a nation, a people, or a cause. Nor is it the function of history to make us feel good about the accident of our birth in the best of all possible countries. In 1971, in an essay in *Key Issues in the Afro-American Experience,* I wrote of the need to argue that same point against the popular view that the reason for writing and studying Afro-American history was to learn about heroes and heroines in "our" past, to discover "our" identity, and to create alternative myths to those of the dominant culture. Such history serves all America and a "common culture" no better than it does black Americans.

Yet, after all of this has been said, a real problem remains for teachers of American history in the schools. Even granting the radical diversity of the country—and recognizing the importance, in the school subjects children study, of legitimizing different heritages—should not American youngsters learn something in common? Should not some basis for discourse span ethnic and regional borders? To ask the question is to answer "yes." Yet, how does one teach American history to a class in San Francisco—the class being made up of Irish-, Italian-, Chinese-, Japanese-, Filipino-, African-, Jewish-, and Native-Americans? Should they not all know something in common with their peers throughout the country? How can one teach that and still be open to the variety of perspectives implicit within that heterogeneous class?

I believe that there is an irreducible body of information about the American past that all high school graduates ought to know. That "core" should comprise mainly the history of political and social institutions, their development, and their practice. Students ought to know how American institutions developed, and how and why they differed from those in the "Old World," including England. Naturally, this would expose students to the ideological foundations of American institutions; and through such instruction they would become familiar with those values and principles through which American political and social life have found sustenance. Such a "core" is essential to active and constructive life as a citizen in the United States. In that sense, it is a skill—like literacy or practical arithmetic. One can share this kind of knowledge with everyone else in the country, seeing oneself defined either by the generality of America or some particular part of it.

Aside from this "core," history has another important role to play, a role peculiar to the discipline and having nothing to do with promoting "common cultures." History is one of the humanities; by studying it, one is forced to look seriously at experiences *other than one's own*. Even when we look at the lives of our forebears, we should understand they *are not ourselves*. It is essential to understand this point. Black Americans, for instance, who fail to recognize that they are not the same as slaves will never understand slavery. The present provides us with a different perspective as well as a different knowledge from the past, and that makes historical study informative and exciting. Maintaining that distance, we can analyze and attempt to understand the process of change and speculate on cause.

That, in my view, defines what is peculiar to history as a discipline, and why one studies it as an intellectual endeavor. It is not to celebrate heroes or the good fortune of our birth. It is not to develop patriotism; and, except as it draws us into the common human experience, it is not to make us feel one with our countrymen. Though these may be good things to do, they are not reasons why one should study, teach, or write history.

The discipline required by history is indifferent to content. Any history will do: Greek, Chinese, African, Native American. All that is required is data that can be used for historical analysis and the will on someone's part to organize that data so as to give meaning to the whole. For the American historian, the pluralism of American life could inspire excitement in the possibilities rather than anxiety over the ever illusory "common culture." There again, it matters whether one sees the glass as half full or half empty.

19

American Myths and Afro-American Claims

The legitimization of descent of the Afro-American people is a particularly problematic subject, because relative to other peoples, Afro-Americans originate as a people in very recent times. As well, they are part of a society which itself is a product of revolution and deliberate, conscious, rational construction.

The features most distinctive to the United States are owing to its being a founded nation, established by men in a self-conscious break with the past and in defiance of those traditions and legacies on which men and nations normally depend for their legitimacy. Furthermore, with the exception of the Native Americans who peopled the nation, all would have to go through a severing process, rupturing links with their own traditions, abandoning any birthright claims. To become American meant to become part of a modern (not traditional) world, to find one's legitimacy not so much in tradition, in the past or precedent, but in the present and future potential.

Emigration was, thus, a modernizing process, common to all who would become Americans. It was true for Africans no less than for Europeans. While no one would be so naïve as to describe the Euro-American and the Afro-American immigration experiences as identical, they do share this common deracination, the rending of ties to the past. On the part of Africans the process was forced, while that of the European was in some degree voluntary. The effect, nevertheless, was the same.

If anything, the uprooting of the African was more total, more traumatic. With the closing in 1809 of the slave trade to the United States, Americans of African descent ceased having their numbers augmented by fresh immigrants, and they were effectively cut off from communication with their native cultures. This, plus deliberate mixing

*This lecture was given at a conference during the early 1980s.

of peoples in the slave trade and on American plantations, had the effect of obliterating ethnic distinction among Africans. By the 1820s, it is fair to say that Americans of African descent were no longer Ibos, Yorubas, Mandinkas, Fulani, Fante, etc. Having lost their specific ethnic identities, they had become a new people—Afro-Americans—few of whom could speak of their ethnic past with any certainty.

This, too, is but an exaggeration of an American trait. American mythology would have it that not only a new nation was created, but a new people as well. "What is this American, this new man?" asked Hector St. John de Crèvecoeur. He found his answer in the newness of the experience.

> Here individuals of all nations are melted into a new race of men, whose labours and posterity will one day cause great change in the world.
>
> . . .
>
> I only repeat what I have heard many say. . . . From nothing to start into being; from a servant to the rank of master; from being a slave of some despotic prince, to become a free man, invested with lands, to which every municipal blessing is annexed! It is in consequence of that change, that he becomes an American.[1]

Crèvecoeur's rhetorical question as well as his answer implied a therapeutic break with the past—a new nation and a new people.

Being a new nation and a new people made it more difficult to establish legitimacy. The break with the past required a justification and rationale—a mythology of its own. Given a past which roots itself in history, folklore, and myth, how does one justify breaking with it so that it is a right and proper act, so that the new nation can be seen as legitimate, not a spurious issue? I believe this aspect of the subject will be taken up by another at the conference. I need, however, address a kindred question: the establishment of a new myth of legitimacy to comport with the "new nation and a new people."

Traditional societies and peoples rest upon legends from a pre-recorded past. These myths of national (ethnic) origin, whether in the oral traditions of Africans, American Indians, or Hebrews, serve to define tribal origins, asserting or implying legitimacy in those origins, serving birthright claims into the present. All such peoples, it would seem, have their own equivalents to the *Iliad, Morte d'Arthur,* or the *Old Testament.*

Such claims, indeed, are antecedent to the nation state itself and persist long after political hegemony has seemingly obliterated ethnic particularism. Lest we doubt the power and persistence of such claims to legitimacy, merely reflect on the twentieth century vigor of Magyars and

---

1. Hector St. John de Crèvecoeur, *Letters from an American Farmer* (London, 1782), quoted in Merle Curti, et al., eds., *American Ideas: The Social Record* (Philadelphia, 1960), Vol. I, pp. 104–5.

Serbs, Croats and Macedonians, Bretons, Welsh, Scots, and Basques, all defying historical hegemonies. Certainly, the difficulties of newly forming nations in Africa and Asia rest upon the resistence of ethnic groups (the origins of some no more ancient than colonial administrative edicts which established them) to hegemonic and nationalizing forces. Even the United States, which has thought of itself from time to time as a melting pot, has seen in recent years the strong resurgence of particularistic identities we have called ethnicity.

The United States, being created by the deliberate choice of men—within known and recorded and remembered time—established itself as modern simply in the act of revolution. The audacity of that act in 1775 was less a radical ideology which would overturn political order than the challenge to the legitimacy of tradition. The modernizing force was in the rationale justifying independence, breaking the tyranny to continuity of institutions, and openly disclaiming the right of heritable privilege and power. It is not coincidental that among the societal casualties of that revolution was the institution of primogeniture and entail. The most radical element of the rationale was the seeming justification for "revolutions" with each generation. To paraphrase the Declaration of Independence, "When a past becomes limiting to change, it is the right of a people to abolish it and create a new one."

The radical heterogeneity of the United States is another way in which it differed from traditional societies. Even when you set aside the dramatic differences Native Americans and Afro-Americans posed to the European, this latter group, by itself, represented a variety of native stocks. How does one claim one people out of such diversity? How does one discover mythic and legendary legitimacy in what would seem a denial of tradition?

These were troubling questions to the first generation of Americans, and they are troubling still. Some, like Crèvecoeur, could applaud the "new man" and the "new nation," but others were anxious to ground the new experiment in a venerable past. Not surprisingly, men could and did hold both sentiments at once without seeming to contradict themselves.

Finding a usable past on which to rest the new took some effort; it was not automatic. Revolution had made the mother country and its past virtually unusable. The founding generation of Americans turned to the classics. This was no easy thing. No battered statues are dug up in America as they are dug up in Greece or Israel or Italy; no arches like that of Titus in Rome, no Colosseum, no ancient theater still in use, no palace ruins like the palace of Diocletian at Split. There was nothing in the physical fact of America to resonate Rome or Greece. Yet Americans gave their towns, villages, and cities such names as Rome, Troy, Athens, Syracuse, Ithaca, Utica, Alexandria, and Augusta.

The founding fathers spoke of a republican form of government, not a commonwealth. The term *res publica* came into that particular English usage in the seventeenth century. Some wanted to call the new head of government "high mightiness," "protector," "regent," or "serenity." But they settled on "president," from *praesidens,* this sense of the term dating from 1783. The national legislature was not to be called a general assembly or a parliament but a congress, from *congressus,* a coming together. The English term first appears in 1768 but was not used to mean legislative assembly until 1775. The congress meets not in a parliament house, a state house, a palace, or a government house but in a capitol, that word originally designating a citadel or temple on a hilltop. The first political parties were Federalist and Republican; our present ones are Republican and Democrat; the first coming from the Latin, the second from Greek. The fact that these classical derivatives were fresh in their time indicates they were deliberately adopted.[2]

The great seal of the United States is a composite of classical allusions. The American eagle, however, is bald, unlike the Roman. It clasps in one talon an olive branch, a sheaf of arrows in the other. These emblems of peace and war have classical connotations and were not common in America before the Revolution. Over the figure is the motto: *E pluribus unum.* On the obverse is a truncated pyramid over which is a triangle with the eye of God, and above this appears: *Annuit coeptis*—he has favored our beginnings. Below the pyramid is *Novus ordo seclorum*—a new order of the ages. At the bottom of the pyramid, in Roman numerals for greater dignity, is MDCCLXXVI, when the new order began. All of this hints at the desire by the founding fathers to attach to their endeavors of 1776 an ancient virtue.[3]

Thus, while breaking from the past, the founding fathers created myths which would place them in a tradition. It was in the same spirit that some wanted to write the American epic, the story that would do for the new nation what the *Iliad* did for Greece. Convention would have such epics as poetry. Joel Barlow, the poet and statesman, would write his *Columbiad* with such a vision in mind.

> Here social man a second birth shall find,
> And a new range of reason lift his mind,
> Feed his strong intellect with purer light,
> A nobler sense of duty and of right,
> A sense of liberty; whose holy fire
> His life shall temper and his laws inspire,
> Purge from all shades the world-embracing scope
> That prompts his genius and expands his hope.[4]

So, in seemingly endless stanzas, Barlow poured out a heroic claim for the new man and new nation not unlike that of Crèvecoeur. The new

---

2. Howard Mumford Jones, *O Strange New World* (New York, 1964), chap. 7.

3. Jones, pp. 228–29.

4. Joel Barlow, *The Columbiad* (Philadelphia, 1807); an earlier and shorter version was his *The Vision of Columbus* (Philadelphia, 1787).

man, however, would not take to such old epic forms. The *Columbiad* never caught on.

George Bancroft would become the American Homer. Bancroft had a broad and varied career. A Jacksonian Democrat, he was appointed Secretary of the Navy, he served as minister to England and to Germany, and he wrote history. His master work was his history of the United States. The first volume appeared in 1834 and the tenth, and final, volume in 1876 (forty-two years of eventful history themselves). These ten volumes carry the story from the exploration and colonial settlements through 1782 and independence in volume 9, the tenth volume being on the Constitution.

It was a mammoth work which captured the public's sense of its history. As one contemporary put it, "Bancroft gave voice to the common understanding." In this sense it was living folklore in the garb of written history.

The history was simple but powerful. It told of a people (mainly English) who fled from social and economic restrictions of the old world—religious intolerance, class discrimination, the decadence and corruption of inherited privilege. They came to the new world—held virtually empty awaiting their coming—and struggled against the wilderness (of which the Indians were a part) to establish societies which were open and free even before the Revolution made a nation so. Through that struggle and experience, they established institutions of government which would leave the human spirit untrammeled, free to realize its own potential—a potential which assumed perfectibility, divinity in fact. It was a free land for free men, uninhibited by outmoded laws and customs based on rank and privilege of birth. The very existence of this free nation and people set freedom against despotism and monarchy; innocent self-interest against corruption; dynamism, progress, and perfectibility against static, stagnant, decadent order.

Nor was that all. It was providential. God was the prime mover. He had established from time immemorial a blueprint for mankind, and through history His plan was to be realized. Nowhere was this more evident than in the creation of the "new empire of democracy."[5]

History, in general, marked the "foot steps of Providential Intelligence."[6] America was more, it was covenantal, resting heavily on Old Testament imagery and the Hebraic understanding of history. This idea of a national covenant that one finds in Hebraic history had been central to Puritan thought. Bancroft's history perpetuated this myth, affirming that America had been chosen to complete God's final plan for mankind—to inaugurate the millenial rule of democracy. The new world was the "new Israel," and the colonists were the "chosen emis-

5. George Bancroft, *History of the United States*, 10 vols. (Boston, 1834–1876), quote from Vol. IV, p. 15.
6. Ibid., IV, p. 10.

saries of God" who, "like Moses, escaped from Egyptian bondage to the wilderness," where in a promised land the "new gospel of freedom" might be lived and proclaimed.[7]

The point would not be so telling if such views were written by only one nineteenth-century historian. But his contemporaries said much the same on a more global scale, claiming that decadent culture and races (Catholics, Jews, Moors, and Indians) were moved aside by a providential hand to permit the Anglo-Saxon forces to achieve the inevitable and moral progress.[8] These themes and assumptions, furthermore, were the *common sense* beliefs Americans had about their past. They were so deep and pervasive as to form the unarticulated major premise of all American policy and thought into our time. It is a history and myth perpetuated by such eminent American historians as John Fiske, Woodrow Wilson, Edward Channing, Vernon Louis Parrington, Frederick Jackson Turner, and, in our own time, Edmund Morgan and Carl Degler.

I have described at length this central myth of American history because it forms the broad context into which any Afro-American myth of ethnic origin must fit. Rather, I should say that such a myth would have to fit within the national legend or find an alternative. The latter option is problematic because, as I have already pointed out, by the second or third decade of the nineteenth century there were few Afro-Americans who could know a specific African ethos.

For African migrants from the seventeenth century to 1808, America had become a melting pot as it would for no other immigrant group. Ibo, Mandinka, Yoruba, Fante, and Angola had become Afro-American, individual language, myths, and culture dying with the first generations. That is not to say that African influence was erased. Rather, it became generalized and muted, remaining in indistinguishable folk tales, music, dance, and religious sensibilities. Even these became so general and defused throughout American culture as to be forgotten as African until later generations set out to rediscover them. Of course, there would always be black efforts to rediscover themselves in an African past, but that would be difficult if not impossible. I will take that matter up at a later point; here, I want to discuss the problems of those who would claim a legitimacy within the dominant American myth.[9]

It requires no great knowledge of American history to know that Bancroft's myth did not comport well with the facts of American history,

7. Ibid., I, pp. 347, 362–63.

8. See the works of Francis Parkman, William H. Prescott, and John L. Motley. For an excellent discussion of these historians as they relate to the themes I am discussing see David Levin, *History as Romantic Art* (New York, 1963).

9. Melville J. Herskovits, *The Myth of the Negro Past* (New York 1941); Arthur Schomburg, "The Negro Digs Up His Past," in Nathan I. Huggins, ed., *Voices From the Harlem Renaissance* (New York, 1975).

especially where blacks were concerned. Where the myth described men
fleeing despotism and tyranny for freedom, Afro-Americans had been
snatched against their will from a normal social condition (sometimes
despotic, sometimes not) into forced labor and the tyranny of slavery.
Where the myth celebrated the discovery in America of free institutions,
the black presence in America was nearly coterminous with the institution of slavery. Where the myth assumed the moral force of God's will
working through history, the condition of the Afro-American was a
boisterous immorality in the eyes of the western world. Slavery was an
American institution, developed by Americans to serve American
needs; no other nation Bancroft would have called civilized had such an
institution in the mid-nineteenth century. How could God's "foot steps"
lead to chattel slavery?

More troubling still was the fact that it was racial slavery. It was not
a matter of merit (or demerit); one did not earn the status of master or
slave. One was born into it, no less than aristocrats and serfs of decadent
Europe. In the United States, being white was a privileged status. In the
antebellum South, a black was presumed a slave without his having
proof to the contrary; the onus was his. Free blacks were social oddities;
denizens rather than citizens, as one historian has noted.[10] In the North,
black Americans were a marginal population, although free. They were
generally denied the right to vote, hold property, attend public schools,
or even settle in many communities.[11] Indeed, as the democratic impulse
swept across the northern states in the 1820s—extending liberties, opportunities, and political power to all citizens—the inhibitions and restrictions mounted against Afro-Americans.[12]

In the American myth, both slavery and blacks were, thus, anomalies. Slavery was a "peculiar institution." Even as Abraham Lincoln
declaimed against it, saying "a house divided against itself cannot stand,
half slave and half free," he would go on to dream of America as a place
where "white men may find a home," not just American whites but *"free
white people everywhere*—the world over—in which Hans, and Bap-
tiste, and Patrick . . . may find homes and better their conditions in
life."[13] Crèvecoeur's "new man" was a white man as Lincoln would see
him, and America was supposed to be a white man's country. Afro-
Americans were a mistake of history.

In considering the colonists' grievances against Britain, Thomas Jefferson complained that the mother country had imposed slavery on the
colonies through the Royal Africa Company. George Bancroft, and
American historians into the twentieth century, have treated racial slav-

10. Marina Wikramanayake, *A World in Shadow: The Free Black in South Carolina*
(Columbia, 1973); Ira Berlin, *Slaves Without Masters* (New York, 1974).

11. Leon Litwack, *North of Slavery* (Chicago, 1961).

12. Eugene Rerwanger, *Frontier Against Slavery* (Urbana, Ill., 1967).

13. Abraham Lincoln, "Speech" at Springfield, Ill., June 17, 1858; "Speech" at
Chicago, Ill., July 10, 1858.

ery similarly, as a given, something inherited about which nothing could have been done. As Bancroft put it, "had no other servitude been known in Virginia than of men of the same race, every difficulty would have been promptly obviated. But Ethiopian and Caucasian races were to meet together in nearly equal numbers beneath a temperate zone."[14] It was clear to him who must dominate; both could not be free.

From the white side, to deal with this anomaly was to write the story as if black Americans, like American Indians, were incidental and not legitimately part of the story. American history actually conformed to the mythic ideal; blacks were egregious, accidental, external to the theme, explained as exceptions, not contradictions. That has been the principal trend of American historiography until the last half of the present century. It has only been in the past twenty years that historians have addressed themselves seriously to the American role in the establishment of racial slavery.[15] That goes a long way to explain the often heard complaint of Afro-Americans that they have been left out of the history.[16]

Another direction of white American thought was to deny that black Americans were men quite like themselves. One could hold to democratizing and egalitarian theory and justify blacks as slaves if they were not included within the sweeping claim that "all men are created equal, that they are endowed by their Creator with certain unalienable Rights . . . Life, Liberty, and the pursuit of Happiness." Both myth and science could serve this end.

The mystic source of alienation most commonly used was the story of Noah's curse of Ham and his Canaanite progeny (Gen. 9:21–27). It was the well-known story of Ham and his children being charged for all time as "hewers of wood and carriers of water" for other men; that is, menials and servants. The story had persisted through Judeo-Christian history as an oppressor's rationale and justification for his role as oppressor or slave holder. It had been a standard explanation of slavery throughout the Mediterranean and western world.[17] In the American

14. Bancroft, I, pp. 119–34.

15. This issue was first seriously addressed by Oscar and Mary Handlin in "Origins of the Southern Labor System," *William and Mary Quarterly,* Ser. 3. VII (April 1950), pp. 199–223; answered by Carl Degler in "Slavery and the Genesis of Race Prejudice," *Comparative Studies in Society and History,* II (October 1959), pp. 49–56, and Ibid., (July 1960), pp. 488–495; Winthrop Jordan, *White Over Black* (Chapel Hill, N.C., 1968), chap. 2; but also see Edmund Morgan, *American Slavery, American Freedom* (New York, 1975).

16. The rationale for Afro-American history as a field of study was actually that blacks had been "left out" of the standard history. Of course, blacks had been treated in the histories of the United States and the histories of slavery, but from a perspective other than their own, making them external to the history. The revisions brought about by the "revolution" of the 1960s has changed American historiography profoundly. Nothing has been more changed than the history of slavery in the United States itself, much due to the use for the first time of sources of slaves themselves.

17. William McKee Evans, "From the Land of Canaan to the Land of Guinea; Strange Odyssey of the 'Sons of Ham,' " *American Historical Review,* Vol. 85, no. 1 (February 1980), pp. 15–43.

argument, blacks were merely the "sons of Ham" and justly kept as slaves—their natural if not their proper moral condition.

American science, too, found a way to set Afro-Americans aside. The so-called American School of Ethnology committed itself to the proposition that blacks and whites were separate species. Josiah Nott, a medical doctor from Mobile, Alabama, argued from theories of polygenesis that there were, in fact, several "types of mankind," and that whites and blacks were separate creations. He even claimed, despite what would seem compelling empirical evidence to the contrary, that miscegenation resulted in a weakened and sterile issue. Like crosses between donkeys and horses, "cross-breeding" between whites and blacks would result in a sterile "muleism." Whites were men; non-whites (blacks, Indians, etc.) were something less.[18]

Science and Biblical myth could be combined, as in the argument of Dr. Samuel Cartwright and Charles Carroll. In their view of polygenesis, blacks were "Pre-Adamite." That is to say, they were created by God as "Beasts of the Field," the penultimate creation before the white man's progenitor, Adam. In this story, the black, as the most intelligent of the beasts of the field, was actually Eve's tempter and seducer. Thus, it would seem, the original sin was miscegenation.[19]

Given the distance Afro-Americans had to the mythic tradition, and given the white desire to consider them outside that myth, it would be a difficult task for American blacks to explain themselves as Americans and find a legitimacy within the dominant myth. The principal tactic of antebellum Afro-Americans was to describe slavery not only as an anomaly but as a moral (if not mortal) flaw in the American mythology. After emancipation, it was to establish birthright legitimacy.

Slave culture, like free American culture, found appeal in the Old Testament. Much of slave song and story found a connection between the Afro-American and the Hebrew children. They, too, had been enslaved in Egypt. They were delivered by God.

> Didn't God deliver Daniel from the lion's den?
> Jonah from the body of the whale?
> The Hebrew children from the fiery furnace?
> Then, why not every man?[20]

This theme is ubiquitous in Afro-American culture. But as a "chosen people," they had a chosen destiny. It was a mythology which fed millenial hopes and muted voices of defiance. It is out of this tradition

18. Josiah Nott, *Types of Mankind* (Philadelphia, 1854); and his *The Negro Race* (Mobile, 1866); William Stanton, *The Leopard's Spots: Scientific Attitudes Toward Race* (Chicago, 1960).

19. George Fredrickson, *The Black Image in the White Mind* (New York, 1971), chap. 8; Charles Carroll, *"The Negro a Beast"* (St. Louis, 1900).

20. Traditional song. See also Lawrence Levine, *Black Culture and Black Consciousness* (New York, 1977).

that we discover the strong current of Christian Stoicism which was finally marshalled into protest by Martin Luther King, Jr.[21]

The providential hand was there. Some, like Maria W. Stewart, claimed that Africans suffered because of "our gross sins and abominations." In this view, the African sojourn in America as slaves was owing to "disobedience, rebellion, and neglect of God."[22] These were Christians, of course, and their view of the providential cause of Afro-American slavery could not be shaken from their view of Africans as pagan idolators. One of the first black historians, George Washington Williams, distinguished the early imperial glory of primeval Africans from the present degraded "Negro type," who occupies "the lowest strata of the African race," because "he early turned from God" to idolatry, losing his civilization and finding "the cold face of hate and the hurtful hand of the Caucasian against him." But it would turn to good—"the elevation of the African race."[23]

This argument suggests the mainstream of antebellum black argument on the subject. It accepted the providential view of Bancroft's history; accepted, also, some of the views of decadence and corruption of the old world. But it would see the African sojourn in America (even as slaves and oppressed) as redemptive. It would bring the fruits of modern, republican institutions and modern commercial enterprise to Africa. Anglo-Saxons, in some versions of this story, had been instruments of evil, or had perpetuated evil in slavery, although they knew better. They would be subject to divine vengeance.[24]

Like whites, then, black Americans could conceive a "manifest destiny." They were a "nation within a nation," as Martin Delany, the nineteenth-century advocate of expatriation, would say.[25] The early expatriates would indeed argue that their mission was to return to Africa, to uplift that "dark continent" and that "benighted people." But, significantly, it was not a specific African people. Africa had become a generality, standing for black people—there had been an obliteration of ethnic differences. For black Americans—as for whites—race had become more meaningful than ethos.

In the years following emancipation, the main thrust of Afro-American identity was to establish birthright claims. Blacks were Americans and citizens, entitled to all rights of citizenship. Leaders and spokes-

21. Nathan I. Huggins, *Black Odyssey; The Afro-American's Ordeal in Slavery* (New York, 1978), chap. 8.

22. Maria W. Steward, "An Address Delivered at the African Masonic Hall, Boston, February 27, 1833," in Dorothy Porter, ed., *Early Negro Writing, 1760–1837* (Boston, 1971), pp. 130–31.

23. George Washington Williams, *A History of the Negro Race in America From 1619–1880* (New York, 1883) Vol. I., pp. vii, 109, 110, 114.

24. Stewart, op. cit.; Leonard I. Sweet, *Black Images in America, 1784–1870* (New York, 1976), chap. 5.

25. Martin R. Delany, *The Condition, Elevation, Emigration, and Destiny of the Colored People of the United States* (New York, 1852).

men from Frederick Douglass to the present would accept the basic tenets of Bancroft's myth, but they would claim slavery to have been an aberration, a corruption. America would not achieve its destiny until black Americans would be accepted as men and citizens. Thus, Afro-Americans became the litmus test for America. The nation approached or distanced itself from the ideal as it accepted or rejected blacks. The argument depended on white Americans concurring in such a standard. Most did not, of course, continuing to view black Americans as an accidental element in a story of liberal, progressive, and democratic history.

Plans for expatriation continued into the twentieth century, marking the despair some blacks felt in their exclusion from mainstream America. Africa in the postbellum period persisted as an equivocal appeal. How Afro-Americans viewed Africa is reflected in the shifting fashions in names identifying with Africa or not. In the early nineteenth century, it was not uncommon for Afro-Americans to refer to themselves as Africans, even using the adjective to distinguish their institutions: e.g., the African Methodist Episcopal Church. It was preferable by many to be called "colored," while "black" tended to be seen as a term of derision until the 1960s. "Negro," as long as it was capitalized, was always acceptable in print, but the spoken form sometimes came close to sounding like "nigra," and that was unacceptable. In the 1960s, however, many blacks began to decry that label. It was an artificial term, invented by white men to designate African peoples. It had no specific ethnic or cultural referent. There was no "Negro" ancestry, no "Negro" heritage. It symbolized the obliteration of the past by the slave trade and the diaspora. The new, preferred term would be "black," or "Afro-American." The latter dates back into the early nineteenth century, where some men, like Martin Delany, used the term "Aframerican." Some continued to be uneasy with the use of "black," pointing to the fact that they are not black in color, but brown or tan, etc. Nevertheless, black and Afro-American are the current, popular usages. The shifts are merely nominal, but they do suggest changing attitudes about color and African heritage. Black Americans became more willing to identify with Africa after World War II, perhaps as a consequence of African independence and the end of colonial rule. Yet for the Afro-American, such identification remained problematic, whatever the will.

When nineteenth-century black Americans spoke of Africa, they tended to imagine a dark continent, a pagan and backward people whom destiny would have them uplift and enlighten. In the twentieth century, the emphasis changed. There remained a sense that the black world needed to be redeemed, but the inspiration was in the ancient African past. When men like Marcus Garvey spoke of Africa, it was of a glorious and remote past. There were the great kingdoms of Songhay and Mali, great universities like Timbuctu. It was not a contemporary Africa, nor was it an African people with which to identify. It was a mythic past. The fact that the West had for so long acted as if Africa had no history and the fact that there was not much written history of Africa covering the period of European expansion made it the easier to ignore present realities for a mythic past. Blacks would not be alone in claiming that the obliteration of African history was deliberate and willful, removing from the New-World black as well as colonized peoples their legitimacy of descent. Thus, in the opening decades of the twentieth century there began an energetic effort to rediscover that history.[26]

Significantly, Afro-American history itself did not seem a usable past for myth-making. Slavery and oppression within a land of free men and free institutions did not serve to nurture myths of a glorious black past or a legitimacy. So Afro-Americans have been tempted to want to discover martial heros in slavery (Nat Turner, Denmark Vesey, Gabriel Prosser, etc.), and point to the African contributions from the first days of settlement to American economic and cultural development. They would say again and again that without black Americans there would be no distinctive American culture. Or, they would want to point to the martial valor of blacks in all American wars, from the colonial period to the present, and, like so many other people, claim that the shedding of blood in national wars gave one a claim on community. When such arguments failed (as they always did) some would surely turn to the glories of an African past.

The 1960s and 1970s brought profound changes both to the perception of the myth and to the black role in the American past. The American faith in the myth had been shaken by perceived limits to American progress, the failure of American ideology abroad, and by the questioning of the American past by blacks, women, and ethnic groups. Furthermore, Afro-Americans became more assertive, placing themselves forcefully in the way; they could no longer be ignored. America's role in the post-war world forced it to confront the contradictions between myth and reality for the first time in its history. On the one hand, the myth of the American past that had dominated American imagination from the first days of the nation was losing hold; more were beginning to doubt it, to question it, to challenge it. On the other hand, black Americans were the more vigorous in making their claims to citizenship, in fact as well as in principle.

It is well, then, to end at this point by mentioning the most successful recent effort of myth-making—engaging through mass media almost the entire nation—Alex Haley's *Roots*. It cannot escape attention in a conference of myths of descent. I would here set aside all questions of historical accuracy, whether or not Haley actually found his "people." He, and most white and black Americans, want to think he did; and that is the stuff of myth. I wish merely to reflect on this phenomenon in the context of this conference.

26. To be seen in the works of Melville Herskovits, Arthur Schomburg, and W. E. B. Du Bois.

The power of the *Roots* phenomenon is precisely that it placed the Afro-American experience—from Africa, through slavery, to freedom—within the dominant American myth. George Bancroft might well have incorporated it into this master work. It was a satisfying myth to blacks because it achieved, in story and symbol, the link between a living black man and a particular African people (and family), tying Haley into a particular lineage and past—into unrecorded time. Because the means was oral history, that traditional link with progenitors, the work seemed to acquire the legitimacy of legend—something truer on a deeper level than history. It was also satisfying to whites because it exculpated the society and culture through catharsis, removing from the present the onus of the past. It brought the black experience into the white sense of the mainstream experience. It was like making a new beginning. "Now that we have acknowledged that, we can start anew."

Furthermore, it made slavery a part of that story without ever implying that it was systemic in America, that what whites called freedom could not have existed without what blacks knew as slavery. There were bad white men and not so bad white men, but never was it suggested that the America they all defined permitted them few choices and that their "pursuit of happiness" presupposed an owned and exploited labor. So, *Roots* managed to incorporate the black experience without damaging or challenging the dominant myth.

Still, it was an Afro-American myth; it was not mere genealogy. Alex Haley, like most black Americans, had white forebears. While this story takes them into account, it never accepts them in his line of descent. It should not have mattered whether those white genes came by way of rape, seduction, or affection, they are part of what made him. The point is, however, that Haley had no curiosity about those "roots," and no one noticed they were missing from the story. Even with this "phenomenon," black people are no more identified with their white kin than whites with their black kin.

That remains curious about the United States. We may, one day, find a new American myth which discovers and acknowledges the blood lines, wherever they go.

20

Humanities, Humanity, and History

We have been properly warned about the muddled and confused state of thinking about the humanities. There are many unanswered questions. What are the humanities? What use are they to ordinary people? Are they essential to the formal education of the public in a democracy? How much is enough? Such questions beg for answers because we, as humanists, educators, and policy makers, are unclear about our own understanding and our own values on the subject. This paper sets out not to resolve these questions but to set them in the context of conceptual frames which might give useful focus. I wish to discuss three particular questions: (1) the practical question of the utility of the humanities; (2) the question of ethnocentrism implicit in the American tradition in the humanities; and (3) the question (or, rather, the problem) American history poses for education in the humanities.

The Useful and the Good

Most of us in the humanities are made uneasy by the practical question. "What good is it anyway? How is reading Homer or Shakespeare or Dante going to pay off in my life?" We are uneasy because we do not have a persuasive answer. If we are lucky (and not all of us are), we have answered the practical question to our own satisfaction. We feel personally enriched, empowered to live life more fully, because we have made literature, art, music, philosophy, and history a central part of our lives. But that is not persuasive to someone who has not been so blessed. In this sense, it is like faith to those who have been "born again." Once one has been "touched by the Spirit," it is impossible to imagine life without

*This paper was presented at the N.E.H. Conference on Excellence and Humanities in Secondary Schools, Phoenix, Arizona, March 13–15, 1985.

187

it and difficult to understand those who remain unregenerate and dumb to the call.

We are made uneasy also because there is something in the tradition of humanistic studies which is hostile to practicality, to applicability. We like to think practical education is, in the end, marginally useful; that it trains one for obsolescence; that it leaves one ill prepared for necessary career and life adaptations; that it trains for a living rather than a life. Some think the humanities analogous to the pure sciences: the value cannot be measured in terms of immediate pay-off but in terms of distant, long-term, and often unrelated benefits made possible because of a healthy and lively theoretical community. Our colleges and universities have institutionalized this distinction even in the degrees they offer. Originally, the Bachelor of Arts differed from the Bachelor of Science, the Ph.D. from the Ed.D. on parallel grounds of theory against practice (the former often defined in terms of a humanities content). Tradition has it that the more practical and particular the study, the less esteemed the degree.[1]

As a measure of quality, *inutility* has been a major influence in Anglo-American education. John Henry Newman, in his *Idea of the University Defined* (1873), characterized "useful knowledge" as a "deal of trash," and that characterization has continued to resonate in the teaching of the liberal arts and humanities in America. Educated men and women should be wrenched from the provinciality of youth, home, and region and introduced to a "world" of learning—"the best that has been known and said in the world." The very process of distancing oneself from purely private concerns, of transcending mundane matters to glimpse the universal is, we have thought, educational. Professional and trade schools are where one should learn to do something—to make a living—following, one would hope, an education for making a life.

Still, the idea does not rest untroubled in the American mind. It is difficult to shake the Veblenian assessment that the pursuit of inutility is merely a conspicuous display of wealth and leisure; who but the rich could afford the time to pursue an education with no practical end? Formal training in the humanities and the liberal arts has been essentially class distinguishing (and gender distinguishing), dividing those with the urgent need to get into the workplace from those more favorably situated.[2] It is thus difficult to dissociate the liberal arts and the humanities from a class bias.

---

1. This tradition explains in part the chronic low esteem teachers have had in the United States, a low regard held not only by the business and professional world outside of education but by many academics as well.

2. A rough distinction, perhaps, but meaningful I think. It divides the eastern liberal arts colleges from the land grant colleges and the different weight of the humanities within each. Regarding the gender question, until recent years, middle-class women's career expectations were strongly influenced by presumption of marriage as a preferred alternative to professional work. Women could, therefore, indulge the "luxury" of hu-

Furthermore, there is deeply embedded in the American character a strong appreciation for the practical and a corresponding distrust for that which cannot demonstrate its purpose and use. It came with the first European settlers to North America, creatures of a Reformation which reconciled God and Mammon—the practice of piety and the accumulation of wealth—by sanctifying work in the world. Asceticism, monasticism—what later generations would call the Ivory Tower—the purely contemplative life away from the work of the world lost favor for the Godly call.

In a book much read in seventeenth-century Massachusetts, William Ames's *Conscience with the Power and Cases Thereof, Divided into Five Bookes,* the doctrine of two callings is plainly set forth. In Chapter V., Book Two, he gives us the reasons:

> First, It is the ordinance of God, that every one by helping others in some particular calling, should glorifie God. Secondly, Every one hath received his talent, or some part of a talent from God to that end: which cannot bee buried or hid without sinne; Thirdly, Idlenesse is too bee flied [*sic*], as the mother and nurse of many vices, especially of evil thoughts, desires, curiousities, and wicked contrivements. Fourthly, the Glory of God, publique and private wellfare, as also the peace of conscience, may and ought to bee sought by some honest calling.

More to the point of education, the Reverend Cotton Mather, author of *Bonifacius. An Essay Upon the Good* (1710), lays down directions for reading, for the education of children, for the management of servants, and for the conduct of various vocations. It was this book, Benjamin Franklin says, which changed his thinking and influenced the principal events of his life.

Read good books, Mather commands, not *"the Devils Library"* of *"foolish Romances, or Novels, or Playes, or Songs, or Jests that are not convenient."* Mather would "endeavor for my *Children* . . . the *Daughters* as well as the *Sons,"* that they "have so much Insight into some *Skill,* which lies in the way of *Gain* . . . that they may be able to Subsist themselves." Children and servants were to read only improving books, avoiding "Pestilential *Instruments of Wickedness."* Mather would purge education of Greek and Latin "Vain Fictions, and Filthy Stories." Instead, he would have them read "Books containing Grave Sayings, and things that may make them truely Wise and Useful in the world."[3]

Such automatic association of education and practical calling in life has persisted in American thought, not simply that education should

---

manities and a liberal education. Practical fields in engineering, the sciences, social sciences, and certain professions (law, business, engineering, architecture) had the reputation of being masculine.

3. Cotton Mather, *Agricola. Or, The Religious Husbandman: The Main Intentions of Religion, Served in the Business and Language of Husbandry* (Boston, 1727), p. 63.

result in some skill to do rewarding work but that the calling itself is a
moral injunction. Idleness—undirected and unpurposeful activity—
encouraged evil. By Benjamin Franklin's own admission, Cotton Mather
turned him around; we cannot read Franklin without recognizing that
debt and, further, our inheritance from them both. Only those of us who
have had the gift of ample time, who have been unhurried by living
necessities, could remain untroubled by the obligatory association
Mather makes of the useful and the good.

In later, affluent years, idleness was most to be associated with
wealth, and wealth with luxury—a corrupting influence. It was endemic
of lasciviousness, effeminacy, and spent vigor. "On the soft beds of
luxury most kingdoms have expired," wrote Edward Young. Luxury, of
course, included the fine arts. Traveling in Europe in the 1770s, Josiah
Quincy had an interview with Colonel Isaac Barré, which he recorded in
his journal. Quincy proudly told the Colonel that the Harvard College
library had acquired a set of prints depicting the ruins at Herculaneum
and was startled to hear Barré admonish that they be kept there, not
opened to the public for the sake of the country.

> They will infuse a taste for building and sculpture, and when a people
> get a taste for the fine arts, they are ruined. 'Tis taste that ruins whole
> kingdoms, 'tis taste that depopulates whole nations. I could not help
> weeping when I surveyed the ruins of Rome. . . . Mr. Q., let your
> countrymen beware taste in their buildings, equipage and dress, as a
> deadly poison.[4]

While Americans have not continued to disparage and distrust luxury, the suspicion of unproductive (unprofitable) idleness remains. In
the long run, taste, like most things in America, is very much defined in
the marketplace. The "bottom line," as we say, is the pay-off.

The practical question is, therefore, a fair one to pose to supporters
of the humanities and the traditional liberal arts. Fair or not, it is bound
to be asked as the cost of education soars. In another year or so, it will
cost approximately $15,000 a year to keep a student in a liberal arts
college. It does not matter how the bill is paid (family savings, grants,
loans, work), $60,000 for a B.A. is an awesome amount to contemplate,
and it will force parents, children, and those making educational policy
to consider differently the value of a college education. What is it for?
What is one to get out of it? We already notice an unrelieved pre-
professionalism among undergraduates and their parents, even among
those we would consider affluent and presumably less anxious about
jobs and career.[5]

For those of us who have been touched by the Muses, who have
found our proper selves in the study of the humanities, who believe for

4. Neil Harris, *The Artist in American Society* (Chicago, 1982), pp. 82–83.
5. The costs in state institutions have risen substantially too. The question is no less a
real one.

some reason in the superiority of the liberal arts over the strictly practical education, it is an unfortunate shift in values. We are eager to tell students that fine arts, literature, philosophy, music, classics, and history are as reasonable tracks to the schools of law, business, and medicine as economics, political science, sociology, or biology. Even in this, however, we have ourselves accepted the validity of the utilitarian imperative; the humanities, too, can serve professional ends. Still, we are not able to persuade anyone that the formal study of the humanities will make one a better lawyer, doctor, merchant, or a better person for that matter.

Until a few years ago, humanists, too, had pre-professional inclinations. We encouraged the brightest and the best of our students to go to graduate school and train for an academic career. That we are now less inclined to do so, that we are less successful in the efforts we make at it, is evidence of the shrunken market rather than our diminished interest in utility or professional generation.

American education is now in trouble. It is universally agreed that primary and secondary schools are failing, and some would include colleges as well. The evidence is everywhere: in student test scores, the lack of basic skills of even the college bound, functional illiteracy among a growing number of the population, drop-out rates, teenage pregnancies, and the list goes on. We did not need commission reports to tell us the general story, but now we have them confirming our worst suspicions. The measure of that failure is utilitarian more than anything else. It is the failure to provide children with "Insight into some *Skill,* which lies in the way of *Gain*" that is basically the fault. Our schools have for some time been problematic in the teaching of the humanities. Until now, we have responded to that problem with mild indifference. We can no longer ignore the problem of the schools because they cannot be counted on to prepare children for the workplace or suitable performance in college.

We have both the National Commission on Excellence in Education's report, *A Nation at Risk,* and that of the Carnegie Foundation, *High School,* to confirm our fears. Oddly, both reports recommend as part of the solution a minimum core of common learning—an academic core curriculum for the high schools—with a heavy humanities component for all children regardless of occupational destiny. Naturally enough, we are apt to consider the present crisis as analogous to the Sputnik scare of thirty years ago. We met that crisis by learning to take mathematics and the sciences seriously in privileged high schools. The present crisis is very different, and the Sputnik-like solutions cannot be the answer. Surely no one could be opposed to improved teaching and better offerings in the humanities. Since that is something we as students and scholars in the humanities can work at, we should certainly lend a hand and our minds to it. Yet it is odd because, like the humanities themselves, it is so epiphenomenal, unrelated to mundane and practical problems.

We are faced with vast numbers of young people who finish (or fail to finish) high school unequipped to find useful and legal occupations. The numbers are growing each year; the impact is cumulative. Our economy appears to be evolving into one which will be less and less able to offer this range of young people jobs even if they were to acquire the marginal skills of basic literacy, simple calculation and communication. Even if we were able to keep these youths in school and train them to read, write, and figure, we would still not equip them for a useful calling in their world. The numbers are large, and at the moment most are poor, black, and Hispanic; but one can count on the problem leaching into the children of clerical and blue-collar families and into the lower middle class.

Like everything else in American society, schools are supposed to produce a result, to pay off. Children who go to our schools—even poor children—have a right to expect their investment in time and substance to have a desirable result. For poor children we have never been able to guarantee that; but we are now, if we are honest, forced to confess that their investment will result in nothing at all, except for those who can and want to go to college. Why finish high school? However badly educated, few children can fail to see the futility of it. It is pointless to cite statistics showing higher earnings for those with a diploma if you cannot give reasonable assurance to the marginal student that there is a job to be had.

For the student who was not college bound, the American schools have never served this very practical role. Those on the academic track have had clear enough signals: do well in the prescribed courses and one could get into some college. For the rest, there has been little direction at all, and relatively little of one's success had to do with the quality of performance in school. One did not step automatically from commercial classes or vocational classes into the workplace. Success depended on family, on friends, on connections, on labor unions and their apprenticeship policies. School had little to do with success. Few educators felt a responsibility. Little has changed except that entry-level jobs are harder to come by, and the easy faith and optimism of youth that school is worthwhile can no longer be relied on to keep them at the task of learning the basics.[6] Considering this to be, as I think it is, the central crisis of the schools, it is bizarre to discuss how reform in the humanities will make a significant difference.

I am reminded of an earlier debate about education. It occurred in the late 1890s, and the question was how best to educate the mass of black people, most of whom were in the South and living within the shadow of slavery. The level of literacy, of work skills, of experience in the world of business and competition was extremely low. We all know

---

6. The lack of alternatives and the lack of a system within schools to train for practical alternatives leading to actual work may account for the growing number of young people choosing some form of college.

of Tuskegee and how Booker T. Washington led the crusade for practical, vocational education. We know, too, of his belief that training blacks to be masons, carpenters, or blacksmiths would be the quickest and surest way to make them self-sufficient and independent. W. E. B. Du Bois, then professor at Atlanta University and later to become one of the founders of the N.A.A.C.P., argued against Washington's single-minded support of industrial education, insisting on the crucial importance of the classical curriculum in higher education for future black leaders and teachers. Not denying the value of practical training for most black Americans, accepting the importance of gaining skills for self-sufficiency, Du Bois nevertheless championed what we now call the humanities as essential to the race's advancement and to an informed leadership in a democracy.

That debate is familiar enough, but we are apt to forget that Washington's reforms were part of a larger movement for industrial education in the United States. It had begun a little after the Civil War and was spurred by the belief of some in northern cities that the "common school education" was of marginal usefulness to growing numbers of poor children of immigrants who would likely find employment only in domestic work or factories. They should be taught to use their hands and learn useful skills and the dignity of labor. Individual philanthropists supported, with their own money, classes in sewing and cooking for girls and shop for boys. Coinciding with the introduction of "manual training" into the schools, industrial training was a reform designed to make the schools useful to a certain class of pupil (of poor and immigrant stock) who would not find a calling in one of the genteel occupations. Like Washington, these reformers were acknowledging the fact of class distinctions within the society and the workplace and were asking the schools to accommodate to that reality.[7]

Class was very much the issue. Washington's polemics were always on that mark, attacking the uselessness of classical education, not only of Latin and Greek, but of modern languages as well. One did not need to know French grammar to shoe a horse, build a barn, or lay brick. There was a pretense and a falseness in the aspiration to higher education. Against his assertion that "the opportunity to earn a dollar in a factory just now is worth infinitely more than the opportunity to spend a dollar in a opera house," the humanist had little defense.

Our present crisis invites comparison, not merely because it recalls the useful and the good, but because there are other matters in common. Growing numbers of our youth in schools and out are, relative to their time, little better off than freedmen in terms of their capacities to earn an honest living and to support themselves and their families. Institutions which should support them—family, school, church—are in disarray or moribund. There is vast confusion as to what the problems are

7. Nathan I. Huggins, *Protestants Against Poverty* (Westport, Conn., 1971), chap. 3.

and how they can be solved. Most freedmen at least had the skills and the opportunity to eke out a marginal living in sharecropping, but most of our kids are urban, with welfare and petty crime their margin. The present generation of youth and adults lack the automatic faith in progress shared by the contemporaries of Washington and Du Bois.

In any case, one would hope today for a school reformer in the style of Washington who could devise an industrial education scheme suitable to our own times and to our complicated industrial and technical economy.[8] Or, even better, a Du Bois who would have the vision to see the need for training both for useful skills and education in the humanities.[9] We are, rather, searching to discover a fresh rationale for the humanities in the schools, promoting our faith that since "it is good for you," a "new and improved" humanities will be even better. Do we really believe that the very best possible courses in art and literature, history and philosophy, taught by the most skilled and enlightened teachers will make a dent in the problems I raise?

The state and the prospects of a significant number of school-age children are so reduced and so dim that one must now say with Washington that the opportunity to earn a dollar in a factory is worth more to them than the chance to read *Gatsby* or *Lorna Doone*. That fact brings into focus the traditional association of humanistic studies and the liberal arts with privileged social classes. Advocates and defenders have never made a case for those for whom college was not a possibility. Since, for all practical purposes, serious study and teaching of the humanities has been done in college, its class-bound character has been moot. But as one gives greater emphasis to the humanities in the high schools, the question of usefulness—and to whom—becomes very real.

The children who will benefit will be those on an academic track, and they in several ways. Better classes in the humanities will likely replace other courses that are a waste of time. They will prepare students better for college. More sophisticated training in high school may permit students to avoid some college courses. For some students this may make possible a richer and deeper college selection in the humanities, but it may also mean easier and earlier specialization for those in the sciences and social sciences. At the present dollar-cost per course credit and the increased course demands in technical and pre-med programs, such savings can be significant. In 1966, James Perkins, then president of Cornell University, delivered lectures at Princeton on the transition of the university. He predicted a growing specialization and training for technical skills. For Perkins, useful knowledge was far from

---

8. Actually, Booker T. Washington trained students for trades and crafts which were becoming obsolete. The future was industrial, and Washington had no plan to meet that future. Tuskegee would support the argument some educators make that practical training can likely be a training for the past.

9. Du Bois was not hostile to industrial education. He insisted on the classical education as a means of training leaders, whom he called the "talented tenth."

a "mess of trash." It was what financed and pointed to the future health of the university. Humanities might be necessary, but they were in the way of efficient, useful training. Perkins predicted that the humanities and the liberal arts core would, one day, be taken over by the secondary schools.[10] That was where they belonged in a modern, technical world. The growing complexities of education owing to technological changes combined with the growing costs of higher education and the consequent pressures to serve pre-professional demands may yet result in Perkins's vision being realized, desirable or not.

Not to be misunderstood, I am not suggesting that poor children and those not destined for college cannot benefit from improved instruction in the humanities. They can and they should. I think, rather, that for systemic and social reasons (many not directly related to the schools), they will not. Few, if any, will be touched by an "academic core curriculum," and despite rhetoric suggesting democratic goals, it is difficult to believe that the proponents of such reforms have these socially alienated youth in mind.

At best, the minimum core of common learning (as was, some would say, the common school curriculum a century ago) is but a device to sustain the "saving remnant," those children on whom the society *must* depend to survive. The rest, lacking some other plan, are left to their ditch—stoically, remorsefully, without perhaps the moral revulsion of William Graham Sumner—but abandoned nonetheless. That remnant, like their counterparts a century earlier and in the Sputnik years, is a privileged youth whom society has every reason to offer the best possible training. However, as the rest are numerous and growing, poor, and in dramatic proportions non-white, it is foolish to ignore the social implications and consequences of such reform. We are either insensible or insincere when we cover these blatant class and ethnic fissures with vague and pious words about democracy and humanistic virtue.

Humanities and Ethnocentrism

When Matthew Arnold wrote of "acquainting ourselves with the best that has been known and said in the world," we know he did not mean *the world*. Rather, the world he meant was the one with which he was well acquainted through the arts and letters. This circularity bothered him no more than it would any "cultivated" western man, assuming no doubt the "best" would naturally come to his attention. However small Arnold's world, it was probably larger than that of most Americans who call themselves humanists. While Eurocentric and Western, Arnold was doubtless *acquainted* with the Islamic, Hindu, and Chinese cultures. American humanists, on the other hand, seldom claim more for the world than the West.

10. James Perkins, *The University in Transition* (Princeton, 1966).

There are two reasons for Americans being, if anything, narrower than our nineteenth-century paragons. For one thing, humanities and the liberal arts have served an acculturative function for Americans. We have wanted to assert our "birthright" in Western civilization, tracing the course of that civilization from ancient Greece to the establishment of our own republic. As provincials to the European metropole, we have been too preoccupied defining ourselves within that tradition to acquaint ourselves with much beyond. Also, we have, especially in recent years, emphasised particular and specialized knowledge, giving little value to mere *acquaintance* with anything. American humanists are likely to be narrower and deeper than Matthew Arnold could have been.

It poses a problem when we want to teach general or core courses in the humanities. We would like to cover our "world," as narrow and limited as that happens to be. That world would at least include Greece, Rome, southern and northern Europe, Russia, England, and possibly the United States. Yet, we like to think that our courses—particularly those which analyze literary texts—are best taught by experts. (We have thus wedged ourselves smugly on the horns of a dilemma.) Perhaps that would be less a problem in the secondary schools, where generalists are more likely to find approval than in colleges.

A few years ago, Professor Edward Said of Columbia University gave an apt critique of general humanities courses in the "core." These courses, he pointed out, are most often taught by faculty not expert on everything read in class, for students who are not expected to become expert on anything by taking the course. He noted four desired results: (1) a sense of "our Occidental humanity"; (2) some practical training in reading texts in translation; (3) a sense of a sequence or continuity within Western culture and an acquaintance with what this culture values; and (4) a general approbation of the books read and of oneself (whether teacher or student) for having read them.

Professor Said went on to challenge three assumptions about such courses: (1) it is illusory to assume students can acquire a humanistic education without any acquaintance with the original languages, with only sketchy knowledge of history, with amateurish instructors (as opposed to experts on every book), and with a sizable list that demands rapid reading; (2) we assume the humanities courses can provide an authoritative canon, but then the authors and their books easily become status symbols and the experience of reading Homer may reduce rather than increase the student's openness of mind; (3) by giving priority and legitimacy to writings in the mainstream of the Judeo-Christian tradition, the humanities course constructs a particular myth of humanity, excluding by ignorance and predilection those of other traditions. When included, non-Western writing is treated as exotic and not fully human, revealing a provincial ethnocentric bias. To the extent that such courses address non-Western culture, they tend to present self-confirming stereotypes.[11]

The points about language and adopted authority should be taken seriously. We risk adopting a false consciousness, or at the least a faulty interpretation, if we read Homer or the Bible in English without paying attention to the crucial problems of translation. The standard answer is: "Better to read _____ (fill in the blank) in English than not to read _____ at all." That response shifts emphasis from the genuine concern of the humanities with inquiry into authentic values to the canonized books and authors. Further, it misses the point. Were I to fill in those blanks with the *Quran* or al-Shadhili could I expect an automatic chorus of "amens" from American scholars and intellectuals? Hardly, despite the fact that intrinsically, from a purely humanistic point of view, one set of options is no more compelling than the other.

We like to make canons. It is convenient to imagine a basic list of authors and texts common to all educated men and women—something akin to a social register, including everything about which there is consensus, excluding anything discomfiting to any arbiter. It helps define the range of civil discourse. It establishes the criteria for what is and what is not worthy of study. In establishing canons, however, we apotheosize authors, transforming their texts into writ. Thus, ironically, we disarm the humanist of his most essential weapons: skepticism, critical distance, and self-criticism.

A nostalgia for a classical education which has all but died out and the quest for the sense of unity which that old order assumed is nevertheless compelling. Professor Walter Jackson Bate addressed what he sees to be the fragmenting and disintegrating state of English Studies. He recalled a tradition of Humane Letters which seemed unparalleled in its achievements, holding together our civilization from the Renaissance with the power and energy of its creative spirit.[12] What Bate saw occurring in English Studies (and parallels can be found throughout the humanities) was an olio of disparate voices and claims: black literature, women's literature, Chicano literature, gay and lesbian literature seemed to swamp what had once been (would likely continue to be) a unified literary field. Professor Bate is not alone in wanting to return to that earlier sense of order and coherence. We cannot go back again, however; the "world" has changed too much for that.

Scholars working in the humanities make qualitative judgments about everything which falls outside the canon; the best ones judge the great works themselves. After all, the humanist's responsibility is to the "best" that has been known and said. Humanists assume the

---

11. Edward Said's comments were made at a conference at Columbia College in 1979.

12. Walter Jackson Bate, "The Crisis of English Studies," *Harvard Magazine,* LXXXV (September and October 1982), pp. 46–53.

pretense of arbiters of quality, taste, and civilization, provoking invidious response. What is included become "great works," what is excluded is unworthy. That is bad enough when we think only of authors and texts. It is a far more serious matter when it is civilizations and peoples who are erased through our studied ignorance, civilizations which some of our students have more reason to identify with than with Greece and Rome.

It is curious how we think about culture and the humanities. None of us would question the importance of language study. It is a crucial introduction into cultures and civilizations not our own. Most of us would support increased language requirements both in the schools and in college. Yet our unanimity ends when we think of a second language in terms of bilingualism in the schools, and our problems are not over pedagogy. We are uneasy about the certification through our schools of a language other than English as a primary language. There are practical reasons, but also chauvinistic ones.

A few years ago, I taught at a college which was serious about maintaining its liberal arts core. There was a solid language requirement, obliging undergraduates to take two years of course work in an ancient or modern Western language. A responsible faculty member turned down a student's request to meet that requirement with Italian. The professor gave two reasons: (1) the point of the requirement was to introduce students to a major literature, enabling them to work in the original language; Italian, according to this professor, had no significant literature, save Dante; and (2) the student came from an Italian-speaking home. Perhaps there would have been a different response had the student come from a French- or German-speaking home, or if he were from a more elevated social class.

In both subtle and obvious ways, the humanities are judgmental as other fields are not. As long as the bulk of students involved in its formal study shared the provincial limits of their teachers, there was little problem. But as the other world crashes in upon us—awakening us to our vast ignorances of lives, cultures, and civilizations we can no longer ignore—and as our own students show a healthy skepticism when we employ the pronoun *our* to link us all with a Western civilization, we are forced to ask new questions and rediscover what the humanities are all about. Failing that, the humanities risk becoming what they have too often been in the past, a resource of genteel bigotry.

It is important to remain alert to this danger, because the enterprise in the United States has been heavily burdened with this fault. We have too easily confused our role of student and scholar with that of abiter and cultivator of tastes and protector of civilization. When our "world" remains small and provincially Western, that is a dangerous role.

This has not merely to do with an academic tradition confronting a pluralistic society. The wholeness and order which Professor Bate recalls with such fondness could have troubling effects when imposed on even the mainstream youngster in the good old days. Malcolm Cowley recalls his own education at Harvard before the first world war.

Cowley remembered Harvard as "salesrooms and fitting rooms of culture." They were not "ground-floor shops, open to the life of the street." The task of that classical education was to transform him from a Pittsburgh lad from a big-town high school into a young man Matthew Arnold might praise. His professors were eager; only "the world they pictured for our benefit was the special world of scholarship—timeless, placeless, elaborate, incomplete and bearing only the vaguest relationship to that other world in which fortunes were made, universities endowed and city governments run by muckers."

So Cowley and his classmates were systematically wrenched from the places and contexts which had nurtured them, encouraged in their alienation from their roots, and then cast into a world which their professors had protected them from knowing. Cowley called his generation *deracinated*. To Gertrude Stein, it was simply *lost*.

> In college we never grasped the idea that culture was the outgrowth of a situation—that an artisan knowing his tools and having the feel of his materials might be a cultured man; that a farmer among his animals and his fields, stopping to plow at the fence corner to meditate over death and life and next year's crop, might have culture without even reading a newspaper. Essentially we were taught to regard culture as a veneer, a badge of class distinction—as something assumed like an Oxford accent or a suit of English clothes.[13]

The Challenge of American History

"The land was ours before we were the land's." The opening line of Robert Frost's "The Gift Outright" is an apt text for thinking about American history and its special challenge to the humanities. As Americans, our relationship to our history must be different from that of other peoples. We are a founded nation, a creature of history. The nation has its story, we all have our stories—varied, sometimes discordant, but somehow complementary. The single experience, common to all but Native Americans, is that our forebears came to this land and adopted it so that our stories must be told here, together.

The land has its proper history, different from our own. That fact illustrates best the historical peculiarity I have in mind. The land does not hold for us, as it does for other people in the world, the material evidence of our past civilization. No battered statues are dug up in America as they are dug up in Greece or Israel or Italy, and we see no weathered arches resembling that of Titus in Rome, no Colosseum, no palace ruins, no ancient temples such as in Sri Lanka, no artifacts of continuous kingdoms such as in Ethiopia. We would instead hope to find

13. Malcolm Cowley, *Exile's Return* (New York, 1962), pp. 31, 33.

the shards of our "civilized" beginnings in the archaeology of other lands, to which we have no true connection.

When we do dig into the land upon which we have built our houses and schools—in Arizona or New Mexico, Maine or Minnesota, Indiana or Arkansas—we find the stuff of a human civilization which belonged there in a sense we can never claim. Layered on top of those remains are strata of artifacts of Euro-American civilizations other than the Anglo-Saxon that we tend now to think of as our tradition.

In truth, Spanish sovereignty once extended as far north as the Carolinas on the Atlantic and beyond San Francisco Bay on the Pacific, embracing at one time or another the Carolinas, Georgia, Florida, Alabama, Mississippi, Tennessee, Louisiana, Texas, New Mexico, Arizona, Arkansas, Oklahoma, Missouri, Kansas, Colorado, Utah, Nevada, Iowa, Nebraska, Wyoming, Idaho, Minnesota, the two Dakotas, and California.

American history begins there rather than in the story of our forebears, or in the Anglo-Saxon legend of the "Pilgrim Fathers." Humanists most of all should know that the traditions they cherish were well in place in the Americas long before Anglo-American institutions transmitted them.

The ideas of Erasmus and Sir Thomas More were taught in Spanish America long before the ideas of Ramus were taught at Harvard College. As early as 1537 Fray Juan Graces, bishop of Tlaxcala, wrote Pope Paul III from Mexico about how Indian children could learn Latin, Castillian and other subjects as easily as whites. Over a century later, Harvard was to graduate, Class of 1665, its solitary Indian alumnus, Caleb Cheeshahteaymuck.[14] The University of Mexico (which had twenty-three chairs by the end of the seventeenth century) dates from 1553, the University of San Marcos in Lima, 1572. The first printing press in the New World was set up in Mexico in 1539, a century before Stephen Day started his in Cambridge, Massachusetts. "When in 1585 a forlorn little band of Englishmen were trying to stick it out on Roanoke Island, three hundred poets were competing for a prize in Mexico City." In 1604, three years before Jamestown, Bernard de Balbuena (Valbuena) produced his great poem—eight cantos, a prologue, and an epilogue—*Grandeza Mexicana,* to celebrate the beauty of a great city, the loveliness of its gardens, the splendor of its buildings, the elegance of its people. Two centuries later, Alexander von Humboldt announced that there was no city in the Western Hemisphere, including the United States, that had such large and well-established scientific institutions as did Mexico City.[15]

This is all well worth remembering because when we contemplate

14. In modern times, of course, there have been Native American undergraduates at Harvard.

15. Howard Mumford Jones, *O Strange New World* (New York, 1964), pp. 84–85.

the Spanish presence in what is now the United States, which lasted past the mid-nineteenth century, we should understand it as something more than military outposts, half-comic factotums, and a mild nuisance to the inevitable Yankee hegemony. The Spanish influence remains in buildings, in place names, in an "atmosphere" in the Southwest. But we have virtually erased the genuine and complete Spanish past from our history of the United States, and even the region of its greatest influence. Perhaps it is because like the Indian, being more ancient than the story we like to tell as our own, the Spanish challenge our priority, legitimacy, and monopoly as Americans.

If present demographic patterns continue, a vast region of the United States will once again be dominated by a Hispanic people. That prospect provides us with a practical reason to rediscover through Spanish-American history a tradition which has been lost to us. It is an opportunity, also, to introduce Hispanic youngsters to the classical humanities, which are an ancient tradition in their native tongues.

The problem just starts here. American history must begin well before any of us or our people become a part of the story. And each of our particular stories joins the narrative at different times, for different causes and reasons, and with different consequences for American history and our own. It is not a unitary story, and to tell it well one must respect both the particular and the general. Not simply because we don't want to leave anyone out, but because the sum is better than any of its parts.

In short, our past contains a multitude of histories, infinite in possibilities. What American historians have chosen to write is only one possible version or, rather, variations around an orthodox convention. If we were to start the story from the Pacific Coast, the steppes of the Southwest, or the Mississippi Valley rather than in Virginia and Massachusetts, the same assortment of events would unfold differently, with different impact and meaning. It would be valid history nonetheless. Even now, one can conceptualize, with interesting results, certain regions of the country in non-conventional histories. Florida, for example, is rediscovering its historical place in the Caribbean Basin, outside the United States proper. And as I have suggested, a considerable part of the Southwest may rediscover its historical place in Hispanic America. They have those historical resources to draw upon.

Similarly, students of American history, with various regional and ethnic identities, bring a different consciousness to the past we present them. The conventional narrative of American history, from the "Pilgrim Fathers" to the present, is not *our* story to all Americans. Those with distinctive ethnic identities—Asian, African, European, Latin American—must come to that story with special sensibilities, which must be honored if we are serious about our humanism. The regional case is also compelling. The southerner and westerner have a right to expect our history to give them a firm, historical sense of their place and region, as much, certainly, as they are asked to have of the "rock-ribbed coast of New England," the Hudson or Shenandoah valleys. The question is, can you write one history that does it all? Probably not. The answer may be multiple histories or, perhaps, a narrative or structure so flexible and open as to permit multiple variations.[16]

This is not meant to be just another argument for pluralism or relativism in history. It is rather to recognize that every formal history is a selection from many valid possibilities. They are deliberate constructs to explain and often to justify national and civic values. As such, histories are deeply ideological, having often invidious implications for groups consciously marginal to the historically defined mainstream. It is therefore not unreasonable to expect that heightened ethnic consciousness will result in different expectations from history. Since the orthodox and traditional version is not *the truth* and sacrosanct, we should welcome the variety.

Despite the possible variety, historical study has a single or common humanistic purpose. Sound historical study achieves it, regardless of specific content. What is it about this study that qualifies it as training in the humanities? We study a people other than ourselves (separate from us in time, place, or culture), considering them within their own context. We try to understand them and their preoccupations in their own terms first, then with the advantage of distance and hindsight, apply useful knowledge and analytical techniques unavailable to them. We consider it all in terms of process, development, and change; and we reflect as much as we can on causal questions. Why did things happen the way they did?

Essentially, that is the historian's discipline. Because, when rightly done, it takes us out of our strictly private, personal selves, forcing us to contemplate universal human issues and values. It is properly a part of the humanities. Yet this discipline is indifferent to specific content. One could study China, Japan, India, Ethiopia, the Arab world, the United States, or Afro-Americans. If, therefore, we want to teach history because it provides good training in the humanities, it should be a matter of indifference to us which history we study. It may, on the other hand, make all the difference to students who want to study a particular past. Let them. Help them to do it right.

Nevertheless, there remains another purpose for teaching history, especially in the schools. It is an unavoidable necessity. We are obliged to educate our children to have a functional understanding of our laws and our social and political institutions. That basic, minimal political and institutional history should be the spine on which any and all versions of American history should be presented in the schools. However, these institutions must be presented not as fixed, but as changing with histori-

16. Hayden White, *Metahistory, The Historical Imagination in Nineteenth-Century Europe* (Baltimore, 1973), Introduction.

cal circumstances. I consider this bare minimum akin to functional literacy. We should equip the graduates of our schools, at the very least, to have enough of an acquaintance with the institutions and laws which govern their lives (and the lives of their fellows), as well as their basic rights and responsibilities as citizens. History will be one way they can be helped to this ground floor.

With that as a foundation, a common ground, some few will go on to discover enough about America to, at last, belong to the land as a "gift outright."

21

Afro-Americans

Nineteen forty-four—it was a good year for Americans to reassess social values and ideals. The Allies' cause in their war against fascism seemed at last destined to triumph. With the defeat of fascism—defined as much in terms of racist ideology as totalitarianism—what would be the conditions under which the world would be reordered, the ideals to which people would be asked to give assent? Clearly, racism and fascism were evil, not only because they were self-serving and corrupt ideologies, but because, as the war had testified, they were ultimately destructive of humanity. So, if the war with its awful costs was to have any redeeming qualities, they would have to be found in life-supporting principles which dignified all mankind, regardless of race or culture.

Sensitive Americans could not reflect on such matters without being aware of their own society's culpability. For the racism that left blacks defenseless against mobs, violence, and murder; that effectively excluded them from the commonweal through social, political, and economic discrimination; that framed legal and customary instruments, engendering a deep social corruption, maintaining one law and practice for whites and another for blacks; such racism was akin to what had inspired the Brownshirts and led to concentration camps and the ultimate "solution" of the holocaust. They were different to be sure, related not identical. The mind that could conceptualize "our Negro problem" was bound in sympathy with the one that could speak of "our Jewish problem," and such minds could find attraction in the same solutions. So, it would be hard to imagine "winning the peace" that was to follow the war, and the bright new world that was to be redemptive, without contemplating how such wartime ideals, as comprised in the Four Freedoms of the Atlantic Charter, would be applied to race relations in the United States. The times called for a hard and dispassionate view of American racial realities as well as a rededication to American ideals for the future. This

*This essay is reprinted from *Ethnic Leadership in America,* ed. by John Higham. Copyright © The Johns Hopkins University Press, Baltimore/London, 1978, pp. 91–118.

preoccupation suggests that the timing of Gunnar Myrdal's *An American Dilemma*—that "definitive scientific study" of American race relations—was not fortuitous.[1]

It was in 1944 also, the same year as Myrdal's study, that Edwin R. Embree, president of Julius Rosenwald Fund, wrote a book comprising the biographies of the thirteen "Negroes who are tops today."[2] His intent was to show Afro-American achievement in various fields, to celebrate individual victory over adversity, and to suggest the potential social benefits of a future of racial justice. To write his book, Embree had queried more than two hundred Americans, white and black, "who know the group best," giving them no guidelines. He asked them merely to use their own judgments in listing the black leaders of the day. He derived from this canvas a consensus of thirteen names, an interesting and strangely mixed group. There were two women, three educators, one research scientist, two writers of poetry and fiction, one labor organizer and leader, one "elder statesman" and intellectual, one composer of "classical" music, two singers (of "classical" and spiritual repertoire), the executive secretary of a protest organization, and one professional athlete. No professional politicians, clergymen, or businessmen made the list.[3] It was Embree's assumption, which was shared by many others, that these thirteen names constituted the top leadership of the race.

In the same year Rayford Logan edited a book of essays by notable Afro-Americans, assessing the status of race relations in the United States and defining some of the contours of that "new world" that must follow the war.[4] Unlike Embree, Logan collected the statements of prominent black Americans. He sought to make the book representative by offering a range of opinions from "conservative" to "radical." While only four of those in Embree's book reappear in Logan's, the lists are nevertheless remarkably similar in the occupations represented. Professional politicians and businessmen are conspicuous by their absence, and clergymen appear only in the guise of university and college administrators.

There would have been little argument that Embree's and Logan's lists constituted the recognized "leaders" of the Afro-American community, at least in one sense of the term. They were men and women who

1. Gunnar Myrdal, *An American Dilemma: The Negro Problem and Modern Democracy* (New York, 1944).

2. Edwin R. Embree, *Thirteen Against the Odds* (New York, 1944).

3. They were: Mary McLeod Bethune, Richard Wright, Charles S. Johnson, Walter White, George Washington Carver, Langston Hughes, Marion Anderson, W. E. B. Du Bois, Mordecai W. Johnson, William Grant Still, A. Philip Randolph, Joe Louis, Paul Robeson.

4. Rayford Logan, ed., *What the Negro Wants* (Chapel Hill, 1944), includes essays by Mary McLeod Bethune, Sterling Brown, W. E. B. Du Bois, Gordon B. Hancock, Leslie P. Hill, Langston Hughes, Rayford Logan, Frederick D. Patterson, A. Philip Randolph, George S. Schuyler, Willard S. Townsend, Charles H. Wesley, Doxey A. Wilkerson, and Roy Wilkins. This volume also contains an academic defense of caste from the point of view of a white Southerner in the "Publisher's Introduction," written by W. T. Couch.

had achieved greatness, as Embree said, against the odds, or who were assumed to stand for some point of view that was shared by a significant number of black Americans. Leaders perhaps, but only three, those attached to labor organizations, could be said to represent an actual constituency.

These books were signs of the times in the kinds of leaders they identified. Similar canvasses at other times would have had quite different results. In 1900, for instance, almost everyone would have agreed on Booker T. Washington, but beyond him most white people would have been ignorant and most black people would have disagreed. Or, in the mid-1970s, it would be impossible to draw up such a list without including those with precise constituencies—politicians and leaders of community-based organizations—while intellectuals, artists, and ministers-as-college-presidents would have lost status. These differences reflect several things: the changed perceptions of Afro-Americans and the society in general, the changes brought by experience in politics and social interaction, the changed self-definition of blacks, their changed goals and strategies, and the changed realities—political, economic, and demographic—of the Afro-American people.

At best it is a difficult matter to identify a group's leadership. We are seldom certain what we are looking for. As for the Afro-American, much of the historical leadership is lost to us because we have not been much interested in the process by which individuals such as Harriet Tubman—or the numberless anonymous black men and women who helped to organize the underground railroad or to disrupt the administration of the antebellum fugitive slave laws—were identified and accepted by others as leaders. We have focused on the *hero* rather than on the *process*. Thus, even the names of the courageous men and women who formed the Loyalty Leagues during Reconstruction and the "Redemption," who tried to keep alive the political voice of blacks in the South, braving the violence of the Klan, are lost to us. Their fate was generally an early grave, unknown and unsung. We have not, even with the arrival of sophisticated social science techniques, chosen to examine the "little community" with an eye to discovering how and under what circumstances leadership emerges on a neighborhood level. The Afro-American leader has almost always been thought of as one who had weight in the "large community." That is why books like Embree's and Logan's made sense.

We are never clear in distinguishing between leadership and achievement. Edwin Embree's thirteen were certainly "tops" in their fields, they had made it against great odds, but only a few of them could be considered leaders in any programmatic sense. Successful black men and women were naturally applauded by Afro-Americans in general, because they showed possibilities that might otherwise have been in doubt and because they stood as symbols of the race. Thus, a black millionaire in the early decades of the twentieth century, like Madame C. J. Walker, could generate the same respect as a hero of athletic contests. But, like

Jack Johnson, Joe Louis, and Mohammed Ali, such respect did not imply goals or strategies for the race's betterment nor a group that was willing to follow.[5] We should not be surprised that achievement evoked resentment as well as respect. Much was expected of black men and women of prominence. They were to "lead," to be agents of change. But in reality their influence was quite limited and their efforts for the race frustrated, resulting in the appearance of empty pretensions. Thus black people might applaud them as leaders of the race at one moment and dismiss them as "dicty" at the next.

We have assumed that a significant black leadership began to emerge in the antebellum period—centering in the convention and abolitionist movements—and came to maturity in the four decades between 1890 and 1930. We have thought of a personal leadership, the mantle shifting from Frederick Douglass to Booker T. Washington to W. E. B. Du Bois as each leader passed. And, despite the problems to such a model posed by the development of national protest organizations such as the NAACP and the Urban League, in which policy necessarily became corporate and not individual, we have identified the black chief administrators (the Walter Whites, the Roy Wilkinses, the Whitney Youngs) by virtue of their places in the organizations, ignoring the question of the base of their support in the Afro-American population. Of course, the advent of Dr. Martin Luther King, Jr., reminds us that an individual may personify so completely and perfectly the spirit and ideals of a movement or epoch that he becomes leader by common consent. Twentieth-century developments have made it more difficult for us to personify leadership. Activities on behalf of the race have become the province of organizations. Government, local and national, has become so highly bureaucratized, and blacks have become so dispersed within government, that it is impossible to imagine a single "Negro advisor" to the President. Thus, we can hardly expect to find, after World War I, a personality to dominate the age as Booker T. Washington did his.

Scanning the past, searching for the personal leader, historians have focused on the era dominated by Booker T. Washington and W. E. B. Du Bois as the coming-of-age of Afro-American leadership. Since the two men articulated so clearly (in full respect of complexity) the Afro-American psychological, social, economic, and political predicament, we have been satisfied by that assessment. But from the point of view of the generation of the 1970s, which does not share those men's faith that

5. The hero as leader is at least suggestive. The three heavy-weight champions mentioned had different public images—reflective of their respective epochs. Jack Johnson was a black man who beat white men and consorted publicly with white women at a time when both were acts of audacious defiance. Joe Louis was the personified challenge to theories of Aryan superiority, a gentleman, and "a credit to his race." Mohammed Ali reflects the spirit of black pride and defiance of the 1960s—both in his rejection of Christianity and his refusal to fight in the Vietnam War—representing the "black" as opposed to the "Negro" image.

ultimate justice is available within the system, their leadership between 1890 and 1930 appears as an interlude of great indulgence and good will (albeit forced), breaking a dominant current of distrust in the system's ability to reform itself without the force of power coming into play. Seen in this light, the attitudes, tactics, and style of black protest from the depression years, culminating in the civil rights movement in the 1960s, has more in common with the convention movements of the 1840s and 1850s, the underground railroad, and the obstruction of the fugitive slave laws than they do with the Washington-Du Bois era.[6] Of course, the mid-twentieth-century movements have been informed and affected by the interlude of "soft" protest, but they returned more and more to antebellum views on the need for power and direct action to bring about necessary changes in the American society.

It is useful, nevertheless, to focus on the roles of Booker T. Washington and W. E. B. Du Bois, for they and the era in which they dominated serve to illustrate the predicament of all Afro-American leadership, whatever the time or assumptions. All leaders have had to contend with a caste-like arrangement separating the races, defying all strategies. That is to say, race relations in the United States presumed a system of a dominant white and a subordinate black group, where there might be parallel social stratification but where the bar would remain immutable along racial lines. In practice it meant that blacks were not accepted as part of the political process; even where they were allowed to vote they were not given entrée to the political machinery. Their participation as citizens was so circumscribed that the instruments of neither political nor economic power would be in their hands. It is in this caste-like reality that the styles and strategies of black leadership have been defined over time.

Although caste has been used by others to define the special relationship of the Afro-American to the white society,[7] it is well to make clear that there are differences between American racial practices and the classical caste arrangements such as have existed in India. The most important difference is that in the United States there has always been a presumption of equality, which is not the case in classical caste societies.

6. Comments by Professor William W. Freehling at the Schouler Symposium at The Johns Hopkins University, February 5, 1976, were suggestive of this thesis.

7. Myrdal, *An American Dilemma;* Allison Davis et al., *Deep South* (Chicago, 1941); John Dollard, *Caste and Class in a Southern Town* (London, 1937); Paul Lewinson, *Race, Class, and Party: A History of Negro Suffrage and White Politics in the South* (London, 1932); Robert Weaver, *The Negro Ghetto* (New York, 1948); W. Lloyd Warner and Paul S. Lunt, *The Social Life of a Modern Community* (London, 1941); Frank U. Quillin, *The Color Line in Ohio* (Ann Arbor, 1913); Leslie H. Fishel, Jr., "The Negro in Northern Politics, 1870–1900," *Mississippi Valley Historical Review* 42 (December, 1955): 466–89; St. Clair Drake and Horace R. Cayton, *Black Metropolis* (New York, 1945); Robert S. Lynd and Helen M. Lynd, *Middletown* (New York, 1929).

All Americans would deny that constitutional inequality character-ized their society, and blacks, quite unlike the classical low-caste person, have accepted an inferior status as neither just nor permanent. Neverthe-less, the difference between principle and practice in American history in regard to white-black relations is too dramatic to ignore. It has only been in the last twenty years that the laws and official practices that sustained inequality as custom have been rescinded. Presumptions of inequality in social practice (in one guise or another) persist. Through-out our history, blacks have been considered "outlaws" in the sense that they could become victims of violence and vigilante groups without any expectation of protection from established peace officers. Until World War II, thirty-one of the states had laws prohibiting intermarriage, pro-tecting the dominant group from loss of identity.[8] Even in northern cities, where blacks had the vote, the major political machines have preferred to leave them unorganized rather than share power with them.[9] While it can be said that caste, as one thinks of it in India, cannot be used to define the black American's position, the word does help to make important distinctions between the experiences of white and black Americans. And it marks the crucial difference between the experiences of Afro-Americans and white ethnics. Ignoring these distinctions, some scholars have been too sanguine about the ease with which blacks could move into the mainstream of American life.[10] Caste, as I use it, is not mere rhetoric; it denotes the special and persistent subordination of Afro-Americans which has made certain leadership styles inescapable. Barring the word "caste," we would have to invent a new word.

Caste is the principal determinant of any discussion of historical Afro-American leadership. It defined the styles and possible strategies. The white and black groups were separate to be sure, the one dominant and the other subordinate, but they were not independent. While the separation suggested the possibility of a kind of "nationalism" on the part of blacks, the system would not tolerate the development of racial power blocks. Thus, in whatever other ways the dominated caste might

8. Aside from seventeen southern states, fourteen northern and western states had statutes prohibiting the marriage of whites with blacks. Arizona, California, Colorado, Idaho, Indiana, Michigan, Montana, Nebraska, Nevada, North Dakota, Oregon, South Dakota, Utah, and Wyoming abolished their laws after World War II. Such state laws were declared unconstitutional by the United States Supreme Court: *Loving et ux, Apellants v. Virginia* (1967). Cf. Harry A. Ploski and Ernest Kaiser, comp., *The Negro Almanac* (New York, 1971), pp. 252–63.

9. Martin Kilson, "Political Change in the Negro Ghetto, 1900–1940s," in *Key Issues in the Afro-American Experience,* ed. Nathan I. Huggins, Martin Kilson, and Daniel Fox (New York, 1971), 2:167–92; Ira Katznelson, *Black Men, White Cities* (London, 1973), chaps. 6 and 7.

10. Nathan Glazer and Daniel P. Moynihan, *Beyond the Melting Pot* (Cambridge, Mass., 1963), and also Glazer, "Blacks and the Ethnic Groups: The Difference and the Political Difference It Makes," in Huggins et al., eds., *Key Issues,* pp. 193–211; Oscar Handlin, *The Newcomers* (Cambridge, Mass., 1959).

mirror the dominant, separate political machinery was not one of them.[11]

Despite differences of class and culture, blacks were easily viewed by whites as a monolith and, for practical purposes, outside the body politic. It was convenient to imagine an individual or two who might be called the "Negro Leadership." They might be persons of notable achievement, respect, and reputation who could be understood to speak for the race. Lacking mechanism for popular choice, such people simply "rose to the top." This pattern is in many ways suggestive of styles of management by colonial powers. Some have referred to such leadership style as clientage or patron-client politics.[12] There was no expectation that a black leadership would arise from the people and be selected and sustained by them.

Between 1890 and 1930, the interlude of "soft" protest, caste imposed two styles on black leadership. From his position in schools, church, or journalism, the spokesman for the race could be an advocate of social change, envisioning a caste-less society where all artificial and arbitrary barriers were removed and all men and women would be able to rise according to merit. Such leaders were of a reformist mode, leaders more of a movement than of a race. While the focus of their reform was racial, the audience was understood to be all right-thinking men and women, regardless of race. Such reform leaders were not uniformly applauded by whites. Monroe Trotter, of Boston, was thought too outspoken and "radical." W. E. B. Du Bois was seldom on good terms even with his white colleagues in the NAACP. Others, like James Weldon Johnson or Walter White, seemed more congenial. Regardless of how whites felt about them, prominent black reformers were acknowledged as "spokesmen."

There were those, on the other hand, who attained prominence and respect, often by remarkable personal achievement, whose principal concern was not reform but the effective manipulation of the system. Caste patterns, and the continued subordination of blacks and whites, were accepted as real, perhaps inevitable. One needed to find ways to serve onself and one's race in terms of that reality. Such men, who were to serve as leaders, had first to be recognized by white men of power as exceptional persons who had influence in the black caste. Such leaders became conduits through which whites channeled their patronage and philanthropy to blacks. It was much easier and more efficient to deal with one such spokesman than it would be to respond to the multiple interests that actually comprised the group.

To act on the assumption that there was one "Negro leader" was, in effect, to capsulate, externalize, and alienate the group from the body

11. Kilson, "Political Change"; Katznelson, *Black Men, White Cities;* James Q. Wilson, *Negro Politics* (Glencoe, Ill., 1960).

12. The term and image is that of Martin Kilson, "Political Change."

politic. Such leaders, who were so identified and used, necessarily became influential and powerful figures among blacks. But they were not products of popular choice, and what power they wielded was that of the white politicians and philanthropists they served. They were, thus, emblems of the black caste, and I call their style emblematic as opposed to reformist.[13] The capital example of this mode was Booker T. Washington, who combined genius, character, great personal vision, and opportunism to bring the emblematic style to perfection. But every city and town having a black population was likely to have its own such figure, most often lacking in Washington's redeeming features.[14]

Seldom was any leader exclusively reformist or emblematic throughout his career. Frederick Douglass, for instance, had both characteristics, reformist predominating the antebellum years and emblematic toward the end of his life. And men of compellingly reformist bent, such as W. E. B. Du Bois, showed evidence of being open to invitation to advise white men of power. While not mutually exclusive styles, they do characterize black leadership from Reconstruction to the onset of World War II.[15]

This was a leadership of personality. Never did such men work to organize black voters. While many talked of a time when the "Negro vote" would make a difference, few wanted to solicit that vote, and most were distrustful of those, like Marcus Garvey, who appealed directly to black masses.[16] They were something of an anomaly in an age of urban political machines, when the spoils of political office were being parcelled among white ethnics, and when ethnocentric and caste patterns were being institutionalized into public and civil service cadres and labor unions. Lacking power, excepting that of their white patrons, there was no basis for the kind of coalition politics fondly imagined by those who speak of an American pluralism. Caste does not make coalitions. The best that could be expected was antagonistic cooperation across caste lines. The situation was fraught with contradictions and dilemmas for the black leader.

Three characteristics marked the black leader: he did not derive his power from a democratic source, he was a self-styled exemplar, and his

13. I prefer the dichotomy "Reformist-Emblematic" to Gunnar Myrdal's "Protest-Accommodation" because I think the former more descriptive of the actual roles and intent.

14. While the word "token" could serve the same meaning as "emblem," I do not intend the pejorative connotations with which the word "token" has become charged.

15. Frederick Douglass, *The Life and Times of Frederick Douglass* (London, 1962).

16. Frederick Douglass's refusal to enter elective politics is interesting and pertinent here. Douglass, *Life and Times,* pp. 398–99; the argument against Marcus Garvey often turned on his "manipulation" of the masses; cf. A. Philip Randolph, "Garveyism," *The Messenger* 3 (September, 1921), reprinted in *Voices from the Harlem Renaissance,* ed. Nathan I. Huggins (1976), pp. 27–35. It is too seldom remarked how often the political thought of Afro-Americans has reflected an antidemocratic distrust of the masses; cf. Louis Harlan, *Booker T. Washington* (New York, 1972), pp. 300–303.

position was tenuous and vulnerable. This last feature resulted from the other two, but it was his role as paragon that was to place special limits on the Afro-American leader. He had to be acceptable in polite society, not threatening to decorum and order. He was to illustrate to whites that blacks could be respected and successful citizens and set an example to blacks of propriety, decency, and achievement.

After the Civil War there would have certainly been a consensus that Frederick Douglass was the single black leader of national stature, even though there were several blacks who held, for a time, important public office. Douglass had played a forceful and assertive role in the abolitionist movement. The Union victory, tied as it was to emancipation, was the ultimate triumph of Douglass's position. He was an extraordinary man; his life comprised slavery, escape, freedom, and public renown as a speaker and writer. He symbolized the dreams and hopes of the freedman. When American presidents, from Grant through Harrison, wanted to demonstrate their administration's recognition of blacks and their obeisance to the ideals of the war, they found a good symbol in Douglass. Of course, other blacks got political jobs, but with Douglass it was something more than mere political appointments.

After Douglass's death, the consensus passed to Booker T. Washington. There might have been other claimants, but Washington had special virtues.[17] As principal and founder of Tuskegee Institute, he was clearly working for the uplift of the freedman; he was a demonstrated builder, leader, and administrator. Furthermore, Tuskegee was a black institution (although supported by white funds), and its principles and goals seemed to accept and validate the de facto system of racial castes. In fund-raising for Tuskegee, Washington was in useful contact with very wealthy, powerful, and influential white men and women. While Washington did not have a power base in a political sense, he had in Tuskegee an institutional base which freed him from a primary dependency on anyone's political fortunes. Washington always, indeed, declared himself to be free of political motives and ambitions—keeping Tuskegee away from overt partisanship. Washington was also a southerner, his place and future was to be in the South where the bulk of the black population was to remain for decades and where one imagined the locus of the "Negro problem." Time also worked to Washington's advantage. With the death of Douglass, February 20, 1895, the representative of that generation of abolitionists and antebellum activists had passed. The resulting question of succession came at precisely the moment of Booker T. Washington's ascendency as an important national figure. Tuskegee had already proved successful, and Washington was already spending much time away on speaking and fund-raising tours. But the single most important event in Washington's career was to occur in September of the

---

17. Harlan, *Booker T. Washington*, pp. 222–23; Emma Lou Thornbrough, *T. Thomas Fortune* (Chicago, 1972), chaps. 5 and 6.

year of Douglass's death. It was then that he delivered his famous address at the Atlanta Exposition, affirming a prosperous New South based on caste arrangements. It would have been, from the moment of that speech, impossible to have challenged his claim as successor to Douglass. And, finally, Washington had the ability, despite controversy among blacks, to keep their loyalty and support.

Neither Douglass nor Washington was the product of a democratic process, nor were they chosen by their people to be spokesmen. Rather, it was as if one day Afro-Americans awoke to find someone everyone concurred was their leader and whom no one in his right mind would challenge. Since there was no effective political apparatus for blacks, how could it have been otherwise?

Few would have expected a different kind of leadership from the one that emerged. Their role was the uplifting of a downtrodden people. Thus, it was a leadership of aristocratic and elitist assumptions, not democratic ones. The black leader should not be one of his people; he should, alas, be better than his people. "It is not enough to have rights, but one must deserve and earn them," was a sentiment repeated so much by Washington and his white and black contemporaries as to become cant. It cast onto the Afro-American the task—required of no immigrant from Europe—that he prove himself deserving of the rights which the revolutionary fathers had declared to be natural and unalienable to all men.

It was in this context that black leaders served as exemplars, presenting themselves as living proof that blacks could perform as citizens in ways that were above reproach. They could, thus, serve as agents of white society's philanthropy and good will, and they would serve blacks as a symbol of racial pride and self-esteem. This exemplary characteristic of black leadership made for very limited possibilities.

An exemplar could not make the mistakes of normal men or democratic leaders. Consider Frederick Douglass's problems with the Freedmen's Bank.[18] As one of the trustees of the bank (he was made president in its final weeks), he had seen it as a practical instrument for improving the condition of freedmen. The newly freed slaves had to be taught and encouraged to save, and this bank was an especially attractive opportunity because it would allow black men to serve as officers and to learn to manage finance. Even the bank's magnificent Washington offices were inspirational. The success of the bank would be both an example of and a means for black achievement. But, alas, the Freedmen's Bank fell in the wake of the bank failures set off by the collapse of Jay Cooke & Company in 1873. Like any other bank failure of the time, those with small savings were most vulnerable, but more was the pity that with this bank many of the savings were the freedmen's first meager efforts at accumulation. Most of the officers of the bank, seeing the coming col-

18. Douglass, *Life and Times*, pp. 399–406.

lapse, were able to make timely withdrawals, thus cutting their personal losses. Douglass could not. The loss of the bank, to him, was a personal and racial setback as well as an institutional failure. As a black man and president, he was embarrassed. He did not want to abandon his people; he had to try to preserve his honor.

It is also in this light that one understands Booker T. Washington's insistence that neither scandal nor criticism fall on Tuskegee. It explains the autocratic character of his administration at the school, where the staff and the students were forever on display to local and distant white visitors. And we see this quality when we read the autobiographies of Douglass and Washington. So much did they see their lives as *public* that there was little room in their imaginations for *private, personal* reflection and self-criticism.

The exemplary role also perpetuated assumptions of racial inferiority; not a constitutional or genetic inferiority of blacks to whites, but a recognition that the present status of blacks was marked by a lack in education, industrial skills, cultural refinements, and experience in government. It presumed the need for uplift. Necessarily, such leaders were cast as apologists for the race. "It may be true," they would say, "that our present status is lowly, but there will come a time when we will earn and, therefore, deserve our proper place in your respect."

Ultimately, the exemplary black leader was enmeshed in contradictions. He was assumed to be exceptional. Could a handful of such exceptional leaders do more than mark the distance between themselves and the masses? Often implied in their autobiographies (explicit in *Up from Slavery*) was the notion of the self-made man, who by dint of character and commitment overcame the odds; while the inequities and handicaps were real enough, sound character and methods had been surpassing. Doubtless Afro-Americans could be thrilled by the stories of such individual black achievement, but one could not help but suppose that those who remained lowly were lacking something in character. Thus, the blame for continued poverty could be turned inward and become personal or racial fault rather than remain outwardly focused on circumstances and the system. Such leaders were, therefore, speechless before the comments they invited: "You made it, so it isn't impossible; why not the others?" and "But you are an exception; one cannot expect much from the others."

Booker T. Washington's rise to prominence and influence epitomizes the mode of emblematic leadership. His teachers, those who had a shaping influence on his life such as Mrs. Viola Ruffner of Malden and General Samuel Chapman Armstrong of Hampton Institute, were strong-willed, tough, self-righteous Yankee missionaries who were certain of the proper formula for Negro uplift. This formula reduced itself to the familiar Protestant virtues: industry, frugality, cleanliness, temperance, order, decorum, and punctuality. With such traits, men and women (even freedmen) could do what they set out to do; or, failing, could at least be of good character. The message was attractive, even compelling, to men and women like Washington because it was so reasonable, clear, and simple; and it focused on self-improvement and self-reliance rather than on conditions of inequity which one might have been powerless to change. The characteristics that were celebrated were conveniently opposite to traits ascribed to the typical freedman. It was easy to assume that if the freedman only learned these virtues, all would be well. The formula had morality, almost a religious quality; success went to the deserving. And the ministers who preached this gospel to Washington were so certain and self-assured as to be truly overpowering.

It should be remembered that this gospel formed a major part of the conventional wisdom and lore of American culture. It was reiterated throughout: from McGuffey's Readers, to Orison Swett Marsden, to Reverend Russell Conwell, to Horatio Alger, to Andrew Carnegie. It pre-empted any consideration of compensation for blacks or any other group that might have been exploited unfairly in the past. And, most importantly as far as race was concerned, since any useful reform was personal and focused on character, this formula in no way challenged racial caste patterns.

The significance of this education and background is in the way it prepared Washington to function within the system of caste. His special success was in his ability, emotionally and ideologically, to make the most of it that anyone could, more than most would have dreamed possible. His was a schooling in the narrowest form of pragmatism, where even the smallest success and achievement became the object. There was little room for speculation or concern about what *should be,* rather one disciplined one's mind to what *was* and what *was possible.* It was a training for a narrow maneuvering within given and unchallenged limits. Deferring ethical considerations, it appeared as opportunism.

One of the difficulties of assessing Washington's real character is the unquestioning and unself-conscious way he made himself an evangelist of the gospel of wealth and success. It would seem that he shaped himself to be a model of that prescription. Knowing the importance of appearance, we suspect that there was a private Booker, calculating his public image and managing himself to appear right before the world. The public Booker T. Washington was only a mask. But it is difficult to verify such suspicions. Recent scholarship has demonstrated that there was more to Washington than he allowed to meet the eye. He initiated and supported, anonymously and often in the most deceptive guises, court cases and projects designed to reverse trends of disfranchisement and racial violence in the South. But he was forever careful to protect his public image, and true to the emblematic style, he was ruthless against those who took more forceful public positions, who were agitators likely to antagonize white friends and supporters.[19]

As an emblematic leader, Washington accepted caste patterns and

19. August Meier, *Negro Thought in America, 1880–1915,* (Ann Arbor, 1963), pp. 112–13; Harlan, *Booker T. Washington,* pp. 296–98, 300–303.

was fundamentally in conflict with those of the reformist mode. There could, therefore, be little tolerance among the Washington loyalists for black leaders and organizations who were critical of caste. There were organizations and agitation for specific reforms, such as for federal antilynching legislation. There were those organizations, heirs to the antebellum convention movement, like the Afro-American League and the Afro-American Council, that would agitate for general reform. The Washington faction's style was to mute such agitation and to keep the appearance of a united black community under the leadership of Washington; one dare not frighten away white friends. In practice, the Washington faction, under the leader's specific instructions, worked within such organizations to see that nothing really happened. In effect, to disarm them.[20]

On the other hand, organizations that Washington thought might be useful, like the National Negro Business League, he was quick to take under his control and help support. Such practices had a deadening effect on black protest organizations into the twentieth century. Those who began the Niagara Movement criticized the Washington group not so much for philosophy as for the stultifying effects they had on others who would choose different paths. Many, including W. E. B. Du Bois, thought it possible to have several different, coexisting strategies. But Washington's instincts were correct. The emblematic leader survives best in a world of peace and complacency, and, above all, a good emblematic leader must be peerless.

When W. E. B. Du Bois criticized Booker T. Washington, it was in part for his tendency to stand mute before the great indignities against black people. But, more pointedly, Du Bois attacked Washington's program of education because it lacked any sense of a need to train a black leadership. To compete in the work-a-day world, one need merely be fitted with a useful trade and with industrious habits and attitudes; the rest would take care of itself. And, since Washington presumed not to change caste patterns, he saw only mischief from the kind of leaders Du Bois would have. As a reformist, antagonistic to caste arrangements, Du Bois wanted a cadre of college- and university-trained men and women who would challenge customary racial attitudes.

It may have been unfortunate that Du Bois used the term "talented tenth" to describe this group of leaders, because he has since been accused of elitism as against the assumed humility of Washington. Certainly, Du Bois was elitist in that he expected that only highly intelligent and educated black leaders could design and bring about effective reform. But Booker T. Washington was elitist in his own way, believing that blacks needed to be lifted up and that men like himself would be their models. Of the two, Du Bois was the more at ease with notions of

20. Thornbrough, *T. Thomas Fortune*, chaps. 5 and 6; Harlan, *Booker T. Washington*, pp. 263–67.

political democracy where even the unlettered and soiled would have the vote. When Washington wrote of rural blacks, his language was often heavy with condescension. On the other hand, some of the most moving passages of Du Bois's *Souls of Black Folk* are informed by his respect for the honor and dignity of a rural, unlettered people struggling futilely to better themselves. Both men were elitists, but whereas Du Bois called forth superior black men and women, demanding that their superiority be respected by whites as well as blacks, Washington's superior black would be properly humble, acting in deference within the precincts of caste.

A product of nineteenth-century higher education at Harvard and Berlin, Du Bois fed on romanticism both from New England transcendentalism and the German source. It was, therefore, no contradiction to celebrate both the exceptional man and the immanent spirit in the souls of all black folk. It had been that spirit which sustained their humanity through generations of enslavement, and it would be its redemptive spark in the days of trial that followed freedom. That humanity had to be honored; there could be no compromise. Du Bois saw the educated mind being able to transcend the mundane, ugly, and contentious circumstances so that one could feel a personal superiority whatever others thought. His dominant metaphor for the educational process in *Souls of Black Folk* is that of climbing a steep and rugged mountain. At the top, one would be buoyed and exhilarated by the experience of great personal achievement, and one would be open to the grand vistas of all past human experience and knowledge. That, in itself, would belie all superstitions and tendentious arguments justifying racial caste. Black men and women had to win at the white man's games—law, science, the arts, finance, business; it was not enough to be trained in useful trades.[21]

W. E. B. Du Bois was correct in seeing the close relationship between questions of leadership for Afro-Americans and systems of training and higher education. Colleges defined leadership characteristics. In the years following World War I, several black colleges witnessed uprisings of students, faculty, and alumni protesting their schools' failure to promote black leaders.

Raymond Wolters has recently brought the stories of these campus struggles into a single volume.[22] Black schools, colleges, and universities had continued patterns of management and control from the late nineteenth century. Most were sustained by northern white philanthropy; some were church supported. Howard University was supported by yearly congressional appropriations, while Lincoln of Missouri received state funds. Of the schools that Wolters discusses, Wilberforce, alone, was in theory supported by a black organization, the A.M.E. Church.

21. W. E. B. Du Bois, *Souls of Black Folk* (Chicago, 1903), chaps. 1, 4, 6, and 8.
22. Raymond Wolters, *The New Negro on Campus* (Princeton, 1975).

All of these schools, to a greater or lesser extent, had the tutelage of the interior as their institutional purpose. Most were little better than high schools. It was strongly held that training for the liberal professions was likely to be a waste of time, if not dangerous. All insisted that black students needed the closest supervision in matters of morals and social discipline, and, therefore, instituted regulations for student conduct considered excessively strict even for that time. Except for Tuskegee, where Washington had maintained a tradition of a black-dominated staff, these schools seemed to prefer white teachers and administrators and would have presumed it unwise to have had a black president.

It makes little difference whether these habits were from genuinely felt need or whether they were merely calculated to placate a white society that was indifferent and even hostile to black pretensions to quality in education. The black faculty and administrators, students, and alumni felt them to be holdovers from the Reconstruction era, vestiges of a system of tutelage where the students were never expected to emerge as men and women of real responsibility. Most of the protests were against such a mentality, and for the most part they succeeded in opening the way for the more general employment of black teachers and administrators, the eventual choice of black presidents at schools like Howard and Fiske, and some easing of parental regulations.

The struggle at Tuskegee was different in an important way. The issue there was the staffing and direction of the newly established Veterans' Administration Hospital. Consistent with caste patterns, it had been difficult for black veterans to receive care in normal facilities, especially in the South. The government decided that a hospital for blacks should be established, and that it should be in the South at Tuskegee. It was assumed by President Robert Russa Moton and other black spokesmen that blacks could, at least, reap the limited benefits of caste: employment of black staff and administrators in top positions of responsibility as well as in subordinate positions. The chief administrator certainly should be black. This seemed even more likely as Tuskegee had always been under black administration with a predominantly black staff.

But white Alabamans and other white southerners were caught in a dilemma. They did not approve of blacks being cared for in white hospitals or by white nurses. Yet, they were not prepared to concede easily to the presence among them of a highly professional cadre of black medical personnel. Whites were in the habit of assuming that such jobs belonged to them. And while they might have been persuaded to accept all of this as one of the realities of caste, they wanted at least to be placated by having a white man in charge of the institution. It was a classical dilemma of American racial caste: separate institutions are fine, but it is extremely hard to allow the inferior caste the implied power and perogatives.

Tuskegee managed to win its point. Its medical and administrative staffs were to be black, and the chief administrator and medical officer was to be black as well. But the story of the Tuskegee Veterans' Hospital and the struggles on the black campuses in the 1920s illustrate the difficulties for the subordinated caste to find in separate institutions the means of developing and training a leadership cadre that would be free to manage those institutions independently.

The realities of racial caste patterns forced all who would aspire to black leadership to confront several dilemmas, those who would attack caste as reformers or those who would exploit caste as emblems. For to deny caste was likely to mean denying the potential power in race as well. It was difficult to imagine how one could achieve a society free from racial discrimination in which all had a fair chance on the basis of merit through the use of organized racial power. Yet any significant reform, from the elimination of discriminatory laws to an anti-lynching bill, was only likely to come as a result of organized political pressure. Reformist leaders tended to shy away from the political organization of the black vote, even in northern cities where that might have been possible. Rather, they tended to place themselves in reform-oriented organizations such as the NAACP and the Urban League, to work with white allies to improve conditions and bring about a better society. The favored tactic of legal tests in the courts was attractive because there seemed to be visible results and because it conformed to a notion of reform coming from justice rather than from power. For obvious reasons, reformers looked askance at those who would mobilize blacks along racial lines. Racialist leadership, after all, contradicted the ultimate goal of a society that was color blind.[23]

Emblematic leaders were no less victims of dilemma. Accepting the reality of caste, one had to accept the de facto supremacy and authority of whites. To the mind of the pragmatist-opportunist, de facto implies de jure. Even the presumed advantage of apartheid, where blacks are free to build and to control their own institutions, has to be qualified by the necessary white dominance. Nor could the emblematic leader be comfortable with the political organization of blacks, for his status depended upon a complacent "constituency." Even the most modest political organization would lead to pressure and demands for change that the emblematic leader would not be able to deliver.

These dilemmas could be torturous, as illustrated in the many twists and turns in the development of W. E. B. Du Bois's political thought. He was fundamentally opposed to caste. He saw the capital problem of the twentieth century to be the "color line" and was certainly not tailored to the emblematic role. Yet, he could give his support to a segregated officer's training camp in World War I because it meant the possibility of commissioning black officers. He could applaud the establishment of the

---

23. Although W. E. B. Du Bois on occasion supported the idea of a "Negro Party," he never worked to organize one.

Veterans' Hospital at Tuskegee because it opened positions of authority to black professionals. And, frustrated by the intransigeance of race in America, he could articulate one of the earliest and clearest positions for black nationalism.[24] It wasn't easy to be a black leader.

There were men who attempted to defy these modes and, instead, would use black organization as an instrument of change. A. Philip Randolph saw his Brotherhood of Sleeping Car Porters as such a lever.[25] He tried to keep that organization free from white financial support and white dominance. He imagined that his Brotherhood, as an Afro-American union within the AFL, could bring about change. As a member of the AFL's councils, he imagined that he could prod the American labor movement to open itself to blacks. "A movement within a movement," he liked to say. At the session at which the Brotherhood was admitted into the Federation, Randolph warned its members that he intended to be a "spearhead which will make possible the organization of Negro workers." Without minimizing Randolph's influence, it is fair to say that by the 1960s the AFL was still the bastion of caste as well as of craft unionism.

Others, perceiving the intractableness of race, took a different course. Numbers of Afro-Americans have advocated some form of expatriation or escape from American society with its castes and its dilemmas. Names like Paul Cuffee, the early Martin Delany, Bishop Alexander Crummell, Bishop Henry McNeil Turner, and Marcus Garvey come to mind. There are others, and we might place among them those "nationalists" who have dreamed of (and on occasion built) separate black communities in the United States.

While I have focused on the "large community" in this discussion of black leadership between 1890 and 1930, this analysis pertains to the "small community" as well. For no city or town, north or south, with a significant black population was without its emblematic or reform leaders. They might vary in effectiveness, competence, and character, but they played similar roles. During this interlude of "soft" protest, these leaders were not challenged by black political organization or by white politicians who wanted to win the black vote. Except for Chicago, where blacks were included in the political machine as early as 1915,[26] white

24. W. E. B. Du Bois, "A Negro Nation within the Nation," *Current History* 42 (June, 1934), reprinted in Huggins, ed., *Voices,* pp. 384–90; see also W. E. B. Du Bois, *Dusk of Dawn* (New York, 1940), chap. 7.

25. A. Philip Randolph seemed always to have had mass organization in his mind. He was one of the few notable black leaders who worked to mobilize Harlem voters in the years before and after World War I. Significantly, however, his efforts were for the Socialist Party and not for major party organizations. Jervis Anderson, *A. Philip Randolph* (New York, 1973).

26. Ralph Bunche, "The Negro in Chicago Politics," *National Municipal Review* 17 (May, 1928): 261–64; Harold F. Gosnell, *Machine Politics: Chicago Model* (Chicago, 1939); Katznelson, *Black Men, White Cities,* chap. 4, n. 73, sees the black machine in

bosses preferred the emblematic leader to an organized black constituency. It was only as late as 1944 that Adam Clayton Powell, taking advantage of the disarray of Tammany, was able to carve out for himself a stable political constituency which would keep him in office until his forced removal in 1968.

Doubtless this exceptional use of political power brought more services, amenities, and jobs to blacks than they might otherwise have received. Yet, by World War II, blacks in no way reflected their numbers in police and fire departments, and jobs in public transportation were all but closed to them. Even in New York and Chicago today, caste marks with unerring definition the civil service administrations and staffs. Regardless of their numbers in these cities, power and policy are not in the hands of blacks.

Local, emblematic leaders, those who would be most likely to affect the day-to-day lives of black people, would not be identified by such books as Edwin Embree's or Rayford Logan's. They were not likely to be known outside their communities, and they were not likely to be seen as being extraordinary achievers. Yet they were more typical of Afro-American leadership before World War II than those who would be named by a canvass of two hundred white and black "who know the group best." But as early as the 1930s we can detect changes in style and attitude that would challenge the reformist and emblematic modes and that would move ultimately to the assumption of power rather than prestige as the instrument of reform.

An attitude of defiance, which had been common among the abolitionists, was rekindled in the 1930s and marked an end to the era of "soft" protest. It was strikingly evident in the depression decade, persisted during the war years, and literally exploded in the 1960s. Since World War II the language of black politics has been amplified in crecendoes of *demands* rather than *hopes*. The word "demand" was hardly in the vocabulary of black leaders until the 1930s. Those who announced a "New Negro" in the 1920s spoke of black "militancy" and of fighting back against white violence, they often warned of dire consequences from continued neglect and duplicity on the part of white leaders, but none of them demanded anything.[27]

Demands imply power, and most black reformers knew that the little power they had was in the logic of their positions and the morality of their claim. It depended, therefore, upon the perception, moral sensitivity, and conscience of whites. Little changed in the real power of blacks in the 1960s, but there was a new attitude among Afro-Americans: a willing-

---

Chicago to have been "co-opted" in the 1930s; for Adam Clayton Powell, see James Q. Wilson, "Two Negro Politicians," *Midwest Journal of Political Science* 4, no. 1 (1960).

27. Nathan I. Huggins, *Harlem Renaissance* (New York, 1971), chap. 2; Huggins, ed., *Voices,* part 1.

ness, like their abolitionist forebears, to break the peace and to become agents of disorder.

The tactic of direct action brought into play a power always implicit in democratic politics. The ability to make a public display, to embarrass, to disrupt, to overburden jails and courts is power of a certain kind. It gives politicians who would otherwise be unmoved a sense of crisis and the excuse to act. It can persuade a normally complacent public to at least remain complacent while reforms are enacted which might restore the peace. With little actual political clout and a willingness to use direct action, a minority can win limited objectives.

The willingness of black leaders and reform organizations to take direct action was rather slow in coming. Until the 1940s the style and rhetoric was similar to that of other progressives, relying on the exposure of inequities, agitation through journals, alliances with influential white liberals, and lobbying for favorable legislation. What was to become the prevalent tactic of court tests of discriminatory laws and practices was begun in the late nineteenth century, gaining dominance until its ultimate triumph in 1954. All the while, it was hoped that blacks would in time form a sufficient political weight to be effective in national and local politics. Little was done by black progressives, however, to organize the black voter. The closest that they would come to direct action were the various protest parades, calling attention to the rise in racial violence against blacks around World War I. But even these "demonstrations" were statements of moral outrage, were themselves quite circumspect, and were not at all intended as confrontations.[28]

While the organizers of the NAACP saw themselves as evoking the abolitionist tradition, while they shared the earlier sense of moral purpose and the racially mixed membership, they had a crucial element that their forebears lacked. The NAACP founders believed in the fundamental rightness of the American society and in the system's ability to reform itself. To them, racial inequities were a fault, but a sound system and essentially right-thinking people would ultimately correct them. Most of the abolitionists, on the other hand, knew that slavery was evil, that it was protected in the Constitution, that it corrupted the entire social fabric, and that it would not simply disappear. Abolitionists often claimed a "higher law" than the laws of the nation which sustained slavery, and most were prepared for direct action to defy those laws. Slaves, like Frederick Douglass, who ran away, stealing their freedom, blacks and whites who served the underground railroad, who defied federal officers enforcing fugitive slave statutes, who gave money (or their lives) for the raid on Harper's Ferry, these were agents of direct action. There was little of that in the NAACP.

Few blacks or whites by the 1930s were prepared to take the position

---

28. Charles F. Kellogg, *NAACP* (Baltimore, 1967), 1: 224–27, for that organization's response to the East St. Louis riots.

that a corrupt nation and corrupt laws and practices deserve no respect, or that civil disobedience was the proper course for the righteous. Most would have insisted that the reformer not only be personally above reproach, but that he should not adopt tactics or language that would fail a test of propriety. Above all else, black people should be models of rationality, decorum; they must be the most unflinching supporters of law and order. It must be the racist opposition that would be cast as demagogues and law breakers. While this position could result in a sense of moral superiority and self-satisfaction, it did not move a nation to act against lynchers, rioters, or those who would deprive blacks of their citizenship rights. Neither did it open to Afro-Americans jobs, better housing, or schools. And while the legal tactic achieved striking and important victories in the courts, it was impotent to translate the de jure to de facto.

The narrowness of life in the 1930s sparked a different kind of black reaction. The riot in the urban ghetto, striking against merchants and police, was first evidenced in that decade. The Harlem riot of 1935 foreshadowed in style and character those which would erupt in the 1960s. The Harlem community had been deeply shaken by the Depression. Before the "crash," Harlem had been a symbol of Afro-American optimism and possibility. Despite the poverty that was there even in the 1920s, there were clear signs of a developing middle class of professionals and working people. Blacks had equity in over 35 percent of Harlem real estate. But with an unemployment rate that was as much as three times that of whites and a chronic difficulty of capital accumulation, most of that promise had been wiped away by the 1940s. The Harlem riot of 1935 seems too familiar to us now. It was spontaneous, as if the people just exploded into violence. It was hard to equate the apparent cause with the magnitude of the reaction. No one seemed responsible for it. Some wanted to blame the Communist Party, but in the end all agreed that people were just fed up. In that instance, as was to become the case in the 1960s, black leaders neither provoked, nor led, nor controlled, nor ended the outburst. Their role, at best, was to explain the phenomenon to white officials and the public.[29]

The Communist Party, in its efforts to organize blacks in Harlem, while by no means the instigators of changes in attitude and tactics, serves to illustrate the new mood. There were forms of direct action by blacks in several northern cities. For instance, the "buy black" campaigns were effective in Chicago and New York. Such efforts were lead by "nationalist" types like Sufi Abdul Hamid in uneasy alliance with some black ministers. They tended to be local, however, with little larger political importance. The Communist Party, however, tapped into such issues as employment for blacks in Harlem, attempting to make it a

29. Claude McKay, "Harlem Runs Wild," *The Nation* 140 (April 1935), reprinted in Huggins, ed., *Voices,* pp. 381–84.

wedge of white-black cooperation in the labor movement. The Party used direct-action tactics to frustrate the evictions of blacks from their tenements, moving furniture and belongings back into the dwelling after they had been placed on the street by city or county officers. In such action, as well as in parades and demonstrations (often without a permit), black and white Communists were attacked and bloodied often enough by the police. It was the Communist organization and press, then, that joined in the standard and chronic black complaint against police brutality. In all of this, the Communist Party seemed in the forefront of changing attitudes about proper and effective protest.[30]

The NAACP's embarrassment over the Scottsboro case illustrates another aspect of this shift in attitude. The Communist Party took over the defense of the Scottsboro boys from the outset. Despite acrimony and repeated charges that the Party was cynically using the boys and their parents, the NAACP was never able to wrest the case completely from the Party's control. The NAACP was simply too slow in acting. It was always very careful in the investigation of cases before taking them on and equally careful in the choice of legal staff and preparation of briefs. Generally, its cases were argued by conservative white lawyers whose strength was in their prestige and experience and who were careful not to antagonize legal authority. The Communist Party, on the other hand, was not burdened by such fastidiousness. It was a corrupt and oppressive society that should be on trial, not the black youths. The speed with which the Party's lawyers could act, the directness and simplicity of its stand, was responsible for gaining the confidence of the boys and their parents. And while the NAACP and other liberal forces persisted in trying to alienate the boys and their parents from the Party's lawyers, they were never able to succeed. For even black officers, like William Pickens, found it impossible to disguise a felt superiority to these southern black peasant folk. After all, their principal argument was that the boys and their parents were dupes of the Party; that was patronizing enough. So it was easy to tag the reformists, black and white, as elitists and bourgeois.[31]

The Party's tactics in the case were also at issue. There was little hope that the Scottsboro case could be won by legal brilliance in the courtroom. Unless the boys could be proved not to have been in the boxcar with the white girls, or unless the girls could be made to recant (and even then), there was no chance that the court in the little Alabama town would move for acquittal. Given procedural correctness, one could

30. Claude McKay, "Sufi Abdul Hamid and Organized Labor," in his *Harlem, Negro Metropolis* (New York, 1940), pp. 143–81; Mark Naison, "The Communist Party in Harlem, 1928–1936" (Ph.D. diss., Columbia University), chap. 3.

31. Naison, "Communist Party in Harlem," chap. 4; Dan T. Carter, *Scottsboro* (Baton Rouge, 1971); for an interesting discussion of the NAACP's style in legal advocacy see, August Meier and Elliot Rudwick, "Attorneys Black and White: A Case Study of Race Relations Within the NAACP," *Journal of American History* 62 (March 1976): 913–46.

not depend on the United States Supreme Court to reverse the convictions. With the best legal talent in the world, the Scottsboro youths were most likely to be executed. Unless, that is, it was made too embarrassing to do so. So the trial and the case became an international *cause célèbre,* exposing the ugliness of southern and American justice. The Party wanted to put southern officials and courts, and the entire American system, on trial before the world. That was not the way the game was normally played. While the tactics justified the charge that the Party was using the case to serve its larger political interests, it is true, nevertheless, as many blacks observed, that without such tactics the Scottsboro boys would have been dead. What was the price of propriety?

Such tactics were not new, nor were they exclusive to the Communist Party. But they foreshadowed the spirit of direct action used by A. Philip Randolph in "demanding" of Franklin Roosevelt some federal fair employment instrumentation. Randolph threatened a march on Washington, which would certainly embarrass a nation fighting against Nazi racism and disrupt the war effort. In Randolph's March On Washington Movement was the kernel of the direct-action tactics later used by CORE, SNCC, and other groups in the 1960s. It was the same mood and spirit (perhaps with different motivations) that inspired Paul Robeson to announce at the height of the Cold War that Afro-Americans should not fight in a war against the Soviet Union, and for A. Philip Randolph to threaten President Truman with a national appeal for civil disobedience if blacks were drafted into a segregated army.[32] Congress and the President were deeply shaken by such threats. Lacking an emblematic leader of the national stature of Booker T. Washington, congressional committees called upon a wide assortment of "Negro spokesmen" to repudiate Robeson and later Randolph. True to the role, such a figure as Jackie Robinson (newly admitted into a major league system) could be counted on to testify that blacks had always been loyal to the United States and always would be. It was such pressure, nevertheless, that forced President Truman to desegregate the armed forces.[33]

The Brown Decision in 1954, by overturning *Plessy* v. *Ferguson* and the "separate-but-equal" doctrine, shattered the legal and constitutional rationale which had protected racial caste patterns. It would seem that one had only to wait for a law-abiding citizenry to comply for racial justice to be established in the land. But the defenders of caste had never been respectful of the law, as it applied to the rights of blacks. Defiance of the law, civil disobedience, and even mob rule had long been major weapons in their arsenal. Defiance seldom involved risk for them because the coercive power of the state was generally in their hands. Almost in tandem, the defiance and direct action of the protec-

32. Anderson, *A. Philip Randolph;* Virginia Hamilton, *Paul Robeson* (New York, 1974), pp. 131–34.
33. Anderson, *A. Philip Randolph,* pp. 274–82.

tors of caste provoked new and massive direct action by those who
wanted change.

The genius of Martin Luther King and the early leaders of CORE
and SNCC was their combining of direct action and civil disobedience
with the high moral tone of those on the side of the law (the "higher law"
at times) and justice. Nonviolence was the ligament that held these
volatile forces in tension. With national TV coverage, even for the most
complacent, it was always easy to tell the bad guys from the good guys.
It was the bad guys who assassinated black and white, men and women,
who burned churches and exploded bombs killing little children. The
moral weight could never be questioned. Such direct action provoked
crises, it obliged federal response. It is clear enough that the Justice
Department, lacking any policy and itself supportive of maintaining
caste, was in no way prepared to manage change in a peaceful way. In
the vacuum of national leadership, the civil rights organizations were
obliged to provoke crises in order to make federal officers approach
their duty.[34]

Nonviolent, direct action brought victories but exacted a heavy toll
on those in the movement. Lives were lost. There were beatings, harass-
ments, and constant threats against life. It took extraordinary and sustained courage to persist. Certitude in one's moral correctness was hardly
enough to feed on. While the action was dramatic, the changes seldom
were clear or immediate. Little wonder that many black youths began to
wonder if nonviolence was not ineffective and a sign of weakness. But
direct action without nonviolence lost its claim to the public conscience
and justified retaliation by means of overwhelming public force.

Young black leaders were understandably restive about a movement
which was not black in its character and dependency. Like earlier reformist groups, the civil rights organizations, while having strong black leadership, were heavily dependent on white allies, influential whites, and
white money. Seldom did their organizations tap down into any black
constituency, except as they moved into voter registration in the South.
The question could well be raised: Should not black goals and priorities
be established by blacks themselves? What would happen if some other
issue were to capture the imaginations and the enthusiasm of the white
allies, as the Vietnam War was to do? Thus, the cry for "Black Power"
reflected the historical need for the political organization of black
masses, that their will be articulated through a black leadership. So
leaders of the black revolution turned toward building a "positive black
consciousness" and to organizing the "black community." The basic distrust of their white allies was merely an awareness that coalitions were
impossible without a true power base. The organization of such a power
base has been going on in the North and the South since the 1960s,

34. Steven Lawson, *Black Ballots: Voting Rights in the South, 1944–1969* (New York,
1976), chaps. 9 and 10.

sometimes with and sometimes without the young militants of the civil rights decade.

Direct-action tactics had their limitations. They could provoke complacent people and agencies into action; they could call up public funds to support the community and to keep the peace. Once the edge of moral superiority was lost, or once the public and officials became indifferent to moral appeal, legal force could be used with impunity. And once the threat behind the demands (escalating often to feed mass media's insatiable need for sensation) came to imply violence against police, these public forces could rationalize even preemptive violence against putative assassins. Northern police as well as southern sheriffs could become agents of official murder. And, of course, direct action and civil disobedience had always been the tactics of those who supported caste, and they would be again. Adopting slogans like "white power," "Irish power," "Italian power," and "Hard Hat power," northern whites were willing to use these tactics in northern cities to redraw caste lines in jobs, housing, and schools.

The vitality of caste, surviving the civil rights decade and the black revolution, has been remarkable. Nothing shows it more than the continuing struggle over civil service occupations and standards for employment, and, most of all, the struggle against de facto segregation in the public schools. White opponents of busing have not been subtle in their defense of caste lines. Many are quick to say that race is not an issue. In a way they are right. For it is not a question of whether or not blacks should be admitted into white schools; the question is how many? The term "tipping" is indicative, for at some point the character of the school stops being white and becomes something else. For as the numbers of blacks grow in the student body, they are able to affect the important nonacademic features of the school: its dances (the music and style), its athletics, and even its student government. In schools of small black populations, those blacks who play important roles reflect upon the liberality of the school and the community. But in schools with 35 percent or more, blacks become prominent because they have the power to be. These are often more important issues than academic excellence or the "quality of education" most often talked about.

It is hard to be persuaded that there is a meaningful difference in academic quality between South Boston High and Boston English. Both are pretty bad, as is most of the Boston public school system, victim of more than a decade of acrimonious conflict to protect caste and ethnic prerogatives. Black Bostonians do not have the alternative of accepting caste, saying, "let the Irish have their school, we will have ours under our community's leadership." That has been the argument of those who have placed themselves against "integration." Whites in Boston, in their school committees or in their unions, will be no more willing than their New York counterparts have been to permit the implications of caste which would allow control of institutions (and jobs) to fall into the hands of blacks. So the issue becomes the maintenance of caste under white subordination or the breaking of caste patterns; schools and jobs become the occasions. Blacks in Boston and other northern cities have no alternative but to destroy caste as it is manifested in primary public institutions, even if it means a continued white and middle-class exodus and decline of the cities. Alternatives to that result are not in the hands of blacks at all.

The "tipping" metaphor applies equally to cities as well as to schools. We have seen the exodus of whites (and many middle-class blacks) from cities as the non-white population has increased. Such demographical factors have been said to be central in the general decay of the cities, although there are other factors. But the result in many northern cities has been that blacks have come into their own as an effective political force at a time to inherit growing problems and costs and fewer rewards and opportunities. Be that as it may, the evidence is clear that in the cities, as in the South, black political organization is coming into maturity. Black reformers and those who would be emblems, or stand for the Afro-American people, must give way to the black leader who has popular support and a power base among black people.

Such a result is to be preferred over a leadership of prestige and pretense, but it has problems nevertheless. As the history of ethnically dominated city machines illustrates, political leaders whose power has come from a popular base have not always been equitable or wise in delivering service to their constituency. That is why white ethnics, although organized and represented for a long time, still feel disaffected, alienated, and powerless. Sophisticated political machinery, as we have good reason to know, is no protection against venality and opportunism of leaders. And as events since the 1950s, and especially Watergate, indicate, real power in the United States has become corporate and plutocratic and is likely to continue to be so. The much awaited advent of political maturity among Afro-Americans may have arrived in time to be an anachronism.

After a century of experience struggling with the reality of caste, where leaders of the black community were only so effective as their reputations, connections, and influence with whites would permit, we are beginning to see evidence of something new. Black officials, elected to local and national office and appointed to the high places in state and national administrations, reflect power rather than prestige. The Black Caucus in Congress indicates a consciousness and willingness to use that power as a lever with which to bargain. We will see in the next few years whether caste is sufficiently weakened to allow more than token power in the hands of blacks. Whether or not, or rather to what extent, coalition politics can work across racial lines remains to be seen. Antagonistic cooperation may remain a better description of interracial politics. But the true test of theories of coalition politics had to wait until blacks had the organized political power that could be measured in the balance.

It is well that we applaud the advent of political maturity among Afro-Americans. Yet we must be attentive lest a quality be lost in the process of change. Those leaders who lacked political clout—Booker T. Washington, W. E. B. Du Bois, A. Philip Randolph, Martin Luther King, Malcolm X—embodied a vision, passion, and integrity that is generally lacking in the political mechanic. However much we might denigrate the notion of leader as exemplar—as well we should when it is empty of power, pretentious, self-righteous—Americans, white and black, in this post-Watergate era, can only pray for leaders who see their role as public figures to be examples of dignity, honor, and the selflessness of genuine statesmanship. But that is a problem and challenge for the national community, not merely for Afro-Americans.

The analysis of Afro-American leadership in terms of caste patterns illuminates the fundamental difference that race has made in American life. In very few ways can it be said that the Afro-American experience is analogous to that of white ethnics. While all have shared some forms of discrimination, and most may have felt the contempt of their fellow Americans, blacks alone, as a native population, have been systematically excluded from effective political coalitions. If spokesmen for white ethnic groups complain today that their people's aspirations are not being realized, that they feel powerless to control their futures, that they are victims of social and demographic flux, it is not because their groups have been historically excluded from political machines, from labor unions, from power in civil service and government. It may be that their leaders have delivered only superficially, that their definition of group interests has been so parochial and self-serving as to be indifferent to class or community interests. In any case, white ethnics have been all too willing to find primary identity in race and color (even prior to ethnic identity), strongly defending caste and failing to invite linkages where interracial coalitions might be effective.

The standard preoccupations of ethnic leaders have been quite different from those of Afro-Americans. White ethnic leaders have been mainly concerned with the defense of the group—its identity, its culture, its neighborhood—against the acculturating and assimilating vortex of American society. They have also had to struggle with the problems of dual loyalties, to the United States and to the motherland. These problems have never been central to black Americans.

Ironically, ethnic defensiveness is often caused by the ease with which certain groups can assimilate into American society. Foreign language disappears, young people move into the suburbs, customs and the old ways are lost. In a society where class loyalties have been weak, a perceived loss of ethnic coherence can produce anxiety, especially for those who are immobile because of poverty or age and, therefore, unable to move as the neighborhood changes. The sense of a cultural vacuum at the center of American life has provoked what some have called a romantic ethnicity[35] which tries to recapture some elusive quality that has given the group meaning in the past.

The defensive concern of some ethnic leaders sometimes comes from the possibility that the group may disappear. Some Jewish leaders have, therefore, struggled against the trend toward intermarriage. A relatively small ethnic population with a low birthrate, Jews might well imagine that the group may lose numbers and cultural integrity if intermarriage continues at a high rate.

This kind of ethnic defensiveness has not been a major element in the programs of Afro-American leaders. Color, itself, has been a safeguard against the fear that black Americans would disappear. Afro-Americans have made much of having a distinctive culture, but few have worried that it was losing its vitality or integrity. And caste has worked in such a way in America that even the children of intermarriages are additions to the group rather than losses from it. While mulattoes were a distinct category in the United States' censuses from 1850 to 1910, they never had in this country the semiofficial social status enjoyed by their counterparts in the West Indies, Haiti, and Latin America. In the United States, for all practical purposes, one was either black or white. So, while black Americans have had conflicting views about intermarriage (often negative), they have not been motivated the same as white ethnic leaders.[36]

Often, white ethnic leadership has been most pronounced about issues regarding dual loyalties. Events in the motherland naturally inspire sentiment and emotion among those who have migrated and their children. At such times, ethnic leaders have wanted to resolve conflict by identifying with American interests, or, as has been far more often the case, insisting that American interests are identical with the perceived interests of the motherland. Thus, ethnic leadership has been enmeshed in struggles for the Irish Republic, for the German and Allied sides in World War I, against communist regimes in Eastern Europe, against Castro in Cuba, and for Israel against its Arab antagonists. It is fair to say that the United States has found it impossible to design a foreign policy since World War II independent of particular ethnic interests.

Black American leaders have been free of this kind of dual loyalty. Like it or not, Afro-Americans' single national identity is with the United States. It is true that there is a propensity to be in sympathy with Third World countries. But Afro-Americans have so far not insisted that the United States' interests are identical with any given nation. There

35. Gunnar Myrdal, "The Case Against Romantic Ethnicity," *Center Magazine* 7 (July/August, 1974): 26–30.

36. Especially if we consider Anglo-Saxon as an ethnic group.

has been strong support for African nationalism, but until the recent events in Rhodesia and the Union of South Africa there has been little effort to affect American-African policy. Perhaps, until now, the issues in Africa have been too ambiguous and Afro-Americans have been without effective leadership. But the conflicts in southern Africa have ripened at a moment when black Americans have the kind of political leverage to affect policy. It remains to be seen whether an American mentality, habituated to a tradition of caste, can adapt itself so as to promote a smooth transition of power from the hands of white men to those of black men.

22

Slavery and Its Defense

The problem of slavery in the United States grew out of contradictions between the system and its social and historical context. It was a permanent and arbitrary condition of unfreedom in a society which, as it developed historically, defined itself as free. It was a hereditary social status in a society that revolted against, among other things, heritable rank and class. In a society that proclaimed human rights were natural rights, it defined certain human beings as property, chattel, and, therefore, devoid of rights others needed to respect. Although believing themselves equal in the sight of God, Christians debased Christians as slaves for profit and power. Because American slavery was racial slavery, it created and sustained a population thought exotic and unable to be assimilated with the dominant race and culture.

Such contradictions have plagued the course of human bondage in the New World. They raise questions that need to be explored. What were the American origins of slavery? Why did slavery develop in a nation that continually gave expression to the goal of human freedom? What were some of the early antislavery expressions? Why did slavery continue to thrive? And what were the justifications invented by a moral people to affirm and defend it?

From 1619 (the date of the first reported slaves imported to a continental British colony) to the Civil War three and a half centuries later, these contradictions just noted plagued American society, both those sections having slaves and those that did not. From the beginning, there were persons who found the system repugnant, those who argued for abolition, as well as those who could tolerate it only at a distance. They all pointed to the conflict between deeply held values and the ownership and exploitation of other human beings. As one might expect, opposition and criticism of the institution brought forth rationalizations, apologies, and defenses, most often couched in terms of similar principles: the

*From *Main Problems in American History,* ed. by Howard Quint, et al., University of Massachusetts Press, 1986.

right to property, the defense of civilized culture against "savage" culture, and so on.

Given such conflict from the beginning, it is perplexing how slavery began and took hold in the British American colonies. Englishmen had said that English air was too free to abide slavery. Why in the colonies, if not in England? There were obvious reasons. Building new colonies required a large supply of cheap and controllable labor. The open and frontier conditions of seventeenth-century Virginia and Maryland gave English labor options not available to them at home. It was difficult to exploit the indigenous peoples. The well-established Atlantic slave trade made Africans available for purchase, and having neither place nor status, they became especially vulnerable to the total control of a slave system.

Still, most historians write about the establishment of slave labor as an "unthinking decision" made by colonists. They simply started using more African labor and discovered themselves, in time, as masters of slaves. The generation of the Founding Fathers could hardly imagine their own forebears as responsible, and they tried to blame the slave system on the British Royal Africa Company and the mother country's need for a favorable trade balance. By the Revolution, few Americans were willing to admit that slavery was the deliberate choice of Americans.

In recent years, historians have conceived the origins of slavery in various ways. Oscar and Mary Handlin saw it as an outgrowth of the early-seventeenth-century labor shortage. If English and African labor had been equally available to the colonists, they argue, Africans would not have been used in large numbers and racial slavery would not have developed in Virginia, Maryland, and the Carolinas.

Furthermore, they pointed out, English servants and laborers, customarily tied as they were to their masters by indenture, long contracts, and custom, were not free men and women in our sense of the term. Thus, the argument goes, early in the century there was slight real difference between English and African servants. By mid-century, however, a sharp drop in the availability of English workers made Africans more attractive. Since Africans had no legal or customary rights within the English system, laws that formalized their "unfreedom," making it permanent and heritable, were possible and desirable. Such laws were enacted in the 1660s in Maryland and Virginia, and these laws became the model for slave codes and statutes elsewhere.

Never claiming the English colonists were without race prejudice, the Handlins argued that legal and institutional differentiation between English and African servants defined the one as free and the other as a permanently enslaved class. These status distinctions in law and society became the basis of American racism.

Other scholars reverse cause and effect. Historians Carl Degler and Winthrop Jordan have stressed English antipathy toward nonwhites from virtually their first contacts. In other words, the English colonists brought with them such deep-seated racial fears and suspicions that the very presence of Africans in the colonies resulted in a special status outside normal community life.

Slavery was a means of capturing an exotic and vulnerable population for a permanent labor force, generating in turn, racial attitudes to rationalize and support the institutions thus created. For the other, racial attitudes predetermined a special status for Africans. There is documentary evidence to support either emphasis. Records from the earliest time show that blacks suffered heavier penalties than whites for the same offenses, that blacks and not whites were likely to be considered "lifetime" indentures. On the other hand, the very laws that defined blacks as slaves complained that "diverse freeborn English women do . . . marry with" Africans, and often black and white servants stood accused as co-conspirators. This suggests that racial fears and hostilities may have reflected norms the governing classes wished to impose, but they did not pervade servant classes as much as had been imagined.

The historian Edmund Morgan has focused on this point in locating the origins of racial slavery in Virginia at the insurgency culminating in Bacon's Rebellion. The social disorders leading to this seventeenth-century uprising raised the specter of class conflict uniting black and white against the governing and propertied classes. Racial slavery, according to Morgan, served to divide permanently the classes most likely to rebel against established authority. Racial slavery defined all whites as free and gave them, in principle, a common status to defend regardless of class.

White men and women, regardless of socio-economic condition, knew they were free because they had the example of slavery conspicuously before them. American freedom, thus, was defined by American slavery.

Despite different emphases, all these scholars share one common insight: however one might explain its origins, racial slavery made the basic social divisions in America along race lines rather than class lines. Affluent and impoverished whites would concur in the enslavement and oppression of blacks, assuming an equality in race that could not exist in class. This concurrence formed the ground for the unlikely alliance of slave-owning and nonslave-owning whites in defending the institution against its critics.

Slavery existed in almost all the colonies. Only Georgia, a colony founded on philanthropic principles, prohibited slavery for a time; the prohibition was repealed in 1749. Under frontier conditions, the attraction of a totally controlled labor force in which one held capital value—being able to profit from price appreciation and natural increase through reproduction—was too compelling for settlers to resist. The number of slaves were few in New England colonies like Massachusetts; however, Rhode Island and Connecticut had a sizeable slave population. The Middle Colonies of New York, Pennsylvania, and New

Jersey had significant slave forces. In none of these northern colonies, however, would slave labor have such a dominant economic and social effect as it would on the South.

Northerners were no more morally sensitive than southerners. Differences in slave population and, therefore, differences in the influence slavery would have, economically and socially, had less to do with principle than with colonial circumstance. The early diversification of the economies in New England and the Middle Colonies made slaveholding less necessary than in the South, where a virtually monolithic economic and social order developed around the slave system. Smaller, more diversified holdings made slave labor only marginally efficient. With a substantial portion of the governing classes not slave owners, it was harder to fashion laws and social practice designed exclusively to protect and sustain slavery. Furthermore, New England life especially centered on community and social control. Puritans, who grew anxious about the threat to their social order from Quakers and other such interlopers, could hardly feel easy about the prospect of large numbers of Africans in their midst.

They were not uneasy, however, about slavery elsewhere. Few New Englanders had qualms about profiting from trade in slaves. Great merchant fortunes were built in Rhode Island and Massachusetts from the Atlantic slave trade.

Both New Englanders and southerners held that slavery and the slave trade was justifiable since the Scriptures acknowledged it as proper to enslave "captives in just wars." Thus, the ongoing colonial conflict with Indians resulted in the enslavement of Indians, and the rationale was extended to assume that the African cargo in the Atlantic slave trade were such "captives."

In one of the earliest abolitionist tracts, Samuel Sewall attacked this reasoning as willful (and sinful) self-deception. Notably, however, Sewall's attack of slavery was only a partial condemnation of the oppression of innocent people for profit. It also rested on the belief that such an exotic people as the Africans could not be absorbed into the Christian community and would remain a source of social disorder. Sewall's argument, like much abolitionist writing to follow, was not so much pro-black or pro-African as it was antislavery. Sewall's ideal community had no blacks in it.

From the earliest time, we can see two broad approaches to the prospect of an African presence: (1) capture them into a cheap and controllable labor force, but remove them from the community through the institution of slavery; (2) reject the advantages of African labor, but exclude blacks from the community, making them unwelcome. These basic patterns characterize the differences between South and North on matters of race and slavery throughout the antebellum period.

The American Revolution brought the contradictions of slavery in a free society sharply into focus. Most Americans of that generation found it difficult and embarrassing to both proclaim the ideals and principles of the Revolution embodied in the theory of the "natural rights of man" and defend the ownership of humans as slaves. Some slaveholders freed their slaves. George Washington was among them. We can trace most of the free black population of southern cities like Baltimore, Charleston, and Savannah to these manumissions.

Other slaveholders held their slaves. Thomas Jefferson was among them. For some, it was due to a belief in the system. For others, the cost of abrogating a large capital investment was the determinant. Most persons who continued to hold slaves shared Thomas Jefferson's views, as expressed in his *Notes on the State of Virginia,* that blacks and Indians were not quite *men* in the sense of the Declaration of Independence and that a republican community of equals could not survive if it was racially mixed. For three decades following the Revolution, Virginia and Maryland slaveholders complained about slavery as a burden rather than a boon, but felt trapped into continuing slavery because the alternatives were unthinkable.

One way out of this dilemma was to "colonize" free blacks (and slaves freed for that purpose) in Africa. As early as 1776, Jefferson proposed a plan for African colonization. Pro-colonization resolutions were passed by the Virginia Assembly in 1800, 1802, 1805, and 1816, and the American Colonization Society was established in 1817. Out of 143 emancipation societies in 1826, 103 of them were in the South, including four abolition newspapers.

Antislavery sentiment and the revolutionary ideals were able to prevail in New England and the middle states of New York, Pennsylvania, and New Jersey. Abolition was most easily accomplished in Massachusetts where, in a 1783 case involving a master's rights over his slave, the Supreme Judicial Court declared that by virtue of the Commonwealth's Declaration of Rights, "slavery in this State is no more." So, by judicial decree, slavery was ended in Massachusetts.

Nowhere else was it so simple. Slave owners, asserting the principle of property rights, wanted just compensation to free their slaves. Nonslave owners did not want to be taxed to compensate owners, who had received labor from slaves throughout their lives. Moreover, nonslave owners wanted owners to guarantee the welfare of slaves too young, too old, or too infirm to be self-supporting. Their fear was that masters would free slaves only to make them wards of the state and burdens on taxpayers.

The debate, particularly in New York, Pennsylvania, and New Jersey, was long and bitter. Each state, however, hit upon a form of gradual emancipation without compensating slave owners. New Jersey's last slave was freed in 1836.

However ambivalent about slavery the Founding Fathers were, they were not prepared to address the problem directly. Neither slavery nor Africans are mentioned in the Constitution, but compromises written into the text have much to do with them. Slaveholding states wanted slaves counted for purposes of representation although they would clearly have no voice in that representation. At the same time, Southerners did not want slaves counted for purposes of tax assessments. Nonslave states wanted the reverse. Article I, Section 2 words the compromise by the reckoning, "three fifths of all other Persons" for purposes of representation and direct taxes.

The Constitution provided for the ending of the importation of slaves in Section 9 of the same Article. Again, the language is revealing: "The Migration or Importation of such Persons as any of the States now existing shall think proper to admit, shall not be prohibited by the Congress prior to the Year one thousand eight hundred and eight. . . ." Yet, in Article IV, Section 2, slave property is guaranteed: "No Person held to Service or Labour in one State, under the Laws thereof, escaping into another, shall, in Consequence of any Law or Regulation therein, be discharged from such Service or Labour, but shall be delivered up on Claim of the Party to whom such Service or Labour may be due." From 1793, there would be federal statutes obliging federal authorities to assist in the apprehension and return of fugitive slaves.

While the Constitution did not mention slavery, it supported the institution in several ways. By means of the three-fifths clause, it gave slaveholders added political power through added representatives. It placed the federal government against those slaves who managed to escape slave masters and cross state lines. By empowering the new government to call forth the militia to execute the laws and repel invasions, it also obliged the government to "suppress Insurrections." Thus, the whole power of the United States could be marshaled against slave uprisings.

While the Founding Fathers, in drafting the Constitution, seemed anxious not to attack slavery as it existed, there is reason to believe that they thought (or hoped) it would not extend far into the nation's future. The decision to end the foreign slave trade in 1808 indicates some expectation of a dying institution. Many of the same men who drafted the Constitution, while serving in Congress under the Articles of Confederation, designed a clearly nonslave future for the United States. The Northwest ordinance of 1787 provided a blueprint for the future United States. It laid out the procedure by which the Old Northwest Territory (to become the states of Ohio, Indiana, Illinois, and Michigan) would come into the Union. Article Six of the Ordinance prohibited both slavery and involuntary servitude in the territory. It nevertheless provided for the return of fugitives.

From the Revolution to the 1820s, there were few who could predict slavery would continue being economically viable. The severe economic depression following the Revolution and the loss of those advantages tobacco and rice growers gained from being part of the British mercantile system placed Virginia, Maryland, and the Carolinas in serious distress. The market price of slaves was low despite the end of the importation of Africans. Commodity prices were no longer subsidized by the British, and overused land was becoming less productive. Many southern spokesmen gloomily predicted a day when slave owners would run away from their slaves to avoid the cost of caring for them. Yet, they could not be moved to convert to a free labor system. They feared the consequences of a racially mixed society (especially one based on republican principles). They could not discover a practical way to remove the black population, especially as there was no alternative labor force. Yet, at the same time, they feared slave insurrections such as the 1794 Haitian uprising. It's little wonder that some southerners were likely to express themselves tragically regarding slavery: they were victims of historical choices from which they could not escape.

Such tones changed in the 1830s. The English textile industry created a large and expanding market for cotton, and the cotton gin (invented in 1793 by Eli Whitney) made possible the profitable marketing of short-staple cotton. It was a crop suitable for cultivation throughout the South, and it could benefit from the economies of scale possible with mass slave labor. Furthermore, the Indian policy of Andrew Jackson succeeded by the mid-1830s in removing Indians from the Old Southwest to the trans-Mississippi West. The whole of the deep South was now open for settlement and exploitation. Like the original southern frontier on the Atlantic Ocean, this new land would be opened with slave labor.

These changes revitalized slavery. Even old South planters could shift into cotton production. Or they or their sons could move onto new lands in the Southwest, taking along some of their slaves. They could sell their slaves at a profit to the growing demand. Early in the 1830s, Southerners ceased their plaintive apologies for the "peculiar institution" and began to speak of it as a "positive good."

But never quite escaping the sense that slavery was morally corrupting, Southerners developed a rather elaborate intellectual defense of the peculiar institution. There was a racial and cultural ground; they argued that Africans and Afro-Americans were a savage people who were better off in American slavery than they would be in Africa. They were not ready to belong to normal, civilized society, and slavery was a kind of school that would, after a few generations, bring blacks up to European standards of civilization. Before then, blacks would either be enslaved or destroyed by white superiors.

Slavery's defenders also found support in the Bible. Both the Old and New Testaments acknowledged the existence of slavery and did not condemn it as such. They turned to Genesis and argued that blacks were Canaanites, descendants of Ham, and thus cursed to hew wood and carry water. And they liked to quote Saint Paul's admonition: "slaves, obey your masters."

The most original defenses for slavery were the political and sociological arguments of John C. Calhoun and George Fitzhugh. Calhoun, the spokesman for slaveholders' interests, considered slavery as a political interest. By the 1840s, the South was a minority section of the country, and it had to defend itself against growing northern and western power. Calhoun wanted to design a defense of the South and of slavery through the Constitution and through guarantees of minority, that is southern, rights. Furthermore, he hoped for an alliance of northern conservatives and southern planters to maintain political control over the nation's future. In his *Cannibals All, or Slaves Without Masters,* and *Sociology for the South,* Fitzhugh attacked the very basis of "free society" and *laissez-faire* capitalism, which left the working classes exploitable without institutional support or defense. Slaves, he claimed, were better off than free workers in the North or elsewhere in the world.

As slavery became more central to southern growth and development, and as the defense of slavery became more ardent, the South closed itself off from criticism. The southern abolitionist movement, which had been quite lively in the 1820s, was dead a decade later. Antislavery advocates and journalists either left the South, were forced out, or retreated into silence. Fearful of criticism, the South silenced its internal critics. Fearful of disorder through slave insurrection and uprisings, they tightened slave codes, enforcing them through citizen patrols, and made it illegal to manumit slaves in most of the South. By the 1850s, the South had become a totalitarian society—all in defense of slavery.

The revival and expansion of the southern slave economy shattered the hopes of those who imagined slavery would not expand, dying of its own weight. Militant abolitionism, thus, began in the 1830s just as Southerners were rediscovering value in their peculiar institution. Many southern voices that were critical of slavery found the only way to be heard was from northern cities. The abolitionist movement picked up the contradictory themes that had been felt from the beginning: slavery was an offense against Christian principles of human worth; it was an offense against democratic principles based on the natural rights of man; it corrupted the master, oppressed the slave, and sapped the moral character of the nation. The same mid-century reform spirit that fed movements for public education, care for the mentally ill, temperance, rehabilitation of criminals, women's rights, and so forth, fed the abolitionists, sharing as they did a common assumption of the divine nature of man and man's perfectibility. It was a powerful force for reform that passed by the South altogether due to slavery.

White and black abolitionists challenged in their papers and on the platform the moral basis of slavery and the moral character of slave owners. Blacks like Frederick Douglass, Sojourner Truth, and Harriet Tubman, all former slaves, were examples of the potential of all slaves. Douglass's newspaper, *The North Star,* along with others like the *Liberator* kept the moral issue before the public. Those not opposed to political action, like James G. Birney, Gerrit Smith, and Salmon P. Chase, formed the Liberty Party in 1839 which, in the election of 1844, was responsible for the defeat of Henry Clay. Along with the Free Soil Party in 1848, it helped defeat Democratic candidate Lewis Cass.

Abolitionists, however, never accounted for large numbers of followers. William Lloyd Garrison's *Liberator* had a circulation of only 3,000 at its height. Their influence, however, reached far beyond their numbers. By the 1850s, they had succeeded in getting northerners, including persons uninterested in freeing slaves and even hostile to blacks, to characterize southern slaveholders as a corrupt planter aristocracy that was willing to oppress all labor for power and wealth. Many settlers in the West were themselves yeoman farmer refugees from what they considered an arrogant and tyrannical slaveocracy.

Northerners were no more ready to accept a racially mixed society than southerners. Even with their hostility toward slavery and slaveholders, they were seldom sympathetic with blacks, and many feared that general emancipation would free hoards of blacks to migrate north into free states. Each of the northwestern states, as they entered the Union, prohibited slavery but also placed major restrictions against black residents, requiring bonds of those who would settle permanently denying them the right to vote, own property, or otherwise live as a citizen. Anxiety about black residence grew as the society became more democratic and extended the suffrage to all men. Generally speaking, universal suffrage meant white, manhood suffrage.

Northerners increasingly saw the future of the nation, particularly the future of the western territories, in light of the Northwestern Ordinance's prohibition of slavery and involuntary servitude. The states of the Old Northwest had come into the Union as "free states." They fought over this principle in the territory west of the Mississippi that had been acquired in the Louisiana Purchase of 1803. That struggle seemed to be resolved in the Missouri Compromise of 1820—Maine was admitted as a free state and Missouri was admitted as a slave state, and the remainder of the Louisiana Purchase would be organized along the line forming the southern border of Missouri (36°–30″ latitude); south of that line would be slave territory, north of the line would be free states.

But the issue was not settled. Following the Mexican War, the territory ceded to the United States included land west to the Pacific Ocean. The issue of slavery in the territories was reopened. Southerners and slaveholders claimed that the West was as much a part of their patrimony as it was for Northerners and free farmers. Persons who called themselves "Free Soilers" wanted the West open for free white men—to establish free institutions without the unsettling presence of blacks and the dominating presence of a planter, slave-owning class.

The "free soil" position about slavery in the territories was incorporated into the Republican Party when it was formed, and Abraham Lincoln's views best represented that position. Speaking before the Illinois Republican State Convention in 1858, Lincoln declared, "A house divided against itself cannot stand." Neither Lincoln nor the Republican Party was prepared to attack slaveholders and slavery where it existed, but they stood against its extension into the territories and, thereby, its continued growth in the United States. It was this position, finally articulated in the Republican platform and the Lincoln candidacy of 1860, which the South found unacceptable and led to secession and civil war.

Lincoln wanted to maintain that the sanctity of the Union—not human rights—was the principle for which the war would be fought. He made attempts in the early war years to assure the South, particularly the border states, that slavery could continue within a Union under a Republican administration. Very reluctant to exploit the South's vulnerability, due to its dependency upon slave labor, Lincoln was willing to accept black volunteers into the Union army only after November 1862. By the end of the war, more than 250,000 blacks served in the military— greatly contributing to the Union victory.

North–South conflict brought into sharp focus the contradictions that slavery created in a free society. They could no longer be avoided or compromised as the politicians thought they had done in 1820 and 1850. Wartime exigencies forced Lincoln to issue his Emancipation Proclamation, freeing, as of January 1, 1863, all slaves in areas still in rebellion against the United States. Yet, the ambivalence about the consequences of a racially mixed society remained. Along with others, Lincoln continued to seek a way to colonize blacks elsewhere, in Africa or in Central America, and he was reluctant to suggest extending the franchise to freed men.

These matters were settled in the law by the constitutional amendments that grew out of the war. The Thirteenth Amendment (1866) prohibited slavery and involuntary servitude. The Fourteenth Amendment (1868) defined citizenship so as to include blacks and extended federal protection of their rights. The Fifteenth Amendment (1870) denied to states the right to exclude persons from the vote on the ground of race, color, or previous condition of servitude. By these amendments, slavery was ended, freed men were defined as citizens with the rights of other citizens, and not to be denied the vote because of race or past slavery. The end of slavery was an expropriation of property. Four million slaves, the capital investment of their owners, were freed without compensating slaveholders for their loss. However, the slaves were also losers; their patrimony was expropriated in that they were set free without compensation. For over three centuries, their forebears had labored and produced wealth, compensated only by subsistence. Unlike other populations, slaves could accumulate nothing, build nothing, and pass nothing of material value to their heirs. When they were freed without compensation for the generations of labor and the creation of value, they were set loose with nothing. They had, as one historian has put it, nothing but freedom.

23

Plus Ça Change . . .

Beware victory most is a lesson all history teaches; Afro-American history most of all. We have wanted so much to believe in progress that we have welcomed each change, each new achievement, each apparent political triumph as another step along the way to racial justice—hoping to see that ultimate goal in improved statistics of black professionals, political office holders, and suburbanites. In time, though, we are made to realize however much the privileged have gained, the lot of the race has changed little. We seem destined to relearn each generation that racial justice can come only when all Americans decide to play a different game, not the old one better.

Some called it the Civil Rights Revolution, others the second Reconstruction. Now it is part of two decades of our history. It began with the Supreme Court's overturning the separate-but-equal doctrine which for over a century had given government sanction to racial segregation. There followed federal legislation protecting blacks in their civil and voting rights—reiterations and amplifications of legislation enacted a century earlier. Then there was affirmative action, which would rectify a history of race and sex privilege in the job market and professional training. So spectacular were these achievements that we have been easily blinded to their shallow effects. Blinded and bartered too. Those of us advantaged enough to cash in, to call ourselves part of the great middle class, have too easily adopted its bourgeois concerns—our property, our neighborhoods, the schools of our kids—finding the threat to our way of life the so-called underclass, rather than the social and economic malignancy which spawns it. You give up something in perspective when you join the team.

The story of the first Reconstruction is instructive. "Now we are a nation; we have yet to become a people" is how Frederick Douglass defined the task of national leadership following the Civil War. His personal achievements had even then surpassed the most extravagant

*This unpublished article dates from the 1970s.

American dream. Born a slave, he escaped to become a leading abolitionist. Self-taught, he became a foremost journalist and orator in the
cause of black Americans' and women's rights. He helped to see black
combatants in the Union Army and fought to assure that their service be
weighed in post-war policy. His voice, along with events, conspired to
persuade Abraham Lincoln that the war had to be fought to end slavery
if the Union hoped to win. The forces of history seemed to be propelling
even the most grudging Republicans beyond themselves as champions of
human freedom.

Victories were strung like beads, one after the other: three constitutional amendments—abolishing and outlawing slavery, defining Afro-
Americans as citizens, and granting them the right to vote. The elective
power of black Americans would help put Ulysses S. Grant in office and
sustain the Republican party for over a decade. Congress would enact
civil rights bills and legislation to empower the federal government to
protect the citizenship rights of Afro-Americans. The change was dramatic, not just from slaves and outsiders to citizens; there were also,
overnight it would seem, black congressmen and senators and petty
office holders. Frederick Douglass himself would serve as U.S. marshal
for the District of Columbia, recorder of deeds, and later consul to the
Republic of Haiti.

Alienation has its advantages. Being an insider, part of the team,
makes one rely too heavily on would-be friends and sunshine compatri-
ots. It makes it harder to protest vigorously against systemic injustice.
Soon the Supreme Court denied the federal government power to act in
defense of citizens' civil rights, something it had shown little will to do
anyway. The Republicans abandoned southern blacks, and by the mid-
1880s they were effectively disenfranchised. Powerless, southern blacks
were left to the mercy of local injustice and northern blacks to system-
atic discrimination and mob violence.

In the 1890s, near the end of his life, Frederick Douglass had come
again to see himself as an outsider. As a black man, he had never been
an insider at all; it had been a deception. So, as an old man, he would
again use the voice of the agitator. He had discovered that the American
people were "disposed to be generous rather than just." Justice, after
all, implies a communality which Reconstruction had failed to achieve.
Americans had yet to realize themselves as a people.

Such dreams and deceptions have been part of the second Reconstruction as well. On the announcement of the Supreme Court's decision
in the school desegregation cases, a southern black woman was quoted
as saying: "It's like having a check for a million dollars; but it's the
weekend and the banks are closed. Come Monday, though. . . ." Well,
the banks opened with deliberate anguish, and now some people question how much the check was worth. Time and inflation have done their
work. Black children won victories in school systems which were bank-
rupt and disintegrating. Battle lines, indeed, were formed to bus black

children into such unmitigated mediocrity as South Boston High. Cities have become shells almost in proportion as black Americans gained political influence in them. And while one can point to moderate growth of a black middle class, there remains a chronic unemployment which reaches 45 percent in some categories of black youth.

We can say that things are better, certainly for the few. But there can be slight comfort in a historical relativism which celebrates the present because the past was worse. The so-called underclass must bear its plight as if no one had ever suffered before. Anyway, how do we measure the advantages over slavery to a family three generations under welfare with no hope but to rear a fourth? Poverty-induced criminality, racial and class inequities in the criminal justice system, prisons that are little worse than ghetto freedom, an alien police with virtual license to kill and brutalize the poor and non-white—what calculus can exult such a present over the past?

"Those who cannot remember the past are condemned to repeat it." A positive restatement of this negative dictum of George Santayana does not follow. We are, in fact, condemned to repeat the past precisely because of the way we remember it, as a justification for smug self-congratulation. We are destined to have more "Reconstructions," one after the other, until we do "become a people."

Less than a month before he died, Frederick Douglass was asked to suggest a strategy for black Americans entering the twentieth century. The old man's answer came from the depths of his being and the fullness of his experience—deceptions and humiliations as well as triumphs—"Agitate! Agitate! Agitate!" He continues to speak to all of us who would discover the real America.

24

Passing Is Passé

Black people, it seems, don't "pass" anymore. The Black Revolution may have had little effect on real power relationships between blacks and whites, improving the opportunities of advantaged blacks yet changing little in the circumstances of the desperate poor and deprived. But the Revolution's insistence on race identity, race consciousness, race pride, and race beauty has made anachronistic the game of hide-and-seek traditionally played by whites and blacks in America.

If, indeed, appearances are real, we have witnessed the end of a phenomenon that has persisted throughout American history. It revealed an abiding American anxiety about racial identification. It spawned suspicions and rumors about people even in the highest places. The story never died that Thomas Jefferson sired children by a black mistress, that they and their progeny lived as white. Andrew Jackson's enemies circulated stories that gave him an African ancestor. Warren G. Harding's domestic life would encourage almost any rumor, so there were those who whispered about "colored blood." Such confusion and uncertainty made "nigger in the woodpile" a common coin in the American language.

"Passing" has been a product of the single consensus in American race relations: the promise of American life and the American Dream actually applied to white men only. Throughout American history to our own day, laws, customs, and brute force have compelled Afro-Americans to know that they were not citizens. To use political power, to hold office, to own property, to get ahead, to protect one's family, and to survive may have been presumptions of the white American's existence, but they were often impossibilities for black Americans. At best, these conditions of citizenship have been problematic. Since being white made all the difference in American life, who would not be white if he could? But such reasoning exacted a psychic penalty. The man who worked as white but kept alive relations with black family and friends knew the immediate fear

*This unpublished article dates from the early 1970s.

245

of detection. On the other hand, he who tried to play it safe by moving to another place and "disappearing" into the white world doubtless nurtured guilt because of deception and the abandonment of race and family. And the fact that Afro-Americans did "pass" only served to deepen white anxieties about racial identification.

Nevertheless, until the 1960s most Americans would agree that, given the inconvenience of blackness, anyone who could be accepted as white would likely grasp the opportunity. Blacks might think it disloyal and unfortunate, whites might think it deceptive and dishonest, but both understood and expected it to happen. Some even fancied that the final solution to race problems would come when everybody looked more or less alike in color.

What I think has happened in recent years is that the assumptions of reasonableness have been undermined. True, it is still an inconvenience to be black in the United States, especially if you are poor. But being white and middle class is not as desirable as it once was. There has been a great turning away by American youth from what has traditionally stood as norms and models of life-style. To most black people, white Americans are emotionally ill and morally corrupt—from the President and Billy Graham to the "hard hat." To become white, therefore, means to take that sickness and corruption as part of the bargain.

It is for this reason, as well as the reassertion of race pride, that it has become important for Afro-Americans to be black, if nothing else. Lest there be doubt, a wide assortment of symbols—hairstyle, clothes, speech—are adopted to assert that blackness. Those black Americans who might otherwise be taken for white, rather than "pass," are even more anxious than their darker brothers and sisters to remove all doubt as to their blackness.

The change is not faddish, but profound and significant. Its importance will not be discerned in changes in power relationships, employment statistics, or institutional practices. But it is likely to bring white and black Americans to a healthier and more objective sense of who they are. Identity can be less burdened by guilt and fear. If that is so, the change will be well worth the trauma and hysteria that has so often marked it.

25

Two Decades of
Afro-American Studies
at Harvard

The year 1989 marked twenty years of Afro-American Studies at Harvard. Born in the tumultuous days of the takeover and "bust" at University Hall and the "strike" that followed—when the air was freighted with charges, claims to principle, and non-negotiable demands—the Afro-American Studies Department is one of the few recognizable survivors of the "student revolution" of the 1960s. As it presently stands, it would hardly be recognized or perhaps approved of by its original student advocates. Its survival, in fact, has been due to modifications and adaptations of those "demands": the nurturing of that germ within the students' concept which had sufficient legitimacy within the University to root itself and take hold.

The student demand for Afro-American Studies was essentially an extension of the civil rights movement, which had by the late 1960s come out of the South and set itself to expose and attack racism endemic in American society and institutions. Those students who would not go on a "freedom summer" in the South could attack racism in the colleges and universities where they were. Universities were attractive targets for good reason. They pretended to be better, more rational, more tolerant, more liberal than the rest of the society. They were more ready than most segments in the society to be publicly embarrassed and apologetic for the historical racism they shared with other American institutions, but they were no more ready than others to change in more than superficial ways.

Harvard, like most American colleges and universities, was willing

*This essay is reprinted from *Blacks at Harvard: A Documentary History of African-American Experience at Harvard and Radcliffe,* by Werner Sollors, et al. Copyright © New York University Press, 1993.

to open its admissions to a broader social spectrum that might increase the numbers of blacks and others from the inner-city. The numbers of black undergraduates did increase in most major institutions by the end of the sixties, and with larger numbers came different expectations, problems, and tensions. In earlier years, when there were seldom more than six blacks in any Harvard class (one or two at Radcliffe), expectations of "fitting in" encouraged black students to suffer any racial problems privately. With larger numbers and with fundamental changes in national sensibilities about race, however, even personal malaise could be taken as symptomatic of the broad, social pathology.

Certainly, black students of the fifties and earlier decades would have noticed that Harvard offered little about black Americans, or other non-whites for that matter. Very little scholarly attention was paid to Africa, Latin America, or what we now call the Third World.[1] Western Europe and the United States were the hub of Harvard's universe, and everyone seemed satisfied that was as it should be. Harvard was little different from other universities in these regards; ubiquity fed complacency. The newly enrolled undergraduates in the late sixties, however, had little reverence for an order and tradition that seemed to them to be part of the problem, defining the world and civilization so as to sustain and encourage genteel bigotry and even racism. They would demand changes in curriculum so as to make their education "relevant" to their lives. That would require focusing on black people and issues affecting them in ways few scholars in the United States were interested (or equipped) to do.

The painful irony was that the gesture of the colleges toward greater inclusion and uplift was met not only with little gratitude but with hostility and non-negotiable demands. It is little wonder that faculty at Harvard and elsewhere recoiled at the thought of undergraduates, hardly any from college-educated households, presuming to challenge the fundamental principles of liberal arts education. It seemed as if some were saying that Langston Hughes was as important to read as Shakespeare, Eldridge Cleaver as important as Machiavelli. Doubtless, some said as much; reasonableness was nowhere in great supply. But the central issue was the shattering of the complacency of the "hub," that self-created and self-sustaining center of the universe which was exclusively white and male, all else being relegated to the margins.

Harvard responded positively to the need and the demand. A faculty committee led by Henry Rosovsky (which included students as non-voting members) issued a report that recommended a "program" of study in Afro-American Studies. That program would call upon the

---

1. In this particular regard, Harvard has hardly improved in the past thirty years. Africa and Latin America were better represented in the fifties than they are in the eighties. A strong and important tradition in Asia (China and Japan) guarantees Harvard continuity and leadership in that region.

various departments to provide courses and appoint faculty.[2] The report also recommended increased graduate fellowships for black students and a variety of measures to improve black student life on campus. The student members of the Rosovsky Committee were unable to win for the report the general approval of Harvard's black students. Nevertheless, the report was adopted by the Faculty and a committee was established to implement it.

In two months, however, unrelated matters of the University Hall sit-in, the bust, and the strike radically changed the political atmosphere, and the Association of African and Afro-American Students was emboldened to make new demands. It wanted Afro-American Studies to be a *department* rather than a *program,* and it wanted a student voice in the selection and appointment of its faculty. On April 22, 1969, the faculty were asked to vote on these propositions without altering them. Although deeply divided, the faculty voted for the changes the students demanded.

It was a bitter decision, many of those voting in favor doing so under a sense of intimidation. In that mood of crisis and perceived threat, the department was born. It would suffer, during its first ten years, from the lingering doubts and resentments harbored by faculty never fully convinced of Afro-America as a legitimate field of study, doubtful of it as a "discipline," and suspicious of what often appeared to be separatist tendencies on the part of its advocates.

Adding to the problem was a general confusion of aims by student advocates. There seemed to be three underlying (not necessarily compatible) expectations.

1. *To Have Something That Is Ours:* Ironically, the larger number of black undergraduates seemed to increase or intensify their feeling of isolation. The institution in all its aspects—courses, student activities, facilities—could easily be divided into "theirs" and "ours." Black students could call little of what normally existed at Harvard as "ours." Among a range of other demands for reform, that for black studies was a demand for legitimacy of place. In such a view, the traditional curriculum in the liberal arts—excluding non-whites and non-western culture with scarcely a thought—was "theirs." It was assumed that courses on African and Afro-American history, literature, etc. would be the answer. Some advocates cared about the content of those courses; others cared mainly that the College make room for them, that they appear in the catalogue. For the former, it would not matter much who taught the courses. For the latter, it was often of great importance that the subject matter be taught by blacks. In both senses, however, black studies was a matter of defining "turf" in the university community.

2. *Quest for Identity:* Ironically, it was the very liberalization of

2. The model was similar to one later adopted by Yale, which for over a decade exemplified the best of Afro-American Studies programs.

America—residential desegregation, greater prospects of upward mobility—that threatened black identity. In the past, all blacks had been pretty much in the same boat, regardless of class and education. Now, prospects for the fortunate few seemed to include admission into the best colleges, positions in corporate America, and escape from the ghetto. Did a step along this road to an "integrated" and mainstream future mean the abandonment of one's people and one's past? Increased mobility made the question, "Who am I?" all the more compelling. The identity crisis was exacerbated in white colleges where little if anything was taught about blacks, and where teachers would announce without embarrassment that William Faulkner was the best delineator of "Negro character" in American literature. Too often, however, the quest for identity intended the discovery and veneration of black heroes and heroines, the celebration of black people's "contributions," running counter to the recognized scholarly values of disinterested analysis.

3. *Field of Study:* Too often lost in the rhetoric was the idea that Afro-American life, history, and culture constituted a legitimate field of study independent of the demands of the time. Few of the student advocates would have known about the lifelong commitment to the promotion of that field by such major figures as W. E. B. Du Bois, Carter G. Woodson, Arthur Schomburg, J. Saunders Redding, Benjamin Quarles, and John Hope Franklin. The central idea was that the Afro-American experience was worthy for what it told about black people and their history in America and for what it tells, through refraction, about American history and culture. It should be studied by scholars, like any other area of human experience, and it should be drawn from the remote edges, from oblivion, to the center of American studies. That was a concept different from what most students advocated, and it is interesting to note that respected black scholars, such as John Hope Franklin, were more than a little suspicious of the programs that were being created in the name of black studies.

As we enter the twentieth year, much of the dust has settled. Afro-American Studies seems an established fact at Harvard. Arguments about its legitimacy as a field of study or a suitable field of concentration for undergraduates are no longer heard. Its students, in course enrollment as well as concentrators, are remarkably racially balanced. Its faculty contribute to the Core and to other university-wide offerings. There is every reason to believe that the department will remain at about its present strength for some time into the future.

Although it was created in an atmosphere of crisis, with confusing and conflicting justification, the present ground on which the department stands is solid and rather conventional. It represents and advances Afro-American life, history, and culture as an important field for scholarly inquiry and study. And it is sustained in this by a remarkable growth of interest in the field over the past two decades. Increasingly, the field has been recognized in the United States and throughout the world. A glance at any of the major professional journals in the humanities and the social sciences will reveal a growing scholarly interest in problems and questions centered in what we now call Afro-American studies. Students of American life in Europe as well as in the Third World have increasingly turned to topics of Afro-American history and literature.

One sees the changes (often clumsy and insufficient) in textbooks of American history or literature. In literature the "canon" is being challenged and opened to include black writers among others. Course content in American history and American literature is beginning to reflect the change. And interdisciplinary programs such as American Studies and Comparative Literature are often leading the way for the mainstream disciplines.

Problems remain, nevertheless. The most difficult task we will have in the future is the recruitment of young people to become scholars in the field, and the identification and appointment of the best of a very small group to faculty positions. For the past decade and more, the best and the brightest of undergraduates have chosen law, medicine, and business over academic and scholarly careers, and that has been an even more exaggerated trend among minority students. At the same time, the demand for scholars in Afro-American Studies has been growing as new schools and programs establish themselves.[3] An additional problem of recruitment is that all too often institutions see appointments in Afro-American Studies as a way to address affirmative-action needs. That is to say, good white scholars are likely to be rejected even if a black scholar cannot be found. The Harvard department has stressed that we are interested in making the best possible appointments, regardless of race, and that the University's legitimate affirmative-action goals be met through university-wide recruitment.

Our strength into the future will be a measure of our meeting the challenges: to maintain an unwavering focus on our principal responsibility—the development and enrichment of our field of study; to maintain the highest standards of teaching and scholarship; to explore the intriguing frontiers of interdisciplinary scholarship.

3. Demographic factors will be important. California, for instance, expects that in the 1990s it will become a state with a majority of its population non-white. Its state colleges and universities are reconsidering and reinvesting in a variety of ethnic studies programs, including Afro-American Studies.

26

The Deforming
Mirror of Truth

Like a morning eagle . . . purblind among . . . wolds
—Keats

It is difficult to know whether to be more astonished by the boldness and courage of the Founding Fathers in their conception and framing of a "more perfect union" or at their purblind avoidance of the inescapable paradox: a free nation, inspired by the Rights of Man, having to rest on slavery. They were forthright enough in confronting certain paradoxes: the reconciling of liberty and order, of majority rule and minority rights. The devices they created to meet these challenges are familiar to us all: a written constitution, a bill of rights, checks and balances, judicial review. Yet, in no official document of their creation did they address, frankly and openly, the conspicuous fact of racial slavery.[1] As far as race and slavery were concerned—both primary facts of their life and times—the Founding Fathers preferred to avoid the deforming mirror of truth.

It is as if the Founders hoped to sanitize their new creation, ridding it of a deep and awful stain. If the evil were not mentioned or seen, it would be as if it were not there at all. By burying the most flagrant contradiction to all their values, there would remain an ideal and perfect monument to republicanism. The nation would, in time, become somehow as pure in fact as in idea.

1. The language of the Constitution that deals with slavery, i.e., the Three-Fifths clause, provision to end the international slave trade, and that referring to fugitive slaves, can only be called a language of avoidance. At no place in the document is slavery or are blacks expressly mentioned.

It was, however, a bad way to start. It encouraged the belief that American history—its institutions, its values, its people—was one thing and racial slavery and oppression were a different story. Nothing so embarrassing, however, nothing so fundamentally contradictory to the social ethos, can be kept at a discreet distance for long. It will intrude, and rudely.

American historians, nevertheless, have conspired with the Founding Fathers to create a national history, teleologically bound to the Founders' ideals rather than their reality. They have chosen to see American history from even before the Revolution as an inexorable development of free institutions and the expansion of political liberty to the broadest possible public. Like the framers of the Constitution, they have treated racial slavery and oppression as curious abnormalities— aberrations—historical accidents to be corrected in the progressive upward reach of the nation's destiny.

National history belongs to everyone and to no one, and thus may claim a universal authority. Insofar as it has succeeded, American history has managed such universality because its diverse population has accepted the Founders and their values as its own. Historical scholarship has served merely to add or take away some detail from the monumental edifice that was the nation. The story was unified, no discontinuity between the colonies and the Revolution, nor between the founding and the Civil War, nor between Reconstruction and the present. All this in a progressive construction of an ever "more perfect union" with each generation.

The holy nation thus acquired a holy history. A conspiracy of myth, history, and chauvinism served to create an ideology as the dominating historical motif against which all history would resonate. This master narrative, like the Constitution itself, could find no place at its center for racial slavery, or the racial caste system that followed Emancipation.

Even such a holy history, however, cannot ignore the imperious demands of the present for explanation through the illumination of the past. Race caste, racism, has been an undeniable and unignorable presence in American life since World War II. Its aggravating persistence has made challenging demands on the past, demands that cannot be comprehended through the sanitized and innocent master narrative. The present to which it must answer, furthermore, has been so fragmented by social trauma that the old master narrative no longer serves as universal authority. The Founders' hope that idea, defying fact, would become reality was vain. The American dogma of automatic progress fails those who have been marginalized. Blacks, the poor, and others whom the myth ignores are conspicuously in the center of our present, and they call for a national history that incorporates their experience. Whatever shape that new national history will take, it must have racial slavery as a structural part of the foundation of the edifice. It is not surprising, therefore, that in the past fifteen years slavery has been one of the most written about subjects in American history.

The Founding Fathers could rightly claim not to have invented slavery. It was of ancient date. The practice is known to have begun when conquerors began to take prisoners of war rather than kill them. The captives lived by the grace of their captors, and were, thus, merely the extension of the master's will. The sociologist Orlando Patterson argues that, throughout history, regardless of the people involved, slavery has had the common trait of the total and deliberate social debasement of those enslaved, as if they were, in fact, dead. The death that would have occurred, but for the capture, remains symbolically definitive of the slave's condition.[2]

Slavery is not, therefore, simply an absence of freedom. We do not, for example, think of convicts, military conscripts, hostages, and other such people with limited or no freedom as slaves. For Patterson, slavery involves a "social death" where the slave's existence and presence in a community is wholly contingent on the will and power of the master.

This theory has a particular meaning for American slavery. An early and continuing Euro-American rationale for slavery was that those Africans involved in the slave trade were "captives in just wars" who had been purchased by traders from their captors.[3] The institutionalization of racial slavery in the North American colonies was accompanied by a debasement of Africans beneath the status of other unfree and indentured labor. Afro-American slavery nurtured a rationale of constitutional and permanent racial inferiority that, by denying blacks elemental humanity, went far beyond ordinary bigotry and color prejudice. Emblematic of that social death is the Founding Father's exclusion of slaves in their declaration of "We the People."

By the mid-nineteenth century, after two hundred years of institutionalized racial slavery, the Chief Justice of the United States Supreme Court, Roger B. Taney, would write for the Court's majority that Americans of African descent had "no rights a white man need respect."[4] In other words, free blacks as well as slaves existed contingent on the will of white men. Race, itself, by the eve of the American Civil War, had become the shroud of a social death.

Two centuries of racial slavery had so confounded race with slavery that black and slave, white and free, became assumed categories. Free blacks, in the North as well as the South, were thought to be anomalous—denizens rather than citizens.[5] Unfree whites were unimaginable. The

2. Orlando Patterson, *Slavery and Social Death: A Comparative Study* (Cambridge, Mass., 1982).

3. Samuel Sewall's *The Selling of Joseph* (1700) is an early antislavery tract that refutes the claim made by traders and owners that slaves were captives in just wars.

4. Roger B. Taney's majority opinion in the Dred Scott case (1857).

5. A useful distinction made by Marina Wikramanayake, *A World in Shadow: Free Blacks in Ante-Bellum South Carolina* (Columbia, S.C., 1973).

emancipation of slaves could not transform a legacy of denied humanity and contingent existence. Slavery was a social phenomenon more extensive and profound than what is suggested by the concept of unfree labor.

In saying that slavery "was above all a labor system," the historian Kenneth M. Stampp wanted to correct a generally accepted view that slavery was an inescapable system of race relations, a school for an exotic and backward people. Stampp and other thoughtful scholars knew, however, that blacks continued in the mid-twentieth century to suffer under "what remains of the caste barriers first imposed upon them in slavery days."[6] What had survived once the labor system ended was slavery's legacy of social death. Black people's rights would remain contingent on white people's willingness to respect them.

American historians have been especially troubled by the fact of racial slavery in the United States. It jars so rudely with what are taken to be the main currents of American life and thought—the realization of the Founders' ideal through the development and expansion of freedom and democracy. Slavery is discordant with what we have taken to be the themes and directions of each period of our history: the settlement and the development within the colonies of the seeds of democratic institutions, the Revolution propounding the rights of man, the expansion of the nation and the extension of the franchise, the age of reform based on beliefs in human perfectibility. None of this comports well with the fact of racial slavery, nor with the persistence into our own time of racial caste and its consequences.

American historians, guarding the ideological integrity of the center, have wanted to treat race and slavery as matters apart from the real, the central story of American history.

Slavery has been seen as a pathological condition, studied as a disorder which had consequences leading to the Civil War. At most, it was the Old South's particular pathology to be ultimately excised for the health of the nation. Racism and racial caste—which issue from racial slavery—have been, in their turn, studied as the "tangle of pathology" of blacks and the so-called underclass. Very little thought has been given to the general health of the society that created and sustains them. Society and its historians have treated all these phenomena as aberrations, marginal to the main story, to be quarantined if we extend the metaphor. Thus, our national history has continued to amplify the myths of automatic progress, universal freedom, and the American Dream without the ugly reality of racism seriously challenging the faith.

Whenever we write history, we do so with a sense of transcendent meaning. No matter how limited or particular our study, we assume a

---

6. Kenneth M. Stampp, *The Peculiar Institution: Slavery in the Ante-Bellum South* (New York, 1956), vii, 34; for the emphasis on race relations and education see Ulrich B. Phillips, *American Negro Slavery* (New York, 1918), among his other works, and Lewis C. Gray, *History of Agriculture in the Southern United States to 1860* (Washington, D.C., 1933), Vol. I.

broader and grander context in which what we say has meaning and makes a difference. Any coherent historical account is underwritten by the assumption of a cosmic comprehension—God's presence if you will—that shapes our work ideologically and morally as well as scientifically. In writing our national history, we do so with a master narrative in our heads that sustains our collective sense of national purpose and identity, and resonates with our most compelling myths. That master narrative, with its dogma of automatic progress, cannot explain racial slavery and caste except as eddies of a grand, progressive, and ultimately engulfing current.

As we enter the final decade of the twentieth century, however, we are daunted by the intractableness of race. With a vast array of other circumstances challenging our faith in our historic sense of mission—our unlimited capacity for expanding and extending democracy, our power to command the future, and the meaning of progress itself—we may be forced to face the deforming mirror of truth as never before. The outcome would have a profound effect on the master narrative that commands our story. In fact, the result would be a tale more like Jean Paul Sartre's *No Exit* than John Bunyan's *A Pilgrim's Progress*.

The social death implicit in slavery and racial caste was carried over into the writing of American history until the 1960s. Black historians aside, American history, almost universally, was written as if blacks did not exist and their experience was of no consequence. It was as if, to paraphrase Roger B. Taney, black Americans had no word, thought, or act historians need take into account. This was more than oversight or accident. White historians shared the view of the general white public— the view of the Founders—that black people did not exist in the world that mattered.

Even in the writing about slavery, where blacks might logically be considered the principal subject, the habit was to write about it as an abstract social or economic institution, to see it as provocative of sectionalism and as a contributing cause of the Civil War. The slave's testimony was never sought and never recorded by historians. It was quite audacious for Kenneth Stampp to conclude his 1956 study of slavery with a former slave voicing a "simple and chastening truth for those who would try to understand the meaning of bondage":

> 'Tisn't he who has stood and looked on, that can tell you what slavery is—'tis he who has endured. . . . I was black . . . but I had the feelings of a man as well as any man.[7]

Even so, it was a singular reference in a book that, consistent with its time, made no other use of slave testimony.

In 1971, I observed that most "people think American history is the

---

7. Stampp, *The Peculiar Institution,* 430.

story of white men, and that is why blacks want a history of their own."[8] It was common then to claim that blacks had been "left out" of the standard histories of the United States. Along with that claim went the demand for an African-American history that would do justice to the role blacks played in the building of the nation. It was, in its way, a claim and assertion of *birthright*. For, as the historian Lerone Bennett stressed, blacks were on this land from "before the Mayflower," legitimizing them as among the "founders" and claiming them as central to the American story.[9]

In the nearly two decades since I wrote those words we have seen remarkable changes in the writing of American history, particularly in the attention paid to African-Americans and to whites' response to the black presence. Coinciding with the demand for black history was the larger challenge to include other marginalized groups, such as the poor, women, Native Americans, laborers, Hispanic-Americans, and Asian-Americans. New questions had to be asked calling for the techniques of demographers and quantifiers in the triumphant "new social history." As one historian put it, the "obvious but radical bottom line of sound demographic work is that everybody counts."[10] Being counted in, however, is only the first step.

As late as 1968, the president of the Organization of American Historians could still warn against the danger posed by African-Americans—"a newly formed hyphenate group"—clamoring for historical recognition. It was a simple matter of dominance. "Pressure-group history of any kind is deplorable, especially when significant white men are bumped out to make room for much less significant black men in the interests of social harmony." He worried that we might have "hard-backed Negro histories of the United States, with the white man's achievements relegated to subsidiary treatment."[11]

Professor Bailey was reacting to changes in historical writing already under way. Those changes took American pluralism seriously and did not assume that a dominant culture, class, and ethnic group could define the national experience. Not all, but most, American historians now accept the view that multiple perspectives on an event are valuable, if not essential.

The governing word is "perspective." The object is not merely to mention and discuss African-Americans, women, Hispanic-Americans,

8. Nathan Irvin Huggins, Martin Kilson, and Daniel Fox, eds., *Key Issues in the African-American Experience* (New York, 1971), Vol. I, 5.

9. Lerone Bennett, *Before the Mayflower: A History of Black America*, rev. ed. (New York, 1984).

10. Peter H. Wood, " 'I Did the Best I Could for My Day': The Study of Early Black History during the Second Reconstruction, 1960–1976," *William and Mary Quarterly,* 3rd Ser., XXXII (April 1978), 190.

11. Thomas A. Bailey, "The Mythmakers of American History," *Journal of American History,* LV (1968), 7–8.

Asian-Americans, white ethnics, and Native Americans—those who had been marginalized in the standard history. Rather, it is to understand the past through them, to see history through their eyes, making them essential witnesses to the events historians discussed. Because the "new social history" focused on multiple particulars, it seemed to defy efforts at synthesis and to confound narrative history. Out of many, it seemed impossible to tell one story.[12]

The search to find the African-American's voice in history, quite naturally, took off from studies of slavery. The first questions had to do with slave personality and slave culture. In little more than a decade our understanding of slavery, and of the life experience of the slave, has been dramatically expanded.

Kenneth Stampp had written with all good will that he assumed that "slaves were merely ordinary human beings, that innately Negroes *are,* after all, only white men with black skin, nothing more, nothing less."[13] When he wrote those words, in 1956, that comment was taken, as it was doubtless intended, as an assertion of the slave's common humanity with white men. But black consciousness came into its own in the early 1960s, and Stampp was roundly criticized for failing to consider blacks as black, having a distinctive culture and quality. It was no longer enough to think of black men as would-be white men. They were persons—a people—in their own right.

Stanley Elkins's *Slavery* was just the book to start the argument.[14] It characterized historical writing on slavery as divided into two camps: those following the abolitionists against those following the defenders of slavery. The defenders had dominated the literature from the end of Reconstruction through World War II, Ulrich B. Phillips presenting the fullest and final statement of that position.[15] Kenneth Stampp, according to Elkins, was the last of the abolitionist school, and *The Peculiar Institution* could be said to be the final and best word on the subject.

Elkins described the debate as basically about morals, turning on several basic questions: Were blacks by character or by culture especially suited for slavery? Did slavery in any way serve to acculturate Africans to American life? Was slavery profitable to slave owners? Was slavery in

12. Bernard Bailyn raises this problem of synthesis and narrative in his presidential address to the American Historical Association: "The Challenge of Modern Historiography," *American Historical Review,* CXXXVII (February 1982), 1–24. Bailyn's concerns, it must be said, are different and unrelated to those of Bailey.

13. Kenneth Stampp, *The Peculiar Institution,* vii–viii. Stampp meant nothing more than what is intended in Shylock's speech: "If you prick us, do we not bleed? if you tickle us, do we not laugh? if you poison us, do we not die?" (*The Merchant of Venice,* Act III, Scene 1). In fact, he goes on to say, "This gives quite a new and different meaning to the bondage of black men; it gives their story a relevance to men of all races which it never seemed to have before" (viii).

14. Stanley Elkins, *Slavery* (Chicago, 1960).

15. Ulrich B. Phillips, *American Negro Slavery* (New York, 1918).

the American South benign? Were slaves content with their lot? Did slaves resist? Would slavery have survived had there been no Civil War?

Phillips had assumed that Africans were racially and culturally inferior to whites and would not have survived outside the guidance and protection of the institution. Slavery was, to him, a school from which, at some future time, persons of African descent might be graduated into some form of freedom. To Phillips, slavery had been a tragic legacy, which slaveholders bore manfully as *noblesse oblige*. Profit had not been the slave owner's motive; almost any other investment would have given him a better return. He had paternal responsibilities and obligations to civil order, otherwise he would have run away from his slaves. As for the slaves, they were content and happy. Except for those of criminal or antisocial bent, there was no serious resistance or violence. Slavery, according to Phillips, was already moribund in 1860. If abolitionists and other provocateurs had not fanned the flames of sectionalism, bringing on the Civil War, slavery would have fallen of its own weight.

Kenneth Stampp disagreed at every point. Slaves were "white men with black skin, nothing more, nothing less." They got no more and no less from slavery than white men would have. Slavery was a labor system, not a school for civilization. As a labor system, slavery relied on force. It was coercive, often brutal. With proper accounting, the slave plantation showed a healthy return on investment. Slavery was a coercive labor system, and slaves resisted as best they could. They were far from contented and happy. Seeing no signs in 1860 of a declining slave economy, Stampp held that, without the Civil War, there was no prospect of slavery's end.

Stampp got the last word because the evidence and the strength of his argument were compelling. It was also true that in the 1950s—in the aftermath of the war against Hitler and in the midst of the Cold War's struggles for the hearts and minds of the Third World—few scholars would defend Phillips's blatantly racist position.

Elkins wanted to call a halt. The Civil War (the "lost cause") and the rights and wrongs of slavery were dead issues to him. He challenged scholars to raise different questions: about moral reform in a federalist system, about the effect of America's chronic institutional weakness (regarding church, state, family, class), about the effect of a "total institution" (his characterization of slavery) on the personalities of its subjects. He invited comparisons of slavery in the Caribbean and Latin America so as to better understand the distinctive characteristics of slavery in the United States.

Elkins's book stirred up quite a fuss. It took some audacity for a young scholar, without archival research, to dismiss all previous scholarship as answering the wrong questions. Nor did it help matters that the questions Elkins posed often rested on dubious assumptions. It was understandable, however, that a new era—preoccupied by the daunting reality of totalitarianism, anticipating a new day of racial freedom—

would demand that new questions be asked of the past. Most historians were willing to give Stampp the last word in the old arguments and to get on to something new.

Elkins's assumption that slavery was a "total institution" reflected the new era. It seemed to him fitting to compare slavery with German concentration camps and, using the words of Bruno Bettelheim, to speculate about the effects on personality of the two experiences. He thought there was enough similarity to claim that slavery, like the concentration camps, produced an infantilized, submissive, dwarfed personality, characterized as Sambo. And he found in contemporary literature what was to him sufficient evidence that Sambo was ubiquitous in slavery.[16]

An intriguing argument. It seemed to be the ultimate denial of Phillips and the pro-slavery claim that American slavery was benign and benevolent. It seemed powerful support for those who wanted to stress the victimization of blacks in slavery and the inherent evil of the institution.[17] Yet the argument also gave support to those who would deny slaves the capacity to be free men. A Sambo-citizen would be inconceivable.

Buried in the argument were racist implications—different from those of Ulrich Phillips—but racist nonetheless. Whether or not Africans were inferior to Europeans at the outset, they had been made so by the "total institution" of slavery. Based on Elkins, it would be fair to ask if, following the Civil War and the Thirteenth Amendment abolishing slavery, it would not have been best to have placed the freedmen under some form of wardship of the state.[18]

Whatever its problems, or perhaps because of its problems, *Slavery* led to a transformation and renewal of historical writing on the peculiar institution. Little in Elkins's book would be left unchallenged, yet it directed attention away from the abstract institution and onto the slave and the slave experience. Until the 1960s, historians cared little what the slave felt, thought, or did. The claim was that slaves left too slight a

16. Elkin's argument on this point has been roundly and effectively challenged. He misread, or misunderstood, Bruno Bettelheim. His personality theory was problematic. Relying mainly on accounts of a pro-slavery writer, Nehemiah Adams (*A South-Side View of Slavery*), he had a very limited and distorted view of the range of slave personality.

17. It should be noted that a large body of sociological literature had grown up since the 1930s that stressed the crippling and limiting effects of slavery on African-Americans. The "Chicago School," led by Robert E. Park and including E. Franklin Frazier, Charles S. Johnson, and Edward Byron Reuter, had characterized slavery as having destroyed what African culture and social structure might have survived the Middle Passage and as having strictly limited slaves' acculturation in America. Thus, they saw the slave family, church, moral order, etc. as feeble, dysfunctional caricatures of white, American institutions. This view prevailed in the 1950s, cf. Abraham Kardiner and Lionel Ovesey, *The Mark of Oppression: A Psychosocial Study of the American Negro* (New York, 1951), "Introduction." It is also the historical assumption of Daniel Moynihan, *The Negro Family: The Case for National Action* (Washington, D.C., 1965) and Thomas Pettigrew, *A Profile of the Negro American* (Princeton, 1964).

18. Elkins suggests as much in *Slavery*.

record to be studied significantly. There was a record, but it was not used. The profession seemed to assume that a slave's testimony was self-interested special pleading and, therefore, uncreditable. The word of slave owners and other whites, however, could be assumed fair and believable as long as it seemed reasonable. Slave narratives and the reminiscences of former slaves were sources considered problematic, to be avoided.[19] Elkins's superficial pass at slave personality served to open the question so that the mind, spirit, and culture of the slave could no longer be ignored.

John Blassingame's *The Slave Community* made full and extensive use of previously ignored slave testimony and challenged Elkins point for point.[20] Personality formation, Elkins had argued, requires institutional validation and reinforcement. Slaves, he claimed, had no such validation within the general society, and masters, hostile to any signs of independence, undermined the creation of strong adult personality among blacks. Blassingame argued that slaves had created, and were sustained by, their own institutions (family, church, community), which supplemented or substituted for the master's world. The slave created his own means of validation.

The slave's religion was not merely a would-be white man's Christianity. It expressed and reflected an African culture, spirituality, and cosmology. Through the "invisible institution" of slave religion, the slave found place and identity in an ethical, cosmic order.

Blassingame stressed the importance of the slave family, which he described as "extended" rather than "nuclear." Like the slave church, he argued, the slave family followed African patterns. Far from being without family reinforcement, the slave's personality was formed and sustained in a community-wide family that mitigated the personal traumas of family breakups. Blassingame emphasized the importance of black male figures in the slave community, claiming they served as leaders, teachers, role models, and sources of sustaining affection for women and children.[21]

Thus, Blassingame answered each point. Elkins, for instance, had

19. Kenneth Stampp, for instance, did not make use of these sources in *The Peculiar Institution*. Had he done so, the professional authority of his book would have been compromised.

20. John Blassingame, *The Slave Community* (New York, 1971).

21. In describing the slave family, Blassingame was not only rejecting Elkins's argument but he was explicitly denying the conventional wisdom about the slave family that has prevailed from the antebellum period. Both abolitionists and proslavery writers would, for different reasons, claim that family life and feeling did not exist among slaves. The Chicago School of Sociology supported that view, claiming that African tradition was dead (killed in the Middle Passage) and slavery made the nuclear family impossible. Blassingame, of course, was responding immediately to the latest version of this argument in the Moynihan Report, which stressed the authority (albeit by default) of black women and the chronic absence of the black male. Blassingame's emphasis equates humanity, family, and strength of character with the presence of strong (not "emasculated") black men.

taken what he considered to be the small number and minor effect of slave uprisings in the United States (compared to those in Brazil and Latin America) as support for his claim of a ubiquitous Sambo personality type, incapable of rebellion. Blassingame, for his part, found more evidence of slave uprisings and counted escapes, sabotage, and day-to-day resistance as clues to a different slave personality.

Blassingame did not challenge Elkins's fundamental assumptions about personality theory. He merely brought the slave's own testimony into the picture. This, in itself, was a major advance in 1971. He insisted that Elkins had not gone far enough. Blassingame accepted Sambo as a valid slave personality type, but he would add two of his own to complete the picture. Besides Sambo, he would add Jack (the trickster) and Nat (the rebel).[22]

Until the 1970s, no historian—neither Stampp, nor Elkins, nor Blassingame—had explored the experience and consciousness of the slave as would Eugene Genovese and Herbert Gutman.[23] Both came to the study of slavery with a keen and conscious political[24] orientation, and both had flirted with, but rejected, American communism and its rigid Marxian formulas. Both were compelled to explain slavery and slave culture, but they came at their studies from opposite and antagonistic directions: Genovese, through theory, from the top; Gutman, empirically, from the bottom.

Genovese's initial and abiding interest has been with the power and reach of the planter class. Strongly influenced by the writings of the Italian Marxist revisionist Antonio Gramsci, Genovese insisted on a reconceptualization of class struggle. The power of the ruling class was to be found not in domination by force, but in its control of the culture

22. It is worth noting the strength and persistence of paradigms even when, as with Elkins, they issued from seriously flawed original conceptions. Even if Elkins's thesis had rested on sound personality theory and on a better grounding in history, it is questionable what value a personality type like Sambo would be to historical analysis. Blassingame did not much improve things by adding two more "types." He slightly increased the range and variety of slave expression, but he is by no means comprehensive. One is obliged to complain, for instance, that none of these "types" represented female consciousness or experience. But where does one stop adding? With sufficient variety, "types" give way to individual difference. Even in rejecting Elkins's argument, his critics unwittingly extended the life and influence of some bad ideas. Cf. Mary Agnes Lewis, "Slavery and Personality: A Further Comment," *American Quarterly*, XIX (1967), 114–121; Eugene Genovese, "Rebelliousness and Docility in the Negro Slave: A Critique of the Elkins Thesis," *Civil War History*, XIII (1967), 293–314; Ann J. Lane, ed., *The Debate Over Slavery: Stanley Elkins and His Critics* (Urbana, Ill., 1971); Kenneth Stampp, "Rebels and Sambos: The Search for the Negro's Personality in Slavery," *Journal of Southern History*, XXXVII (1971), 367–392.

23. Eugene Genovese, *Roll, Jordan, Roll: The World the Slaves Made* (New York, 1976); Herbert G. Gutman, *The Black Family in Slavery and Freedom, 1750–1925* (New York, 1976).

24. I use "political" here to indicate their use of history to challenge and displace from authority the liberal-conservative consensus that dominated American historical writing, as well as to politically educate a new generation of students.

shared by ruled and ruler. Genovese would come to stress the hegemony of the planter class as the "world the slaveholders made."[25]

The intellectual and articulate spokesmen for the planter class displayed, for the mid-nineteenth century, a remarkably radical political and economic critique. That was their attraction to Genovese. They were open and forthright in their consciousness of class, seeing in class struggle the principal threat to order. They were unflinching in asserting their class interests and their willingness to die for them. They were sharp in their critique of capitalism. Ironically, their views of political economy and the forces of change comported well with a Marxian analysis. This irony drew Genovese to a curious appreciation of the slaveholder and his power and to a seeming reassertion of Ulrich Phillips's notion of a patrician master.[26]

Like Phillips, Genovese saw the Old South as a neo-feudal political economy. The culture of slavery preempted capitalistic decision making. The master class had created and been nurtured in a culture of obligations and responsibilities of master and slave that obviated choices capitalist owners took for granted. Master-slave relations were familial, the master paternalistic. Also like Phillips, Genovese saw plantation slavery as being only marginally productive, generating a rate of profit too low to attract investment by a rational, self-interested capitalist. True to his "pre-capitalist" mentality, the slaveholder was not in it for profit.[27]

Focusing on power and dominion, Genovese in his early work was not much interested in slaves. They were what their paternalistic masters allowed them to be, part of a culture created out of the necessary interplay between master and slave conforming to the self-concept of the master class. Genovese's view of the slave was little different from that of Elkins.[28]

The tumultuous events of the late 1960s, as well as the exciting scholarly exchanges during those years, pushed Genovese to both revise his views and turn his attention from the master to the slave. He modified his views of paternalism so as to correct any implication of a benign and benevolent order and to admit the possibility of slave influence. He opened himself to the study of slave culture for its own sake.[29] He

25. Eugene D. Genovese, *The World the Slaveholders Made: Two Essays in Interpretation* (New York, 1969).

26. This irony had been observed before. Cf. Richard Hofstadter, "John C. Calhoun, the Marx of the Master Class," in his *American Political Tradition* (New York, 1948).

27. Eugene D. Genovese, *The Political Economy of Slavery Studies in the Economy and Society of the Slave South* (New York, 1965).

28. Eugene D. Genovese, "The Legacy of Slavery and the Roots of Black Nationalism," *Studies on the Left*, VI (1966), 3–26. His views were much changed in a revision of this essay written for *In Red and Black: Marxian Exploration in Southern and Afro-American History* (New York, 1971), Chap. 6.

29. In this, he was most influenced by Lawrence Levine's *Black Culture and Black Consciousness: Afro-American Folk Thought from Slavery to Freedom* (New York, 1977).

continued, nevertheless, to insist on the precapitalist character of plantation slavery and the hegemony of the master class.

Roll, Jordan, Roll, published in 1976, contains some of the finest,
most moving, and comprehensible writing on slave religion, culture, and
imagination to be found in historical literature. It contains perhaps the
fullest discussion of the institutional structure within which slaves had to
live and cope. Genovese is fulsome in his analysis of how he imagines
slaves to have exploited the masters' paternalism and ideology to win
control over some portion of their lives.

These were, however, concessions possible only through acceptance
of the world the slaveholders made. That, to Genovese, was a fatal
compromise, for while it permitted slaves to create their own world,
they did so at the price of power and means to oppose the masters'
dominion which held them enthralled. They were locked, ideologically
and culturally, into a condition where their being could be defined and
indulged only within the masters' limits. They had no alternative. As
Genovese's masters were precapitalist, his slaves were prepolitical.

Genovese's writings on slavery began with bloodless theoretical studies of political economy focused on the master class but developed to
become a rich and fully textured exposition of slave life and culture. Yet,
in over a decade of highly original and provocative work, he remained
remarkably consistent. He persisted in seeing the subject from the top
down. Rejecting the challenge to write from the bottom up, Genovese
insisted that history is "the story of who rides whom and why."[30] He was
consistent in viewing the political economy and culture of slavery in the
United States as precapitalist, the slaves' reactions (even in resistance)
as prepolitical.[31] The shaping subtext of all his work was a Marxian
dialectic that perceived power and historical change in terms of class
struggle.

Herbert Gutman's work differed in fundamental ways. While he was
not uncritical of the new social history's tendencies to balkanize and
romanticize the poor, powerless, and inarticulate, he insisted that one
could not understand workers by studying employers, or understand
slaves by studying the worldview of slaveholders.[32] Writing history from
the bottom up—from the point of view of the worker and the slave—
was not merely a concession to their humanity and resiliency (and to
their tragedy), but it was elemental to an understanding of their cultures
and the historical changes they effected. Gutman was an empiricist who
wanted massive data (interpreted within an ideologically specific frame-

30. Eugene D. Genovese and Elizabeth Fox-Genovese, "The Political Crisis of Social History: A Marxian Perspective," *Journal of Social History,* XX (1976), 219.

31. For Genovese's distinctions between a political, or prepolitical, resistance and
true rebellion as related to Afro-American slavery, see Eugene D. Genovese, *Resistance
and Rebellion* (New York, 1979).

32. Herbert G. Gutman, *Work, Culture, and Society in Industrializing America:
Essays in American Working-Class History* (New York, 1976), xii.

work) to provide the grounding of history and its generalizations. As for his ideological framework, he saw slaveholders as capitalist entrepreneurs just like the American factors and merchants to whom they sold their cotton, produce, and human chattel. Slaves, therefore, were unfree workers in a peculiar capitalist enterprise.

Gutman's work on the black family grew from cross currents of scholarly debate. Not only had Elkins and nearly all American historians dismissed the slave family as nonexistent or dysfunctional, the authoritative work in sociology (by both white and black scholars) found slavery to be the source of modern, black family instability. Those views had gone virtually unchallenged until the mid-1960s when the Moynihan Report brought them forward as part of an argument for a public policy of "benign neglect." Moynihan used Stanley Elkins as his authority and found in the black family a "tangle of pathology" and proof that "white America broke the will of the Negro people."[33]

What Moynihan took as conventional historical wisdom was nothing more than the impressions and deductions of earlier sociologists who had gone no further in the way of historical research than to study the *laws* of slavery as they might relate to family. They assumed (as did Stanley Elkins) that without positive legal support the family could not exist. Historians had provided no respectable knowledge about the black family in slavery or in freedom. To say, as Moynihan did, that the destruction of the black family in slavery had caused "deep-seated structural distortions in the life of the Negro American," was to make a historical assertion about the cause without historical literature to support it. Were the twentieth-century disabilities of the black family (whatever they were) an inheritance of slavery and history, or were they traceable to contemporary conditions of labor and employment? Gutman sought to find out.

He began by working backward, from the postbellum manuscript censuses, into the Freedmen's Bureau records, back into eighteenth-century plantation journals and records. The data base was massive. He studied it as an archeologist would the remains of a past civilization, and he brought to his work the assumption that slaves had a culture worthy of study. He also brought a methodology that could construct meaning from vast and sprawling data.

Gutman's work established the terms in which the slave family could be said to have meaning. Using plantation records, among other data, he was able to place families together. The most spectacular result of his work was the graphic display of "family trees" on several plantations.

His work showed how kinship networks among slaves extended beyond a particular plantation or holding, extended throughout county

33. U.S. Department of Labor, Office of Policy Planning and Research, *The Negro Family: The Case for National Action,* prepared by Daniel P. Moynihan (Washington, D.C., 1965), 5. The phrase "tangle of pathology" had earlier been used by the black social psychologist Kenneth Clark in his *Dark Ghetto: Dilemmas of Social Power* (New York, 1965).

and state, and in time throughout the entire South. Through analysis of naming patterns, Gutman showed how slaves were self-governing in the naming of their young, how the chosen names honored kin across generations, and how male figures were recognized and respected. His analysis of Freedmen's Bureau records showed how family consciousness defied time and space. He showed how spouses and children, long separated by great distances, sought to reunite despite enormous hardship. Finally, he found in the naming patterns (particularly in the choice of African names) and the exogamous character of slave marriages support for his contention that slaves shared a belief system separate and independent from the master. They were not, therefore, simply victims and creatures of the world the master made. Rather, they created their own culture out of an African past in a world in which they were a constructive, human agency.

This remarkable outpouring of studies in the 1960s and 1970s extended and deepened our understanding of the African-American experience in slavery, giving us a fuller and richer appreciation of African-American mind and culture. It was as if historians were bringing to life a people who had been both socially and historically dead.[34]

As a consequence of all this work, we were no longer content to understand slavery simply as an institution in which blacks labored under white dominion, mere victims subjugated to the rule and will of whites. While there remained grounds of intense dispute among them, Blassingame, Genovese (in his later work), Gutman, Fogel, and Engerman all would give slaves an important role in the shaping of their lives and culture. They were instrumental in the creation of the world they shared with the master. Such an idea had been out of the question in the late 1950s when Kenneth Stampp wrote his book.

Stanley Elkins had demanded new questions. But were the questions really new? The focus had certainly changed to include the slave, and the work was more subtle and sophisticated about matters of economics, culture, and personality. Yet the questions continued to focus on profit,

---

34. Aside from these works, the writing of two economic historians was promoted (with much fanfare and press attention) as an overturning of all earlier historical understanding of slavery: not only did they claim that plantation slavery was profitable and economically efficient, but slaves received over their lifetime 90 percent of what they produced in some form of compensation. Robert M. Fogel and Stanley L. Engerman, *Time on the Cross: The Economics of American Negro Slavery*, 2 vols. (Boston, 1974). The excitement was shortlived, however, as the work was challenged on almost every point it made. Its principal innovation was the extensive application of economic models to slavery issues (i.e. efficiencies of scale on plantations, efficiency of slave labor, in-kind compensation for slave labor, coercion, etc.). Historians and economists effectively challenged both the generalizations and the methodology of the book. See Herbert G. Gutman, *Slavery and the Numbers Game* (Urbana, Ill., 1974); Paul A. David, et al., *Reckoning with Slavery: A Critical Study in the Quantitative History of American Negro Slavery* (New York, 1976).

efficiency, racial capacity, productivity, coercion, resistance, family, slave culture, and paternalism. Apart from his provocative and audacious attitude, Elkins himself was merely putting old wine in new bottles. He assumed that in the garb of social science and in the nonmoralistic tones of inquiry and speculation, the assertions of racial incapacity could pass muster as a new idea.[35]

New and different questions will not be asked as long as slavery is studied in and of itself, apart from general American history.[36] Our master narrative denies it place, marginalizing both the institution and African-Americans. Governed by that fact, the questions will remain the same until our national history and myth can incorporate both slavery and racism. Until then, slavery and slaves will remain only accidentally and tragically American.[37]

It is in deference to the master narrative that historical studies of slavery, from the nineteenth century to the present, have presented the subject prototypically, frozen in time (the 1840s and 1850s) and space (the Deep South's large plantation). The historiographical discussion has seldom ventured beyond those limits. (Of recent scholarship, only Herbert Gutman and Lawrence Levine can be said to have breached the form.[38])

Such static and fixed views strengthen the illusion of slavery as aberrant and marginal to the main story of American history. One is not

35. Elkins's interest in the slave and slave personality was only incidental. There is no evidence in *Slavery* that he thought it important to know about slave life, thought, and culture. The thrust of his argument implied that there was not much there to study or understand except as it might reveal the crippling effects of total control and domination. There were other issues Elkins thought more important. He revealed a dominating aversion to moral issues in historical writing. He saw strong institutions (i.e. the church, the state, the family, etc.) as necessary bastions against moralistic (irrational) public behavior. The particular pathologies of slaves (and the curious impotence of abolitionism) in the United States were owing to relatively weak social and political institutions in the United States (as opposed to Britain). What Elkins was calling for was not new questions about slavery but historical writing about slavery and related matters that was amoral, taking its methodology from social scientists.

36. Much of the heat behind both the support and criticism of *Time on the Cross* was due to an implication (vigorously denied by the authors) that their book defended slavery as a viable and efficient labor system that rested on the self-interested bargaining between master and slave.

37. The words "tragic" and "peculiar," commonly used to describe American racial slavery, suggest that slavery has an aberrant and perhaps fortuitous place in American life and history. The assumption is that the American life would have been more purely itself had Africans and slavery never been introduced to the British colonies.

38. Gutman's *Black Family,* while resting heavily on the records of large plantations, extends his study over generations and he augments his work by extensive use of nonplantation records (censuses, probate and court records, Freedmen's Bureau records, etc.). Levine's *Black Culture and Black Consciousness* ranges across time and cultures, explaining African influences, and the changes in African-American experience through the 1940s.

obliged by the picture they present to understand race and slavery in the founding of America, in colonial life, in the American Revolution, and so on. Rather, one is encouraged to continue to treat the mainstream of American history as if racial slavery were merely a curious nuisance, complicating and temporarily drawing attention away from the central American story.

It has been more than a decade since the colonial historian Peter Wood remarked on the slight and seemingly haphazard historical attention to slavery in colonial America.[39] Until the 1960s, in fact, historians of early America typically wrote about Massachusetts, calling it New England, "and when speaking of New England, they called it America. Some among them wrote of white male Virginia periodically, referring to it as the South."[40]

Nor, as far as blacks and slavery were concerned, did Wood find matters much improved at the time of his article. Using the *William and Mary Quarterly* as a rough guide, he observed that of the 407 articles published from 1960 to 1976, only 26 (a mere 6.4%) were directly on slavery, racism, or blacks "even though Afro-Americans constituted more than 20% of the English North American colonies by the 1770s." Oddly enough, more articles focused on slavery in Massachusetts than in Virginia. "In fact, over two-fifths of the 26 articles related to the small black population north of the Mason and Dixon's line while less than one-fifth concerned the far larger enslaved population to the south."[41]

Here we see most clearly the influence of the master narrative in shaping and defining historical significance. The story of the United States is of the development of the North (read Puritan New England) rather than the South. It is of whites unrelated to or unengaged with blacks. It is of freedom and free institutions rather than of slavery. It is as if one wrote a history of Russia without serious consideration of serfdom; a history of India ignoring caste. The distortion would be jarring did it not serve so well the national mythology and an idealized national character.

The myth and the master narrative explain why, until the late 1940s, historians paid no attention to the origins of slavery in the British North American colonies. George Bancroft, the father of American historians, saw American colonists as innocent actors in a drama of cosmic scale. He took great pains to outline slavery's history, among many peoples, reaching into ancient times; how it had ended in England and most of Western Europe; how it remained common among Africans. That is to say, slavery was not created by Americans. Furthermore, left to their

---

39. Peter H. Wood, " 'I Did the Best I Could for My Day': The Study of Early Black History during the Second Reconstruction, 1960–1976," *William and Mary Quarterly,* 3rd Series, XXXV (April 1978), 185–225.

40. Ibid., 187.

41. Ibid., 188, footnote 5; Wood credits Professor Steven Creiert for the count of articles in the periodical.

own devices, the American colonists would have avoided racial slavery. For had profits from the slave trade "remained with the Dutch," the traffic would have been checked. The Royal Africa Company and the Crown's demand for profit forced large numbers of Africans on the colonists, and that determined the issue.

> For the first time, the Aethiopian and Caucasian races were to meet together in nearly equal numbers beneath a temperate zone.[42]

For Bancroft, no more need be said. A large number of Africans in an American colony had to result in either racial slavery or annihilation.

This view of the origins of African-American slavery reflected one that had been expressed during the Revolution. An early draft of the Declaration of Independence listed as one of the colonists' grievances against George III the imposition on them of Africans through the Royal Africa Company. That particular item met objections from some representatives of slave-holding colonies and did not appear in the final draft.[43]

None of the major works on slavery addressed the question of origins, neither Phillips nor Stampp. Stampp, for his part, saw the tragedy of a system that

> Southerners did not create . . . all at once in 1619; rather, they built it little by little, step by step, choice by choice, over a period of many years; and all the while most of them were more or less blind to the ultimate consequences of the choices they were making.[44]

A series of "unthinking" decisions merely dismisses the question of origins in order to focus on the nineteenth-century prototype. The implication is, nevertheless, that had those decisions been *thoughtfully* made—in conformity with American values—racial slavery would not have been the outcome.

It was 1950 when Oscar and Mary Handlin became the first American historians to take the question of origins seriously.[45] Ten years after it appeared, their article became the source of considerable controversy.

The Handlins argued that the actual status of African servants in the early seventeenth-century colonies was confused and unclear, but not in any legal or formal sense were they slaves. The servant classes in the England of that period lived a kind of quasi-freedom. Owing to traditional class ties and responsibilities—English laws against vagrancy, occupational ties to households and masters—English servants were, by

42. George Bancroft, *History of the United States*, 10 vols., rev. ed. (New York, 1882), 177.

43. See Garry Wills, *Inventing America: Jefferson's Declaration of Independence* (New York, 1978).

44. Stampp, *The Peculiar Institution*, 6.

45. Oscar and Mary Handlin, "Origins of the Southern Labor System," *William and Mary Quarterly*, 3rd Series, VII (1950), 199–222, reprinted in Oscar Handlin, *Race and Nationality in American Life* (Boston, 1957), chap. 1.

our standards, "unfree." That was certainly the case for indentured servants in the American colonies, who were bound sometimes for lengthy terms of service.

In the early seventeenth century, the Handlins argued, African servants in the North American continental colonies had a similar "unfree" status. The duration of their service was assumed to be long, sometimes indefinite, sometimes lifelong. They were not dealt with, in law or practice, as slaves. While the Handlins did not go so far as to say English and African servants were the same, they did claim both shared a common status of "unfree" labor without blacks being distinguished as slaves.[46]

The Handlins' point was that racial slavery was not foreordained from the importing of the first Africans into Virginia in 1619. It was something that grew out of special problems of labor supply and demand in the colonies.

The demand for labor grew over the middle decades of the 1600s. The American colonists would prefer English (or even Irish) labor to meet their needs. The period, however, witnessed a sharp decline in the numbers of the English servant class willing to migrate, while the supply of available Africans remained steady and actually increased.

To attract the dwindling supply of English workers, the American colonists greatly improved their terms of indenture. The length of obligatory service was drastically shortened, and the amount of "freedom dues" increased. In contrast, the status of African servants declined. They began to be treated as a caste apart. Their term of service—previously indefinite—became lifelong. Shortly, the African's status became defined in law as well as in practice as that of slave. He was owned as chattel, as would be his issue.

The Handlins' rather mechanistic view of the process by which Africans became slaves had several striking features: racial slavery was not an automatic consequence of the African's presence; slavery developed out of labor-market considerations, not as a result of "unthinking" decisions; the degradation of Africans into slavery was concomitant with the elevation of the white servant class into a presumptive freedom.

Perhaps the most provocative assertion by the Handlins was that the establishment of racial slavery created sharp distinctions between slave labor and free labor, where there had been none between white and black servants. Racial slavery in a "free" society begged explanation and justification. The rationale would come to be race. Slavery, therefore, not only heightened racial difference, it rested on and in turn reinforced racism and racist assumptions.[47]

46. Supporting this argument, the Handlins stressed the similarities of treatment and condition of white and black servants. They minimized differences while not flatly denying them. They never claimed that whites were unconscious or indifferent to race, or that they had no preference of English over African servants.

47. The Handlins do not argue, as critics accused, that slavery *created* racist attitudes and assumptions. Racial bigotry, prejudice, preference, etc., were present from the begin-

The Handlins' argument remained unchallenged—or, rather, not commented upon—for a decade. That was, however, a decade of great ferment over the civil rights of blacks. Agitation and debate brought race and racism into public and scholarly discourse as never before. Everyone would agree that the historical roots of American racism were bound, somehow, to slavery. The Handlins, alone among historians in addressing the origins of slavery, came under sharp attack. They were viewed as saying that slavery created racism rather than the other way around. To the remaining question—What caused slavery?—they had answered that it was labor-market forces particular to the American colonies in the mid-seventeenth century. That would not stand uncontested at a time when race and racism seemed the necessary and sufficient cause for everything having to do with blacks and whites in America.

The historian Carl Degler was first to venture a refutation of the Handlins. In a subtle shift of focus, Degler stressed early evidence of racial discrimination and the use of the term "slave" for blacks before the legal establishment of slavery. For Degler, racism antedated the formal establishment of slavery, which was an inevitable outcome of existing racial attitudes and the presence of Africans in sizeable numbers. The evidence seemed ample. Blacks were given harsher penalties than whites for the same offenses even when they were co-conspirators in crime or escape. There were stricter penalties for miscegenation than for fornication. And the statutes establishing slavery made distinctions between "freeborn" English and African "slaves."

> . . . the status of the Negro in the English colonies was worked out within a framework of discrimination . . . as slavery evolved as a legal status, it reflected and included as part of its essence this same discrimination which white men had practiced to cite a different case against the Negro all along.[48]

Like Degler, Winthrop Jordan found race and color prejudice to have been general among Englishmen and other Europeans in the sixteenth and seventeenth centuries. He found the inclination to degrade or disparage dark-skinned people to be general in Europe and of ancient

---

ning. Slavery, however, was established owing to specific economic and social needs and circumstances, not because of such racial sentiments. Once established, however, racial slavery required a sophisticated racist rationale to justify and sustain it. That rationale was not created by slavery, but a slave society drew upon already existing assumptions and attitudes to produce it.

48. Carl N. Degler, "Slavery and the Genesis of American Race Prejudice," *Comparative Studies in History and Society,* II (1959), 49–66. The quotation is on p. 52. To assume, as many did, that the Handlins denied difference in attitude about English and African servants is a distortion of their argument. For them, it was a matter of emphasis, and early confusion and uncertainty counted more to them than observed race difference. Indeed, their analysis turns on a clear colonial preference for English over African servants. The outlines of the debate that ensued is in Raymond Starr, "Historians and the Origins of British North American Slavery," *Historian,* XXXVI (1973), 1–18.

origin. Under the circumstances of American colonization, therefore, it was inevitable that Africans would be degraded.[49]

On the face of it, this seemed an argument about the precedence of chicken or egg. Which came first, slavery or racism, could not be finally resolved to everyone's satisfaction. All would agree that color and race prejudice existed before the legal establishment of slavery, and no one would doubt that the establishment of racial slavery gave a meaning and authority to racial and color prejudice that would dominate race relations in the new society. Still unexplained, however, was what compelled Anglo-American colonists to choose to make Africans into slaves and build a society dependent on that slave labor.

The Handlins saw it as a forced option of the labor market, supply and demand. Degler, and those who agreed with him, saw slavery as the logical and inevitable consequence of the presence of Africans among Anglo-Americans who were dominated by racial antipathy. The Handlins stressed class over race; it was the servant classes rather than race that mattered initially. For Degler, on the other hand, race drove all before it, overwhelming class and all other social considerations.

The Handlins had been quite audacious in finding the establishment of slavery to be a result of rational and self-interested choices made by colonial planters in need of labor. Slavery was thus an *American* (New World) institution, created out of American needs and circumstances. And the special kind of racist rationalizations needed to explain slavery were American also.

Degler and Jordan echoed and updated the conventional wisdom voiced by Bancroft (and Thomas Jefferson before him). Slavery was a consequence of the races meeting in equal numbers "beneath a temperate zone."[50] Degler, Jordan, and Bancroft all could assume their readers would accept race and demography as sufficient explanation for the establishment of slavery. Like Bancroft, they, too, would find racial slavery an unavoidable inheritance from the Old World, its attitudes and its pressures. The idea that American settlers—the founders in the myth—might make deliberate choices to establish chattel slavery, basing the future of the colonies on it, was subordinated to a compelling racial determinism.

However, it is by no means certain how pervasive and commanding race and color prejudice was among the settlers. Reading Degler and Jordan, one would expect to find much evidence of white servant complaints against the possible confusion of their status with that of black

49. Winthrop Jordan, *White Over Black: American Attitudes Toward the Negro, 1550–1812* (Chapel Hill, N.C., 1968). See also his "Modern Tensions and the Origins of American Slavery," *Journal of Southern History,* XXVIII (1962), 496–498.

50. Bancroft, *History of the United States,* Vol. I, 177.

servants. No one has found such evidence, which certainly would have strengthened one side of the argument.[51]

Indeed, even that evidence cited to prove distinction of treatment along racial lines proves far more than that. Documents that prove blacks received harsher punishment that whites for the same offense also prove that white and black servants conspired in crime and escape. Similarly, documents reflecting official disapproval of miscegenation, even more than fornication, also indicate that interracial unions were frequent enough to be perceived as a threat to order. The very language of the laws first defining the African as a slave reveals a complex, biracial picture. The Maryland law of 1661 began:

> And forasmuch as divers free-born *English* women, forgetful of their free condition and to the disgrace of our nation, do intermarry with negro slaves, by which also, divers suits may arise, touching on the issue of such women. . . .[52]

This becomes evidence both of official disapproval and of a practice sufficiently large to warrant legislation. Even so, masters were known to encourage marriages of black men and English women so as to capture the women and their offspring into slavery or lifelong indenture.

The point is not to deny historical and societal attitudes of race and color prejudice among English and European settlers. It is, rather, to observe that such attitudes did not universally and automatically determine behavior. What the laws and judicial practices indicate is that the governing classes found in racial distinctions a means of social control.

That is central to Edmund Morgan's argument in his study of seventeenth-century Virginia.[53] He points to early dreams and failed hopes for racial and cultural pluralism in the colony. He stresses the social fluidity but growing tensions of the early years, and the relative advantages of free servants over slaves. The turning point, for Morgan, was Nathaniel Bacon's Rebellion of 1676, when colonial order was threatened by the uprising of an assortment of western freemen and gentlemen against the pretensions and power of the Tidewater aristocracy, in which a common hatred of Indians kept white men

51. Negative evidence, of course, is never fully persuasive. The absence of such complaints is certainly noteworthy, demanding explanation. From the establishment of slavery into our own time, white workers, servants, professionals, etc., have been quick to complain at the sight of black would-be peers, arguing a degrading of their labor and status.

52. John C. Hurd, ed., *The Law of Freedom and Bondage in the United States* (Boston, 1858), Vol. I, 249.

53. Edmund S. Morgan, *American Slavery, American Freedom* (New York, 1975). Morgan analyzes intermarriage and miscegenation, 333–336; "Slavery and Freedom: The American Paradox," *Journal of American History,* LIX (1972), 5–29; Theodore Allen, " '. . . They Would Have Destroyed Me': Slavery and the Origins of Racism," *Radical America,* IX (1975), 41–63.

from social upheaval. The lesson in Bacon's Rebellion was that an alien, racially exotic threat (real or imagined) could weld white men in a common bond that would hold against all other class and political fractioning.

To the governing class, the chilling prospect of class war was one additional reason to import African slaves. They would have as readily enslaved their English servants or Scottish and Irish prisoner imports except for a likely veto by the Crown. Englishmen, even servants, were presumed to have rights. Scots and Irish were very likely to become a source of disorder, especially when entrapped in permanent servitude. One did not have to enslave Africans by some official act of the colony. They could be purchased as slaves, the terms, duration, and conditions of their servitude to be worked out over time. The adoption of African slavery in Virginia was made easier because they were thought a "brutish sort of people," and because there was no institutional or legal restraint against their enslavement. Race, in short, made it possible and easy, but was not the cause.

The governing classes felt little kinship or affection for white servants, who under different circumstances might themselves have been enslaved. These servants were defined as free by the fact of African slavery. Thus, Morgan's paradox. Freedom among the white servant classes and lower orders had meaning precisely because of slavery. Racial slavery created among white men a kind of equality (in freedom) and a common bond which could be made to take precedence over all other interests.

In Morgan we find the most radical departure from the conventional wisdom of Bancroft and his followers. His work begs to amend the master narrative. Rather than American history being a story of the creation and development of free and democratic institutions, we now have the argument that American freedom itself is the creation of slavery.[54] Whereas the master narrative detached the origins of American slavery and the slave experience from the central story, Morgan's thesis, in contrast, makes slavery (and unfreedom) a formative and necessary part of the story. He forces us to see slavery and freedom as inseparably a single, albeit paradoxical, phenomenon. And as American slavery was *racial* slavery, the badges of servitude in racism makes white and black a persistent American paradox. Just as American freedom finds its meaning in American slavery, whiteness and white power found their meaning

---

54. The idea of slavery creating a *herrenvolk democracy* is frequently observed; cf. Pierre L. Van den Berghe, *Race and Racism: A Comparative Perspective* (New York, 1967); George M. Fredrickson, *The Black Image in the White Mind: The Debate on Afro-American Character and Destiny, 1817–1914* (New York, 1971); and his "Toward a Social Interpretation of the Development of Racism," in Nathan Irvin Huggins, Martin Kilson, and Daniel M. Fox, eds., *Key Issues in the Afro-American Experience* (New York, 1971), Vol. I, 240–254.

in the debasement of blacks. A master narrative about free whites creating free institutions lacks the context in which whiteness and freedom have meaning. The narrative evades the paradox by ignoring or marginalizing slavery and blacks.

If the problem were merely one of exclusion and lack of recognition, the response could be to work for inclusion and appreciation of the black contribution to American history. The end-product would be an "integrated" history in which the African-American role—ordeals, contributions, great men and women, achievements, etc.—complements what has been a powerful white male-dominated story.

The paradox of American slavery and American freedom, however, challenges the master narrative itself. It demands more than mere racial "integration" of American history. It does more than say—as was the standard complaint of the 1960s—that blacks and other powerless groups have been left out of the history. It goes, rather, to the ideological and conceptual basis of conventional history, exposing it as unsound.

The "nationalistic" alternative to integrated history is also no response to the paradox.[55] The invaluable work done in recent years to unearth and reveal previously disregarded aspects of African-American life, history, and culture has served to bring to life a people who were socially and historically dead. Left as "black history," however, it merely moves the story of the black experience from the margins to the center, marginalizing in turn the "mainstream" history. The challenge of the paradox is that there can be no white history or black history, nor can there be an integrated history that does not begin to comprehend that slavery and freedom, white and black, are joined at the hip.

However much black and white, slave and free seem to be polar opposites, we must see them not only as interdependent but as having a common story and necessarily sharing the same fate. That is another way of saying "community," albeit unilaterally antagonistic, parasitic, and exploitative. It is in this sense, therefore, marginalizing and distorting to write, as John Blassingame does, of a "slave community."[56]

Some of the works produced in the 1970s at least address the question of master-slave accommodation. Eugene Genovese, particularly, finds "the world the slaves made" a result of bargaining and manipulation within the hegemony and dominion of the master. There was, at least, a dynamic tension between master and slave that created the

55. I use the term "nationalistic" simply to delineate those who would see the end of their historical work to be the black experience itself, and not a part of a more general discourse.

56. I do not mean to suggest that the slaves' experience in family, religion, etc. that Blassingame illuminates is unworthy of consideration. My point is, rather, that there is a community beyond that delineated by Blassingame, which is both defined by the slave and which defines him. That larger community is at the center of the American experience.

world in which they both lived. That is a large step beyond the view of slaves as victims, pure and simple.[57]

The most successful and thoroughgoing effort to address the slave community (e.g., master and slave, white and black) is Peter Wood's work on colonial South Carolina. Wood tells of the founding and development of that colony with African-American slavery at its center rather than on its margin. The fact of the colony's black majority by no means compelled that focus. Earlier histories had managed to treat South Carolina as white men's country no less than North Carolina, Virginia, or Maryland. Wood's attention to the full significance of a white minority in a black man's country helped him weave the African heritage and culture into one fabric, describing an African-European-American culture based on racial slavery.[58]

The master narrative persists despite this new and sophisticated work. It persists because it feeds and satisfies our most profound sense of identity. For generations, American children of all races and backgrounds have learned the story of "our Pilgrim fathers" landing on Plymouth Rock, dissenters establishing in the New World the germs of democratic institutions; freeing themselves from Old World decadence and corruption; establishing a government under a "more perfect union"; ridding themselves of an inherited chattel slavery; moving West, despite wilderness (and Indian) resistance, to build a continental nation, to be the envy of the world; being a peaceful, industrious, and progressive nation; becoming the exemplar of freedom and democracy throughout the world.

No mere patriotic litany, this narrative forms the backdrop against which all American history is written. Its most vulgar form made national history a Manifest Destiny: the Anglo-Saxon race in the vanguard of the westward march of "civilization," always with more than a hint of providential guidance. The seemingly irresistible, relentless, and triumphal procession into the American Century begged for divine or cosmic explanation. That sense of destiny gave moral authority to national purpose.

From the beginning, and all along, there would be voices gainsaying the myth. Some Puritan divines, while considering all events providential, distrusted the hubris that converted the idea of a "city on a hill" from onus to self-satisfaction. Writers like Nathaniel Hawthorne and

57. Slave culture, however rich and varied, was merely that which slaves wrested or salvaged from within the bounds of masters' paternalism. Genovese, *Roll, Jordan, Roll*. Herbert Gutman insisted on an African-American "belief system," independent of the master. Gutman, *Black Family*. Neither he nor Genovese takes up the question of the Africanization of Anglo-Americans and the Europeanization of Africans. Lawrence Levine's *Black Culture and Black Consciousness* is one of the few books that does.

58. Peter H. Wood, *Black Majority: Negroes in Colonial South Carolina from 1670 through the Stono Rebellion* (New York, 1974).

Herman Melville warned of the corruption of the human heart, distorting motives, ends, and means. Theologians like Reinhold Niebuhr reminded us of the inescapable gap between human aspirations and our limited capacity to perform. Something about the reality of America would always be far less than the dream and the dream's story. Rightly understood, racial slavery tells us that truth from the beginning.

The dream has been compelling to black no less than to white Americans. African-Americans, too, have insisted that slavery was a tragic departure from the American destiny. Black abolitionists, like their white counterparts, were voices of the American conscience alerting their audiences to the disparity between American purpose, destiny, and slavery. Even those blacks who would emigrate to Africa saw the African sojourn in America (even in slavery) as ordained to enlighten and uplift Africa. Frederick Douglass, the great black abolitionist, was convinced the Civil War was a divine scourge brought upon an otherwise moral, Christian nation by slaveholding. W. E. B. Du Bois, in the mid-twentieth century, would see the destiny and challenge differently: America was the laboratory in which *the* problem of the twentieth century—the problem of the color line—would be observed and understood, or tragically misunderstood.[59]

The desire to merge national and racial identity into a single myth explains the compelling persistence of the story of Sally Hemings—the slave and servant of Thomas Jefferson who, the story goes, bore his children. The evidence is circumstantial; we will never get a truth everyone will accept. Custodians of the Jefferson legacy seek to protect his historical reputation and demand substantial and irrefutable evidence. I venture to say that most black people *know* the rumors are essentially true despite gaps and problems with the evidence.

Why is it so important? Why the fuss? Sally Hemings was certainly not the first or the only black woman to have been so used by a master. It is Thomas Jefferson who makes this story different.

Jefferson was a "founding father" of the nation, and it is rumored that he sired children by an African-American woman, his slave. It does not matter whether the story is *actually* true. It is *symbolically* true and will, as a result, never be fully discredited for those on either side. Like other legitimizing myths, the Sally Hemings story ties a people to the founding of the nation, reinforcing birthright claims.[60]

To cite a different case, Alex Haley's *Roots,* for all its many historical problems, captured the imaginations of whites and blacks as has no recent work of American history. It evidenced the direct and specific

---

59. For nineteenth-century attitudes of blacks, see Leonard Sweet, *Blacks' Image of America* (New York, 1973); for Douglass, see Nathan Irvin Huggins, *Slave and Citizen: The Life of Frederick Douglass* (Boston, 1980); W. E. B. Du Bois, *Dusk of Dawn: The Autobiography of a Race Concept* (New York, 1950).

60. Legitimizing myths and myths of national origin are commonly set in illicit sexual unions.

connection between an African-American and a traditional Old World culture. Creating a personal story, it defied the massive anonymity of the Middle Passage. It evoked an oral tradition—like the *Old Testament* and the *Iliad*—establishing a "prehistoric" people's experience. It authenticated an individual black man and his family as symbolic of the whole African-American people. Most important, it integrated itself into the dominant Bancroftian myth of providential destiny. The story ends with that onward, upward, progressive vision fundamental to the American faith. Through *Roots,* black people could find a collective memory and be mythically integrated into the American dream.[61]

Reality seems, nevertheless, more and more to deny the myth. The present challenges the past in ways that cannot be denied. History, even as national myth, must tell us who we are, how and why we are where we are, and how our destinies have been shaped. Particularly with regard to race relations and the relative status of whites and blacks, we enter the final decade of the twentieth century with more reason to doubt the progressive myth and the master narrative than ever before. We are even more racially divided now than we were in the seventeenth century. Rather than moderating and disappearing along with a general social advance, race in the United States seems to have been overlaid and reinforced after countless hopes and false starts. As we stand in the backwash of the so-called Second Reconstruction, we are once again dismayed at the feeble results from seemingly herculean efforts.[62]

Taking our cue from Orlando Patterson, it would seem that the "social death" of slavery came to be the embodiment of race distinction. It persisted as a badge of servitude after slavery was ended. Seeing slavery and freedom as absolute conditions, we have never understood properly the peculiar condition of blacks who were not slaves, before or after the Thirteenth Amendment and general emancipation.

Freedom and unfreedom remained blurred from the seventeenth century. Slavery was only the most conspicuous form of American unfreedom. Being white and not owned as property did not guarantee the attributes we associate with freedom. Individual slaves, on the other hand, might be so well situated as to be virtually free, while some whites might well have been so oppressed by place and circumstance as to have been little better than chattel.[63] One of the favorite arguments of those

61. It does not matter whether Haley *actually* found his family members in Africa, his forebear's home village and people. The story stands in powerful resonance with the master narrative, as symbolic truth for white and black Americans.

62. The Kerner Commission Report warned of two nations—one white, the other black. The decade of the 1980s has compounded the division by reinforcing the division between affluence and poverty because of the shrinking prospects for the middle class. The term "Second Reconstruction" was introduced by C. Vann Woodward and has since been generally applied to the period from roughly 1948 through the Civil Rights Movement. See C. Vann Woodward, *American Counterpoint* (Boston, 1976).

63. Consider, for instance, the condition of seamen in the mid-nineteenth century.

who defended slavery was that slaves were more free than their masters because they were unfettered by responsibilities for subsistence or family. Some would describe slavery as a kind of "work-fare" system in which employment and subsistence were guaranteed (regardless of age or state of health). Whatever truth there might be in such a concept would imply that it was this freedom from care and responsibility, rather than chains, that was lost with emancipation.

The status of free blacks in the South reveals that there was no clear line between slavery and freedom. Vagrancy laws held in jeopardy what liberty blacks had. They were restricted in their right to hold property, to vote, to hold office, to defend themselves and their families in or out of court. Nor were they free to choose how they might earn a living.[64]

Northern blacks fared little better. They, too, were seriously restricted in their political and economic freedom. Jim Crow practices forced them into separate schools, churches, places of public accommodation. They, too, were limited as to how they might earn their living. In this regard, they might well envy some southern blacks who were free to practice trades denied to northern blacks by presumption of racial privilege. According to the ideology and rhetoric of the Revolution, they were slaves, not free persons.[65]

White people in the South also had to cede freedom to racial slavery. They could not speak or write freely on the subject of slavery if their views were critical. The state controlled the mail and, therefore, what citizens read. There was no freedom of speech and press in the South. Those who owned slaves were restricted in the ways they could handle their human investment. If they wanted to free their slaves, they would often have to transport them to a northern state. White men and women were not permitted to marry blacks or effectively acknowledge their own children by interracial unions. Abolitionists were run out of the South, and in the North they were subject to violence against themselves and their property.

Were this catalogue of limits descriptive of Eastern European nations or Central American republics, we would be quick to recognize it as tyranny. Our national mythology, however, cannot accommodate such an idea. Our traditional thinking about race and the ultimate "end" of slavery clouds the issues and makes us see it all as an aberrational result of historical accident.

That a majority of whites, then and now, have failed to recognize these limits on their own freedom is of little importance. A society that

64. Marina Wikramanayake, *World in Shadow: Free Blacks in Ante-Bellum South Carolina* (Columbus, S.C., 1973); Ira Berlin, *Slaves Without Masters: Free Blacks in the South* (New York, 1977).

65. Leon Litwack, *North of Slavery* (Chicago, 1961); Eugene Berwanger, *Frontier Against Slavery: Western Anti-Negro Prejudice and the Slavery Extension Controversy* (Urbana, Ill., 1967).

indulged racial slavery necessarily encouraged tyranny and totalitarianism, which infected life well beyond the slaves and slave management.

It is a distortion to imagine an antebellum America neatly divided between those who were slaves and those who were free. That distortion becomes all the more problematic when we consider emancipation and Reconstruction. For then, as our mythology would have it, slavery ended and freedom was extended to everyone.

At the time, whites and blacks alike were confused as to what freedom would mean to the emancipated slaves. For African-Americans, as for all Americans, the condition of freedom depended on the existence of slavery. With slavery abolished, what could freedom mean for everybody since "black" and "unfreedom" were nearly synonymous? Everyone—legislators, judges, the general public—seemed to know that blacks would likely carry with them "badges of servitude" after emancipation. The framers of the Civil Rights Act of 1875 and the Fourteenth and Fifteenth Amendments hoped to protect blacks against such a servile legacy. In less than a decade after the Civil Rights Act, however, the Supreme Court in effect legitimized as natural the de facto unfreedom of blacks.[66] The observation by freedmen that "emancipation did not make them white" may be best understood not as color envy but as the astute observaton that the real issue had not been slavery and freedom. It was, and would continue to be, black and white.[67]

By the mid-nineteenth century, freedom had become associated with free-market assumptions of liberal economics. Classical liberalism, notions of the free market, and the Protestant ethic were strong ingredients in antislavery sentiment. Free labor and the free market were efficient; slavery was not. With slavery ended, faith in the market (efficiency gaining its just reward) made the freedman the sole measure of his own destiny. The onus was on the freedmen to prove themselves worthy of being free. They were responsible for their own condition and, by implication, for their own past. They were free, indeed. Free to rise or fall, do or die, and it would go according to what they could command in the market. In this sense, the emancipation of the slave converted him from an object in the market to a victim of the market.

The "free market," however, was as much an illusion as freedom itself. Blacks, when they were allowed to compete at all, would never be in *fair* competition with whites. Race intruded into and superseded ra-

66. Congressional debates over this civil rights legislation and these amendments are filled with the phrase "badges of servitude" regarding freedmen. Likewise, in arguments before the Supreme Court in the Civil Rights Cases (1883), this intent was made clear. Justice John Marshall Harlan, in his lone dissent, addressed himself to this legacy as being exactly the target of the Fourteenth Amendment and the legislation. The majority court, in effect, said it was impossible to legislate freedom for blacks where it did not exist in the white, public mind.

67. See Leon Litwack, *Been in the Storm So Long: The Aftermath of Slavery* (New York, 1979), for the broad range of white and black reaction to emancipation.

tional self-interest. Freedmen could not command a fair market price for their labor because the alternatives to exploitative wages were narrow or nonexistent.

The oppression and exploitation of blacks would not end with emancipation. As freedmen, however, their oppression and exploitation could be rationalized by liberal ideology as natural, given their backwardness. "Freedom" meant leaving to the "natural forces" of evolution and the fictive, competitive, "free" market the ultimate resolution of racial status. That is what freedom meant.

Accepting two absolute conditions—slave and free—black leaders, like whites, assumed that freedom (not being a slave) meant something ultimate and absolute. Once free, in a free society, one could not question the character of a freedom that allowed some free men to freely exploit other free men. Nor could one wonder how exploitation could leave the victim's freedom limited and encumbered. Nor could one conceive of a permanent tax and chronic disability stemming from a historical condition. Black leaders of every persuasion, from left to right, would look forward to the day when black Americans, through their industry, skill, and enterprise, would command a place in American society commensurate with their numbers and weight in the economy. Because they believed so strongly in fundamental racial equality,* American freedom, and liberal capitalism, it took nearly three quarters of the century for that automatic faith to be shattered.

White Americans were well aware that the abolition of slavery would affect their own freedom. Would everyone be treated alike? Custom and self-definition made whites say "no." Slavery and race had been crucial terms of white identity as much as of black. Slavery had been only one means of defining blacks apart from the community. Discriminatory practices in residence, employment, and use of public facilities defined America as a white man's country. Badges of servitude borne by blacks, emblems of racial privilege, were pervasive and assumed in American life—North as well as South. Emancipation did nothing to change those assumptions. While some features of Reconstruction were intended to undermine caste and race privilege, by the *Civil Rights Cases* (1883), and certainly by *Plessy v. Ferguson* (1896), there could be no doubt remaining that much of what whites had lost with the end of slavery could be reinstituted through legislation and judicial interpretation. It was a matter of local option—whatever the will of the majority of whites in a state or locality—that determined the quality of life and freedom for blacks.[68]

---

*Any random selection of whites and blacks would reveal among them the same range of potential and capacity.

68. Consistent with the Revolutionary rhetoric of John Dickinson, this would be the imposition (a tax, if you will) on blacks "without their own consent expressed by themselves or their representatives." According to Dickinson, that made them slaves.

It was not slavery but a caste-like system that effectively excluded blacks from the community and from a share of power that perpetuated racial privilege. Emancipation and Reconstruction did little to alter that system of racial caste.

Of course there were significant changes in the lives of freedmen. It is better not to be owned as property, to have some say (albeit small) over one's life, to be able to have one's marriage recognized in the law, and to be able to aspire, however vainly, to something better. All better than being chattel. But the continuation of racial caste patterns contained all of these improvements within a system excluding blacks from power.

Changes would come and our progressive ideology would call them advances. Over all, the apparent improvement of individual blacks made little fundamental difference. The basic features of caste were left unchanged. Following periods of great hope—of important advances in property ownership and capital accumulation—came shocks of depression, when most gains were wiped away. The line of advance was conspicuously thin. Continued discrimination in employment, housing, education, and the delivery of legal and public services made blacks most vulnerable during times of recession, when whites—imagining black achievement to be at their expense—were willing to cede less. Signs of individual achievement persisted: higher literacy (between World War I and the 1950s), longer years in school, increased property ownership. But these seemed to amount to little in the final analysis because, relative to the gains made by whites, the gains by blacks had been small. A century after emancipation, the badges of servitude remained.

Caste and race privilege were the targets of the civil rights movement and the Second Reconstruction. Integration was the accepted issue for most blacks because segregation was the most obvious example of caste being defended by public authority. But African-Americans remained divided over how important or how desirable it was to live among or go to school with whites. All agreed, however, that to be denied admission and access because of color was unacceptable. Most argued for desegregation and integration on the assumption of white privilege. That is to say, the only way to guarantee equal treatment was to be in the same boat with whites. Racial separation invites discrimination and white privilege. *De jure* integration, however, was met by the flight of those whites who could afford to move, and impoverished whites and blacks were left to squabble over disintegrating schools and cities.

The events of the past two decades contradict our master narrative and its faith in automatic progress, assuming an always expanding and improving world where each "today" is better than each "yesterday," where "tomorrow" remains our El Dorado. Even at our most optimistic, we have been obliged by reality to trim our sails and explain: "A rising tide lifts all boats." Our faith blinds us to the fact that rising and falling tides have little to do with who rides steerage and who dines at the captain's table. Just as slavery was the acid test of our liberal faith in the eighteenth and nineteenth centuries, race—its legacy of social death, its badges of servitude—is the acid test for us, now.

As we enter the final decade of the twentieth century, despondency weighs heavily upon us. The tide seems not to be rising for us. The middle class—miracle of the American century—is shrinking as the poles of wealth and poverty rudely mark the social divide. Living standards are falling as more have to work more hours to stay in place. Industry and investment weakens at home and shifts abroad. Education and health care are in crisis. The future of social security remains in jeopardy in an aging nation whose youth are unemployable in growing numbers. Drugs and crime are rife and uncontrollable. The infra-structure—roads, bridges, harbors—deteriorate. The prospects of repair and reform are narrow, given an enormous public debt and a citizenry unwilling either to save for the future or tax themselves for the common good.

Our times seem to call for new myths and a revised master narrative that better inspire and reflect upon our true condition. Such a new narrative would find inspiration, for instance, in an oppressed people who defied social death as slaves and freedmen, insisting on their humanity and creating a culture despite a social consensus that they were a "brutish sort of people." Such a new narrative would bring slavery and the persistent oppression of race from the margins to the center, to define the limits and boundaries of the American Dream. Such a new narrative would oblige us to face the deforming mirror of truth.

NOTE: Nathan's sudden death precluded his final revision of this new Introduction. I had the privilege of working with Peter Dimock and Werner Sollors, whose wise comments and caring guidance were invaluable to the completion of this work.

27

Nathan Huggins:
A Personal Memoir

LEON F. LITWACK

Nat thought of himself as somewhat of a truant in his early formative years. He had a penchant for asking the wrong questions in the wrong places of the wrong people. And that got him into trouble, particularly when he insisted that the questions he asked ought be answered in a way that made sense, that bore some relation to reality. In a story Nat loved to recall, his high school biology teacher one day asked the class to repeat the five fundamentals of life which they had been expected to memorize from the textbook. Nat recited the proper answer, "Response to stimuli, locomotion, reproduction, respiration, & excretion," and his teacher nodded in approval. But Nat still held the floor, his curiosity aroused. "You know," he told the teacher, "a flame does all those things." The teacher was not amused. "The man who wrote this book knows a great deal more than you," he observed. Nat remembered saying something impertinent, to which the teacher impatiently retorted, "Well, I studied under the man who wrote this textbook." Nat was unimpressed, as he quickly made clear. "What difference does that make?" he asked. That abruptly ended the exchange, and Nat was on his way to the principal's office where he would be punished for his impertinence. The incident no doubt helped to terminate his less than memorable high school experience. But it did not squelch Nat's irreverent, combative, questioning spirit. That quality never diminished. He would always ask the toughest questions, and he would persist until he got answers. (Nat would finish high school in the army, then enter the University of California at Berkeley on the GI Bill.)

For some forty years we knew each other, meeting as undergraduates at Berkeley, sharing the same politics, the same commitment to social activism, many of the same friends, and sharing as well a passionate interest in a history we would ultimately teach and research. We had both manifested an early interest in the history of black Americans, but that interest had not been satisfied in a high school curriculum which essentially defined blacks out of American identity, treating their history (if at all) as a history of submission patiently and passively if not gladly endured. It was our good fortune at Berkeley, however, to encounter in the classes taught by Kenneth M. Stampp a strikingly different version of reality. "He gave evidence about brutality, coercion, and resistance," Nat would recall of Stampp's lectures on slavery, "that one couldn't find in existing texts. He came up with more satisfying conclusions."

We both found Berkeley an exhilarating experience, all the more so for its political diversity, its proximity to San Francisco, and its size. "Because Berkeley was so large," Nat recalled, "they didn't know what color I was until they got to know *who* I was, and by then I had established a track record." For most of our undergraduate years, however, we were increasingly lonely rebels in a sea of student apathy, caution, and conservatism, confronting an administrative apparatus that discouraged even as it carefully monitored radical student activism. (Students in those years were not said to be influenced by radical ideas but infected by them.) Nat lived in the Oxford Cooperative, and he would serve as President of the University Students Cooperative Association. He also chaired the Student Welfare Board (where he campaigned to improve wages and conditions for working students), and he sat on the student executive committee (where he introduced a resolution in 1953 protesting the House Un-American Activities Committee and government loyalty probes of teachers, affirming that the investigation of thought was "above and beyond the scope of any agency in a free society"). Even then Nat had a way of persuading people, usually through the sheer reasonableness of his argument. That same year he was narrowly defeated for student body president. Before graduation, he was named to the Student Hall of Fame, and I vividly recall walking Nat through the ceremony initiating him into the Order of the Golden Bear, a secret men's society composed of selected students, faculty, and administrators. We both wondered what we were doing there.

Nat occupied a very special place in my life. The political activism we shared no doubt influenced the way we looked at history, but history had also helped to inform and shape our politics. The many conversations in those years revolved around a variety of subjects and concerns, including our futures. After receiving his M.A. at Berkeley, Nat was undecided about the next step. He wondered whether he should stay at Berkeley (and work with Kenneth Stampp) or accept a generous fellowship to Harvard. It was not an easy decision to make: Berkeley or Cambridge, each with its attractions and traditions. Still another question troubled Nat. Few prospects existed outside the black colleges in the early 1950s for a black Ph.D. in history. "Expectations then were so different," he recalled. "Certainly in 1951, one couldn't imagine a black getting his Ph.D. in history and expecting to teach anywhere. Folk wisdom taught us that a black person with a Ph.D. ended up pushing a broom, or working at the post office if he was lucky." Hoping to enhance his chances, Nat elected to go to Harvard, but as he quickly discovered, Harvard was not Berkeley. Harvard, he recalled (characteristically, in an interview with Harvard's alumni magazine), was "the most austere, uptight place I'd ever seen. In class, nobody talked about anything that was being done by anybody outside of Harvard. Everything was here—or it wasn't worth talking about." Berkeley had few of those pretensions. "Berkeley was much more democratic. People were apologetic about being 'socially better,' or if they weren't, they would get into fraternities and would be treated with contempt by anybody of real consequence."

We enjoyed our reunion in Cambridge. It was my first trip to the East, and I was collecting materials for my dissertation at Berkeley on free blacks in the antebellum North. Nat was pursuing his graduate studies, also holding forth as one of Cambridge's preeminent coffee house philosophers and conversationalists. At Harvard, Nat was anxious to establish his identity as a historian, rather than as an Afro-American historian. "I was anxious that no department could pick up my vita and say, 'Well, he's a Negro historian and that's a field we don't teach.' " The state of Negro or Afro-American history in the late 1950s forced both of us to establish our academic credentials in other areas. Nat wrote his dissertation with Oscar Handlin on Boston charities. Although my dissertation had been in African-American history, I went off to teach Jacksonian America at the University of Wisconsin.

Some decades later, when Nat returned to Harvard as the W. E. B. Du Bois Professor of History and of Afro-American Studies, he worked (in the tradition of Carter G. Woodson and Du Bois) to establish the legitimacy and intellectual respectability of Afro-American studies. He remained adamant, at the same time, in opposing efforts to reduce the complexities, ambiguities, and paradoxes of the black experience to a therapeutic search for "a usable past" or a political agenda. The distinctiveness of the American experience, Nat thought, rested in large measure on its African-American component. After all, he would suggest, "if you incorporate the Afro-American into America, you may be obliged to reinterpret the American experience in such a way that freedom is not the word that defines it. . . . You're going to have to change the terms in which you think and talk about American life."

It was a theme Nat would address most eloquently in his teaching and in his publications. *Harlem Renaissance* will no doubt be the book for which Nat is most remembered. But I think he cherished *Black Odyssey,* and he was in fact delighted to learn shortly before his death that it would be reissued in paperback. The book has a passion, a poetic, epic quality to it, and it reflected Nat's strong feelings about the need for historians to communicate to a larger audience, the need to bring drama, passion, and clarity to the historical experience, not to bury it in the vocabulary and methodology of incomprehensibility. Nat had considerable respect for the complexity of the past, but he also possessed the capacity for sensing what was truly significant in that complexity.

Nat's mind was subtle, richly informed, deeply and broadly inquiring and embracing. I miss him: the camaraderie, his infectious smile, his playful wit and spirit, his humaneness, his presence. The character of his life cannot adequately be described without noting the intensity of his human concerns, his social compassion, his utter honesty, his insatiable curiosity, his intellectual engagement, and, yes, his irreverence, his combativeness, his often quiet rage, and the number of times he forced his audiences (colleagues and students alike) to see and feel and think about the past and present in ways that could be genuinely disturbing and uncomfortable. Few could employ irony and subtlety as effectively as Nat. He used them to unmask hypocrisy, to expose pretensions, to undermine myths and the mythmakers, to afflict the comfortable and the indifferent.

For the forty years I knew him, Nat held steadfast in his vision of a more humane society, even as so many others fell by the wayside of submission, compromise, and fashionable accommodation. A deeply probing radical critic, a skillful disturber of complacency, he was always an individualist, never an ideologue. He distrusted the ideologues, along with the well-intentioned. He rejected the race hustlers and ethnocentric chauvinists. He envisioned a curriculum that would reflect the racial and cultural diversity of this country, and in his last visit to Berkeley, he challenged the Eurocentric bias in education. "How do we get people who believe they are the center of the universe to move over?" he asked. That was vintage Huggins. He spent the last two decades of his life at Columbia and Harvard. But in spirit, I believe, he really belonged to Berkeley, a rebel and dissident in the finest Berkeley tradition.

"Precisely who and what is the people?" an American poet once asked. To seek answers to that question, using a variety of documentation, Nat believed, was to engage in the highest form of historical inquiry. Few historians cared so passionately about the answers. Lionel Trilling once made reference to certain "men who live their visions . . . who *are* what they write." That spirit very much infused Nat's scholarship, particularly *Black Odyssey,* with the evocative closing passage of its Introduction:

> Certainly, adventures more breathtaking than all the sagas of the West, human sacrifices more moving than Iron Curtain melodramas, were the true tales of slaves and free blacks. If our histories, literature, and popular culture have not discovered this lore, it is perhaps because we have been unwilling to call oppression by its proper name.
>
> Within that tyranny, looking beyond the acts of defiance, rebellion, and escape, we will find a quality of courage still unsung. It is in the triumph of the human spirit over unmitigated power. It raised no banners. It gained no vengeance. It was only the pervasive and persis-

tent will among Afro-Americans to hold together through deep trauma and adversity. Much that was in their circumstances would have reduced them to brutes, to objects in the market. It would have been easy to become what many whites insisted they were: dumb, slow, insensitive, immoral, wanting in true human qualities. But slaves laid claim to their humanity and refused to compromise it, creating families where there would have been one, weaving a cosmology and a moral order in a world of duplicity, shaping an art and a world of imagination in a cultural desert.

It is exactly this triumph of the human spirit over adversity that is the great story in Afro-American slavery. It is why slaves, in their art, in their story properly understood, in their faith in themselves and their God, have been a source of inspiration to all who have come to know of them. It is why the spirituals had universal appeal—beauty, yes, but from a people who would have been crushed.

Many slaves lived their lives without much that we would call resistance. They died whole persons nevertheless, able in their souls to meet their God without shame. No black American, and certainly no white American, has cause to apologize for them. Modern history knows of no more glorious story of the triumphant human spirit.

That "triumphant human spirit." Nat exemplified it in his own life and work. He left us a precious legacy of scholarship and social activism. He was a true disturber of the peace. In the passion, irreverence, commitment, and humanity he brought to the study of history, in his appreciation of the extraordinary variety and resourcefulness of the black response to white America, in his appreciation of the fundamental contradictions between this nation's professed egalitarianism and deep inequalities in wealth and in conditions of work and life, Nathan Huggins made his mark on my life—and on the historical profession. "The right to the pursuit of happiness," he once wrote, "when translated into the profit of private individuals and corporations at the expense of human and other resources is ultimately destructive of human values and community." The best way to remember Nat, to honor his achievements, his scholarship and his teaching, is to act on the commitments and concerns he voiced so eloquently.